1984

# children,
# MENTAL
# HEALTH,
# and
# the LAW

**Volume 4, Sage Annual Reviews of Community Mental Health**

**Volume 4**
SAGE Annual Reviews of Community Mental Health

# children,
# MENTAL
# HEALTH,
# and
# the LAW

edited by
## N. Dickon Reppucci
## Lois A. Weithorn
## Edward P. Mulvey
## John Monahan

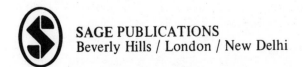

SAGE PUBLICATIONS
Beverly Hills / London / New Delhi

*For information address:*

SAGE Publications, Inc.
275 South Beverly Drive
Beverly Hills, California 90212

SAGE Publications India Pvt. Ltd.
C-236 Defence Colony
New Delhi 110 024, India

SAGE Publications Ltd
28 Banner Street
London EC1Y 8QE, England

Printed in the United States of America

**Library of Congress Cataloging in Publication Data**

Main entry under title:

Children, mental health, and the law.

   (Sage annual reviews of community mental health ; v. 4)
   1. Children—legal status, laws, etc.—United States—
Addresses, essays, lectures. 2. Mental health laws—
United States—Addresses, essays, lectures. I. Reppucci,
N. Dickon. II. Series. [DNLM: 1. Mental health—In
infancy and childhood. 2. Child advocacy. W1 SA125TC
v.4 / WS 105.5.M3 M549]

| | | |
|---|---|---|
| KF479.A75M46     1983 | 346.7301'35 | 83-21116 |
| ISBN 0-8039-2813-7 | 347.304135 | |
| ISBN 0-8039-2184-5 (pbk.) | | |

FIRST PRINTING

# *Contents*

*This book is dedicated to*
SEYMOUR B. SARASON
*for his wisdom and humanity.*

# Acknowledgments

An edited book requires the time and energy of many people besides the contributors and the editors. In the present case, the University of Virginia's Institute of Law, Psychiatry and Public Policy, under the direction of Richard Bonnie, provided the interdisciplinary environment that fostered the interactions among the editors, and between the editors and several of the contributors, that resulted in the decision to compile this manuscript. Under the auspices of the Institute, and the University of Virginia School of Law, Elizabeth Scott, at times in conjunction with Gary Melton, Lois Weithorn and Dick Reppucci, has regularly taught a legal seminar and forensic clinic focused on children and families. Graciously, both graduate and undergraduate students enrolled in courses taught by Dick Reppucci and Ed Mulvey in the University of Virginia's psychology department were encouraged to participate in these seminar-clinics. The experience has been a stimulating one for all concerned, and the interchange that occurred in these seminars has been another major impetus for developing this book. Moreover, the above experiences have culminated in the creation of the University of Virginia's new interdisciplinary Center for the Study of Children and the Law.

A few other people deserve special mention. Debbie Mundie and Louise Spangler of the University of Virginia's psychology department warrant special thanks for the rapid and efficient typing of several chapters in multiple drafts. Mark Aber read and commented on several chapters and always provided helpful feedback. Finally, Christine M. Reppucci has been a major source of encouragement and of the right phrase or word at particularly frustrating moments.

# *Preface*

The "community" perspective in the mental health disciplines could be thought of as having three core concepts: prevention, populations, and institutions (Heller & Monahan, 1977). The overall goal is to prevent the development of behavioral and psychological problems within large populations of people. The means to achieving that goal, the community perspective suggests, lie in affecting the institutions that impinge most fatefully upon people's lives.

Many different populations (e.g., the elderly and minorities) and various institutions (e.g., the health and welfare systems) have been the focus of study and intervention by adherents to the community perspective in the past two decades. Surely, however, the population in which the most intense empirical and social efforts have been made has been children. This emphasis no doubt derives from the belief that the earlier in the process of its development a problem is identified, the easier it is to change. Among the institutions whose effects upon this population have received professional scrutiny, the legal system has figured prominently. This attention may be traced to the fact that changing the law is the most conspicuous way that institutional policy can be altered.

This volume of the Sage Series on Community Mental Health, provides a comprehensive state-of-the-art view of the relationship between mental health and legal concerns as they affect children in the mid-1980s. The book addresses four of the key topics in the area: the relationship of children to their families, to the health care system, to the juvenile justice system, and to the educational system.

The contributors to this volume, among whom are numbered many of the leading scholars in the field, have provided insightful critiques of the current status of empirical research, professional practice, and legal policy on a wide variety of related topics. They have, as well, offered provocative suggestions on where the field may be headed, and where they think it should be headed.

*—John Monahan*

## Reference

Heller, K., & Mohanan, J. *Psychology and community change.* Homewood: Dorsey Press, 1977.

# PART I

## GENERAL ISSUES

# 1

# *Mental Health, Law, and Children*

## *A Brief Overview*

### Edward P. Mulvey
*Western Psychiatric Institute and Clinic*
*University of Pittsburgh*


### N. Dickon Reppucci
### Lois A. Weithorn
*University of Virginia*

Contemporary public policy has witnessed a marriage of legal principles and social science. As in many marriages, the two partners have come to resemble each other over the years. For generations, the legal system has grappled with the delicate problem of maintaining the family as the primary building block of the social order while preserving individual liberties. A store of legal logic about such issues as family privacy, state obligation, and juvenile rights has developed over time to guide these efforts. Since the Progressive Era (approximately 1890-1920), however, applied social scientists have become increasingly influential partners in attempts to foster healthy family functioning and child development. In fact, the knowledge and assistance of mental health professionals have become inextricably linked to many aspects of public policy in this area. There is presently an active use of the legal system to promote goals deemed desirable by extant social scientific theory and an increasing legalization of social service delivery.

This book is an effort to illuminate several of the areas where there is presently an active, vibrant exchange between the legal and mental health systems. It is presented as a state-of-the-art view of the legal and social scientific aspects of many of the key issues. It is not intended to be an exhaustive discussion of all the issues affecting policy toward children and families. Rather, it is a series of focused looks at a complex interaction.

Adequately portraying the larger interaction between legal policy and social science is not a straightforward task, since the content of each family or child policy issue frames the relationship slightly differently. The priorities given certain legal principles change with the particular issue, as does the value and applicability of social scientific theory. A clearer picture of the key questions regarding such seemingly disparate issues as child custody or juveniles' access to abortion can be obtained by examining questions in terms of the most basic general principles involved. Certain frameworks can be helpful for analyzing the general interaction between legal policy and social science across the multitude of sociolegal issues addressed in this book.

### Parent-Child-State

The first general framework that is useful for structuring many of these issues is that of the parent-child-state triad. These are the three basic, identifiable parties whose interests are at stake when policy in this area is formulated, and each element relies on the others for resources or services. For example, the state relies on parents to provide proper socialization for its future citizens, and parents rely on the state to provide their children with formal education. Also, children rely on parents for nurturance, guidance, and support and on the state for protection from cruel treatment within the family. The web of interests between these three elements is the focus of public policy for children and families.

The position that emphasizes parental rights and has as its critical interest the preservation of family stability and harmony is known as "family libertarianism." Basically it supports the view that parents should be autonomous in raising their children as they see fit, except in very dire circumstances. This constitutional right to family privacy is reflected in the laws of all of the states. In the 1972 *Wisconsin v. Yoder*[1] decision, the Supreme Court upheld the position that Amish parents who did not want their children bound by Wisconsin's secondary education provisions had the right to raise their children in their own cultural tradition. This decision was viewed as a victory for the family libertarian position; however, it was based in large part on the notion that the children's best interests were isomorphic with their parents' interests. In a forceful minority dissent, Justice Douglas raised the issue that parents and children may not have an identity of interests.

Therefore, he emphasized that the independent rights of children should be acknowledged.

This children's-rights position focuses on the child in the triad and argues that children should have rights equivalent to those of adults, at least in many instances. This stance has been a powerful motivating idea behind the child advocacy movement of the last 25 years, and it has been strengthened by the Supreme Court's extension of constitutional protection to children as individuals,[2] and its subsequent recognition of their right to privacy.[3] Despite these decisions, the limits of autonomy for minors remain unclear. For example, the abortion decisions have been predicated upon a right to privacy for *mature* (without defining the term) minors.[4] Yet, the autonomy of even a mature minor may be limited by the state's deference to parental decisions about what is best for him or her [5] (Ehrenreich & Melton, 1983).

The state-interventionist position, which stresses the third branch of the triad, is based on the *parens patriae* power of the state (i.e., the state has the authority and responsibility to protect children from serious harm when their parents cannot or will not do so). This power derives from the legitimate state interest in protecting members of society who cannot protect themselves and in assuring that children develop into responsible and productive citizens. This position has powered the juvenile court movement since its inception at the turn of the century and clearly implies that, in many circumstances, the state and its designates in the legal and mental health professions know best. The parens patriae authority has been used to uphold child labor[6] and compulsory eductation laws,[7] to support the termination of parental rights on the basis of abuse or neglect,[8] and to override parental refusals to consent to life-saving medical treatment, even when those refusals were based on religious grounds[9] (Ehrenreich & Melton, 1983). Although the state-interventionist position has become less dominant since the 1967 landmark *In re Gault*[10] decision, it still retains major influence and has many supporters, especially among professional helpers.

It should be obvious that there is, of necessity, an interdependence between these three positions, and that public policy attempts to maintain an equilibrium between the competing interests. Changes in one link of the triad have repercussions for the other two, and policies must be evaluated in light of these possible consequences. Expansion of due process and privacy rights for juveniles, for example, has been primarily rooted in the relationship of the child to the state. Court decisions have established a juvenile's rights to an adversary, due-process, delinquency adjudication hearing and to privacy concerning certain medical procedures. This expansion of individual juvenile interests, however, has not been absolute, largely because of the potentially disruptive effect a granting of total rights would have on the parent-child relationship. In *Parham v. J.R.*,[11] for instance, a juvenile's guarantee to an adversarial hearing when faced with involuntary civil commitment was denied partially based on the logic that such a procedure would undermine the parents' relationship with their child. The rights of juveniles have been circumscribed by the legitimate fear of adversely affecting the parent-child alliance.

Similarly, changes in the parent-child alliance have had repercussions for the relationship between the parent and the state. For example, the increasing frequency of no-fault divorce has necessitated a reconsideration of the role of the state in determining child custody, and has fostered a refinement of the standards for state intervention and priorities. Relying on child development theory (e.g., Goldstein, Freud, & Solnit, 1973) and empirical evidence (Mnookin, 1975) about the potential harm done to children by poorly regulated state intervention, the standards for state intervention have been shifting from an assumption that the state can act *in loco parentis* to an obligation for the state to pursue the *least detrimental alternative*. The increasing number of single-parent and reconstituted families has forced a reappraisal of the state's role in regulating parenting arrangements.

The framework of the parent-child-state triad is useful for understanding the motivations, limiting factors, and seeming inconsistencies behind many legal policies regarding children and families. Because judgments about children and family issues are highly discretionary, however, the tension maintained among child, parent, and state interests is also dependent upon current social scientific thought. Social science theory and practice provide much of the justification for the policy stances affecting the triad. As a result, a second framework is necessary to structure the collaborative process between the legal and social scientific communities regarding these issues.

### Discipline versus Profession

The social scientific and legal communities can be thought of as influencing each other as both disciplines and professions (Musto, 1981). The distinction between a field as a discipline and as a profession is comparable to the distinction between theory and practice or between content and process. Considering a field as a discipline means examining the existing body of accepted knowledge, the assumptions accompanying that knowledge, and the methods for advancing knowledge in that area. Considering a field as a profession means examining the application of an area's existing knowledge through service provision. The discipline of a field is concerned with advancement of knowledge; the profession of a field is concerned with translation of that knowledge into practice. Academics are generally concerned with the discipline of social science; practitioners are generally concerned with the profession of social science. Although seemingly simplistic, this distinction is valuable as a method for sorting out the reciprocal influences between the two fields.

In a number of specific instances, the discipline of social science provides empirical tests of the assumptions that underpin legal logic. Grisso's (1981) work on the ability of juveniles to understand Miranda warnings or Weithorn's work (Weithorn & Campbell, 1982) on children's understanding of treatment consent are clear examples of the empirical examination of legal assumptions. In situations such as these, the contribution of social science to law is one of establishing the validity of an assumption in order to promote clearer legal debate on philosophical and value grounds. The discipline of law will pursue its own issues using its own methods; social science findings can promote, but not resolve, debate. Conversely, the discipline of law can often push social science by providing situations and constructs grounded in the reality of social relations, which challenge the development of externally valid theory. Social scientific thinking about group decision making, for example, has been pushed and refined as a result of trying to understand jury deliberations. The discipline of law provides social scientists with accrued common knowledge and legal theory upon which to base their own theory development.

The professions of law and social science, meanwhile, operate in concert in many matters related to children and families. First, discretionary legal action often hinges on the advice of mental health professionals. Family court judges and personnel regularly interpret social service information and reach decisions based on consideration of these factors. Lawyers serving as guardians *ad litem* often plan strategy to get children what is seen by mental health experts as being in their best interest. In many cases data provided by mental health professionals are the "facts" that underpin court action.[12] Second, on a more organizational level, the legal system and mental health professionals are linked in a reciprocal resource exchange relationship. The court provides clients for mental health providers, and these professionals in turn provide a needed service for the court. In essence, the court acts as a screening and monitoring operation for many mental health agencies, providing referrals and a collaborative working relationship. Court involvement (and the possibility of further court action) may provide mental health professionals with entree into high-risk families (e.g., abusive or neglecting families) who were unlikely to seek services otherwise. In return, the court ensures, at least theoretically, that the least coercive and most treatment-oriented interventions are being used with problem individuals and that, further, more intrusive court action can be justified if these treatment efforts fail.

Clearly we view the mental health and legal systems as being intimately intertwined about issues pertaining to children and families. It is hoped that the two frameworks we have presented (the parent-child-state triad and the discipline-profession distinction) can serve as preliminary organizing principles for the reader in analyses of the dimensions of this interconnection between fields. It is also necessary, however, to emphasize briefly the need for such analysis.

Rapid social change is affecting both the structure of families and the larger ecological context in which parents and children interact. Informed policy regarding these matters can occur only if both fields are clear sighted in structuring the problems ahead. At a general level, we may be witnessing a major turning point in policy emphasis regarding children and families. Since the Progressive Era we have operated under the assumption that the state could provide beneficial care in support of the family and child development. Increased skepticism about the state's ability to identify and provide for people's needs, however, has coincided with an awakening regarding the value of individual rights. As a result of this confluence, there is the possibility that we are moving from a "state as parent" model of services for children and families to a "liberty model" of such services (Rothman, 1974). This movement away from benevolent stewardship will be a period of intense scrutiny of the services spawned by the Progressive Era mentality. Specific changes are already presently confronting us, particularly regarding the scope of family and juvenile rights (Keiter, 1982). Meeting these and developing conceptualizations, strategies, and tactics to deal with the many delicate issues to come will require a broad perspective and an interdisciplinary awareness. It is our hope that this collection will contribute to that expanded perspective.

## Plan of the Book

We have organized the 13 chapters in this book into five parts: (1) General Issues, (2) Children in the Family, (3) Children in the Health Care System, (4) Children in the Juvenile Justice System, and (5) Children in the Educational System. In Part I we have included the present chapter and Lois Weithorn's "Children's Capacities in Legal Contexts." Whereas this chapter has concerned itself with a brief examination of two general frameworks—the parent-child-state triad and the distinction between disciplines and professions—Weithorn focuses on identifying those circumstances in which the legal system concerns itself with the psychological capacities or competencies of children. Discussing contexts such as juvenile justice proceedings, health care decision making, custody disputes, and courtroom testimony, she surveys each of six competencies. In each case she analyzes traditional legal assumptions about children's capacities, current legal standards, and the state of our psychological knowledge about children's functioning according to those standards.

Part II comprises three chapters. In "The Wisdom of Solomon," Dick Reppucci examines the thorny issue of child custody dispute resolution in the context of the changing structure of social institutions and the changing philosophical conceptions of the child. Special attention is given to the best interests of the child standard, the increasing use of joint custody, and aspects of the legal system that either encourage or discourage cooperative parenting after divorce. Reppucci concludes that developing more valid clinical procedures, more legal options, and a firm empirical data base are the major challenges of the future.

In the next chapter, Mindy Rosenberg and Robert Hunt present an overview of several issues confronting the mental health and legal professions in the area of child maltreatment. They review definitional problems in state statutes, the legal context of maltreatment cases, psychological theories of etiology, and intervention strategies. They conclude with an attempt to bridge some of the apparent gaps between the legal and mental health professions by elucidating several research questions relevant to child maltreatment.

In "Children, Families, and Work" Ellen Greenberger discusses the function of children's work in historical perspective, the effects of employment on adolescents' well-being and family relations, and recent legal debates about restraints on child labor. She concludes that the benefits of working are in a delicate balance with the costs to family functioning, adolescents' psychosocial development, and the well-being of society.

In the first chapter of Part III, Elizabeth Scott focuses attention on "Adolescents' Reproductive Rights." In her comprehensive review, Scott addresses legal and psychological issues relating to minors' acccess to contraception and abortion, and to the sterilization of mentally retarded minors. She traces the history and development of current legal standards, identifies the psychological assumptions upon which certain legal standards are based, and reviews empirical research relevant to those assumptions. Where appropriate, she discusses the role of the mental health professional as consultant to the legal system.

In the second chapter Gary Melton provides a critical analysis of the U.S. Supreme Court's decision in *Parham v. J.R.*,[13] a case that addressed questions relating to the civil commitment of minors to mental hospitals. "Family and Mental Hospital as Myths" identifies those notions (about psychological functioning, family relationships, and the mental health system), upon which the majority opinion in Parham appeared to turn. Melton examines those notions from an empirical perspective, concluding that the assumptions underlying this critical decision may be no more than myths.

The longest section in the book is concerned with children in the juvenile justice system. This part contains four chapters. In the first, Tom Grisso examines "Procedural Issues in the Juvenile Justice System" from a unique perspective. He analyzes the impact of decisions made within the juvenile justice system upon the psychological welfare of the juveniles who are the objects of such decision making. He considers the various stages at which decisions about juveniles are made—pretrial interrogation, pretrial detention, transfer to adult criminal court, and postadjudication disposition—and addresses the probable psychological consequences of particular decisions for the well-being of the juvenile. Each section includes the author's recommendations for changes in policies governing systemic decision making.

In the next chapter Ed Mulvey addresses the difficult situation encountered by mental health professionals in advising the juvenile court regarding the likelihood of success in treating juvenile offenders. Putting this clinical judgment into the broader framework of discretion in juvenile justice, he outlines the task in both its practical and theoretical terms. He concludes that the judgment as practiced has only limited connection to the theoretical model commonly used for analysis and research in this area. As a partial solution he proposes that this task be thought of and investigated as a judgment made under uncertainty—one in which the context of the judgment will play an influential role.

Jean Ann Linney's chapter takes a much broader view regarding the provision of services for juveniles, as she examines the rationale and possible impacts of the deinstitutionalization movement. Tracing the history of legislative and case law underpinning deinstitutionalization, she presents an overview of the expected benefits connected to this policy emphasis. Next, she outlines several general systemic impacts (e.g., the process of relabeling youth) that have been investigated as possible macrolevel effects associated with the movement away from institutional care. Throughout, she emphasizes and illustrates the interplay between juvenile rights and the system of services established to meet the perceived needs of adolescents in legal trouble.

In the concluding chapter in this section, Ed Seidman discusses "The Adolescent Passage and Entry into the Juvenile Justice System." He argues that a greater understanding of the normative nature of the adolescent passage is required in order to restrict both the legal and mental health professions from overidentifying youthful misbehavior as deviance. He further argues that youth should be diverted from the juvenile justice system at the earliest possible point and net-widening by community agencies must be reduced. He concludes that the business-as-usual stance of both juvenile justice and mental health professionals requires modification in order to develop innovative, sociostructural, proactive, primary prevention strategies.

The final part consists of two chapters. In the first, Donald Bersoff examines the legal and psychological issues relating to educational placement of children through "Psychological Assessment in the Schools." This chapter provides a focused analysis of the constitutional principles that are invoked by the use of standardized psychological tests to make determinations that affect the welfare of children. Recent legal challenges to the use of standardized intelligence tests to place minority group children in classes for the educable mentally retarded are analyzed. Bersoff concludes with a consideration of children's capacities to serve as involved participants in educational decision making concerning their welfare.

In the book's final chapter Bruce Baker and Richard Brightman explore issues relating to the "Access of Handicapped Children to Educational Services." The authors first review the legal basis for the concept of a right to education for the disabled. They then examine the key provisions of the Education for all Handicapped Children Act of 1975 (PL 94-142) and their implementation. The chapter focuses upon the strategies by which parents have been and can be involved in the educational placement process concerning their children and upon the impact of the act for the children themselves.

## *Conclusion*

Our goal is to provide a series of integrative, critical summaries of the most salient issues that link mental health, law, and children. Although there are two excellent legal casebooks available, Robert Mnookin's *Child, Family and State* (1978) and Walter Wadlington, Charles H. Whitebread, and Samuel M. Davis's *Children in the Legal System* (1983), there are no books suitable for a more general audience of concerned professionals in the social sciences or for courses at either the undergraduate or graduate level. This work attempts to fill that void. As the marriage of the legal system and the social sciences grows more complex, a more thorough understanding of its foundations becomes mandatory not only for mental health and legal professionals, but also for the informed layperson. It is hoped that this book is an initial step in that direction.

## *Notes*

1. Wisconsin v. Yoder, 406 U.S. 205 (1972).

2. Tinker v. Des Moines Independent Community School Dist., 393 U.S. 503, 512-513 (1969); In re Gault, 387 U.S. 1, 31-57 (1967).

3. Carey v. Population Servs. Int'l., 431 U.S., 678 (1973); Planned Parenthood of Central Missouri v. Danforth, 428 U.S. 52 (1976).

4. Planned Parenthood of Central Missouri v. Danforth, supra Note 3.

5. Parham v. J.R., 442 U.S. 584, 603 (1979).

6. United States v. Darley, 312 U.S. 100 (1940).

7. Pierce v. Society of Sisters, 268 U.S. 510 (1925).

8. Roe v. Connecticut, 417 F. Supp. 769, 779 (M.D. Ala. 1976) (dicta).

9. State v. Perricone, 37 N.J. 463 (1962); In re Hudson, 13 Wash. 2nd 673 (1942); Compare In re Sampson, 65 Misc. 2d 658 (N.Y. 1970): overriding parents' decision where no threat of death existed.

10. Compare In re Gault, supra Note 2.

11. Parham v. J.R., supra Note 5.

12. Although the standard of best interests is invoked by both the court (e.g., Finlay v. Finlay, 240 N.Y. 429, 433, 148 N.F. 624 [1925]) and mental health professions (see, for example, the American Psychological Association's 1981 Ethical Standards, which require only that "psychologists take special care to protect the minors' best interests [Principle 5d]"), it should be clearly recognized that this standard is at best a general guide for discretion.

13. Parham v. J.R., supra Note 5.

## References

American Psychological Association. *Ethical standards of psychologists.* Adopted by the Council of Representative in January 1918.

Ehrenreich, N.S., & Melton, G.B. Ethical and legal issues in the treatment of children. In C.E. Walker & M.C. Roberts (Eds.), *Handbook of clinical child psychology.* New York: Wiley, 1983.

Goldstein, J., Freud, A., & Solnit, A.J. *Beyond the best interests of the child.* New York: Free Press, 1973.

Grisso, T. *Juvenile's waiver of rights: Legal and psychological competence.* New York: Plenum, 1981.

Keiter, R.B. Privacy, children, and their parents: Reflections on and beyond the Supreme Court's approach. *Minnesota Law Review,* 1982, *66,* 458-518.

Mnookin, R.H. Child-custody adjudication: Judicial functions in the face of indeterminacy. *Law and Contemporary Problems,* 1975, *39,* 226-290.

Mnookin, R.H. *Child, family and state.* Boston: Little, Brown, 1978.

Musto, D. The search for solutions: Fetching answers from other disciplines. Paper presented at the VI International Symposium on Law and Psychiatry, Charlottesville, Virginia, June 31, 1981.

Rothman, D. The state as parent: Social policy in the Progressive Era. In W. Gaylin, I. Glasser, S. Marcus, & D. Rothman, *Doing good: The limits of benevolence.* New York: Pantheon Books, 1974.

Wadlington, W., Whitebread, C.H., & Davis, S.M. *Children in the legal system.* Mineola, New York: Foundation Press, 1983.

Weithorn, L.A., & Campbell, S.B. The competency of children and adolescents to make informed treatment decisions. *Child Development,* 1982, *53,* 1589-1599.

# 2

# Children's Capacities in Legal Contexts

### Lois A. Weithorn
*University of Virginia*

The law has long recognized that children[1] differ psychologically from adults. As developing persons who have not yet reached full maturity, children are typically viewed as less capable than adults in many spheres of functioning of relevance to the law. That most children have not reached their full psychological potential is indisputable. What is less clear, however, is the degree to which particular capacities of relevance to the law vary with chronological age and levels of cognitive and emotional development. As Rodham (1973, P. 3) has pointed out, a presumption that all children are incapable of exercising legal rights

> obscures the dramatic differences among children of different ages and the striking similarities between older children and adults. The capacities and the needs of a child of six months differ substantially from those of a child of six or sixteen years.

"Capacity," "maturity," "competency," "competence," and "intelligence," are terms often used interchangeably when referring to children's functioning in legally relevant contexts (Weithorn, 1982). More generally, the term capacity refers to having certain abilities, skills, knowledge, or experience, and may imply that an individual is able to perform in a certain manner. The law is concerned with the individual competence of adults in a

Author's Note: I would like to thank Elizabeth Scott for her helpful suggestions in reviewing earlier drafts of this manuscript.

25

wide range of circumstances, including competency to manage one's own financial affairs, write a will, stand trial, plead in a criminal trial, consent to treatment, and testify in court. This chapter will review those childhood competencies or capacities that are of particular interest and concern to the law. Typically, when the competency of an adult is questioned, it is because that adult's functioning is impaired in some way, by mental disability (e.g., emotional disorder or intellectual deficits), altered states of consciousness, or inability to communicate. Although children also might be affected by these conditions, their presumed immaturity is the most common justification for questioning their capacities.

This chapter will focus on six types of capacities across various legal settings. These competencies include (a) capacity to commit a crime; (b) competency to stand trial, including the capacity to assist one's attorney; (c) competency to consent to treatment; (d) competency to consent to research; (e) capacity to express a preference in child custody disputes; and (f) competency to testify. This chapter will not review competency to waive *Miranda* rights, despite its importance, because an excellent summary of legal and psychological issues has been provided elsewhere (see Grisso, 1981).

Each review of the various competencies will include a summary of relevant legal concepts and trends; an analysis of those psychological skills and abilities that appear to be correlated, at least theoretically, with each type of competency; and a discussion of the existing empirical research addressing children's capacities in that sphere.

## Capacity to Commit a Crime

In order for an individual to be held responsible for a crime, it must be proven in court, beyond a reasonable doubt, that the individual both voluntarily performed the physical act in question *(actus reus),* and entertained the requisite criminal state of mind *(mens rea).* Historically, according to common law, children under the age of 7 were presumed incapable of forming mens rea and, thus, could not be held criminally responsible. Children between the ages of 7 and fourteen also were presumed incapable, but that presumption was "rebuttable," in that evidence could be admitted to demonstrate that a particular child, in fact, entertained a "guilty mind." Children age fourteen and older were viewed as adults with respect to criminal capacity.

This so-called infancy defense, which excluded certain children from criminal liability because of presumed immaturity, has been likened to the insanity defense, in that similar legal tests have been applied to both doctrines (McCarthy, 1977). Evidence that might be entered to rebut the presumption of incapacity would attempt to demonstrate that the child in question was "of sufficient intelligence to distinguish right from wrong, and understood the nature and illegality of his act" (Frey, 1973). This standard clearly emphasizes the notion that a person should not be held criminally responsible for actions if that person is not capable of appreciating the wrongfulness of such acts (Low, Jeffries, & Bonnie, 1982).

The infancy defense, like the insanity defense, was derived from legal policy goals defining which persons society is willing to excuse from criminal responsibility, and, therefore, from punishment. That the infancy defense defines an irrebuttable presumption of incapacity for children younger than 7 is an indication of society's resolve not to punish these children in the criminal justice system, regardless of the facts of any individual case.

The development of the juvenile court system, however, has led some jurists and scholars to question the current relevance of mens rea requirements and common law presumptions for the legal analysis of the behavior of children. The juvenile court system gradually developed in the United States during the latter part of the nineteenth century, and was formally initiated in the United States with the Illinois Juvenile Court Act in 1899.[2] By 1917 all states except three had special juvenile court systems (Low et al., 1982). The juvenile courts, as contrasted with criminal courts, were created to help, rather than punish, problem children, by intervening in a positive and corrective manner. Theoretically, adjudications of delinquency were not to be viewed as synonymous with findings of criminal guilt, but with a finding that a juvenile needed the rehabilitative services that the system could offer. As such, the authorizing legislation of most states did not set lower age limits on the jurisdiction of the juvenile court ("Problem of Age and Jurisdiction in Juvenile Court," 1966). In that the goal of the system was to reach all of those children who might benefit from such educative intervention, the courts typically were not prevented by statue from dealing with children under age 7. Most juvenile courts still retain jurisdiction of minors through the age of 18, although in some states minors are automatically referred to adult criminal court at age 16. States vary in the ages at which they authorize juvenile courts to transfer or waive jurisdiction of a juvenile to criminal court for prosecution. Typically, states do not permit the waiver of minors younger than age 14 ("Problem of Age and Jurisdiction in Juvenile Court," 1966).

Given the underpinnings and goals of the juvenile court system, it is not clear to what degree traditional mens rea requirements are applicable. One position was advanced by Judge Ketcham, of the Juvenile Court of the District of Columbia in 1959:

Free will, evil intent, moral responsibility, and proof of guilt beyond a reasonable doubt are the language of the criminal code. They encompass a design of punishment to be meted out to those who offend against the social order combined with a major exception in the case of persons found not to be mentally responsible. . . . But where the protection rather than the punishment of the offender is the aim, where the action of the state is on behalf of the law violator as well as in the interests of the community, such criminal concepts require qualification.[3]

Judge Ketcham's opinion would suggest that mens rea need not be proven in juvenile court, and that common law presumptions regarding capacity are extraneous to juvenile court proceedings. This conclusion appears to be based upon the notion that since the juvenile court system functions to provide treatment, and the mens rea concept is a derivation of a system emphasizing punishment of offenders, the concept is inappropriate to the deliberations of juvenile courts (McCarthy, 1977).

In 1973, Judge Orth, in a case with similar holdings,[4] emphasized that

When a juvenile court has exclusive jurisdiction over a person alleged to be a delinquent child and does not waive that jurisdiction, the result, stated in terms of common law, is that the age under which a person is *conclusively presumed* to be incapable of committing a crime has been raised from seven to 18.[5]

*In re Gladys R.*[6] provided an exception to the above trends. However, its application of common law presumptions of minors' capacities have been viewed as unique to California's particular statutory schema (Low et al., 1982; McCarthy, 1977).

The past two decades have seen the extension to juveniles of a range of due process protections that have been accorded adults.[7] Despite the philosophy and goals of the juvenile court system, the U.S. Supreme Court has recognized that juvenile proceedings frequently lead to deprivation of the juvenile's liberty, and have held that constitutional guarantees related to a fair trial are applicable to juvenile court proceedings. Whereas the Supreme Court has been clear as to the requirement that one must prove actus reus beyond a reasonable doubt, however, it has not dealt directly with mens rea requirements.

It now appears that a more modern, limited concept of mens rea, referring primarily to the individual's intent to commit the crime, may be relevant to, and applied by, juvenile courts (Westbrook, 1965). Rather than focusing on the more "subjective" moral dimension of the concept inherent in notions of appreciation of right and wrong, Westbrook indicates that the concept most relevant to juvenile court is the more "objective" dimension relating to intention of the consequences of one's behavior. Thus, it is an appropriate state-of-mind requirement for the state to prove that a juvenile intended or had "foresight" with reference to the probable, reasonable, or natural consequences of his or her actions (Rosenheim, 1973; Westbrook, 1965). The relevant test might be "whether or not the person realized at the time that his conduct would, or might, produce results of a certain kind" (Westbrook, 1965). The court in In re Glassberg[8] held that there must be a finding of criminal intent, or mens rea, in delinquency proceedings, to distinguish between acts that were performed intentionally, rather than accidentally. The Maryland Court of Appeals, in *In re Davis,* indicated that a finding of delinquency must be predicated upon proof beyond a reasonable doubt that the juvenile actually had formed the criminal intent that was an element of the offense charged.[9]

From a psychological standpoint, notions of whether a juvenile is capable of forming criminal intent would depend a great deal on the specific crime involved. For example, in a case evaluated for juvenile court by this author, a developmentally disabled child, age 7, allegedly set fire to a sofa in an abandoned house. It appeared that he had done so because he enjoyed watching flames. The flames spread through the abandoned house and to an adjacent house, destroying both houses, and killing a person in the adjacent house. The child was charged with arson and murder. Whereas one might contend that the child did intend to set the match to the sofa, it could be argued that the child did not intend, or have the foresight to comprehend or predict, the consequences of that act. Such were the findings of our evaluation. In fact, this child appeared to have little understanding in general of the danger posed by exposure to fire, or of the concept of death and its permanence.

It would seem that conceptualization of the probable consequences of this particular act, under these circumstances, requires that a child be capable of thinking sequentially about certain abstract possibilities. Unquestionably, children who have attained the level of formal operational thinking, which develops between ages 11 and 14, are capable of such thinking (Inhelder & Piaget, 1958). It is possible that somewhat younger children may also be capable, especially if they have had concrete and direct personal experience with the components of their situation. But many, and perhaps most, crimes are less complicated than the one described above. It is possible that a child as young as 4 years old may hit another child, desiring to cause temporary pain and discomfort. That child may be quite capable of intending the assault and its consequences. Thus, depending upon the specific criminal acts and their potential consequences, children of older or younger ages might be expected to be able to foresee the probable consequences of their behavior.

Other developmental research is relevant to concepts of capacity to form intent. Piaget's (1965) work in the area of moral reasoning has led to a corpus of studies examining the degree to which children are able to recognize and apply notions of intentionality when evaluating hypothetical situations. Piaget presented children with vignettes about other children, which were characterized by either of the following two paradigms: (a) a child has good intentions, but the act causes a high degree of damage; (b) a child has bad intentions and causes a low degree of damage. Piaget found that younger children (e.g., age 6) tended to evaluate the children causing greater damage as "naughtier," despite the child's good intentions, whereas older children (e.g., age 10) tended to emphasize intentionality rather than severity of damage, as more relevant to the concept of "naughtiness." This work has been criticized, in part, because the vignettes are somewhat ambiguous (i.e., intent is never clearly spelled out), and because children were not presented with the full range of variations of the vignettes (e.g., bad intent/high damage, good intent/low damage; (Grueneich, 1982; Karniol, 1978; Keasey, 1977a).

Subsequent investigations have attempted to distinguish (a) between an accident and an intentional act, and (b) among the differing *motives,* for intentional acts, e.g., good intent versus bad intent (Berndt & Berndt, 1975). In general, revisions in methodology, and reframing of some of the experimental inquiries, have led to the following conclusions:

> Children as young as three years of age seem able to differentiate between good and bad motives and the concept of bad is learned before the concept of good. In contrast, it is not much before their sixth birthday that children seem able to clearly differentiate between accidental and intentional events. (Keasey, 1977a, p. 256)

Keasey and Sales (1977) examined the judgments of children 5 to 7 years old presented with hypothetical vignettes describing criminal behaviors (e.g., arson, battery, larceny, and homicide). They found that even the 5-year-olds applied concepts of intentionality rather than level of damage, about 66.7 percent of the time, when judging "naughtiness" of story characters. By contrast, 6-year-olds were found to emphasize intention 83.3 percent of the time, and 7-year-olds to do so 89.1 percent of the time.

The findings suggest that by age 6 most children have the ability to reason about others' intentions to do harm. If this is so, how do evaluations of other people's intentions relate to one's own capacity to intend to do harm? Keasey (1977b) contends that children's consideration of intentionality in hypothetical situations involving themselves precedes such considerations when evaluating the behavior of others. The above-cited research elucidates lower age levels at which children are capable of comprehending notions of intent and motive (therefore, at what ages they may be capable of understanding their own psychological processes of this type). Yet, as noted earlier, concepts of foresight of the reasonable consequences of one's acts have been found to be critical in recent analyses of the relevance of mens rea to juvenile court proceedings, suggesting that further research may need to focus on children's ability to *predict* the sequence of events that might follow from particular acts.

It seems that it would be neither productive nor possible to attempt to identify an age at which children are capable of forming criminal intent. The dimensions and elements of crimes and the specific acts that constitute these crimes are so varied and diverse, encompassing enumerable human behaviors, that there is no way to determine children's capacities to intend the consequences of crimes in general. Rather, as the particular acts and their consequences vary, so will the ages at which children are capable of forming intent.

## Competency to Stand Trial

The standard that an individual who is not competent to stand trial due to mental disorder cannot be prosecuted stems from common law notions that criminal prosecution of such an individual violates basic principles of fairness and humanity ("Incompetency to Stand Trial," 1967; Winick & DeMeo, 1980). The U.S. Supreme Court has held that it is an unconstitutional abridgment of due process protections guaranteeing a fair trial to try individuals who, because of mental infirmity, cannot understand the proceedings against them, or participate in their defense,[10] since such a trial would be tantamount to a trial in absentia. The standards defining the test of competency to stand trial most frequently applied appeared in 1960, in *Dusky v. U.S.*[11]

Whether . . . [the defendant] has sufficient present ability to consult with his lawyer with a reasonable degree to rational understanding—and whether he has a rational as well as factual understanding of the proceedings against him.

Later judicial decisions[12] have further elaborated these standards. Typically, under state law an individual who is found incompetent to stand trial may be committed to a psychiatric facility for treatment directed toward restoration of that individual's competency. *Jackson v. Indiana*[13] challenged the constitutionality of extended periods of hospitalization for some defendants whose competency was not restored. The U.S. Supreme Court held in this case that such persons "cannot be held more than the reasonable period of time necessary to determine whether that capacity can be restored "in the foreseeable future."[14] The court further opined that if the individual is determined to be unrestorably incompetent, he or she must be released, or committed under appropriate civil commitment statutes.

There has been little discussion in the legal literature or in the courts of the appropriateness of requirements for competency to stand trial in juvenile court. In his 1959 decision *In re Betty Jean Williams*,[15] Judge Ketcham addressed this question and suggested that the philosophy and goals of the juvenile court system necessitate a somewhat different approach to competency than is applied in criminal courts. Since the proceedings are to be "adversary insofar as the aforementioned purposes (i.e., serving the child's welfare) are to be achieved,"[16] Judge Ketcham's position, further elaborated, might be that rights such as confrontation of witnesses and consultation with counsel are of a different import when contrasted with their meaning in criminal court. However, Judge Ketcham's opinion preceded later developments in the law, whereby the U.S. Supreme Court extended to juveniles certain due process protections accompanying criminal proceedings. It could be argued, therefore, that if a minor is not competent to stand trial, he or she is unable effectively to exercise those newly granted rights. This was the position taken by the Supreme Court of Arizona in 1980 when it held that even in the context of a juvenile delinquency proceeding, the right not to be tried while incompetent is a fundamental right:[17]

Gault establishes that due process requires that a juvenile have notice of the charges against him and the right to assistance of counsel would be meaningless if a juvenile . . . was unable to understand the charges or assist in her own defense.[18]

Yet, despite the direction of the courts that have grappled with this issue, most juvenile courts do not hold pretrial competency hearings, and competency to stand trial, in practice, simply is not raised frequently in juvenile court. This may result from the inherent dilemma posed by requiring juveniles to be competent to stand trial in order for juvenile court proceedings to be held. Clearly, some proportion of juveniles would be found not competent, due to immaturity. Unlike adults found incompetent due to mental disorder, there is no expectation that "treatment," will restore competency to juveniles whose incompetency is a result of their youth. Clearly commitment of these juveniles to some facility with no hope of restoration of competency without an adjudicatory hearing would raise even greater constitutional problems than holding the proceedings with an incompetent child.

The other options available to the court would be to drop its charges, or to wait until the juvenile aged sufficiently to become competent, and then hold the hearing. Obviously neither alternative is practical, particularly in view of the fact that despite its failures and difficulties, the juvenile court system remains one that continues to operate under a theoretical doctrine of treatment rather than punishment. Thus, whether by policy or practice, it appears that unless there are some rather dramatic shifts, competency to stand trial will remain an issue not confronted frequently with respect to juvenile court proceedings.

A fundamental problem remains, however. As noted, many of the due process rights extended to juveniles may be construed as meaningless if the juvenile does not have the capacity to exercise these rights. Perhaps the most fundamental of these rights is the juvenile's right to representation by an attorney, since if the juvenile can assist counsel in a minimally adequate manner in preparation of the case, the attorney can ensure that all of the juvenile's other rights are appropriately exercised. The Institute of Judicial Administration-American Bar Association (IJA-ABA) Juvenile Justice Standards (1980), as they relate to counsel for private parties, indicate that in representing a juvenile, an attorney is to be guided by that juvenile's preferences and judgment regarding the plea to be entered and other matters related to the control and direction of the case. The standards clearly assume competency on the part of most juvenile clients, while providing special guidance to attorneys who represent incompetent juveniles.

From a psychological standpoint, what is required of a person regarding competency to stand trial? In general, a competency to stand trial evaluation performed by a mental health professional should examine the client's capacity for understanding the following: roles of courtroom personnel; courtroom procedures; charges against one; and alternative pleas, including the process of plea bargaining (Institute of Law, Psychiatry and Public Policy, 1982; McGarry, 1973). Further, the individual must be found capable of assisting and relating to his or her attorney. Very little empirical research has focused upon juveniles' capacities in this realm. Most available data focus on attitudes toward and understanding of the roles of courtroom personnel. For example, Caul (1981) examined juveniles' abilities to distinguish between the defense attorney and other court-related professionals. The juveniles included in the sample were males, 14 to 16 years old, who were in temporary detention relating to their contacts with juvenile court. Caul's findings suggest that these juveniles perceived the public defenders as being "on their side," the prosecutors as "against them," with the judge somewhere in the middle. The findings also are supportive of the expectation that these juveniles will cooperate with and trust their attorneys, and that they basically understand the roles of various courtroom personnel.

In a call for research relating to children's ability to work with attorneys, Grisso & Lovinguth (1982) suggest that such research must focus on

(a) children's understanding of what an attorney is, and what the attorney-client relationship is supposed to be; (b) children's expectancies about the consequences of consulting with an attorney; and (c) children's capacities to weigh information provided to them by the attorney, and to make rational choices among the options presented to them by counsel.

Grisso's (1981) earlier research with 431 incarcerated juveniles, ages 10 through 16, supports the notion that most juveniles seen in juvenile court have a basic comprehension of what a lawyer is and does. Further, when presenting juveniles with hypotheticals designed to elicit responses relating to understanding of the intended function and significance of legal counsel, Grisso found that a high percentage of juveniles, like adults, had adequate comprehension of the lawyer's intended role. Interestingly, only one-third of the juveniles, as compared with about 90 percent of the adults, seemed to understand that telling their lawyer the entire truth about their case would be necessary for the lawyer to build an effective case. The juveniles seemed to think that the lawyer might use this information to decide whether or not he or she wanted to represent them, or that the lawyer might report confessions to court.

In general, therefore, there are few studies examining juveniles' capacities to understand the proceedings against them, and to cooperate with their attorneys. Such research is crucial for guiding attorneys in their work with juveniles. The greater the juveniles' capacity for understanding the proceedings, the more the attorney can interact with the juveniles as he or she might an adult, providing information and guidance, and allowing the client to make key decisions in the case. However, where there may be gaps in comprehension, it is incumbent upon attorneys to attempt to educate their young clients. Where such education does not permit juvenile clients to participate adequately in their defense, attorneys must resort to an alternative role in relation to a client's case, perhaps providing greater direction than he or she might otherwise.

Interestingly, in addition to any incapacities that result from juveniles' younger age, confounding factors may mitigate their competency to stand trial. Whereas the roles of personnel, courtroom proceedings, and so on may be relatively standard with reference to criminal court, there remains much that is equivocal with reference to juvenile court. Is an adjudicatory hearing an adversary process? Are the possible outcomes of the hearing really in the juvenile's best interest? The transition and mixed models that have characterized juvenile court proceedings in recent years have been difficult for many scholars and court personnel to define. We would expect that the inherent inconsistencies in the current system would be no less confusing to juveniles.

## Competency to Consent to Treatment

The doctrine of informed consent requires that three conditions be met in order for a treatment decision to be considered legally valid. The decision must be informed (i.e., the patient must be provided with adequate information about the proposed and alternative treatments), voluntary (i.e., the patient must make the treatment decision free from coercion or unfair inducements), and competent (Meisel, Roth, & Lidz, 1977). The predominant legal standard for competency emphasizes that the patient must have an "appreciation" of the nature, extent, and probable consequences of the conduct consented to.[19] Although the notion of appreciation is not clearly defined by the law, it has been viewed by some as a higher level of understanding, requiring the individual to think abstractly and to make inferences about the implications of the proposed treatments for oneself (Appelbaum & Roth, 1981; Weithorn, 1982). In practice, however, competency to consent to treatment is typically evaluated by examining the patient's understanding of the basic factual information presented by the attending professional. Consent forms stress such factual information. Roth et al. (1977) and Meisel (1979) reviewed several additional standards of competency, which may be applied in various contexts. The "rational reasons" or "reasonable decision-making process" standard emphasizes the manner in which the patient arrives at a decision. Did the patient consider the information about the risks and benefits of the various treatments provided by attending professionals (Weithorn, 1982)? The "evidence of choice" test requires that patients merely express a preference regarding treatment. Finally, the "reasonable outcome" test examines the choice the patient has made to determine whether it is reasonable. This judgment may be made by comparing the patient's choice to prevailing professional opinion as to what are the "best" choices, or to a standard of the choice a "hypothetical reasonable person" might select.

While law presumes that adults are generally competent to consent to treatment, it presumes that minors are incompetent. This notion stems from concepts of children as being less capable of exercising informed judgment, thereby requiring the protection of adults. Thus, under most circumstances, parents provide the legally valid consent and refusal for the treatment of their minor children. This predominant policy is strongly entrenched in the courts' respect for family privacy (i.e., the rights of parents to exercise discretion regarding the welfare of their minor children).[20] Therefore, interventions in the autonomous functioning of the family must be justified by certain other policy goals that are determined to outweigh the interests of the parents in particular circumstances. Yet, in recent years the courts have identified several sets of circumstances in which the interests of the state (i.e., in fostering "the healthy, well-rounded growth of its young people into full maturity as citizens"),[21] or the interests of minors (e.g., in liberty or privacy) have, on balance, been judged to outweigh the parents' interests in retaining decision-making authority relating to their children's health care (Weithorn, 1983b). Perhaps the most consistent example of this type of exception has been in the case of reproductive rights of minors. The U.S. Supreme Court has repeatedly affirmed a pregnant minor's right to obtain an abortion, if that minor is considered to be sufficiently "mature" to make a competent abortion decision.[22] Further, the Court has empowered minors to obtain contraceptives independent of parental consent.[23] These decisions have hinged on the Court's assessment that the state's interests (in discouraging unplanned teenage pregnancy and the birth of unwanted children to teenagers) together with the minor's privacy (i.e., autonomy) interests, outweigh family privacy concerns.

As noted above, in Bellotti v. Baird (II)[24] the Court made a minor's access to an abortion independent of parental consent contingent on the minor's maturity, or competency, to consent. As such, the Court invoked the "mature minor" rule, an exception to the doctrine of parental consent on the statutes of certain states, which reads: a minor may consent to any surgical or medical treatment or procedures if that minor is "of sufficient intelligence to understand and appreciate the consequences of the proposed treatment or procedures for himself."[25]

In contrast, the Court has been less supportive of minors' autonomy with respect to another mode of treatment: psychiatric hospitalization. In 1979, in *Parham v. J.R.*, the Court held that a Georgia statute authorizing parents to admit their minor children to inpatient psychiatric facilities on a voluntary basis was not unconstitutional.[26] In the Court's analysis, family privacy interests outweighed the minor's interests in due process prior to the deprivation of liberty that characterizes such hospitalization. The Court addressed the question of whether minors might be able to make such treatment decisions independent and concluded that

> Most children, even in adolescence, simply are not able to make sound judgments concerning many decisions, including their need for medical care or treatment.[27]

Interestingly, the Supreme Court decided the *Bellotti* and *Parham* cases during the same term, contradicting itself on the question of minors' competency. In *Bellotti* the Court allowed that some minors may be sufficiently mature to consent to abortion whereas in *Parham* the Court dismissed the possibility that any minors, including adolescents, would be competent to make treatment decisions. This contradiction, which probably resulted from two different justices' writing these two decisions, clearly reflects the current state of legal controversy on the question of minors' competency.

Weithorn (1982) and Grisso and Vierling (1978) provide discussions of the psychological skills that appear to be required in order to make a competent treatment decision. Based on a Piagetian analysis (Inhelder & Piaget, 1958; Piaget, 1972), these authors predict that most adolescents will have the necessary cognitive skills to demonstrate competency according to the highest standard: appreciation. Since the standard of appreciation requires that individuals understand at a relatively abstract level information about future possibilities resulting from each of several choices, it appears that formal operational thinking would be a prerequisite. Formal operational structures allow individuals to conceptualize multiple abstract possibilities and to hypothesize about the consequences of various courses of action. Since children begin to develop formal operational structures at about age 11, and the stage reaches a point of equilibrium at about age 14, it would appear that 14-year-olds and older adolescents would meet the highest standards of competency.

Weithorn and Campbell (1982) investigated the law's presumptions regarding the competency of minors to consent to treatment. Children aged 9 and 14 were compared with adults aged 18 and 21. All subjects were presented with four hypothetical vignettes about individuals suffering from particular medical or psychological disorders, and who had to choose among several treatment options. The subjects were presented with detailed information about the nature, purpose, risks, and benefits of the alternative treatments, and were asked to choose among them. The subjects were then asked a series of standardized questions about their decisions, and about the vignettes. The responses were scored according to criteria on several scales, each scale having been designed to measure competency according to one of the legal standards reviewed above.

In general, the findings strongly supported hypothetical predictions. Fourteen-year-olds were found not to differ from adults in most instances according to all scales of competency: inferential understanding (i.e., appreciation), factual understanding, reasoning, reasonable outcome, and evidence of choice. By contrast, 9-year-olds were found to perform significantly less well on the understanding and reasoning scales. However, despite the 9-year-olds' poorer performance on these scales, they did not differ significantly from the adults with respect to the choices they selected (i.e., reasonable outcome test), in three or four instances. This finding suggests that full understanding and the most sophisticated reasoning process may not be prerequisites for reaching a reasonable decision, or at least, figuring out what is the socially acceptable or popular choice. All subjects evidenced a choice on the vignettes; thus, no group differences were found on that scale.

As a first attempt to examine minors' competency to consent to treatment by using assessment strategies developed with legal standards in mind, this study provided information about the functioning of healthy children under optimal circumstances. However, if we wish to address questions of the capacities of mentally disabled minors to consent to treatment, further research is necessary. Such questions are currently under investigation by this author.

Research investigating the capacities of mentally disabled adults to consent to treatment yields contradictory findings. Some studies (Grossman & Summers, 1980; Soskis, 1978; Soskis & Jaffe, 1979; Stanley, Stanley, Lautin, Kane, & Schwartz, 1981) suggest that psychiatric patients do not differ from medical patients on competency measures, while other studies (Appelbaum & Gutheil, 1980; Appelbaum, Mirkin, & Bateman, 1981) conclude that psychiatric patients are not competent. Thus, it remains unclear to what extent an emotional disorder will impair the decision-making ability of adults or minors.

## Competency to Consent
## to Research

On March 8, 1983 the Department of Health and Human Services (DHHS) promulgated federal regulations specifying protections for children involved as subjects in research.[28] These regulations authorize the individual Institutional Review Boards (IRBs)[29] to determine what role children are to play in decision making about their own participation in research. Questions of minors' roles in such decision making are influenced by somewhat different policy issues than those pertaining to consent to treatment. Clearly, family privacy and parental discretion remain key when considering consent to both treatment and research. However, unlike treatment procedures, many research procedures do not involve the possibility of direct benefit to the subjects in the form of needed services. Rather, the benefits of the procedures typically accrue to a class of individuals (to which the subject may belong), or to society in general. Thus, when individuals are asked to participate in many research protocols, they are asked to "volunteer" themselves for the good of others. Our society does not require its citizens to perform such activities as part of a social contract. Thus, whereas there is a justification for forcing an individual to participate in treatment, there can be no justification for such coercion with respect to procedures without direct personal benefit. Therefore, it is proposed that even individuals of limited competence should have some say in whether they are volunteered for research, since those procedures are often not expected to yield direct benefit to them.

The DHHS regulations differ somewhat from the initial recommendations of the National Commission for the Protection of Human Subjects of Biomedical and Behavioral Research (1977). This commission, influenced by Ferguson's (1978) work, recommended that the assent of children of age 7 and older be required, together with parental permission, prior to the inclusion of children in most types of studies. The commission used the term "assent" to distinguish the child's "knowledgeable agreement" (Levine, 1981) from legally valid consent, for which one might have to meet higher standards of competency. The term "permission" was applied to the parents' authorization for their child's participation, to differentiate a decision one makes on behalf of another (permission) from a decision one autonomously makes for oneself (consent).

The commission listed the following exceptions to the general formula requiring the child's assent plus parental permission: (a) If the research includes an intervention from which the subject might derive significant therapeutic benefit, and which is not available outside the research context, young children's objections may be overridden; (b) under certain circumstances such as those in which the research procedures relate to a treatment for which minors can provide legally valid informed consent (e.g., abortion), and the research procedures do not present a greater than minimal risk to the subject, the requirement for parental consent may be waived.

The federal regulations retained the spirit of the commission's recommendations, although leaving most decisions to the discretion of the IRB. Thus, rather than providing federal guidance as to the age at which assent should be required, DHHS indicated that the IRB should ensure that "adequate provisions are made for soliciting the assent of the children, when in the judgment of the IRB the children are capable of providing assent."[30] IRBs were instructed to consider the ages, maturity, and psychological state of the relevant children when making capacity determinations. Only under circumstances in which the child is not capable of providing assent, or when the research procedures hold out the promise of critical health benefits to the child, would the requirement for assent be waived. The regulations further indicate that the requirement for parental permission could be waived when such a requirement "is not . . . reasonable . . . to protect the subjects."[31] It was specified that appropriate substitute consent mechanisms (e.g., allowing minors decision-making autonomy) would depend on the children's age, maturity, and condition.

In that the regulations emphasize the importance of the minor's age and maturity to IRB deliberations about minors' role in the consent process, it behooves behavioral scientists to inform IRBs as to the degree to which minors are capable of participating meaningfully in the process. The central questions relate to children's capacities to provide fully informed consent (thus allowing for a waiver of the requirement for parental consent under appropriate circumstances) and children's capacities to provide meaningful assent.

The legal requirements for informed consent for research are quite similar to those characterizing informed consent for treatment (Levine, 1981). The primary differences relate to the types of information that must be provided in individuals, with certain additional elements of disclosure required for research consent.[32] Further, the standards for competency to consent to treatment have been applied to consent regarding research as well (Appelbaum & Roth, 1982).

Given the similarities between consent issues in the treatment and research contexts, the Weithorn and Campbell (1982) findings appear to have direct relevance for questions of minors' competence to provide informed consent for research. The results support the notion that there is a significant group of mature minors—adolescents 14 and older—who are capable of sophisticated decision making. Thus, under circumstances in which an IRB determines that it would be advisable to waive the requirement for parental permission, empowering the minor to provide independent consent would be a suitable substitute mechanism that would adequately protect that person.

The National Commission (1977) seemed to define assent as the general capability "of understanding the procedures and general purpose of the research and of indicating" one's wishes regarding participation. I have suggested elsewhere (Weithorn, 1983a) that the National Commission intended the standards for meaningful assent to be significantly lower than the highest standards for fully informed consent, and I propose that competency to provide assent consists of two elements. First, the prospective subject must comprehend at a very basic level what will be done to him or her, or what he or she will be required to do, if assent is provided. Second, the child must understand the basic purpose of the research. Most children, as a result of school participation, are quite familiar with the concept that we engage in activities in order to learn more about something (Weithorn, 1983a).

Piagetian research (Inhelder & Piaget, 1958) supports the proposal of the National Commission that even children as young as 7 can provide meaningful assent. During the stage of concrete operational thinking—extending from 7 to 11 years—children are able to consider several elements of a stimulus situation, and to employ logical cognitive operations when thinking about problems, as long as the concepts are not highly abstract. Weithorn and Campbell's (1982) study also is supportive. Although the 9-year-old subjects evidenced significantly poorer understanding and reasoning than the adults, the patterns of their responses indicated that they understood a great deal and could play a meaningful role in decision making, even if they were not as capable as adults of self-determination. For example, the 9-year-old children tended to consider the one or two more salient elements of disclosure when reasoning about their choices, while the older subjects considered a broader range of factors when making their decision. Yet, the factors considered by the 9-year-olds were almost uniformly logical and important (e.g., "I'd take the medicine because without it, you can die). This finding is consistent with that reported by Keith-Spiegel and Mass (1981), who found similarity between the reasons offered by minors and adults when presented with vignettes about hypothetical research projects. Finally, Lewis, Lewis, and Ifekwunigue (1978), presented school children, aged 6 through 9, with a real, not hypothetical, choice of participating in a swine flu vaccine program and found that the children responded in a manner suggestive of meaningful decision making.

In summary, barring psychological infirmity, most school-aged children appear capable of providing meaningful assent for participation in research. Furthermore, most adolescents probably are capable of providing competent informed consent for such research under appropriate circumstances.

## Capacity to Express a Preference
## in Child Custody Disputes

Judges typically retain much discretion regarding the disposition of child custody disputes in divorce cases. There remains great variability across states in the degree to which jurists are instructed to take particular factors into account when making custody decisions. Consideration of a child's custodial preference is one of those factors given varying attention across jurisdictions. The statutes of approximately 20 states require the courts to give some consideration to a child's preference, although the case law of almost all states has addressed this concept (Siegel & Hurley, 1977). Some states require that if a child is of a certain age (e.g., 12 or 14), the preference of that child regarding a custodian must be dispositive. Others, adopting a standard similar to that suggested in the Uniform Marriage and Divorce Act,[33] specify consideration of the child's wishes as one of several relevant factors to be reviewed by the courts, but it is left to the court's discretion how to weigh these factors. Other states suggest or encourage that courts consider a child's preference, but they in no way mandate that the child's wishes be reviewed. However, regardless of the specific standard adopted by particular states, one theme emerges in an analysis of appellate court reviews of custody decisions. In order for a child's preference for a custodian to be considered meaningful by the courts, the child must be "of sufficient age and mental capacity to form a rational judgment"[34] or "an intelligent choice," or that the child's preference be based on "sound reasoning" (Siegel & Hurley, 1977). Some states requires that a finding of mental capacity be made prior to the consideration of a child's preference (Benedek & Benedek, 1979). In general, absent specific guidelines emphasizing age rather than mental capacity, it appears to be an accepted standard that courts consider children's preferences only if such preferences are the product of an intelligent and rational decision (Committee on the Family, 1981).

Psychological data investigating children's capacities to express meaningful preferences in custody proceedings might inform the courts on two primary questions. First, what are the psychological correlates, from a developmental perspective, of the capacity to make a reasoned and intelligent choice regarding one's guardian? Clearly, many courts attempt to evaluate on a case-by-case basis such capacities with the guidance of only this rather vague legal test. Second, to what degree are the ages of 12 and 14—cited in case law, statutes, and scholarly writings—meaningful as cut-off points, above which children are assumed to be capable of registering a reasonable custodial preference?

To date, no empirical data have been published, directly addressing these questions. Thus, this discussion will attempt to apply basic psychological theory and research to these issues.

It is beyond the scope of this chapter to review the various procedures for obtaining the child's preferences, as well as the relative merits or disadvantages of involving the child in the decision-making process. For the purposes of this discussion, when referring to a child's preference, it is assumed that the child in question has voiced a direct and clear preference for a custodian, under one set of circumstances or another (i.e., with a lawyer, judge, or mental health professional). I will not refer to inferences made by others regarding such preferences, even if such inferences are considered to be meaningful in such proceedings. In addition, the following discussion accepts the premise that because children are the objects of the custody dispute, and because their future and their welfare may be contingent on the outcome of the dispute, they have a basic right to participate in the proceedings in a manner corresponding to their desires and capacities (Bersoff, 1976-1977; MacDougall, 1980).

It would seem that the most basic criterion of a reasonable decision regarding one's custodian is an understanding of the nature of the question being posed. That is, does the child recognize that he or she is being asked to choose which parent to live with on a permanent basis, and that such a choice will, in most situations, necessitate a dramatic curtailment in one's contact with the noncustodial parent? Conceptualizing what it might be like to live with only one parent rather than another, and to appreciate the permanence of such an arrangement requires a capacity to conceptualize future circumstances and events. Children become increasingly capable of formulating ideas about future possibilities regarding their home lives as they develop formal operational cognitive structures. Furthermore, the ability to balance the short-term versus long-term consequences of each alternative figures prominently in such decision making. One might conclude that reasonable decision making also is that which considers each of the relevant consequences of one's alternatives and weighs the advantages and disadvantages of each (Weithorn, 1982). Thus, can the child discriminate between the relative advantages to his or her well-being of having a parent who chooses good vacation spots from one who evidences daily concern for and attention to the child's basic emotional and physical needs? Clouding our evaluation of the child's ability to weigh these variables is our own inability to determine which factors are most important to a child's well-being.

Yet, need a child actually evidence such clear and reasoned thinking in order to be judged to have made a reasonable decision? If a child expressed just one "reasonable" basis for a preference, is demonstration of a sophisticated risk-benefit analysis really necessary? The law is not clear on this point, since no standards are provided as to how one is to measure or evaluate the reasonableness of preferences. A child may be able to verbalize only one logical reason for a preference (e.g., that one parent is frequently absent). Further, one can envision the court considering more emotional and subjective (rather than cognitive) reasons from children. A child might indicate a preference for one parent over another because the child simply appears to be more emotionally attached to one parent rather than another, or because the child doesn't like one parent's new partner.

The law is relatively clear regarding some of the factors it considers do *not* constitute the basis of a reasonable preference, but it provides little guidance as to precisely which types of reasons *are* acceptable. For example, it has been noted (Committee on the Family, 1981) that the courts are cautious of children's preferences if they believe that those preferences were influenced by the child's desire to be with a more permissive or less strict parent. Further, the courts appear to be wary of what they perceive to be unstable or temporary preferences expressed by children, perhaps as a response to recent pleasant visits with one parent or another.[35] Although we would expect that children who have developed the sophisticated thinking consistent with formal operational structure will be most capable of fully reasoned decision making, which minimizes the above problematic influences, that is not to say that younger children are incapable of expressing meaningful preferences based on sound, albeit unsophisticated, reasoning. The results reported by Weithorn and Campbell (1982) regarding children's competency to consent to treatment suggest that even when younger children (e.g., age 9) demonstrate an inability to apply the more sophisticated balancing of risks and benefits, the options they do select tend to be similar to those choices selected by adults, and the reasons they articulate tend to be eminently sensible.

Independent of factors related to age and level of cognitive development, there are, of course, idiosyncratic and sometimes problematic emotional factors that may impinge on a child's decision making. A child may choose the parent not chosen by a sibling, so as to ensure that one parent isn't abandoned (American Psychiatric Association, 1982). One might question whether such a preference is based on sound reasoning, given that the primary concern is the child's, rather than the parent's, best interests. There are a broad range of affective and family relationship variables that might affect a particular child's expressed preference, and the influence of such variables might or might not vary with the age of the child.

A final factor of relevance is the degree to which a child is capable of expressing an independent and voluntary choice under these particular circumstances. The courts are wary of parental attempts to influence children. Until they have reached adolescence, children typically defer to powerful others (Grisso & Vierling, 1978) and are greatly influenced by their parents. Thus, again, adolescents should be more likely than younger children to express independent choices. Yet, to what degree do more typical patterns of deference to parental influence remain prominent in the face of conflicting demands or requests from both parents?

In summary, it appears that the capacity of children to render a reasonable and intelligent preference regarding their custodian might require rather sophisticated cognitive deliberations, suggesting that the age standards of 12 or 14 are meaningful cut-off points above which children's preferences will be considered. Yet, in that the law has not clearly defined what is meant by an "intelligent" or "reasonable" decision, we cannot disregard the possibility that younger children, who may verbalize one or more sensible intellectual or emotional reason, might also be registering meaningful preferences. Clearly, empirical research will be the key in elucidating developmental patterns in children's decision making regarding custodians and judicial notions of what constitutes sound reasoning, for such decisions.

## Children's Competence to Testify

Whereas evidentiary standards presume adults to be competent to testify in court, presumptions regarding the testimonial competence of children vary across jurisdictions. For example, approximately 12 states have enacted statutes that presume the testimonial competence of children aged 10 and older (Siegel & Hurley, 1977). These statutes specify that children younger than 10 will be permitted to testify if they can demonstrate competency to the trial judge. With few exceptions, most states do not invoke a *per se* rule, barring the testimony of children of particular ages with an irrebuttable presumption of incompetence. Rather, judicial discretion in making case-by-case determinations of children's competency is the rule typically defined in case law (Melton, 1981). Testimony by children as young as age 4 has been noted.[36] Usually the context of the judicial competency determinations will be a *voir dire* examination or interview of the prospective witness by the judge.

In order for an individual's testimony to be considered of value to the court, that individual must have personal knowledge that is relevant to the legal inquiries. In the case of a child, that knowledge might relate to events that were observed (as an eyewitness to an act that might be construed as criminal or negligent); personal experiences (as a victim of a criminal or negligent act); one's own actions (as the alleged perpetrator of an illegal act); or one's feelings, ideas, or attitudes (as a child expressing a preference in a custody dispute). In that the latter subject has been dealt with in some detail above, this section will focus primarily upon the evidentiary standards defining children's competency to testify regarding events they have witnessed, experienced, or performed.

A variety of standards defining testimonial competence have been applied by jurisdictions. In *Laudermilk v. Carpenter,*[37] the Supreme Court reviewed those common and case law standards some variations of which are applied in most states:

(1) an understanding of the obligation to speak the truth on the witness stand; (2) the mental capacity at the time of the occurrence concerning which he is to testify, to review an accurate impression of it; (3) a memory sufficient to retain an independent recollection of its occurrence; (4) the capacity to express in words his memory of the occurrence; and (5) the capacity to understand simple questions about it.[38]

Perhaps most frequently cited is the standard requiring that the child understand the concept of the oath and be motivated to speak honestly. Voir dire investigations have asked children about their religious beliefs or expectations as to the consequence of lying, in order to determine if the children were sufficiently motivated to speak truthfully. Whereas the motivation to be truthful does not appear to be developmentally linked (Melton, 1981), the ability to differentiate reality from fantasy might be. Johnson and Foley (in press), in an excellent review of the relevant developmental literature, report that many writers speculate that children may confuse fact (i.e., what they have observed or experienced in the external world) with internal experiences derived from dreams and waking imaginations. The authors conducted a series of four studies to examine this notion empirically.

Johnson and Foley's (in press) investigations compared children as young as 6 to older children and to adults. Their findings suggest that broad generalizations about children's ability to discriminate perceived from imagined stimuli are inappropriate. Depending upon the nature of the discrimination, differences between children and adults might or might not be found. Young children were as capable as adults of discriminating stimuli they had seen or heard (e.g., visual slides or spoken words) from those they had been asked to imagine. Yet, children were more likely than adults to confuse memories of what they did (e.g., spoke a particular word) from what they thought about doing (e.g., thought about saying the particular word). This finding is particularly meaningful in considering children's capacity to testify about their own actions. The researchers currently are investigating whether there exist developmental differences in ability to discriminate what one perceives other people doing from what one imagines other people doing. It would seem that this latter investigation might be of most direct relevance when a child has been an eyewitness to or a victim of the actions of another. Thus, it would be premature to draw conclusions as to young children's ability to separate fact from fantasy.

One caution should be noted. In generalizing from the laboratory to real incidents requiring testimony, we might consider the degree to which those incidents are similar to or different from ordinary experience. For example, it is a well-accepted notion among child abuse workers that very young children simply do not fantasize or lie about having experienced sexual abuse, and may not even be capable of doing so because what typically occurs in sexual abuse incidents is so unfamiliar to them (Beach, 1983). Thus, whereas young children may confuse fact and fantasy regarding neutral and familiar stimuli, it is not clear to what extent such findings would be generalizable to that proportion of cases in which testimony is required about affectively charged or unfamiliar experiences.

In recent years there has been somewhat greater emphasis on that standard of competency that requires an accurate memory of the events to be reported. Loftus (1979) has demonstrated that the memories of adults concerning perceptions may be less accurate than is commonly presumed and, in particular, may be susceptible to influence from subsequent input. Are children's memories less accurate, or more susceptible to influence, than are those of adults?

Developmental research indicates that children typically recall less information than do adults (Johnson & Foley, in press; Marin, Holmes, Guth, & Kovac, 1979). Marin et al. designed a laboratory analogue of a circumstance requiring eyewitness testimony. Children and adults, ostensibly participating in some other type of study, were surprised by an altercation between the experimenter and a confederate, and their memories of this incident were subsequently tested. Subject groups represented the following grade levels: kindergarten through first; third and fourth; seventh and eighth, and university.

A significant linear trend was observed in the results from the "free recall" section of the inquiry, in that older subjects recalled more facts about the incident than younger subjects. Interestingly, however, the younger subjects' responses did not tend to contain inaccuracies, with the older subjects being more likely to report incorrect information. However, despite younger children's poorer performance regarding the amount of information reported on free recall, no significant age differences were observed when subjects were asked 20 direct objective questions. No significant age differences were found during the photo identification phase of the inquiry, although the adolescent group appeared somewhat more adept at this task than either the older or the younger group, although this difference only approached significance.

The Marin et al. findings may be limited by the time period used in the study (i.e., two weeks). Whereas immediate eyewitness reports may be requested of individuals shortly after viewing incidents, courtroom testimony typically follows by several months or years. Johnson and Foley (in press) suggest, however, that there is as yet no evidence suggesting that long-term retention is inferior in younger children. Related to another point, these authors suggest that if the testimony concerns material that is otherwise familiar to the child subjects, their performance might be superior than that of adults for whom the material was not familiar. In particular, they cite a study by Chi (1978) demonstrating that chess-playing children were better able to remember chess-piece positions than were adults who did not know how to play chess. Overall, the Marin et al. findings are consistent with basic research on memory (Johnson & Foley, in press; Melton, 1981), and would suggest that children will provide more complete information when testifying if asked direct and objective, rather than open-ended, questions.

Are children more susceptible to the influence of input subsequent to the events in question, such as in responding to suggestive or leading questions? Questions such as, "Was the package the man carried small?" (Marin et al., 1979) lead the subject to infer that the man was necessarily carrying a package. Questions such as, "How fast were the cars going when they smashed into each other?" (Loftus, 1979) obviously suggest their own response by the use of such phrases as "smashed into" rather than "hit." Dale, Loftus, and Rathbun (1978) found that young children (ages 4 and 5) were more likely to respond positively about the presence of an entity not actually present in a film when asked questions such as: "Did you see *the* girl?" rather than "Did you see *a* girl?" The form of the question did not affect accuracy of responses about entities that were not present in the film, however. Because Dale et al. did not compare their young subjects to adults, we can only speculate that adults may also have performed in this manner, based upon the findings of Loftus (1979) in similar studies with adults.

Cohen and Harnick (1980) showed subjects (9 and 12 years old and adults) a brief film, then asked 22 questions in either a suggestive or non-suggestive form. One week later, the subjects returned and were provided with a multiple-choice memory test. The younger subjects were more likely than the two older groups to respond initially in the directions of suggestive questions, although all groups were affected by the suggestions. One week

later, it was found that those subjects who had been presented with suggestive questions obtained fewer correct responses on the multiple-choice test.
No developmental differences were found. This indicates that, whereas the
younger children might have been more compliant and less likely to disagree
verbally with the person asking the leading questions, their memories of the
original stimuli do not appear to be affected by such questions to a greater
degree than do the memories of adults (Loftus and Davies, in press).

With respect to the other standards cited in *Laudermilk v. Carpenter*,[41]
some brief statements may be made. Depending upon the specific incidents
the child is to report, younger children may or may not be capable of per-
ceiving the event and verbally expressing that experience. Apparently, the
courts often regard evidence of developmentally normal functioning of a
child in other spheres (e.g., intellectually) as sufficient to determine capacity to perceive an event (Siegel & Hurley, 1977). Regarding the child's verbal skills and capacity to report his or her observations and experiences,
direct questions that permit monosyllabic responses, together with liberal
use of concrete aids (e.g., anatomically correct dolls in sexual abuse cases),
may assist very young children in such expression. Finally, the capacity to
understand the questions asked depends, in part, on the specific questions.
Of course, questions can be simplified for younger children.

In conclusion, it appears that most children who have knowledge of relevance to legal proceedings should not be disqualified as witnesses on the
basis of age alone. Even very young children may, under certain circumstances, meet all of the criteria for competency to testify. Further, the type
(i.e., open-ended versus focused) and nature (i.e., suggestive versus non-
suggestive) of the question may affect responses. Whereas children, more
than adults, appear more vulnerable to the immediate pressure to respond in
the directions of suggestive questions, they do not appear to be influenced to
alter their memories of the original percepts to a greater degree than adults.

## Conclusions

Unfortunately, many writers and professionals—including, but not limited to, social scientists, scholars, policymakers, and health care personnel—fail to differentiate among the various legal competencies discussed in
this chapter. It is not uncommon for these experts to assume that competency to stand trial is the same thing as competency to consent to treatment,
or competency to testify. Obviously, such an assumption is incorrect. As
noted in the introduction to this chapter, the term competency refers merely
to sets of skills or abilities. There is no more similarity between competency
to stand trial and competency to consent to treatment than there is between

competency to drive a car and competency to raise a child. Whereas persons whose functioning is so impaired that they are unable to perform most daily tasks may be incompetent in several spheres, few other generalizations can be made about persons' capacities from one context to the next. The only exception to this rule is where two types of competency are related from a theoretical and policy standpoint (e.g., as noted in this chapter when comparing competency to consent to treatment or research).

It is hoped that this chapter has demonstrated further that very different conclusions may be drawn about children's abilities to meet legal criteria for competency, depending upon the type of competency in question. So, where we might conclude that 4-year-olds could, in some instances, meet the criteria for competency to commit certain crimes or competency to testify, we would rule out the possibility that such a child could register valid consent for a surgical operation, according to the appreciation standard. It is important to note that, in each instance, psychological factors alone are not sufficient to determine whether or not a child should be permitted to exercise his or her capacities in the legal sphere. As noted above, our society values the autonomous decision making of parents regarding their children's health care. It is only under certain exceptional circumstances that the law is willing to overrule parental authority and allow some alternative decision maker (e.g., the child) to choose. Therefore, even if we can demonstrate empirically that adolescents are capable of independent health care decision making, legal policies will not, and should not, automatically shift "across the board" to become more consistent with the data. Whether a minor's competency to commit a crime or competency to stand trial is at all relevant to the legal system depends upon the policy goals and procedures that define the system. As we have moved from the processing of all minors in the criminal justice system to a juvenile justice system that was at first idealized, but is now viewed more realistically, the competencies of relevance have shifted as well.

It has only been in the past several years that social scientists have begun to examine children's capacities in legal contexts (Melton, Koocher, & Saks, 1983). Some of this research may have been a response to requests from lawyers (Leon, 1978; Wald, 1976) that social scientists address such questions. Whereas our data bases are beginning to develop, clearly this field is in its early stages of development. Some of the questions in particular need of such investigation were noted in this chapter. Finally, we would emphasize that in undertaking psychological research that tests the law's presumptions about children's capacities, social scientists must ensure that they are adequately familiar with and informed about the legal standards and policies at which their work is directed.

## Notes

1. For the purposes of this chapter, the term "children" will be used to refer to all minors, i.e., persons who have not reached the legal age of majority. The age of majority typically is 18 or 21, depending upon the jurisdiction and the particular legal issue in question.

2. Illinois Juvenile Court Act of 1899, Act of April 21, 1899, Illinois Laws 131.

3. In re Betty Jean Williams, Memorandum Opinion. Docket No. 27-220-J-Juvenile Court for the District of Columbia (October 29, 1959), as reprinted on pp. 191-192 in Fox, S. J., *Modern Juvenile Justice* (St. Paul, MN: West Publishing Company, 1979).

4. In re Davis, 299 A.2d 856 (Md. 1973).

5. Id. at 859.

6. In re Gladys R., 464 P. 2d 127 (Cal. 1970).

7. In re Winship, 397 U.S. 358 (1970); In re Gault, 387 U.S. 1 (1967); Kent v. U.S., 383 U.S. 541 (1966).

8. In re Glassberg, 88 So. 2d 707 (La. 1956).

9. In re Davis, 299 A. 2d 856 (Md. 1973).

10. Drope v. Missouri, 420 U.S. 162 (1975); Pate v. Robinson, 383 U.S. 375 (1966).

11. Dusky v. U.S., 362 U.S. 402 (1960).

12. Id. at 402.

13. Jackson v. Indiana, 406 U.S. 715 (1972).

14. Id. at 738.

15. In re Betty Jean Williams, Memorandum Opinion. (See Note 3.)

16. Id. at 191.

17. State ex rel. Dandoy v. Superior Court, 619 P. 2d 12 (Ariz. 1980).

18. Id. at 15; see also In re Welfare S.W.T., 277 N.W. 2d 507 (Minn. 1979); In re Jeffrey C., 81 Misc. 2d 651, 366 N.Y.S. 2d 826 (1975).

19. Restatement (Second) of Torts, chap. 45, Section 892A (2), 1979.

20. Parham v. J.R., 442 U.S. 584 (1979); Wisconsin v. Yoder, 406 U.S. 205 (1972); Pierce v. Society of Sisters, 268 U.S. 571 (1924); Meyer v. Nebraska, 262 U.S. 390 (1923).

21. Prince v. Commonwealth of Massachusetts, 321 U.S. 158 (1944) at 168.

22. City of Akron v. Akron Center for Reproductive Health, Inc., ___ U.S. ___ (Docket No. 81-746, 1983); Bellotti v. Baird II, 443 U.S. 662 (1979); Planned Parenthood of Central Missouri v. Danforth, 438 U.S. 52 (1976).

23. Carey v. Population Services International, 431 U.S. 678 (1977).

24. Bellotti v. Baird II, 443 U.S. 662 (1979).

25. Arkansas Statutes Annotated, Section 82-363(g) (1976); Mississippi Code Annotated, Section 41-41-3(h) (Supp. 1972).

26. Parham v. J.R., 442 U.S. 584 (1979).

27. Id. at 602-603.

28. Additional Protections for Children Involved as Subjects in Research, 48:46 Federal Register 9614 (March 8, 1983) (to be codified in 45 CFR Part 46).

29. Institutional Review Boards are those committees established within each facility, agency, or institution where research is conducted, whose responsibility it is to ensure that such research complies with federal regulations and ethical principles.

30. Additional Protections for Children Involved as Subjects in Research, 48:46 Federal Register 9614 (March 8, 1983), at 9619.

31. Id. at 9620.

32. Final Regulations Amending Basic DHHS Policy for the Protection of Human Research Subjects, 46:16 Federal Register 8366 (January 16, 1981) (45 CFR 46).

33. Uniform Marriage and Divorce Act. Uniform Laws Annotated. Vol. 9A, Sections 401-410, 1979.
34. Ross v. Pick, 8 A. 2d 463 (Md. 1952).
35. Gregory v. Gregory, 292 So. 2d 50 (Fla. 1974).
36. State v. Doe, 614 P. 2d 1086 (Md. 1980); In the Interest of R.R., A Juvenile, 398 A. 2d 76 (N.J. 1979).
37. Laudermilk v. Carpenter, 457 P. 2d 1004 (Wash. 1969).
38. Id. at 1010.

## Reference Note

1. Roth, L.H. (Principal Investigator). *Empirical study of informed consent in psychiatry* (Final report submitted on research grant MH-27553, Center for Studies of Crime and Delinquency, National Institute of Mental Health). Pittsburgh, PA: University of Pittsburgh, 1980.

## References

American Psychiatric Association. *Child custody consultation: A report of the Task Force on Clinical Assessment in Child Custody.* Washington, DC: American Psychiatric Association, 1982.
Appelbaum, P.S., & Gutheil, T.G. Drug refusal: A study of psychiatric inpatients. *American Journal of Psychiatry,* 1980, *137,* 340-346.
Appelbaum, P.S., Mirkin, S.A., & Bateman, A.L. Empirical assessment of competency to consent to psychiatric hospitalization. *American Journal of Psychiatry,* 1981, *138,* 1170-1176.
Appelbaum, P.S., & Roth, L.H. Clinical issues in the assessment of competency. *American Journal of Psychiatry,* 1981, *138*(11), 1462-1467.
Appelbaum, P.S. & Roth, L.H. Competency to consent to research: A psychiatric overview. *Archives of General Psychiatry,* 1982, *39,* 951-958.
Beach, B.H. Out of the mouths of babes. *Time,* January 31, 1983, p. 58.
Benedek, R.S., & Benedek, E.P. *The child's preference in Michigan custody disputes.* Paper presented at the Michigan International Year of the Child Conference. Lansing: Michigan State University, 1979.
Berndt, T.J., & Berndt, E.G. Children's use of motives and intentionality in person perception and moral judgment. *Child Development,* 1975, *46,* 904-912.
Bersoff, D.N. Representation for children in custody decisions: All that glitters is not *Gault. Journal of Family Law,* 1976-1977, *15,* 27-49.
Caul, J. *Juveniles' perceptions of lawyers.* Unpublished doctoral dissertation, St. Louis University, 1981.
Chi, M.T.H. Knowledge structures and memory development. In R.S. Siegler (Ed.), *Children's thinking: What develops?* Hillsdale, NJ: Lawrence Erlbaum, 1978.
Cohen, R.L., & Harnick, M.A. The susceptibility of child witnesses to suggestion. *Law and Human Behavior,* 1980, *4,* 201-210.
Committee on the Family, Group for the Advancement of Psychiatry. *Divorce, child custody, and the family.* San Francisco, CA: Jossey-Bass, 1981.
Dale, P.S., Loftus, E.F., & Rathbun, L. The influence of the question on the eyewitness testimony of preschool children. *Journal of Psycholinguistic Research,* 1978, *7,* 269-277.

Ferguson, L.R. The competence and freedom of children to make choices regarding participation in research: A statement. *Journal of Social Issues,* 1978, *34*(2), 114-121.

Frey, M.A. Intent in fact, insanity and infancy: Elusory concepts in the exercise of juvenile court jurisdiction. *California Western Law Review,* 1973, *9,* 273-289.

Grisso, T. Juveniles' waiver of rights—legal and psychological competence. New York: Plenum Press, 1981.

Grisso, T., & Lovinguth, T. Lawyers and child clients: A call for research. In J.S. Henning (Ed.), *The rights of children: legal and psychological perspectives.* Springfield, IL: C.C. Thomas, 1982.

Grisso, T., & Vierling, L. Minors' consent to treatment: A developmental perspective. *Professional Psychology,* 1978, *9,* 412-427.

Grossman, L., & Summers, F. A study of the capacity of schizophrenic patients to give informed consent. *Hospital and Community Psychiatry.* 1980, *31,* 205-207.

Grueneich, R. Issues in the developmental study of how children use intention and consequence information to make moral evaluations. *Child Development,* 1982, *53,* 29-43.

Incompetency to stand trial. *Harvard Law Review,* 1967, *81,* 454-473.

Inhelder, B., & Piaget, J. *The growth of logical thinking.* New York: Basic Books, Inc. 1958.

Institute of Judicial Administration, American Bar Association. *Juvenile Justice Standards: Standards Relating to Counsel for Private Parties.* Cambridge, MA: Ballinger, 1980.

Institute of Law, Psychiatry and Public Policy. *Forensic evaluation training manual* (6th ed.). Charlottesville: University of Virginia, 1982.

Johnson, M.K., & Foley, M.A. Reliability of children's memory: Assumptions and evidence. *Journal of Social Issues,* in press.

Karniol, R. Children's use of intention cues in evaluating behavior. *Psychological Bulletin,* 1978, *85,* 76-85.

Keasey, C.B. Children's developing awareness and usage of intentionality and motives. In C.B. Keasey (Ed.), *Nebraska Symposium on Motivation,* 1977, *25,* 219-260. (a)

Keasey, C.B. Young children's attribution of intentionality to themselves and others. *Child Development,* 1977, *48,* 261-264. (b)

Keasey, C.B., & Sales, B.D. An empirical investigation of young children's awareness and usage of intentionality in criminal situations. *Law and Human Behavior,* 1977, *1,* 45-61.

Keith-Spiegel, P., & Maas, T. *Consent to research: Are there developmental differences?* Paper presented at the American Psychological Association Convention, Los Angeles, 1981.

Leon, J.S. Recent developments in legal representation of children: A growing concern with the concept of capacity. *Canadian Journal of Family Law,* 1978, *1,* 375-434.

Levine, R.J. *Ethics and regulation of clinical research.* Baltimore, MD: Urban & Schwarzenberg, 1981.

Lewis, C.E., Lewis, M.A., & Ifekwunigue, M. Informed consent by children and participation in an influenza vaccine trial. *American Journal of Public Health,* 1978, *68,* 1079-1082.

Loftus, E.F. *Eyewitness testimony.* Cambridge, MA: Harvard University Press, 1979.

Loftus, E.F., & Davies, G.M. Distortions in the memory of children. *Journal of Social Issues,* in press.

Low, P.W., Jeffries, J.C., & Bonnie, R.J. *Criminal law.* Mineola, NY: Foundation Press, 1982.

MacDougall, D.J. The child as a participant in divorce proceedings. *Canadian Journal of Family Law,* 1980, *3,* 141-163.

Marin, B.V., Holmes, D.L., Guth, M., & Kovac, P. The potential of children as eyewitnesses. *Law and Human Behavior,* 1979, *3,* 295-305.

McCarthy, F.B. The role of the concept of responsibility in juvenile delinquency proceedings. *University of Michigan Journal of Law Reform, 1977, 10,* 181-219.

McGarry, A.L. *Competency to stand trial and mental illness* (DHEW Publication No. ADM 77-103). Washington, DC: U.S. Government Printing Office, 1973.

Meisel, A. The "exceptions" to the informed consent doctrine: Striking a balance between competing values in medical decision making. *Wisconsin Law Journal,* 1979, 413-488.

Meisel, A. Roth, L.H., & Lidz, C.W. Toward a model of the legal doctrine of informed consent. *American Journal of Psychiatry, 1977, 134,* 285-289.

Melton, G.B. Children's competency to testify. *Law and Human Behavior,* 1981, *5,* 73-85.

Melton, G.B., Koocher, G.P., & Saks, M. *Children's competence to consent.* New York: Plenum Press, 1983.

National Commission for the Protection of Human Subjects of Biomedical and Behavioral Research. *Report and recommendations on research involving children.* (DHEW Publication No. OS 77-0004). Washington, DC: U.S. Government Printing Office, 1977.

Olin, G.B., & Olin, H.S. Informed consent in voluntary mental hospital admissions. *American Journal of Psychiatry, 1975, 132,* 938-941.

Palmer, A., & Wohl, J. Voluntary admission forms: Does the patient know what he's signing? *Hospital and Community Psychiatry, 1972, 23,* 250-252.

Piaget, J. *The moral judgment of the child.* New York: Harcourt Brace Jovanovich, 1965.

Piaget, J. Intellectual evolution from adolescence to adulthood. *Human Development, 1972, 15,* 1-12.

Problem of age and jurisdiction in juvenile court. *Vanderbilt Law Review,* 1966, *19,* 833-864.

Rodham, H. Children under the law. *Harvard Educational Review,* 1973, *43,* 487-514.

Rosenheim, M.K. The child and the law. In B.M. Caldwell & H.N. Ricciuti (Eds.), *Review of Child Development Research, 1973, 3,* 509-555.

Roth, L.H., Meisel, A., & Lidz, C.W. Tests of competency to consent to treatment. *American Journal of Psychiatry, 1977, 134,* 279-284.

Siegel, D.M., & Hurley, S. The role of the child's preference in custody proceedings. *Family Law Quarterly, 1977, 11,* 1-58.

Soskis, D.A. Schizophrenic and medical inpatients as informed drug consumers. *Archives of General Psychiatry, 1977, 134,* 645-647.

Soskis, D.A., & Jaffe, R.L. Communicating with patients about anti-psychotic drugs. *Comprehensive Psychiatry, 1979, 20,* 126-131.

Stanley, B.H., Stanley, M. Lautin, A., Kane, J., & Schwartz, N. Preliminary findings on psychiatric patients as research participants: A population at risk? *American Journal of Psychiatry, 1981, 138,* 669-671.

Wald, M.S. Legal policies affecting children: A lawyer's request for aid. *Child Development,* 1976, *47,* 1-5.

Weithorn, L.A. Developmental factors and competence to make informed treatment decisions. *Child and Youth Services,* 1982, *5,* 85-100.

Weithorn, L.A. Children's capacities to decide about participation in research. *IRB: A Review of Human Subjects Research,* 1983, *5*(2), 1-5. (a)

Weithorn, L.A. Involving children in decisions affecting their own welfare: Guidelines for professionals. In G.B. Melton, G.P. Koocher, & M. Saks (Eds.), *Children's competence to consent.* New York: Plenum Press, 1983. (b)

Weithorn, L.A., & Campbell, S.B. The competency of children and adolescents to make informed treatment decisions. *Child Development*, 1982, *53*, 1589-1599.

Westbrook, J.E. *Mens rea* in the juvenile court. *Journal of Family Law*, 1965, *5*, 121-138.

Winick, B.J., & DeMeo, T.L. Competence to stand trial in Florida. *University of Miami Law Review*, 1980, *35*, 31-76.

# PART II

# *CHILDREN IN THE FAMILY*

# 3

# The Wisdom of Solomon

## Issues in Child Custody Determination

### N. Dickon Reppucci
*University of Virginia*

As the divorce rate in contemporary American society has risen (Glick, 1979; Emery, Hetherington, & Fisher, 1983), the necessity of deciding child custody has become increasingly common. The courts are now having to determine proper custody arrangements for increasing numbers of children of all ages (Bodenheimer, 1977). The societal changes in sex roles, the family, the legal system, and the makeup of the work place, which have contributed to the rising divorce rate, have also resulted in changed expectations of parents in terms of the social definitions of their roles. Of particular importance is the fact that many fathers no longer accept the definition of their role solely in terms of economic support of the family. Consequently, more fathers are claiming the right to custody of their children when their marriages break up (Folberg & Graham, 1979). As a result, judges are increasingly required to decide between two equally active and interested parents, and they often wind up making arbitrary judgments.

Currently, there is controversy and confusion among lawyers and mental health professionals over the criteria on which custody decisions should be made. In the past, historical trends and social norms supported awarding custody largely to one parent on the basis of his or her sex, with the conception of custody of the child as a property right. Today the indeterminate and ambiguous concept of "best interests of the child" is the most widespread standard. Recent psychological research (Luepnitz, 1982; Santrock & Warshak, 1979) has attempted to delineate the effects of different types of custody situations on children and parents in an effort to develop more spe-

Author's Note: Sincere appreciation is expressed to W. Glenn Clingempeel, Mary Murphy, and Christine Reppucci for their assistance in preparing this chapter.

cific, uniformly applicable criteria for making custody decisions. Legal scholars are also interested in developing more specific criteria in terms of the rights, responsibilities, and competencies of parents and children.

This chapter focuses on how standards for awarding custody have changed from the presumption of the father's right, to the preference for the mother, and then to the rights and interests of the child. At present the standards for awarding custody seem to be in transition, with many states moving toward a presumption of joint custody. There are now several justifications for making child custody adjudications in practice and theory. These justifications will be examined in the context of the changing structure of social institutions and the changing philosophical conceptions of the child. Special attention will be given to the best interests standard, the conceptualizations of Goldstein, Freud, and Solnit (1973), the increasing use of joint custody, and the legal system as it affects custody decisions.

## Toward the
## Best Interests of the Child Standard

From the time of the Romans until the nineteenth century, the custody of the child was presumed to be the right of the father (Derdeyn, 1976; Franklin & Hibbs, 1980). The father was invested with absolute control over the life of his children by the legal doctrine of *patria potestas,* and he was viewed as their natural protector. The father's responsibilities were largely defined as physical maintenance and economic support of the child. There was no conception of the psychological needs of the child in the law. The child was considered a part of the father's property, to be possessed and used to provide services (Franklin & Hibbs, 1980; Gaddis, 1978). Eventually English common law, which was based on these traditional assumptions, sought to recognize some of the responsibilities for care of the child along with the rights of parenthood with the Talfourd's Act of 1839. By establishing the doctrine of *parens patria,* the state recognized its role in abridging the rights of the father, when necessary, to ensure the well-being and care of children under seven. Nevertheless, throughout the 1800s custody was primarily awarded to the father. Decisions in the American legal system about child custody were based on these same principles.

Many social changes concerning women and children occurred around the turn of the century. The changing conception of the child emphasized protecting his or her welfare and providing for his or her psychological well-being. The mother's role as the primary physical and psychological caretaker of the child began to be recognized. Child custody adjudication reflected the new philosophical and psychological conception of the child by recognizing the need for "mother love," especially during the child's early "tender years."[1] At first, the mother's developing right to custody-was considered a temporary condition for young children. The children would be given back into the custody of their father later in their development. But, as the tender-years presumption was adopted by most state courts, it developed into a legal precedent favoring mothers as custodians of children of all ages (Weiss, 1979). Furthermore, the legal precedent of child support developed, removing a significant constraint against mother custody. Previously, when fathers were not given custody of their children, they were also absolved of all responsibility for their financial support (Derdeyn, 1976).

Interest in the welfare of the child was first enunciated in 1881 in *Chapsky v. Wood* [2] and clearly expressed in 1925 in *Finlay v. Finlay* [3] as the "best interests of the child" doctrine (Clingempeel & Reppucci, 1982; Derdeyn, 1976). This doctrine became the cornerstone of most state custody statutes (Folberg & Graham, 1979). However, critics (e.g., Goldstein et al., 1973) have argued that the child's needs and desires are often not important criteria at all. In reality, the best interests of the child have been determined by assessing the characteristics of the parents. By far, the preeminent deciding characteristic has been the sex of the parent, perhaps because it is the least ambiguous criterion (Ahrons, 1980). For the past 70 years mothers have been awarded custody in 90 percent of all custody cases, both contested and uncontested (Victor & Winkler, 1977). Although seeming to absolve any bias toward a particular parent's right to custody, the best interests standard has largely been used to support the mother's claim to custody (Clingempeel, & Reppucci, 1982; Franklin & Hibbs, 1980). In conjunction with the tender-years doctrine, which imbues the mother with superior parenting qualities by virtue of her sex, it has been assumed that the best interests of the child clearly will be served in most cases by awarding custody to the mother. To gain custody, fathers have had to prove the mother was unfit, usually by virtue of immorality (i.e., adultery) or incompetence (i.e., evidence of mental illness or alcoholism).

Another method of determining a child's best interests has been to assess parental culpability for divorce. The parent at fault for causing the divorce has been presumed to be less deserving of custody than the innocent party (Derdeyn, 1976). Although no-fault divorce laws are now in effect in 48 states (Freed & Foster, 1981) and are the most common legal grounds for marital dissolution, vestiges of this historical precedent remain. Findings as to whether a parent is fit are often based on grounds similar to those used in the past to determine fault, e.g., adultery, habitual drunkenness, and gross immorality (Podell, Peck, & First, 1972). Thus these factors, although not a formal part of child custody law, continue to play a role in the exercise of judicial discretion (Emery et al., 1983).

The best interests standard has also been used to, "subordinate, often intentionally [the child's] psychological well-being to . . . an adult's right to assert a biological tie" (Goldstein et al., 1973). This parental-natural-right doctrine[4] has had the effect that biological parents are usually awarded custody in disputes with other caretakers or psychological parents (Kram & Frank, 1982). Although it could be in opposition to the best interests standard, it has often been justified as being in the best interests of the child. Thus, from the early 1900s to the 1980s, the child's best interests have been determined mainly without regard to his or her desires and preferences for a custodial parent and without consideration of the particular needs a parent could fill relative to the child's developmental stage, apart from tender-years considerations for young children.

Major changes in American society in the 1960s and 1970s have resulted in new controversies in child custody adjudications. Changes in conceptions of sex roles, the rising divorce rate, the introduction of no-fault divorce laws, and the increasing number of mothers in the American work force have significantly altered the structure of the typical American family and the roles within it. Many mothers no longer stay at home all day and care for their children, while the father brings home the family income. More women than ever are working full- or part-time or are completing their education, in addition to fulfilling their role as mothers. In some cases it may be due to economic necessity. For other women, psychological well-being requires more than being a success in the single role of mother.

In conjunction with these changes in women's roles and occupations, men's ideas about their roles and responsibilities have also changed. More men are becoming aware of and interested in the psychological and emotional aspects of their roles as fathers (Ahrons, 1980; Fein, 1978; Jacobs, 1982; Lamb, 1976, 1979). Unfortunately, with the rising divorce rate and the presumption of mother custody, "more men are being separated from their children at the same time that they are being urged to take a more active and affective role in their child's growth and development" (Greif, 1979). This separation is not necessarily by choice. However, more fathers seem unwilling simply to hand over the children to the mother and step out of their children's lives. More fathers are filing for custody—shared or alone—of their children. Others are seeking enforceable visitation rights, which allow them enough time and freedom to develop meaningful relationships with their children. Many fathers are unwilling to have their parental relationships ordered by the vicissitudes of the custodial mother (Victor & Winkler, 1977).

Along with these changing conceptions of parental roles and the structure of family life in America, a more complex psychological conception of the child has developed, which necessitates more comprehensive custody adjudication standards. Children are no longer considered totally incompetent to relate their own needs and desires to safeguard their best interests. Gaddis (1978) stated that "family court case workers, mental health professionals, and the legal profession are now responding to the more enlightened approach that children are independent persons with their own needs, rights, and privileges." Although this is still a somewhat more ideal than real consideration, it does allow for the child's best interests to be determined, to some extent, according to child-centered variables. Ideally, such children's best interest criteria would be concerned with maximizing both their economic needs and their development and potential (Alexander, 1980; Krishner, 1978). In terms of legal principles, the children's interests and participation should be solicited because they are substantially affected by the custody dispute (Franklin & Hibbs, 1980).

The legal ramifications of this changing conception of the child have led to an increasing use of consultation with the children involved to identify their preferences as to the custodial parent. At least 20 states now have statutes that *require* consideration of the child's preference of custodial parent if he or she is over 10 years of age. The other 30 states have case law relevant to this consideration (Franklin & Hibbs, 1980). Moreover, a few states go so far as to require that a child's preference for custody be binding if the child is of a certain age, usually 12 or 14 (Siegel & Hurley, 1977). Psychological data indicate that there are both advantages and disadvantages to this new criterion. Kurdeck and Seisky's (1980) research suggests that, although children were distressed by their parents' divorce, they could understand that it was caused by interpersonal difficulties and that there were benefits in terms of personal growth for themselves and their parents. Moreover, recent research on informed consent (e.g., Weithorn, 1983; Weithorn & Campbell, 1982) suggests that young children may be more competent to make important life decisions than was previously thought.

Whether or not their expression of a preference is desirable is questionable. Obviously, many parents may coach their children to ask for them as custodians. Furthermore, having to choose between two parents whom the child loves and wants to be with may cause guilt and depression in the child (Franklin & Hibbs, 1980). As Westman (1979, p. 253) states, "Generally speaking, it is not fair to place a child in the position of making choices between parents." Many mental health professionals object to laws allowing children to testify because of the possible ill effects of forcing a child to choose between parents and because of the great potential that parental coercion will influence the choice (GAP, 1981). Interestingly, a somewhat consistent finding in research on divorced families is that what is most important to children—even very young preschoolers—is free access to and continued relationships with both parents after divorce (Greif, 1979; Kurdeck & Seisky, 1980; Rosen, 1979; Steinman, 1981; Wallerstein & Kelly, 1974). Thus, many children might opt for liberal visitation or shared custody if they are made aware of and can understand the alternatives.

Although there is considerable research and speculation concerning the child's role in determining his or her best interests, this essentially indeterminate standard necessarily incorporates value judgments. As a result, "Custody disputes are now decided on the basis of broad, person-oriented principles that ask for highly individualized determinations" (Mnookin, 1975). But are individualized or child-centered criteria really used? If so, why are 90 percent of all contested custody cases still being awarded to the mother? As of 1975, only 8.4 percent of children of divorce were living in the custody of their fathers (Weiss, 1975). Although adjudicating custody disputes according to the sex of the parent violates the equal protection guaranteed in the Fourteenth Amendment,[5] it is probably still used quite often as a criterion for the decision. This may be the result of the indeterminate standards that Mnookin (1975) highlights. Judges are left with much discretion, due to undefined and unspecified standards, so they may rely on their own value judgments to make custody adjudications. Obviously, many judges still think the mother is most often the best parent.

The issue of parental fitness is also controversial relative to the ambiguity of the best interests standard. A parent may be unfit according to a judge's or mental health professional's personal values if allegations are made about his or her unconventional housekeeping, sexuality, morality, or alcohol or drug use (see e.g., *Painter v. Bannister*).[6] But the values of the judge and/or mental health professional are not necessarily those shared by the family in question or by society at large. Thus, there is considerable subjectivity and inconsistency in determining the child's best interest if that is indeed what is being determined. As Rosen (1979) indicates, the different professions involved—law, social work, psychology, and psychiatry—all weigh competency factors differently. Some alternatives have developed to counter the indeterminacy of the best interests standard. New standards for custody adjudication have been proposed by some, comprehensive evaluations are used by others, and a trend toward joint custody is developing.

### Beyond the Best Interests of the Child

In 1973 Goldstein, Freud, and Solnit proposed a comprehensive set of standards, based solely on psychoanalytic conceptions, for determining child custody adjudication in their extremely influential book, *Beyond the Best Interests of the Child*. Realizing the inherent ambiguities in the best interests standard, they suggested instead a more "realistic" consideration of "the least detrimental alternative for safeguarding the child's growth and development." These authors emphasized the risk of psychological harm to the child as a result of prolonged custody litigation and, thus, the need for speedy and permanent custody placements. They elaborated three criteria involved in determining the child's least detrimental alternative. The criteria seek to ensure that a child will be placed with the adult who is now or who is likely to become the child's "psychological parent." Psychological parenthood is determined by emotional attachments; the results of daily care; and social, psychological, and emotional interactions. Thus, the notion of the primary caretaker is influential in determining the psychological parent. Because of the enormous influence these criteria have had, each will be discussed.

The first criterion for a custody decision is that the child's continuity of relationship with his or her psychological (read "custodial") parent should be safeguarded. Goldstein et al. (1973) discourage joint custody or enforceable visitation rights of noncustodial parents, relying rather on the discretion of the custodial parent concerning appropriate visitation. They emphasize the hazards and conflicts in continuing the relationship with the noncustodial parent, ignoring the possible benefits and the child's need and/or desire for this relationship. Moreover, recent research indicates that often both parents are the psychological parents of the child (Fein, 1978; Rosen, 1979; Steinman, 1981). In several studies, the children most prone to psychological stress and illness after divorce were those who had little contact with their noncustodial parents (Bloom, Asher, & White, 1978; Kurdeck & Seisky, 1980; Lowenstein & Koopman, 1978; Wallerstein & Kelly, 1974). Children often felt abandoned or neglected by the noncustodial parent if they lost contact with him or felt guilty for causing his departure (Wallerstein & Kelly, 1974; Weiss, 1975).

In light of these data, leaving visitation rights up to the discretion of the custodial parent may be dangerous because it could encourage the abuse of this privilege. Children often become pawns in "visitation roulette" (Victor & Winkler, 1977), whereby the parents continue the exchange of hostilities by controlling access to the children (Franklin & Hibbs, 1980; Noble & Noble, 1975). The children may become victims of the arrangements that are supposed to be the least detrimental to their well-being.

Goldstein et al.'s (1973) second criterion is that custody adjudication should proceed in consideration of the child's sense of time, which is based on the urgency of theorized instinctual and emotional needs. They advocate separating divorce and custody proceedings so the latter may be resolved regardless of the merits of the divorce or separation action. Disputes over child custody should be heard and decided promptly, so the child is placed with the custodial parent as soon as possible. In terms of reducing the psychological risks of exposing the child to long periods of custody litigation and uncertainty about his or her status, this may be a positive secondary prevention measure. Perhaps another consideration based on the child's sense of time would be the child's desire to have access to both parents as emotional needs may demand. It is difficult for children and parents to limit contact with each other strictly to periods of visitation.

Goldstein et al.'s third criterion is the incapacity of the state to supervise interpersonal relationships and the limits of making long-range predictions about the future needs of children and parents. They use this principle to advocate for the importance of family autonomy and the private ordering of relationships within the family and for the benefits of limited interference by the state. However, by also advocating single-parent custody and the custodial parent's control of visitation, they are increasing the likelihood of prolonged custody conflicts and litigation (Gaddis, 1978; Franklin & Hibbs, 1980). Gaddis (1978) notes that fewer cases come back to the courts for redetermination when both parents have equal rights of access to their children.

Goldstein et al. counter this possibility by suggesting that all child custody adjudication should be final, regardless of changed conditions that may motivate the noncustodial parent to seek custody, since this finality would contribute to the stability and continuity of the child's relationship. However, they overlook the possibility that it could also be very harmful in some cases. For example, several psychological studies indicate that mothers who get sole custody often have problems adjusting to the demands of their work, child care, and social roles and responsibilities (Noble & Noble, 1975; Steinman, 1981; Wallerstein & Kelly, 1974). Parental custody by the father may be desired later to alleviate the pressures of child-care demands and exercising all the parental responsibilities. As Eider (1978) notes, this de facto shared custody probably exists in many families. Furthermore, children in some cases may desire a change in their custodial parent. If the custodial parent opposes this change, or if the custody decision is final, how would the courts deal with the self-made solutions of the dissatisfied children and noncustodial parents, i.e., persistent runaways and child snatching (Noble & Noble, 1975; Victor & Winkler, 1977)?

The value of Goldstein et al.'s proposals is that they offer comprehensive, determinate standards for adjudicating custody decisions, and they are a major attempt to use "psychiatric knowledge" to interface with the law. Unfortunately, the validity of their assumptions is questionable at best and based on theory rather than on any empirical findings (Felner & Farber, 1980). Further, the theory and research has been based on general studies of parent-child relations, attachment, separation, and loss, which may be only tangentially related to divorce—a situation that has unique features that make these general studies inapplicable (Emery et al., 1983). Moreover, Goldstein et al., have ignored evidence that does not agree with their position (Katkin, Bullington, & Levine, 1974). Nevertheless, these criteria have been influential and are used as decision-making standards in many places.

## Joint Custody

Since the mid-1970s, a new rule—joint custody—has emerged as a panacea. A common component of all joint custody arrangements is that both parents are legally given equal power and authority with regard to their children's upbringing, education, and general welfare (Clingempeel & Reppucci, 1982; Cox & Cease, 1978; Gaddis, 1978). Ordinarily, physical custody is shared more evenly than is the case in sole custody arrangements, although specific patterns of alternating between parental homes, including the duration of stay with each parent and the frequency of environmental changes, may vary widely. Inherent within this arrangement is the assumption that joint custody is in the children's best interests, which results in considerable pressure upon parents to negotiate joint custody (Scott & Derdeyn, in press). Proponents argue that joint custody itself promotes cooperation and reduces conflict (Roman & Haddad, 1978), although there are no controlled empirical investigations to support this claim. It should be noted that a recent (Ilfeld, Ilfeld, & Alexander, 1982) presentation of outcome data on relitigation for joint custody versus single custody purports to support the benefits of joint custody. However, this study is replete with methodological errors that invalidate the results.

Nevertheless, since 1975, when joint custody existed only in the North Carolina statutes, 26 additional states have enacted joint custody laws, and the legislatures in the remaining states currently have joint custody legislation under study (Freed & Foster, 1982). Under most of these laws, judges are permitted to order joint custody in cases in which only one parent wants it (Schulman & Pitt, 1982), although sometimes even when neither parent has requested it.[7] Moreover, eight states have passed statutes containing a legal presumption favoring joint custody, but this presumption usually only applies when the parents agree.

Why the rush toward joint custody? Scott and Derdeyn (in press) suggest that joint custody is attractive to the judiciary because both parents are awarded custody, thereby avoiding an agonizing choice, and because this arrangement discourages adjudication of the custody issue in the first place. In addition, it appears to be in the best interests of the child. There is the promise that the child in divorce will not lose either parent but will be able to maintain close relationships with both (Scott & Derdeyn, in press). What research there is indicates that continued contact with both parents is beneficial for children (Hess & Camara, 1979; Hetherington, 1981; Rosen, 1979) *but only in the absence of significant interparental conflict* (Ellison, 1983; Hetherington, Cox, & Cox, 1978). In fact, Emery (1982) has recently concluded that the level of interpersonal conflict may be more critical to children's postdivorce adjustment than either father absence or the disruption caused by marital dissolution per se. Rutter (1981), in a longitudinal study, found that children continued their problematic behavior after separation if parental conflict continued, but improved when family discord was reduced.

The implication of these findings for joint custody appears to be that where parents can cooperate, joint custody may be beneficial; where substantial conflict exists, single custody may better serve the child's needs (Scott & Derdeyn, in press). However, an investigation by Steinman (1981) of 24 highly motivated and cooperating families who voluntarily chose joint custody suggests caution. Although the parents found the arrangement satisfactory despite some difficulties, their children's experiences were more mixed. About one-third of these children felt overburdened by the demands and requirements of the arrangement, especially the physical movement to and from the parent's homes.

## The Legal System

The legal system may vary in the extent to which it encourages or discourages cooperative parenting after a divorce. Many critics consider the adversarial nature of the system itself to be the central problem rather than the practice of individual judges, attorneys, or other court personnel (Bahr, 1981; Coogler, 1977). One major concern is that interactions with legal system personnel may exacerbate interparental conflict (Spanier & Anderson, 1979) and, thus, have deleterious effects on the postdivorce adjustment of children. Legally contested cases, although a small minority (about 10 to 15 percent), are of particular concern because they are usually conducted within an adversarial, win-lose format and treat the divorcing parties as totally independent legal entities. This translates into attorneys for each parent doing what is necessary to gain the most advantageous position (with regard to custody, visitation, and child and spousal support) for their client. This often entails that each parent divulge derogatory information suggesting that the other parent is unfit. While conducive to winning an adversarial contest, such a strategy probably worsens the interparental relationship and ignores the interdependence of parents and children postdivorce (Clingempeel & Reppucci, 1982). Watson (1969) discussed the essential contradiction in a system advocating the psychological best interests of the child while at the same time obligating the parents' lawyers to a total commitment to their clients. Regarding the role of lawyers in the adversary contest, Watson (1969, p. 65) argued,

> They appear to believe that they can conduct a vigorous adversary contest and then have the contestants return to some kind of working rapport. Such con-

tests in child custody cases will surely produce wounds which do not heal adequately to assure a good subsequent working relationship between the parents.

Of course, it cannot be assumed that attorneys are a homogeneous group with regard to proclivity for either courtroom battles or negotiated settlements. Clearly, lawyers will differ in their performance of various roles (e.g., counselor, negotiator, litigator) at the time of child custody determination (Mnookin & Kornhauser, 1979). Nevertheless, it would appear that lawyers who negotiate out-of-court settlements in a way that minimizes conflict (i.e., without the use of threats, bluffs, and manipulation) are probably doing their clients a service in avoiding litigation (Emery et al., 1983). Empirical research would be useful in relating the roles of attorneys during child custody decision making to the postdivorce adjustment of parents and children.

In recent years, the role of the parents' attorneys has not been the only concern. With the trend toward greater representation of the child, debates regarding the appropriate role of the attorney in custody cases have been extended to attorneys who represent the child, i.e., the court-appointed *guardians ad litem*. These attorneys represent one attempt by the judiciary to counter the indeterminacy of the best interest standard that Mnookin (1975) concludes has resulted in a situation in which a judge is asked to use scanty information to make an impossible prediction for which there are no agreed-upon outcome criteria. However, concern has been expressed about whether a representative for the child would facilitate or hinder dispute settlement. Certainly the process might be more complicated (with three rather than two parties to the negotiation) and costly (Mnookin & Kornhauser, 1979). Moreover, some legal commentators have contended that a third attorney would increase the adversarial nature of the contest (Straus, 1976), while others have argued that the child's representative is in an ideal position to serve as mediator and to attenuate conflict (Watson, 1969).

Landsman and Minow (1978) conducted extensive interviews with eighteen attorneys who had served as representatives for the child in custody cases in New Haven, Connecticut. Their goal was to elucidate the full range of activities that these attorneys performed in their role as representative of the child. While about 50 percent classified themselves as either fact finders or advocates, in practice, all attorneys engaged in these activities, plus others (e.g., counseling parents with regard to the child's best interests and mediation attempts aimed at out-of-court settlements). These findings suggest that at least some representatives of the child do perform tasks aimed at reducing the interparental conflict in custody disputes. Unfortunately, the small and highly selective sample precludes generalization. Future empirical research could potentially guide the formulation of criteria for deciding when, and whether, the advantages of counsel for the child outweigh the disadvantages (Mnookin & Kornhauser, 1979).

Mental health professionals have also been involved in custody decisions for some time. Usually they have been called upon on behalf of one or the other parent to provide expert testimony on the child's best interests. Unfortunately, a major problem involved in using their testimony is that it may be biased or contradicted by other experts and therefore discounted by the judge when the expert represents only one parent. Witness the recent warning by the American Psychological Association's Committee on Scientific and Professional Ethics and Conduct:

> In the experience of the committee, psychologists who become involved in child custody cases are frequently unaware of state statutes regarding rights of the custodial and noncustodial parents. They sometimes become engaged with one parent or one parent's attorney against the other in an adversarial proceeding and sometimes are used by one side or the other in a way that is detrimental to the psychological well-being of the child or children involved. As in other assessments, psychologists who reach opinions that have serious impact on the lives of others based on partial information are liable to a charge of ethical violation. (Hall & Hare-Mustin, 1983, p. 726)

More recently, many courts have been requesting independent comprehensive evaluations and recommendations from mental health professionals. These court referrals for evaluations theoretically have the potential advantage of being from neutral parties and, thus, of determining the best alternative for the child in an unbiased fashion. However, depending upon the evaluator's theoretical inclinations, various criteria are used in deciding child custody.

For example, the Colorado Children's Diagnostic Center (CDC), involves a multidisciplinary team evaluation of the different custody alternatives, in which all the children and potential custodians are interviewed. A report and recommendation for custody adjudication is presented to the court after a week of intensive evaluations and discussions with the parents and among the staff. The CDC's philosophical basis for criteria is essentially derived from Goldstein et al.'s (1973) proposed criteria (Jackson, Warner, Hornbein, Nelson, & Fortescue, 1980). In contrast, John Batt (1976) advocates a procedure that focuses on the child's developmental stage, assessing his or her relevant needs. Then the parents are evaluated in terms of practical and theoretical considerations—time, devotion, attitudes toward the child as well as intentions, objectives, and goals. On the basis of these criteria, the goal is to determine who will best serve the child's needs and interests relative to his or her developmental stage. In yet another alternative, Krishner (1978) suggests the use of a "legal social services" integrative approach. This considers the three important areas of the child's best interests: (1) emotional, (2) educational and developmental, and (3) economic. Once information is obtained that satisfies the evaluator, a child environmental impact statement is written, in which the impact on the child of various custody alternatives are discussed.

In essence, there are many types of custody adjudication evaluation procedures now in use throughout the United States. Since each evaluative procedure has relatively definitive standards, it is likely that cases are being decided with more discriminating criteria than the sex of the parent or the value judgments of judges. Nevertheless, most mental health evaluations share the basic underlying problem that the knowledge base does not exist for making any definitive judgments for what is ultimately in the best interests of the child (GAP, 1981; Mnookin, 1975).

Nonadversary modes of dispute settlement have been proposed as an alternative to custody adjudication under the adversary model (Druckman & Rhodes, 1977; Haynes, 1981; Kay, 1970; Kubie, 1964). Perhaps the most serious consideration has been given to a mediator-arbitrator Model. Under this model, persons functioning as mediators, either attached or unattached to the court, adopt as their goal the parental resolution of custody disputes. Their purpose is to facilitate negotiated settlements that are self-determined by the divorcing parties rather than imposed by the court. In contrast to adversarial out-of-court settlement, the divorcing spouses employ a single mediator who works with both parties in an effort to reach a mutual agreement in regard to their disputes. Mediation is usually designed to be a short-term process that is completed in one to twelve sessions of one or two hours each. Druckman and Rhodes (1977) have argued that a greater percentage of parent-determined versus court-determined custody cases would have at least three major advantages:

(1) The people who know the child best would make the custody-related decisions, and this could provide an example of future cooperative relationships.

(2) The achievement of mutually advantageous solutions would minimize the sense of loss and resentment in one parent and is consistent with the notion that postdivorce adjustment of children is a function of an interdependent system.

(3) The child's fears of losing a parent would be attenuated.

In addition, there is the likelihood of reduced financial burden on both the state and the divorcing parties as well as increased compliance with court orders[8] (Bahr, 1981).

Although nonadversarial modes of custody adjudication could possibly reduce interparental conflict after a divorce, the beginning shift from a presumption of single-parent custody to a presumption of joint custody might also have similar benefits. In American society today, divorcing parents usually assume that one of them must get custody. Joint custody has only recently been considered as an option and is still used sparingly, even though a majority of states have now enacted joint custody laws. Parents who would have agreed on joint custody as a compromise might battle in court for sole parental custody. Therefore, the likelihood of cooperative parenting after divorce might be increased by a presumption of joint custody.

A presumption of joint custody would assure that shared parenting after divorce is raised as an option. Such a presumption may therefore increase the likelihood of out-of-court compromises resulting in a greater percentage of custody decisions determined by the parents rather than the courts. Besides the potential advantages noted by Druckman and Rhodes (1977), the promotion of parent-determined custody arrangements is consistent with the position of several legal scholars that intervention in family and parenting issues, given our limited knowledge, should be minimized commensurate with the societal values of family autonomy and pluralism (Wald, 1976; Mnookin, 1975; Mnookin & Kornhauser, 1979).

While a presumption of joint custody could ultimately have positive effects on the postdivorce adjustment of children, it is possible that such a presumption would make very little difference. Even when custody is awarded to one parent, parents often carry out de facto joint custody arrangements (Abarbanel, 1979). Moreover, there is the possibility that a presumption of joint custody would encourage many parents who are unwilling to put aside their hostilities to attempt joint custody arrangements. As a result, children might be exposed to more interparental conflict than they would under single-parent provisions. Insofar as joint custody fosters more contact between parents, it may exacerbate interparental conflict and its concommitant deleterious effects on children. As previously mentioned, for joint custody to succeed, former spouses who are hostile toward each other would need to separate the parental and marital dimensions of their relationships. Unfortunately, the blend of situational and personality factors that enable certain parents successfully to accomplish such a separation has not yet been determined. Also, the question, "To what extent is the level of interparental conflict—both predivorce and during the custody determination process—a predictor of successful and unsuccessful attempts at joint custody?" has not been addressed by the existing research literature.

The effects of specific legal standards (including a shift to a joint custody presumption) on the out-of-court negotiations and bargaining of divorcing parents has received little attention from researchers or legal scholars. Recently, however, Mnookin and Kornhauser (1979) explored the potential impact of three alternative legal standards—maternal preference, best interests of the child, and joint custody—on the bargaining of divorcing parents. They suggest that each of these standards has its own set of bargaining endowments and that changing the standard should influence the range and frequency of possible negotiated outcomes.

As an illustration, Mnookin and Kornhauser speculate on the impact on child custody bargaining of a shift from the maternal preference rule to the more sex-neutral best interests of the child standard. They suggest that such a shift not only increases the relative power of fathers but also renders the outcome uncertain if the case goes to court. Consequently, assuming that both parents want custody, the parent who is less willing to risk a court battle and possible loss of contact with the child is penalized in the negotiations. The more risk-averse parent would settle for custody half of the time, for example, rather than risk a court battle for sole custody with a chance of losing. This may be unfortunate since the better parent may be the one who is more unwilling to risk a substantial reduction in contacts with the child. The more discretionary standard would thus affect differentially the bargaining strengths of the two parents depending upon their attitudes toward risk.[9]

Mnookin and Kornhauser also argue that the Goldstein et al. (1973) proposals for sole custody and no legally enforceable visitation rights would likely increase the number of contested cases and reduce the likelihood of parents reaching an agreement on their own. They contend that such proposals allow parents to agree only on the outcome about which they are least likely to agree: "total legal custody or none." Therefore, since parents lack the power to make binding promises regarding intermediate allocations (visitation and child support arrangements), this rule would likely create more custody disputes at the time of divorce.

According to Mnookin and Kornhauser, the shift to a joint custody standard would pose a different kind of problem. Since the outcome is certain if the case goes to court (each parent would receive custody half the time), this standard does not penalize the risk-averse parent. It is also sex-neutral and thus consistent with shifting legal trends. The problem, however, stems not from its characteristics as a background rule for out-of-court negotiations, but rather from its inapplicability in adjudicated cases. The forcing of joint custody on parents who cannot agree to cooperate would probably not be in the best interests of the child.

The Mnookin and Kornhauser analysis demonstrates the importance of studying the effects of legal standards on the dispute settlement process and on the ultimate outcome of child custody bargaining. As these authors suggest,

> Divorcing parents do not bargain over the division of family wealth and custodial prerogatives in a vacuum; they bargain in the shadow of the law. (p. 950)

## Conclusion

Fifteen years ago, after conducting a review of research related to child custody adjudication, Ellsworth and Levy (1969) concluded,

> The available data are woefully inadequate. The studies may have some marginal utility in directing the attention of parents, court employed social workers, and judges to the potential areas of vulnerability in children of divorce under varying conditions; but the data can hardly be considered dispositive for purposes of choosing among alternative formulations of custody adjudication doctrines. (p. 201)

Unfortunately, the social science research relevant to the advantages and disadvantages of joint custody versus single-parent custody is today only slightly more informative. A scientific data base for making child custody decisions following divorce is sorely lacking. The standards and procedures used in determining child custody decisions are in a transitory state and are evolving in ways to fit the complex needs of the family in contemporary American society. The present legal standard of the best interests of the child is highly indeterminate and has resulted in a variety of methods for evaluating and adjudicating child custody in divorce cases. The current bandwagon for joint custody seems to be related to a desire to mitigate the pain and loss caused by divorce for both children and parents and to have a rule for making these agonizing decisions. However, there is a marked disparity between the power of the joint custody movement and the sufficiency of evidence that joint custody can accomplish what we expect of it (Scott & Derdeyn, in press). The immediate and urgent challenges for both legal and mental health practitioners and researchers are the development of valid clinical procedures, more legal options, and—perhaps most important—a solid empirical data base for decision making.

## Notes

1. Hines v. Hines, 192 Iowa 569, 185 N.W. 91 (1921).
2. Chapsky v. Wood, 26 Kansas 650 (1881).
3. Finlay v. Finlay, 240 N.Y. 429, 433, 148 N.E. 624 (1925).

4. Portnoy v. Strasser, 303 N.Y. 539, 104 N.E. 2d 859 (1952).

5. Watts v. Watts, 77 Misc. 2d 178, 350 N.Y.S. 2d 285 (Fam. CT. 1973).

6. Painter v. Bannister, 258 Iowa 390, 140 N.W. 2d 152, cert. denied, 384 U.S. 949 (1966).

7. Beck v. Beck, N.J. Super., 432 A. 2d 63 (1981).

8. A note of caution to the euphoria surrounding the adoption of mediation has recently been sounded by Melton and Lind (1982, p. 65): "Recent proposals for nonadversary procedures in resolution of custody disputes have relied on untested assumptions about psychological harms of adversary procedures and the contributions which mental health professions might make in required mediation. There is, in fact, reason to believe that adversary proceedings may result in more sense of control over the process and a strong belief in its fairness. It is likely that these benefits are applicable at least to older children as well as to disputing parents. Adversary procedures may also result in quicker, more lasting resolutions of conflict. Evaluation studies are needed to test effects of various procedures more definitively."

9. Other determinants of the outcomes of bargaining over child custody noted by Mnookin and Kornhauser (1979) include, (a) preferences of divorcing parents, (b) legal rules indicating what the court would do if the case went to court, (c) transaction costs and the spouses' abilities to bear them, and (d) strategic behavior.

## References

Abarbanel, A. Shared parenting after separation: A study of joint custody. *American Journal of Orthopsychiatry,* 1979, *49,* 320-329.

Ahrons, C. Joint custody arrangements in the post-divorce family. *Journal of Divorce,* 1980, *3,* 189-205.

Alexander, S.J. Influential factors on divorced parents of visitation arrangements. *Journal of Divorce,* 1980, *3,* 223-239.

Bahr, S.J. An evaluation of court mediation for divorce cases with children. *Journal of Family Issues,* 1981, *2,* 39-60.

Batt, J. Child custody disputes: A developmental-psychological approach to proof and decision-making. *Williamette Law Journal,* 1976, *12,* 491-570.

Bloom, B.L., Asher, S.J., & White, S.W. Marital disruption as a stressor: A review and analysis. *Psychological Bulletin,* 1978, *85,* 867-894.

Bodenheimer, B.M. Progress under the Uniform Child Jurisdiction Act and remaining problems: Punitive decrees, joint custody, and excessive modifications. *California Law Review,* 1977, *65,* 978-1014.

Clingempeel, W.G., & Reppucci, N.D. Joint custody after divorce: Major issues and goals for research. *Psychological Bulletin,* 1982, *91,* 102-127.

Coogler, O.J. Changing the lawyer's role in matrimonial practice. *Conciliation Courts Review,* 1977, *15,* 1-12.

Cox, M.J.T., & Cease, L. Joint custody, what does it mean? How does it work? *Family Advocate,* 1978, *4,* 10-13.

Derdeyn, A.P. Child custody contests in historical perspective. *American Journal of Psychiatry,* 1976, *133,* 1369-1376.

Druckman, J.M., & Rhodes, C.A. Family impact analysis: Application to child custody determination. *The Family Coordinator,* 177, *26,* 451-458.

Eider, V. Shared custody—An idea whose time has come. *Conciliation Courts Review,* 1978, *16,* 23-25.

Ellison, E.S. Issues concerning parental harmony and children's psychosocial adjustment. *American Journal of Orthopsychiatry,* 1983, *53,* 73-80.

Ellsworth, P.C., & Levy, R.J. Legislative reform of child custody adjudication. *Law and Society Review*, 1969, *4*, 167-215.

Emery, R.E. Interparental conflict and the children of discord and divorce. *Psychological Bulletin*, 1982, *92*, 310-330.

Emery, R.E., Hetherington, E.M., & Fisher, L. Divorce, children, and social policy. In H. Stevenson & A. Siegel (Eds.), *Children and social policy.* Chicago: University of Chicago Press, 1983.

Fein, R.A. Research on fathering: Social policy and an emergent perspective. *Journal of Social Issues*, 1978, *34*, 122-135.

Felner, R.D., & Farber, S.S. Social policy for child custody: A multidisciplinary framework. *American Journal of Orthopsychiatry*, 1980, *50*, 341-347.

Folberg, H.J., & Graham, M. Joint custody of children following divorce. *University of California at Davis Law Review*, 1979, *12*, 523-581.

Franklin, R., & Hibbs, B. Child custody in transition. *Journal of Marital and Family Therapy*, 1980, *6*, 285-291.

Freed, D.J., & Foster, H.H. Divorce in the fifty states: An overview. *Family Law Quarterly*, 1981, *14*, 229-260.

Freed, D.J., & Foster, H.H. Divorce in the fifty states: An overview. *Family Law Quarterly*, 1981, *14*, 229-260.

Freed, D.J., & Foster, H.H. Family law in the fifty states: An overview as of September, 1982. *Family Law Reporter*, 1982, *8*, 4065-4104.

Gaddis, S.M. Joint custody of children: A decision-making alternative. *Conciliation Courts Review*, 1978, *16*, 17-22.

GAP (Group for the Advancement of Psychiatry). *Divorce, child custody, and the family.* San Francisco: Jossey-Bass, 1981.

Glick, P.C. Children of divorced parents in demographic perspective. *The Journal of Social Issues*, 1979, *35*, 112-125.

Goldstein, J., Freud, A., & Solnit, A. *Beyond the best interests of the child.* New York: Free Press, 1973.

Grief, J.B. Fathers, children, and joint custody. *American Journal of Orthopsychiatry*, 1979, *49*, 311-319.

Hall, J.E., & Hare-Mustin, R.T. Sanctions and the diversity of ethical complaints against psychologists. *American Psychologist*, 1983, *38*, 714-729.

Haynes, J.M. *Divorce mediation.* New York: Springer, 1981.

Hess, R.D., & Camara, K.A. Post-divorce relationships as mediating factors in the consequences of divorce for children. *Journal of Social Issues*, 1979, *35*, 79-96.

Hetherington, E.M. Children and divorce. In R. Henderson (Ed.), *Parent-child interaction: Theory, research, and prospect.* New York: Academic Press, 1981.

Hetherington, E.M., Cox, M., & Cox, R. The aftermath of divorce. In J.H. Stevens & M. Matthews (Eds.), *Mother-child, father-child relations.* Washington, DC: National Association for the Education of Young Children, 1978.

Ilfeld, F.W., Ilfeld, H.Z., & Alexander, J.R. Does joint custody work? A first look at outcome data of relitigation. *American Journal of Psychiatry*, 1982, *139*, 62-66.

Jackson, J., Warner, O., Hornbein, K., Nelson, E., & Fortescue, P. Beyond the best interests revisited: An approach to custody evaluations. *Journal of Divorce*, 1980, *3*, 207-222.

Jacobs, J.W. The effect of divorce on fathers: An overview of the literature. *American Journal of Psychiatry*, 1982, *139*, 1235-1241.

Katkin, D., Bullington, B., & Levine, M. Above and beyond the best interests of the child: An inquiry into the relationship between social science and social action. *Law and Society Review*, 1974, *8*, 669-687.

Kay, H.H. A family court: The California proposal. In P. Bohannan (Ed.), *Divorce and after.* New York: Doubleday, 1970.

Kram, S.W., & Frank, N.A. *The law of child custody: Development of the substantive law.* Lexington, MA: D.C. Heath, 1982.

Krishner, S. Child custody: A better way. *Journal of Family Law,* 1978, *17,* 275-296.

Kubie, L. Provisions for the care of children of divorced parents: A new legal instrument. *Yale Law Journal,* 1964, *73,* 1197-1200.

Kurdeck, L., & Seisky, A. Children's perceptions of their parents' divorce. *Journal of Divorce,* 1980, *3,* 339-337.

Lamb, M.E. (Ed.). *The role of the father in child development.* New York: Wiley, 1976.

Lamb, M.E. Parental influences and the father's role. *American Psychologist,* 1979, *34,* 938-943.

Landsman, K.J., & Minow, M.L. Lawyering for the child: Principles of representation in custody and visitation disputes arising from divorce. *Yale Law Journal,* 1978, *87,* 1126-1101.

Lowenstein, L., & Koopman, B. A comparison of the self-esteem between boys living with single parent mothers and single parent fathers. *Journal of Divorce,* 1978, *2,* 195-208.

Luepnitz, D.A. *Child custody: A study of families after divorce.* Lexington, MA: D.C. Heath, 1982.

Melton, G.B., & Lind, E.A. Procedural justice in family court: Does the adversary model make sense? In G.B. Melton (Ed.), *Legal reforms affecting child and youth services.* New York: Haworth Press, 1982.

Mnookin, R.H. Child-custody adjudication: Judicial functions in the face of indeterminacy. *Law and Contemporary Problems,* 1975, *39,* 226-290.

Mnookin, R.H., & Kornhauser, L. Bargaining in the shadow of the law: The case of divorce. *Yale Law Journal,* 1979, *88,* 950-997.

Noble, J., & Noble, W. *The custody trap.* New York: Hawthorn Books, 1975.

Podell, R., Peck, H.F., & First, C. Custody—to which parent? *Marquette Law Review,* 1972, *56,* 51-58.

Roman, M., & Haddad, W. *The disposable parent.* New York: Holt, Rinehart and Winston, 1978.

Rosen, R. Some crucial issues concerning children of divorce. *Journal of Divorce,* 1979, *3,* 19-25.

Rutter, M. Epidemiological/longitudinal strategies and causal research in child psychiatry. *Journal of American Academy of Child Psychiatry,* 1981, *20,* 513-544.

Santrock, J.W., & Warshak, R.A. Father custody and social development in boys and girls. *Journal of Social Issues,* 1979, *35,* 112-125.

Schulman, J., & Pitt, V. Second thoughts on joint custody: Analysis of legislation and its implications for women and children. *Golden Gate Law Review,* 1982, *12,* 538-559.

Scott, E., & Derdeyn, A. Rethinking joint custody. *Ohio State Law Journal,* in press.

Siegel, D.M., & Hurley, S. The role of the child's preference in custody proceedings, II. *Family Law Quarterly,* 1977, *13,* 1-58.

Spanier, G.B., & Anderson, E.A. The impact of the legal system on adjustment to marital separation. *Journal of Marriage and the Family,* 1979, *41,* 605-613.

Steinman, S. The experience of children in a joint-custody arrangement: A report of a study. *American Journal of Orthopsychiatry,* 1981, *51,* 403-414.

Strauss, P. *Professional responsibility of the lawyer: The murkey divide between right and wrong.* Unpublished paper, Association of the Bar of the City of New York, 1976.

Victor, I., & Winkler, W. *Fathers and custody.* New York: Hawthorn Press, 1977.

Wald, M. State intervention on behalf of "neglected" children: A search for realistic standards. In M.K. Rosenheim (Ed.), *Pursuing justice for the child*. Chicago: University of Chicago Press, 1976.

Wallerstein, J.S., & Kelly, J.B. The effects of parental divorce: The adolescent experience. In J. Anthony & C. Koupernik (Eds.), *The child in his family: Children at psychiatric risk*. New York: Wiley, 1974.

Watson, A.S. The children of Armageddon: Problems of custody following divorce. *Syracuse Law Review*, 1969, *21*, 55-86.

Weiss, R.S. Issues in the adjudication of custody when parents separate. In G. Levinger & O.C. Moles (Eds.), *Divorce and separation*. New York: Basic Books, 1979.

Weiss, R.S. *Marital separation*. New York: Basic Books, 1975.

Weithorn, L.A. Involving children in decisions affecting their own welfare: Guidelines for professionals. In G.B. Melton, G.P. Koocher, & M.J. Saks (Eds.), *Children's competence to consent*. New York: Plenum Press, 1983.

Weithorn, L.A., & Campbell, S.B. The competency of children and adolescents to make informed treatment decisions. *Child Development*, 1982, *53*, 1589-1598.

Westman, J.C. *Child advocacy*. New York: Free Press, 1979.

# 4

# Child Maltreatment

## Legal and Mental Health Issues

**Mindy S. Rosenberg**
*University of Denver*

**Robert D. Hunt**
*Yale University*

As our society attempts to extend protection to children who are physically or sexually abused, or severely neglected, we face complex decisions, raising issues of competing interests, values, and resources. Moreover, these decisions often require thoughtful professional collaboration. In an effort to define its role and the boundaries of intervention, the state must decide when a child is in sufficient danger to warrant intrusion into the sanctity of the home. When do the rights of the child and his or her need for physical and psychological protection and nuturance preempt the right of family privacy? What types of physical or psychological abuse are most crippling to a child's development? To what extent should the state acknowledge cultural and social differences in defining appropriate limits of parental discipline? The answers to these and other questions are central to legal decision making about intervention and services for abused children and their families.

The purpose of this chapter is to present an overview of some of the issues in the area of child maltreatment that face mental health and legal professionals. First, we will review definitional problems in state statues, highlighting difficulties professionals confront when deciding whether to intervene coercively in families. Next, the legal context of maltreatment cases will be discussed, followed by a survey of psychological theories of etiology and intervention strategies. Finally, we will attempt to elucidate certain research questions relevant to the mental health and legal professions, with the intent of bridging some of the apparent gaps between them in the field of child maltreatment.

## The Dilemma of Definitions

Researchers and commentators in the field of child maltreatment typically begin their writings by discussing the problems inherent in defining the phenomenon. Few people would argue that severe physical injury or a clear diagnosis of failure-to-thrive constitutes abuse in the first instance and neglect in the latter. Yet, the majority of reported abuse and neglect cases fall somewhere along a continuum of *potential* child maltreatment, and there is remarkably little consensus as to when a court should find a child abused or neglected (Bourne & Newberger, 1977; Gelles, 1980; Wald, 1975). The definitional dilemma in child protection work creates serious problems for professionals, since these definitions are used as guidelines to determine when intervention into family privacy is justified. Furthermore, at the core of this definitional problem is the issue of competing interests between "some groups, including lawyers and government officials, who use the definitions to determine standards for intervention into families, and other groups, including scholars and social service workers, who use it to focus attention and funding on families in need of assistance" (Zigler, 1980, p. 8).

Child maltreatment typically refers to several categories of behavior, including child abuse, child neglect, emotional abuse and neglect, and sexual abuse. The most frequently used definition of child abuse is

non-accidental physical injury (or injuries) that are the result of acts (or omissions) on the part of parents or guardians that violate the community standards concerning the treatment of children. (Parke & Collmer, 1975, p. 513)

Application of this definition raises questions as to the extent of injury necessary for reporting and the pont at which physical punishment becomes excessive and, therefore, abusive (Alvy, 1975). In addition, it is often difficult to ascertain whether any particular injury was inflicted intentionally.

Difficulties in identification of physical abuse create a risk of unnecessary intervention in some families. Mental health and legal professionals disagree as to the evidence needed to prove abuse and the point at which intervention should occur. On one end of the continuum are those who seek to protect family privacy and argue for limiting court intervention to cases in which a child has suffered *serious* nonaccidental physical injury (Goldstein, Freud, & Solnit, 1979; Institute of Judicial Administration/American Bar Association, 1977; Uviller, 1980; Wald, 1975). Critics who agree with this formulation have argued that definitions of abuse need to be more explicit. They have asserted that stated statutes are unconstitutionally vague, thereby permitting decisions based on subjective opinion (Day, 1977; "A Case of Neglect," 1975; *"Parens Patriae* and Statutory Vagueness in the Juvenile Court," 1973). Those who argue to the contrary propose that intervening early when there is evidence of nonserious injuries may prevent more extreme future situations (Bourne & Newberger, 1977). These commentators have maintained that child protection statutes must be broad enough to allow for the examination of facts on a case-by-case basis (see "The Constitution and the Family," 1980). However, problems arise when the vaguely worded statutes allow for multiple interpretations, broad discretion, and excessive interference in family autonomy.

The inclusion of neglect in the concept of child maltreatment was one step toward broadening the definition. Neglect is an extremely difficult concept to define, both psychologically and legally. Attempts to do so force professionals to differentiate those child-rearing patterns that are actually harmful to children from those that are merely different from more generally accepted styles of parenting. Social scientists have defined neglect as

> a condition in which a caretaker responsible for the child either deliberately or by extraordinary inattentiveness permits the child to experience . . . present suffering and/or fails to provide one or more of the ingredients generally deemed essential for developing a person's physical, intellectual and emotional capacities. (Polansky, Hally, & Polansky, 1975, p. 5)

Definitions of neglect in state statutes are typically marked by ambiguous language and are particularly susceptible to great discretion in interpretation. The following examples from legal cases and state statutes illustrate this point:

> a neglected child is . . . "a child who lacks proper parental care or guardianship"[1], [upholding statute permitting the termination of parental rights]
>
> " . . . a child whose environment is injurious to his welfare"[3]
>
> " . . . a child who lacks necessary and proper physical, educational or moral care and discipline"[4] (upholding statute permitting the termination of parental rights)

Emotional abuse and emotional neglect have recently been included in several state statutes (e.g., Arizona, California, Delaware, Idaho, Louisiana, Tennessee, and Texas) as separate, reportable events. The idea that psychological abuse or neglect could have a detrimental impact on child development is not new (Garbarino, 1980; Goldstein, Freud, & Solnit,

1973; Rohner & Rohner, 1980; Rutter, 1979; Spitz, 1945). However, it is problematic to prove psychological harm in a court of law, since its impact on children may not have physical manifestations and may not be noticed immediately. Moreover, efforts to expand child protection legislation to include notions of psychological harm confront one of the basic problems with the current set of standards, which is that the focus of concern is primarily on parental behavior rather than on child outcome ("The Constitution and the Family," 1980; Wald, 1975, 1976). Parental conduct, in and of itself, is an inadequate prediction of the extent of emotional damage in a child (White, 1973). In commenting on the types of standards that should be drafted to guide courts in cases of abuse and neglect, Wald (1975, pp. 1016-1017) cautions that,

> While emotional damage to a child should be a basis for intervention in some cases, it is essential that laws be drafted in a manner consistent with our limited knowledge about the nature and causes of psychological harm. Intervention should not be premised on vague concepts like "proper parental love" or "adequate affectionate parental association". Such language invites unwarranted intervention, based on each social worker's or judge's brand of "folk psychology". Although such language might clearly apply to parents who refuse to hold, talk to, or engage in any contact with their children, it could also be applied to parents who travel a great deal and leave their children with housekeepers, who send their children to boarding school to get rid of them, or who are generally unaffectionate people.

Sexual abuse is another category of child maltreatment for which there is no commonly accepted definition. Sgroi, Blick, and Porter (1982) describe sexual abuse as "a sexual act imposed on a child who lacks emotional, maturational, and cognitive development . . . by an adult or older adolescent perpetrator" (p. 9), and they continue by listing a series of acts that may be included in the definition. Whereas mental health and legal professionals may agree on the inclusion of intercourse within a definition of sexual abuse, opinions vary when the behavior is less specific (e.g., inappropriate displays of affection). A unique legal consideration in cases of sexual abuse is the likelihood that the adult will be criminally prosecuted. These criminal proceedings may have a harmful impact on the child and family (see Sgroi, 1982).

Problems in the identification of child maltreatment are not confined to any single profession. Nagi (1977) asked 1700 hospital, school, court, policy, and social agency personnel to respond to the statement, "It is difficult to say what is and what is not child maltreatment"; 69% of the total sample agreed. Giovannoni and Becerra (1979) asked a similar cross section of 300 professionals to rate whether a series of seven vignettes depiciting incidents of physical punishment would be considered child abuse. Whereas there was agreement for the most obvious forms of abuse (e.g., severe injuries), there was complete disagreement on incidents that hovered at the threshold of maltreatment (e.g., harsh discipline). Gelles (1982) reports general agreement from a sample of physicians, elementary school guidance counselors, principals, social workers, and police on a two-component definition of abuse that included evidence of clear, identifiable harm and clear intent to produce injury or harm. Yet, he was unable to obtain consensus as to whether sexual molestation (an example of clear injury and clear intent) was a situation of child abuse. Emergency room physicians were the only group in complete agreement that sexual molestation constituted abuse.

Clearly, problems in the identification of abusive and neglectful parents are experienced by a variety of legal and mental health professionals, even those who work intensively in the area of child protection. Not unexpectedly, most questions arise when the facts of the case are unclear and open to interpretation. In the absence of clear standards, there is an increased potential for individual values and professional orientation to mold one's perspective. The next section addresses the legal responses to child maltreatment in the context of the state *parens patriae* laws, and recent attempts, through limitations of those laws, to increase specificity in defining conditions that warrant intervention into family life.

## *Legal Response to Child Maltreatment: Expansion and Limitation of Parens Patriae*

Essentially, the law's response to cases of child maltreatment can be characterized as an evolving attempt to balance the often competing interests of state, parent, and child. The interests of the state and the child require that children be protected from serious harm, such as might result from abuse and neglect, and that they be prevented from engaging in antisocial behavior. Parent and child interests require that the family be free from unnecessary governmental intrusion. In situations in which the parent acts in a way that is inconsistent with the child's best interests, the state can exercise its parens patriae power by assuming the role of parent in protecting the child's welfare, thereby overriding parental authority. If intervention is necessary, particularly in out-of-home placements, then the child's interests become paramount, and the state is required to place the child in a situation that will do the child more good than harm. There is debate as to the state's ability to provide alternatives that are as good or better than the child's family situation (Mnookin, 1973; Wald, 1975, 1976, 1982). Thus, the degree to which the child's interests can be served by state intervention is unclear. The following examples of child maltreatment cases and principals illustrate the court's struggle to delineate the circumstances that warrant intervention into family life.

As noted above, the state has an interest in promoting family autonomy and not intruding into the rights of parents to raise their children free from excessive governmental interference. The law acknowledges the state's limitations in its ability to provide guidelines for parenting and its attempts to substitute for parental influence. As written in the custody decision of *Prince v. Massachusetts*, "It is cardinal with us that the custody, care, and nurture of the child reside first in the parents, whose primary function and freedom includes preparation for obligations the state can neither supply nor hinder."[5] This position is generally consonant with the views of mental health and legal scholars: "As parens patriae, the state is too crude an instrument to become an adequate substitute for flesh and blood parents" (Goldstein, et al., 1979, p. 12).

Support for family autonomy promotes pluralism in our society. Thus, the law protects bonds of marriage, parenthood, foster families[6], and extended relatives who function as parents.[7] Increasingly, the presence of psychological as well as biological bonds is considered fundamental to defining family relationships. Legally protected family relationships are defined by both objective factors such as formal marriage and blood ties and by the degree to which family members provide intimacy, support, and protection for the child.[8] Thus, unwed fathers who fail to participate in support of their children have been denied the right to block their children's adoption.[9]

The state recognizes a distinction between the idea of promoting family autonomy and reinforcing parental authority. Parents' rights to authority are premised on two important assumptions: (1) Parents are more mature, experienced, and have better judgment than children[10], and (2) parents will act "in the best interest of their children." The state's interest in deferring to parental authority is diminished if parents do not provide this level of care.

The state's right to intervene in the family derives from two distinct sources—its police power and the concept of parens patriae. The policy power is the state's inherent plenary power to prevent its citizens from harming one another, and its mandate to promote all aspects of the public welfare.[11] The power of parens patriae is the limited paternalistic power of the state to protect or promote the welfare of certain individuals, including children, who lack the capacity to act in their own best interest.[12]

The state's exercise of its parens patriae power over children is defined and limited by three principles. First, the power is based primarily on the presumption that children lack the mental competence and maturity possessed by adults. Second, before intervening, the state must show that the child's parents or guardians are either unfit, unable, or unwilling to care for the child.[13] Finally, the state should exercise the parens patriae power solely to further the best interests of the child (Mnookin, 1973).

Child protection statutes passed in the early 1900s contained broad and vaguely worded clauses allowing juvenile courts much discretion to intervene in family life. Since *In re Gault* in 1967,[14] there has been widespread reexamination of these parens patriae statutes, which had not previously been subjected to constitutional scrutiny. As a result, many parens patriae laws have been challenged as being "unconstitutionally vague and overbroad," thereby permitting excessive, and sometimes unwarranted, intervention in the family (Day, 1977; IJA/ABA, 1977). Others have felt some flexibility and vagueness in these statutes desirable, suggesting that they facilitate more appropriate outcomes for individual cases.[15]

One limitation on the parens patriae power has been the "void for vagueness" doctrine. This doctrine is invoked frequently in criminal cases when there is concern about potential infringement of an individual's due process rights.[16] The doctrine is composed of three distinct, yet related, components that provide the basis for judicial consideration (Day, 1977). The concept of fair warning comprises the central component of the doctrine, and requires that a statute be worded clearly so that an individual is given adequate notice of what behaviors are considered illegal. The second component, the anti-discretionary element, concerns the potential for arbitrary judicial enforcement of ambiguously worded statutes. The third component considers whether the statute is "overbroad," (That is, is it likely that legal as well as illegal behavior could be prosecuted?) This doctrine is best summarized in the case from which it originated, *Connally v. General Construction Company.* The judge ruled that

> [A] statute which either forbids or requires the doing of an act in terms so vague that men of common intelligence must necessarily guess at its meaning and differ as to its application violates the first essential of due process of law.[17]

Involuntary termination of parental rights statutes have been challenged repeatedly on grounds of vagueness. The move to terminate parental rights is the most serious infringement to family integrity since it severs permanently the legal basis of the parent-child relationship. Until quite recently, however, claims of vagueness against termination statutes have been overturned by the power of the parens patriae rationale.

The case of *Alsager v. District Court of Polk County, Iowa*[18] was the first family law case to apply successfully the void-for-vagueness doctrine, and it is illustrative of the tension between the state's parens patriae interests and the parents' autonomy. In the *Alsager* case, the Supreme Court of Iowa acted "in the best interest of the child" to terminate the parents' rights with respect to five of the six Alsager children. The stated grounds were that the parents "substantially and continuously or repeatedly refused to give the child necessary parental care and protection" and that they were "unfit parents by reason of . . . conduct . . . detrimental to the physical or mental health or morals of the child."[19] The parents challenged successfully the state termination statute by contending that the statute was unconstitutionally vague, that the state failed to show a substantial degree of harm to the children, that procedural due process was denied when inadequate notice of the termination proceeding was given, and that the standard of proof required merely a preponderance of the evidence rather than the more stringent standard of clear and convincing evidence.

The appeals court held that evidence presented in the termination proceeding was insufficient to warrant severing the parent-child relationship. For example, the evidence revealed that the parents "sometimes permitted their children to leave the house in cold weather without winter clothing on, allowed them to play in traffic, to annoy neighbors, to eat mush for supper, to live in a house containing dirty dishes and laundry, and to sometimes arrive late at school."[20] The decision to order the initial temporary removal of the children from the home was made on the basis of a twenty-minute home visit by a probation officer, who found that the only occupants at that time included the mother and her youngest child, who was less than one year old. After the children were removed from the home, they spent the next five years in a total of fifteen separate foster homes and eight juvenile home placements. The decision to terminate parental rights failed to provide the children with increased stability or improved lives. In fact, we might speculate that the decision did more harm than good to the children's emotional health.

*Alsager* is a clear example of a situation in which the application of a state statute was in violation of the parents' due process rights. First, the statute's standards were highly susceptible to interpretation and could not inform parents as to what behaviors were required or should be avoided to prevent termination of parental rights (i.e., absence of fair warning). Second, the vague phrasing allowed for subjective interpretations such that arbitrary terminations were inevitable. Third, the fundamental right to family autonomy had been inhibited since no actual or imminent harm to the children was shown to exist as a prerequiste termination. In summary, the judge presiding over the appeal concluded that in order,

> to preserve the best interests of both parents and children, the Court deems that termination must only occur where more harm is likely to befall the child by staying with his parents than by being permanently separated from them.[21]

Since the Alsager case demonstrated the doctrine's successful applicability to civil legislation in family law, numerous attempts have been made to employ the doctrine as a means to clarify standards of adult behavior toward children.[22] In *Roe v. Conn,*[23] a district court overturned a child neglect law that allowed termination of parental rights, due in part to the void-for-vagueness doctrine, and affirmed that the state can "sever entirely the parent-child relationship only when the child is subjected to real physical or emotional harm and less drastic measures would be unavailable."[24] Again, this type of judgment increases the state's burden to define the nature and boundaries of real harm to the child, the potential benefits and risks of removal, and the potential for other, less drastic interventions. It is becoming increasingly important that definitions of abuse and neglect are focused upon the effects on the child, and not simply on the parents' acts.

In a third example of the use of the void-for-vagueness doctrine,[25] the defendant was found guilty on two counts of conduct likely to impair the morals of a minor. The defendant asserted that charges should be dismissed on the grounds that the statute was unconstitutionally vague as applied to the facts of the case, Specifically, the question raised was whether the challenged statute provided fair and unambiguous warning regarding what conduct was illegal. The court held that the defendant was guilty as charged, since the facts of the case (i.e., pornographic photography and attempted sexual intercourse with a 12-year-old girl) were viewed as a clear portrayal of "act [s] likely to impair the health or morals of any such child" and corresponded with other court decisions that defined specific behaviors constituting grounds for misconduct.[26]

### Response of Mental Health Professionals and Social Scientists

The response of mental health professionals and social scientists to the problem of child maltreatment has been twofold: to conduct investigations that attempt to increase our understanding of the phenomenon, and to develop and evaluate intervention strategies. Basic assumptions that underlie the definition of any social problem lead to particular approaches to its solution (Caplan & Nelson, 1973). Therefore, the theoretical model chosen as an explanatory framework will have implications for the type of intervention strategies developed.

Briefly, there have been several conceptual models advanced to explain child maltreatment, and each model posits a different set of assumptions about its etiology. The psychiatric perspective assumes that the parent is the primary cause of the problem. Research is focused on identifying personality characteristics that distinguish abusive from nonabusive parents (Gelles, 1973; Spinetta & Rigler, 1972; Steele & Pollock, 1968). Reconstruction of the childrearing histories of abusive parents is a second emphasis of this approach (Bakan, 1971; Steele & Pollock, 1968). By contrast, societal explanations of child maltreatment shift the locus of blame from parent to society. This approach is concerned primarily with social attitudes towards violence and social stresses that are thought to contribute to the problem (Gil, 1970; Light, 1973; National Institute of Mental Health, 1978; Parke & Collmer, 1975). Finally, an ecological model assumes that the causes of child maltreatment are multiply determined. Maltreatment is viewed as a pathological adaptation between caregiver, child, and the immediate environment (Garbarino, 1977). Advocates of this perspective emphasize the dynamic nature of the individual-environment interaction, rather than studying one or the other variable in isolation (Belsky, 1980; Pelton, 1979; Rosenberg & Reppucci, 1983a). The focus of research is to identify environmental conditions that undermine, rather than support, healthy parent-child relationships and to examine those transactions between environments, individuals, and groups that create a context for maltreatment.

Interventions with abusive and neglectful families have as their goals the prevention of further abuse and neglect and the alleviation of stresses that have contributed to maladaptive childrearing patterns. Services are typically divided into the following categories:

(a) those designed to change the parent(s) and to be therapeutic and/or educational in nature;

(b) those that focus on situational factors with the intent of reducing environmental stress; and

(c) those designed to ameliorate the effects of abuse and neglect.

Services in the first category include individual psychotherapy and counseling, family therapy, casework, parent education, and self-help groups such as Parents Anonymous. Examples of services designed to reduce stress are crisis nurseries, drop-in respite centers, day-care, parent aides, homemaker services, job-training programs and other job opportunities, improvements in housing, and income maintenance programs. The third category of programs includes hospital-based programs, day-school-like programs that often have a parent education component, and out-of-home placements such as foster care.

The remainder of this section will focus on several studies of the effectiveness of interventions with maltreating families. We will discuss methodological problems that have implications for mental health, social science, and law. Since 15-20 percent of child protection cases require court action and the remaining 80-85 percent are handled outside of court (Besharov, 1974), the discussion will not focus on out-of-home placements or termination of parental rights as forms of intervention.[27]

One of the largest evaluations of child protective services was conducted by the Berkeley Planning Associates (1977), and included a sample of 1724 parents treated in 11 protective service demonstration projects throughout the country. Protective service workers provided data about the parents from time of intake through termination of services. The data included demographic information, specification of types of support services utilized, client attitudes and behavior, treatment goals, and life situational changes. Unfortunately, the evaluators did not include a control group, nor were clients observed by anyone other than the protective service worker providing the information. Using the incidence of repeated abuse as the primary outcome measure, 30 percent of the parents abused or neglected their child while in treatment; less than 30 percent improved significantly in behavior, attitudes, or life situation; and less than 40 percent improved in at least one-third of the problem areas defined initially at intake. Overall, the evaluators reported a 40-50 percent success rate by the time of termination, but no follow-up data were collected. Services that demonstrated the greatest success were parent education groups, lay therapy, and Parents Anonymous. Length of time in treatment was associated with the most positive behavioral change.

Other studies report that length of time or intensiveness of treatment is a significant factor in reducing the recurrence of abuse. Shapiro (1979) interviewed 171 maltreating families—27 percent of whom were identified as abusive—and reviewed their social service records. He found that client improvement was related positively to length of time in treatment. Specifically, some improvement in child care was noted with changes in the physical handling of children, but not in the psychological aspects of parenting, (e.g., nurturance and empathy). Fitch (1977) studied 140 severely abused hospitalized infants and randomly assigned each to one of two experimental groups that differed in treatment intensiveness (i.e., up to 30 months of treatment and greater access to services). Fitch included in the sample a treatment control group of nonabused infants. Differences were noted between the treated groups on physical and social developmental tests and on mothers' perceptions of children and their behavior. More positive perceptions and changes were noted for the intensive treatment group. Rate of reabuse was significantly higher for the untreated abused group (8.7 percent) than the treated abused group (2.7 percent), suggesting that treatment had some positive impact on decreasing the recurrence of abuse. (Unfortunately, no follow-up data were gathered.)

Green, Power, Steinbook, and Gaines (1981) attempted to identify the factors associated with successful and unsuccessful treatment outcomes. Their sample included 79 abusive parents who received psychodynamically oriented individual therapy, group therapy, home visiting, and a telephone advocacy service for a minimum of 6 sessions and a maximum involvement of 36 months. Ratings of client behavior and symptoms (e.g., abusive behavior, perceptions of children, depression, low frustration tolerance) were obtained from the primary therapist and validated consensually by additional program staff. Two-thirds of the sample demonstrated some form of behavioral and symptom improvement; 28 percent were rated significantly improved. Favorable outcomes were likely to occur with parents who had had minimally abusive childhoods, who were motivated to participate actively in the programs, and who were able to be self-reflective and respond to verbal therapies. Unsuccessful outcomes occurred with parents who had a childhood history of serious maltreatment, who had inflicted severe injuries to their children and who were court-ordered to participate in the program or who terminated service against staff advice. Members of the latter group were described as persons whose defensive coping style was one of denial and projection; who frequently misperceived others' behavior; and who had abnormal expectations of their children, poor relationships with other adults, frequent court involvement, and their children in out-of-home placements. Overall, parents responded positively to the home-visiting and telephone interventions, and perhaps the success of the second group might have been increased if less traditional forms of treatment had been offered. Research on intervention with multiproblem families argues against the use of traditional therapy in favor of more concrete, practical forms of intervention (Heller & Monahan, 1977).

Four and one-half years after documented child abuse, Martin and Beezley (1976) followed up 58 children whose parents had been treated. Ninety percent of the children had remained at home. Although the children were no longer being physically abused, the investigators found that 68 percent of the children were experiencing "hostile rejection" and/or excessive physical punishment. Generally, those children were functioning better than children whose parents had received no formal therapeutic intervention. Similarly, in a sample of 23 abusive families, Baher (1976) found "slight positive changes" in parental behavior, but the "majority of mothers could not be termed even fairly accepting of the battered children after 21 months of treatment" (p. 171).

Interventions that have used various parenting group approaches (e.g., cognitive-behavioral groups) have met with moderate, short-term success (e.g., Ambrose & Hazzard, 1980), but follow-up studies are rare. One exception is a study conducted by Justice and Justice (1976). These investigators used goal attainment scaling in their group therapy sessions, which met for 4-5 months, 1½ hours per week. Abusive parents identified their own goals in behavioral terms and reported weekly on their progress. After three years there was no recurrence of abuse. However, the fact that 75 percent of the children were in out-of-home placements and their return was contingent on improved parental functioning suggests that this group of parents might have been particularly motivated to *report* their behavior positively as well as having a strong incentive to *change*.

The effectiveness of coercive versus voluntary treatment has received much attention in the literature (Bourne & Newberger, 1977; Wald, 1975, 1976), although the question continues to be an empirical one. Wolfe, Aragona, Kaufman, Sandler (1980) offered a skills program in child management to 71 voluntary and court-referred abusive parents, and reported that court-ordered parents were five times more likely to complete the program than were parents who volunteered. Of the 39 percent who completed, 82 percent were observed to have "benefited significantly," although there were no clear criteria for making these judgments. The authors concluded by supporting the idea of court-ordered treatment for abusive families, primarily on the basis of attendance, rather than as a function of systematically documented changes in parent behavior.

Bourne and Newberger (1977) offer clinical evidence that services provided on an involuntary basis can often be beneficial, since family disorganization, lack of knowledge about social service systems, and mistrust of professional help often prevent families from seeking service voluntarily. In cases of neglect, legal intervention may serve to increase a family's appreciation of services rather than generate hostility (Polansky, DeSaix, & Sharlin, 1972). Some clinicians have even asserted that voluntary acceptance of intervention represents an ostensible acquiescence to authority, though the parent actually opposes the intervention (Steele & Pollock, 1974). The issue is further complicated by the difficulty in distinguishing between voluntary and coercive intervention in abuse and neglect cases. Voluntary requests may actually be the result of pressures from professionals to "take advantage" of these services in lieu of threatened court action. As a result, it is difficult to analyze systematically the differential impacts of voluntary and state-coerced participation on program effectiveness.

Outcome evaluations of the effectiveness of nontraditional services (e.g., parent aides, Parents Anonymous, homemaker services, crisis nurseries, drop-in centers, etc.) for abusive and neglectful families have not been performed. Further, there are no studies that compare the relative effectiveness of traditional and nontraditional interventions, nor the additive effect of a combination of two service types.[28]

In summary, outcome evaluations of interventions designed for maltreating families have produced a mixed set of findings. The majority of reported studies have used traditional forms of treatment (e.g., therapy and casework), and approximately one-third of the clients have demonstrated some form of "improvement." Researchers have been dismayed to learn that halting physical abuse does not necessarily stop physical punishment, nor does it guarantee parental acceptance of the child. Length of treatment has been proposed as an important factor associated with positive change, although that may be a function of the type of intervention used (e.g., psychodynamically oriented therapy). There is some evidence that the option of multiple forms of intervention, particularly nontraditional services, can be quite beneficial to these families. The paucity of outcome data on nontraditional services is unfortunate, considering their potential for effectiveness with families who may not benefit from more traditional, verbal therapies.

The presence of serious methodological problems in some of the studies reviewed above severely compromises the validity of these studies' findings. Their methodological problems thus contribute to the general confusion about the nature of appropriate intervention for cases of abuse and neglect. Moreover, these problems tend to undermine the confidence of legal and social service professionals regarding the utility of psychological information to guide decision making. Methodological flaws—such as lack of comparison groups, inadequate matching of comparison group cases on socioeconomic status, inadequate sample sizes, and bias of studying severely impoverished populations—have been discussed in great detail elsewhere (e.g., Newberger, Newberger, & Hampton, 1983; Parke & Collmer, 1975). The three methodological issues to be addressed here include problems of sample definition, treatment design, and unspecified or vague outcome criteria.

Problems in sample definitions stem directly from the problems of definitions of abuse and neglect in the legal standards and state statutes. Psychological researchers inherit the problems encountered initially by protective service workers when they attempt to define abusive and neglectful parents. It is common for researchers to include subjects in their sample based on the protective service worker's findings alone, without using an additional confirmatory criterion. This can lead to misclassification. Sample homogeneity is further clouded when researchers fail to account for potent variables such as

— severity of injuries inflicted on the child;
— length of time as a protective service case prior to intervention;
— number of previous reports for maltreatment;
— episodic or chronic abuse; and
— the combining of different types of physical, emotional, and sexual abuse, together with neglect, into one sample.

Consequently, there is no way of knowing which interventions are effective for which kinds of problems. Besharov (1981) argues that research samples of abusive and neglectful families lack "comparability, reliability, and taxonomic delineation" and therefore confound the results of studies on incidence, sequelae, etiology, and program effectiveness.

One recent trend in psychological research is to develop an alternative classificatory system for maltreating families that would allow people to distinguish between the severity of different forms of abuse and neglect and relate these to parent-child interactions and child outcomes (e.g. Burgess & Conger, 1978; Rizley & Cicchetti, 1981). Zigler (1979, p. 92) stresses that

> The nature of child abuse is . . . in need of a more differentiated and conceptually based classificatory system. Child abuse is a phenotypic event having a variety of expressions and causes, and we will make little headway so long as we insist on viewing every act of child abuse as the equivalent of every other.

Problems in treatment design stem from two sources. First, few outcome studies on child abuse and neglect outline specifically the nature of the intervention, professional qualifications of the staff, length of time involved, and extent of additional services used. The reports of the studies lead to only a vague understanding of the content and process of treatment. More detailed documentation is needed to assess reliably whether the intervention has been worthwhile.

Second, treatment interventions have often been designed without reference to current etiological theories of child maltreatment. A particular mode of treatment may be implemented because of a professional's theoretical orientation (e.g., clinicians typically recommend therapy), as a result of the prevailing zeitgeist (Rosenberg, Reppucci, & Linney, 1983), or as a function of resource availability in the local community. Frequently there is little indication that parents were assessed prior to treatment in order to match an intervention to their needs.

A prime example of this situation is the proliferation of parent education groups for abusive parents, based on the assumption that abusive parents as a group have poor skills in parenting. Research has revealed that some, but not all, abusive parents have extremely poor child-rearing information and skills. In their in-depth interviews about the contextual factors of abusive incidents with 66 parents, Kadushin and Martin (1981) found that an abusive parent's first reaction to a child's misbehavior was typically low-level, noncorporal response. This response typically was followed by a progressive escalation of a variety of child management techniques before the parent became abusive. Only 8 percent of their sample responded immediately by "whipping, beating, slapping, or punching." In contrast, 40 percent "spoke to the child, reasoning, explaining, instructing," 42 percent used threats or warnings, 4 percent walked away or used time-out procedures, and 5 percent used a "limited intensity punishment," such as "shook child, light slap, or spank" (p. 163). In a study of abusive and nonabusive mothers' perceptions of their own and their children's behavior, Rosenberg and Reppucci (1983b) reported that abusive parents actually offered a greater number of explanations for children's behavior and were able to identify more strategies for intervention in certain situations than were nonabusive mothers. In fact, it appeared that the more they knew, the more desperate and out of control they seemed to feel when their strategies did not remedy the situation. Results such as these would argue against the idea that all abusive parents need training in the acquisition of parenting skills per se; it is clear that some parents may benefit from a slightly different form of intervention that helps them to use what skills they have more appropriately.

The failure of particular forms of intervention does not necessarily mean that maltreating families are untreatable or that the intervention was executed poorly. Rather, it may be that the specific intervention is an outgrowth of an etiological formulation that is inappropriate for the complexity of the problem. In the case of child maltreatment, conceptual formulations that involve an ecological perspective appear to hold more promise than either the psychiatric or sociological model alone. Despite this information, professionals continue to view maltreatment as a result of individual factors and develop interventions accordingly (Gelles, 1982). Given its individual orientation, the legal system is particularly susceptible to ordering individually focused interventions, which may not be the appropriate level, or at least the only level, at which one should intervene in maltreating families.

Vague or unspecified outcome criteria make up the third methodological factor that contributes to confused research findings. Recurrence of abuse is the outcome criterion used most frequently to gauge intervention success. One is reminded of the problems encountered with the use of recidivism as an outcome criterion for interventions with juvenile offenders (Reppucci & Clingempeel, 1978). Once a juvenile is within the purview of social control agencies, it is much harder to escape detection, since that juvenile's behavior is monitored more carefully than that of a nonidentified youth. Recidivism estimates are likely to be inflated as a result, and tend not to be representative of the potential for treatment-induced change. Similarly, the rate of reabuse is susceptible to inaccuracy and, although it is important information to record, it should not be used as the single criterion. Parents who are identified as abusive and/or neglectful are likely to be under increased surveillance by the service network, and behaviors that may hover between acceptable punishment and abuse may be reported as abuse. Some studies report rates of reabuse only if the injuries were severe enough to warrant hospitalization, but these are very few. Certainly, multiple outcome measures that focus on several levels of information (e.g., individual, family, community) and the relationships between levels would be preferable to single outcome measures. The choice of outcome measures is also dependent on one's etiological formulation of the problem.

## Summary and Conclusions

Child maltreatment is a complex, multiply determined phenomenon requiring collaboration across disciplines in order to generate meaningful etiological frameworks and intervention strategies. Law, mental health, and social science are woven inextricably in this collaborative process. Both professional groups confront similar questions in their work with maltreating families: questions of problem definition, specification of parameters for intervention, and choices among intervention strategies. Within each question is a set of competing interests, values, and demands for resources that create tension within and between these professions.

In its most general terms, the tension reflects the problem of trying to decide how broadly or narrowly standards for identifying maltreating families should be defined. Specifically, should only serious forms of maltreatment be reported and investigated, or should nonserious forms also be included? Arguments have been made for both sides (Bourne & Newberger, 1977; Wald, 1975, 1976). Should the need for intervention be based on the manifestation of serious harm, or should one attempt to intervene early with less serious problems, in an effort to prevent future harm? Psychologists who advocate secondary prevention may be in conflict with legal professionals who wish to preserve family autonomy. Finally, which etiological framework would be most informative to guide decisions about the level and strategy of intervention? Mental health professionals need to tie their interventions to conceptual frameworks of maltreatment and then carefully evaluate outcomes before they can provide courts with meaningful information for decision making.

Among the most important research issues that warrant investigation are the following:

(1) Researchers should take advantage of conditions not always possible or ethical to devise certain studies. One example of a naturally occurring experiment is a two-year project that is being conducted by Michael Wald and his colleagues.[29] These researchers were able to compare two groups of 5-10 year-old abused children from neighboring counties. One group remained at home, while the other group were removed from their homes and placed in foster care. A comparison group of school classmates was also included. This study was possible, in part, because of varying legal policies in the two neighboring counties. Results from this study are not yet available to the public.

A second example of a naturally occurring experiment might be one that takes advantage of the diversity in state parens patriae laws, and compares the extremes—i.e., those that protect parental rights more than children's rights (parental autonomy) and those whose concern is primarily the protection of children (parens patriae). Variables to study include

— types of cases identified;
— cases that require court action;
— types of dispositions decided;
— influence of injury severity on disposition choice; and
— factors that influence decision making about service recommendations.

(2) Studies that relate specific variables to child outcomes are needed. Variables of interest might include

— severity of injuries;
— episodic versus chronic maltreatment;
— availability of outside support networks to children; and
— the link between nonserious forms of maltreatment and the potential for future, serious maltreatment.

(3) As previously mentioned, intervention studies that derive from a specific conceptual framework are critical. These studies should carefully

describe the interventions, use appropriate experimental designs including samples and measures, and attempt to collect relatively long-term follow-up information in order to determine effectiveness.

In the late 1960s the problem of maltreatment was conceptualized such that it seemed that some people were fit parents and others were not; the two populations were considered relatively discrete. With the passage of reporting laws and the burgeoning research on the topic, the boundaries between what is and what is not child maltreatment became blurred. It was difficult to circumscribe the phenomenon in a meaningful way. Within the last decade the trend in law, mental health, and social science has been toward specificity and close scrutiny of those circumstances that warrant state intervention. This movement suggests a more seasoned, thoughtful approach to the problem. It is hoped that pursuit of this course will produce fruitful results.

## Notes

1. Utah Code Ann. S78-3A-2 (p. 17).
2. In re Daniel H; 591 P. 2d. 1175 (Okla. 1979).
3. Ill. Ann. Stat. Ch. 37, 702-704.
4. Custody of a Minor, 79 Mass. Adv. Sh. 2099, 393 N.E. 2d 379 (1979).
5. Prince v. Massachusetts, 321 U.S. 158, 166 (1944).
6. Smith v. Organization of Foster Families for Equality and Reform. Offer 431 U.S. 494 (1977).
7. Id. at 504-506.
8. See Harvard Law Review, 1980 at 1270-1283.
9. Quilloin, v. Walcoh, 434 U.S. 246 (1978).
10. See Parham v. J.R., 99 S. CT 2493, 2504 (1979).
11. Jacobson v. Massachusetts, 197, U.S. 11, 24025 (1905).
12. See Harvard Law Review, 1974, at 1207-1219.
13. Quilloin supra Note 9.
14. In re Gault, 387 U.S. 1 (1967).
15. See Harvard Law Review, supra Note 8 at 1232.
16. Connally v. General Construction Co; 269 U.S. 385, 391 (1926).
17. Id.
18. Alsager v. District Court of Polk County, Iowa, 406 F. Supp. 10, 15 (S.D. Iowa 1975), aff'd, 545 F. 2d. 1137 (8th Cir. 1976).
19. Id. at 11.
20. Id. at 12.
21. Id. at 24.
22. See also Linn v. Linn, 205 Neb. 218, 286 N.W. 2d 765 (1980).
23. Roe v. Conn 417 F. Supp. 769 (M.d. Ala. 1976).
24. Id. at 779.

25. Connecticut v. Pickering 180 Conn. 54 (1980).

26. See, e.g., State v. Coulombe, 143 Conn. 604, 124 A. 2d. 518 (1956); State v. Anderson, 152 Conn. 196, 197, 205 A. 2d 488 (1964); State v. Gelinas, 160 Conn. 266, 267, 279 A. 2d. 552 (1971).

27. See Mnookin (1973) and Wald (1975) for information on the subject.

28. Descriptions of these nontraditional services can be found in Parke and Collmer (1975) and from the National Center of Child Abuse and Neglect (e.g., Gifford, Kaplan, & Salus, 1979; Broadhurst, Edmunds, & MacDicken, 1979; Borgman, Edmunds, & MacDicken, 1979; Jenkins, MacDicken, & Ormsby, 1979; Hally, Polansky, & Polansky, 1980; Martin, 1979).

29. Personal communication.

## References

Alvy, K.T. Preventing child abuse. *American Psychologist,* 1975, *30,* 921-928.

Ambrose, S., & Hazzard, A. Cognitive-behavioral parenting groups for abusive families. *Child Abuse & Neglect,* 1980, *4,* 119-125.

Baher, E. *At-risk: An account of the work of the battered child research development.* Boston: Routledge & Kegan Paul, 1976.

Bakan, D. *Slaughter of the innocents.* San Francisco: Jossey-Bass, 1971.

Belsky, J. Child maltreatment: An ecological integration. *American Psychologist,* 1980, *35,* 321-335.

Berkeley Planning Associates. *Evaluation: National demonstration program in child abuse and neglect.* Berkeley, CA: Berkeley Planning Associates, 1977.

Besharov, D. *Juvenile justice advocacy.* New York: Practicing Law Institute, 1974.

Besharov, D. Toward better research on child abuse and neglect: Making definitional issues on explicit methodological concern. *Child Abuse and Neglect,* 1981, *5,* 383-390.

Borgman, R., Edmunds, M., & MacDicken, R.A. *Crisis intervention: A manual for child protection workers.* Washington, DC: National Center on Child Abuse and Neglect, 1979.

Bourne, R., & Newberger, E.H. Family autonomy or coercive intervention? Ambiguity and conflict in the proposed standards for child abuse and neglect. *Boston University Law Review,* 1977, *57,* 670-706.

Broadhurst, D.D., Edmunds, M., & MacDicken, R.A. *Early childhood programs.* Washington, DC: National Center for Child Abuse and Neglect, 1979.

Burgess, R.L., & Conger, R.P. Family interaction in abusive, neglected, and normal families. *Child Development,* 1978, *49,* 1163-1173.

Caplan, G., & Nelson, S. On being useful: The nature and consequences of psychological research on social problems. *American Psychologist,* 1973, *28,* 199-211. A case of neglect: Parens patriae versus due process in child neglect proceedings. *Arizona Law Review,* 1975, *17,* 1055-1089.

The constitution and the family. *Harvard Law Review,* 1980, vol. 93, pp. 1156-1383.

Day, D. Termination of parental rights statutes and void for vagueness doctrine: A successful attack on the *parens patriae* rationale. *Journal of Family Law,* 1977-1978, *16,* 213.

Fitch, M.J. *Prospective study in child abuse: The child study program.* Denver, CO: Denver Evaluation Center, 1977.

Garbarino, J. The human ecology of child maltreatment: A conceptual model of research. *Journal of Marriage and the Family,* 1977, *(November),* 721-735.

Garbarino, J. Defining emotional maltreatment: The message is the meaning. *Journal of Psychiatric Treatment and Evaluation,* 1980, *2,* 105-110.

Gelles, R.J. Child abuse as psychopathology: A sociological critique and reformulation. *American Journal of Orthopsychiatry,* 1973, *43,* 611-621.

Gelles, R.J. Violence in the family: A review of research in the seventies. *Journal of Marriage and the Family,* 1980, *42,* 873-885.

Gelles, R.J. Problems in defining and labeling child abuse. In R.H. Stan (Ed.), *Child abuse prediction: Policy implications.* Cambridge, MA: Ballinger, 1982.

Gifford, C.D., Kaplan, F.B., & Salus, M.K. *Parent aides in child abuse and neglect programs.* Washington, DC: National Center on Child Abuse and Neglect, 1979.

Gil, D.G. *Violence against children: Physical abuse in the United States.* Cambridge, MA: Harvard University Press, 1970.

Giovannoni, J.M., & Becerra, R.M. *Defining child abuse.* New York: Free Press, 1979.

Goldstein, J., Freud, A., & Solnit, A.J. *Beyond the best interests of the child.* New York: Free Press, 1973.

Goldstein, J., Freud, A., & Solnit, A.J. *Before the best interests of the child.* New York: Free Press, 1979.

Green, A.H., Power, E., Steinbook, B., & Gaines, R. Factors associated with successful and unsuccessful intervention with child abusive families. *Child Abuse & Neglect,* 1981, *5,* 45-52.

Hally, C., Polansky, N.F., & Polansky, N.A. *Child neglect: Mobilizing services.* Washington, DC: National Center for Child Abuse and Neglect, 1980.

Heller, K., & Monahan, J. *Psychology and community change.* Homewood, IL: Dorsey Press, 1977.

Institute of Judicial Administration/American Bar Association (IJA/ABA). Joint Commission on Juvenile Justice Standards, Standards Relating to Child Abuse and Neglect, Washington, DC: Author, 1977.

Jenkins, J.L., MacDicken, R.A., & Ormsby, N.J. *A community approach: The child protection coordinating committee.* Washington, DC: National Center for Child Abuse and Neglect, 1979.

Justice, B., & Justice, R. *The abusing family.* New York: Human Sciences Press, 1976.

Kadushin, A., & Martin, J.A. *Child abuse: An interactional event.* New York: Columbia University Press, 1981.

Light, R. Abused and neglected children in America: A study of alternative policies. *Harvard Educational Review,* 1973, *44,* 556-598.

Martin, H.P. *Treatment for abused and neglected children.* Washington, DC: National Center for Child Abuse and Neglect, 1979.

Martin, H.P., & Beezley, P. Therapy for abusive parents: Its effects on the child. In H.P. Martin (Ed.), *The abused child: A multidisciplinary approach to developmental issues and treatment,* Cambridge, MA: Ballinger, 1976.

Mnookin, R.H. Foster care—in whose best interest? *Harvard Educational Review,* 1973, *43,* 599-638.

Nagi, S.Z. *Child maltreatment in the United States.* New York: Columbia University Press, 1977.

National Institute of Mental Health. *Child abuse and neglect programs: Practice & theory.* Washington, DC: United States Department of Health, Education and Welfare, 1978.

Newberger, E.H., Newberger, C.M., & Hampton, R.L. Child abuse: The current theory base and future research needs. *Journal of the American Academy of Child Psychiatry,* 1983, *22,* 262-268.

*Parens patriae* and statutory vagueness in the juvenile court. *Yale Law Journal*, 1973, *82*, 745-771.

Parke, R.D., & Collmer, W.C. Child abuse: An interdisciplinary analysis. In E.M. Hetherington (Ed.), *Child development research*, (Vol. 5). Chicago: University of Chicago Press, 1975.

Pelton, L.H. (Ed.). *The social context of child abuse and neglect.* New York: Sage Press, 1979.

Polansky, N., DeSaix, C., & Sharlin, N. *Child neglect: Understanding and reaching the parent.* New York: Child Welfare League of America, 1972.

Polansky, N.A., Hally, C., & Polansky, N.F. *Profiles of neglect: A survey of the state of knowledge of child neglect.* Washington, DC: Department of Health, Education and Welfare, 1975.

Reppucci, N.D., & Clingempeel, W.G. Methodological issues in research with correctional populations. *Journal of Consulting and Clinical Psychology,* 1978, *46,* 727-746.

Rizley, R. & Cicchetti, D. (Eds.). *Developmental perspectives on child maltreatment. New directions for child development.* San Francisco: Jossey-Bass, 1981.

Rohner, R.P., & Rohner, E.C. Antecedents and consequences of parental rejection: A theory of emotional abuse. *Child Abuse & Neglect,* 1980, *4,* 189-198.

Rosenberg, M.S. & Reppucci, N.D. Child abuse: A review with special focus on an ecological approach in rural communities. In A.W. Childs & G.B. Melton (Eds.), *Rural psychology.* New York: Plenum Press, 1983. (a)

Rosenberg, M.S., & Reppucci, N.D. Abusive mothers: Perceptions of their own and their children's behavior. *Journal of Consulting and Clinical Psychology,* 1983, *51,* 674-682. (b)

Rosenberg, M.S., Reppucci, N.D., & Linney, J.A. Problems of implementation: Parent education for high-risk families. *Analysis and Intervention in Developmental Disabilities,* 1983, *7,* 1-15.

Rutter, M. Maternal deprivation, 1972-1978: New findings, new concepts, new approaches. *Child Development,* 1979, *50,* 283-305.

Sgroi, S.M. (Ed.). *Handbook of clinical intervention in child sexual abuse.* Lexington, MA: D.C. Heath, 1982.

Sgroi, S.M., Blick, L.C. & Porter, F.S. A conceptual framework for child sexual abuse. In Sgroi, S.M. (Ed.), *Handbook of clinical intervention in child sexual abuse.* Lexington, MA: D.C. Heath, 1982.

Shapiro, D. *Parents and protectors: A study in child abuse and neglect.* New York: Child Welfare League of America, 1979.

Spinetta, J., & Rigler, D. The child abusing parent: A psychological review. *Psychological Bulletin,* 1972, *77,* 296-304.

Spitz, R.A. Hospitalism: An inquiry into the genesis of psychiatric conditions in early childhood. In A. Freud et al. (Eds.), *The psychoanalytic study of the child* (Vol. 1). New York: International Universities Press, 1945.

Steele, B.F., & Pollock, C.B. A psychiatric study of parents who abuse infants and small children. In R.E. Helfer & C.H. Kempe (Eds.), *The battered child.* Chicago: University of Chicago Press, 1968 (2nd ed., 1974).

Uviller, R.K. Save them from their saviors: The constitutional rights of the family. In G. Gerbner, C.J. Ross, & E. Zigler (Eds.), *Child abuse: An agenda for action.* New York: Oxford University Press, 1980.

Wald, M.S. State intervention on behalf of "neglected" children: A search for realistic standards. *Stanford Law Review,* 1975, *27,* 985-1040.

Wald, M.S. State intervention on behalf of "neglected" children: Standards for removal of children from their homes, monitoring the status of children in foster care, and termination of parental rights. *Stanford Law Review,* 1976, *28,* 625-706.

Wald, M.S. State intervention in behalf of endangered children: A proposed legal response. *Child Abuse & Neglect,* 1982, *6,* 3-45.

White, S. Federal programs for young children: Review and recommendations, 1973. Cited on p. 986 in Wald, M.S. State intervention on behalf of "neglected" children: A search for realistic standards. *Stanford Law Review,* 1975, *27,* 985-1040.

Zigler, E. Controlling child abuse in America: An effort doomed to failure? In R. Bourne and E.H. Newberger (Eds.), *Critical perspectives on child abuse.* Lexington, MA: D.C. Heath, 1979.

Zigler, E. Controlling child abuse: Do we have the knowledge and/or the will? In G. Gerbner, C. Ross, & E. Zigler (Eds.), *Child abuse: An agenda for action.* New York: Oxford University Press, 1980.

# 5

# Children, Families,
# and Work

### Ellen Greenberger
*University of California, Irvine*

Forty years ago a family that consisted of a father, mother, and school-going children typically had one adult—the father—in the labor force. In only one of ten two-parent families that were raising minor children did the mother work; and school-going teenagers rarely held a job during the academic year. Two dramatic changes in the work life of family members have taken place since that time. One is well known, well documented, and much studied: the increased labor force participation of married women with minor children (Ferber & Birnbaum, 1982; Johnson & Waldman, 1981; Levitan & Belous, 1981). The other change has been much slower to attract interest or scrutiny: the increased labor force participation of minor children, while attending high school (Greenberger & Steinberg, 1980; Steinberg & Greenberger, 1980.

An abundant literature has demonstrated that employment (and unemployment) have substantial impacts on adults' mental health, on the economic and social functioning of the family, and on their children's well-being (Catalano & Dooley, 1980; Cobb & Kasl, 1977; Dooley & Catalano, 1980; Durkheim, 1951; Elder, 1974; Jahoda, Lazarsfeld, & Zeisel, 1971; Kamerman & Hayes, 1982; Special Task Force, 1979; Steinberg, Catalano, & Dooley, 1981).[1] It seems plausible that employment of adolescents has analogous consequences; that is, working also may affect young people's mental health and influence relations among family members. In this chapter I discuss the function of children's work in historical perspective, the effects of working on adolescents' well-being and family relations, and recent debate about restraints on child labor.

Author's Note: I appreciate the contribution of Laurence Steinberg to many of the views expressed in this chapter.

## Children's Work in Perspective:
## A Brief Overview

In most societies of the world, and in most historical periods, children's work has been an important element in the economy of the family and the community. Both their unpaid and paid work contributed to the economic well-being of the family group. When the family was the unit of production in society, children performed unpaid work that directly affected the family's output, e.g., tending animals or harvesting crops. Children also performed unpaid work that indirectly affected household output. With older children taking responsibility for the care of younger siblings, for example, the parents could turn their attention to economically more productive tasks. As well, older children were often sent to work outside the home, for other members of the community, in order to produce additional income for the family. In short, virtually all family members performed work, to the degree that they were able; work, centered in the home, served as a source of family cohesion; and children's work contributed meaningfully to the family's economic well-being.

With the industrial revolution, work was removed from the home and the immediate community to the factories. Working, under the new conditions, was more likely to separate family members in time and space than to join them, or to involve them in shared tasks. Nonetheless, children still had a place in the family economy. Not only fathers and mothers but also the children of poor parents went to work in the factories. Because there was an abundant supply of labor, and strong demand for the cheap labor of children to perform relatively simple industrial tasks, adult men often could not find employment. The work and attendant earnings of their children, in such cases, often were essential to the family's survival.

A number of interconnected factors brought this era to an end. The efforts of humanitarians (chiefly but not only women) to end the abuses of child labor, and the efforts of labor unions (mostly men) to protect jobs from competition from cheap labor (chiefly children), led to the enactment of legislation that greatly curtailed the involvement of children and adolescents in the workplace.[2] Over time, increasing mechanization of the workplace created a labor surplus that rendered children's labor unnecessary and simultaneously created a need for workers with more complex cognitive skills. These developments, taken together, set the scene for the expansion of compulsory education. Secondary school attendance, once the privilege of the well-to-do, was mandated for children of all social classes. The extension of compulsory education and the changed nature of the work place led to a steady disappearance of children and youth from the work force between 1900 and 1950.[3] Especially children who were enrolled in school disappeared from the work force during the first four decades of this century.

Since 1940 the trend for school-going children to be separated from the labor force has gone into sharp reverse: The proportion of children 14 to 17 years old who work during the school year has increased ninefold among boys, and nearly double that figure among girls (U.S. Bureau of the Census, 1943; U.S. Bureau of Labor Statistics, 1980). Currently, at any given point in the academic year, about 42 percent of high school sophomores and 63 percent of seniors hold jobs. Their jobs are concentrated in the service and retail sectors, but students also are employed in manual labor, farm work, clerical work, and the skilled trades.[4] Moreover, school-going youngsters work very substantial numbers of hours: the average sophomore, for example, 15 hours per week; the average senior, 19 hours per week.

It is beyond the scope of this chapter to fully explore this phenomenon—a task undertaken elsewhere (Greenberger & Steinberg, in press). Briefly, economic developments once again have sparked a demand for the labor of the young; and changes in values have prompted children to greet demand as opportunity—for the most part, with their parents' blessing.

The most pertinent economic change behind youngsters' return to the work place concerns the shift from an industrial economy, aimed at the manufacture of products, to an economy directed toward the delivery of a wide range of personal and business services (Ginzberg, 1977). One feature of a service economy is the proliferation of part-time jobs, many requiring little skill and necessitating work at "off" hours (e.g., evenings and weekends). Jobs in the food service industry, especially in fast food establishments, are a case in point. Many of these jobs, especially those that carry remuneration at or below the minimum wage, are ideally suited to teenagers, whose "regular" work hours already are committed to school attendance and whose wage requirements are low, compared to those of self-supporting adults. Among the social changes that have encouraged the reentry of youngsters into the work place are increased consumerism and decreased protectionism in relation to children. Both teenagers and their parents have participated in the increased consumption of goods and services (Levitan & Belous, 1981); and Winn (1983) argues that a fundamental protective attitude toward children has been replaced by a hide-nothing orientation, in which early exposure to the realities of life (presumably including sex, substance use, and—pale in comparison—work) is seen as preparation for the realities of adult life.

As we have shown in this brief historical sketch, the nature of children's work and the place where it is performed—in the fields, the factories, the fast food restaurants—have changed substantially over time. But perhaps the most important change in children's work concerns its meaning for the family. Youngsters' paid employment is no longer motivated primarily by their family's financial need, nor do youngsters' earnings go primarily to the cause of family subsistence. Rather, youngsters work chiefly for their own benefit, and especially for the purpose of enabling a high level of consumption.

Two facts dramatize contemporary reasons for working. First, teenagers who work during their high school years are more likely to be white, middle class, and residents of the suburbs, than to be Black or Hispanic, poor, and residents of the cities (Lewin-Epstein, 1981). Second, much of the money they earn goes for discretionary purchases, including cars, stereos, designer clothing, concert tickets (a phrase that once suggested an evening at Carnegie Hall), and drugs (Johnston, Bachman, & O'Malley, 1982). Based on their ongoing series of national surveys, Bachman and Johnston observe that teenage employment has led to the phenomenon of "premature affluence" (Morgan, 1981a). Children's work has been transformed from an activity performed for the good of others into an activity performed for the benefit of children themselves.

## The Consequences of Work
## for Adolescents and Their Families

Empirical research on the consequences of work for adolescents and their families has gotten off to a late start, as noted earlier, perhaps because of the perception that adolescents' jobs are peripheral to their lives, or because of the pervasive belief that there is no problem, as such, to study. Religious and philosophical traditions with deep roots in American life promote the conviction that work is good for youngsters; it keeps idle hands busy, teaches responsibility, builds character. Research of the past several years, however, demonstrates that adolescent work does present problems to study, and that working during the high school years may have costs as well as benefits to young people and their families. We will consider the two domains of possible impact—adolescents' own well-being and adolescents' families, in that order.

### Work and Psychosocial Development

Any effort to assess the costs and benefits of working to adolescents' well-being must establish a standard of healthy development against which the outcomes of working are to be judged. Greenberger (in press), based on an earlier formulation by Greenberger and Sorensen (1974), has proposed an interdisciplinary model of psychosocial development that emphasizes the importance of growth in the directions of autonomy and social integration. These two constructs—autonomy and social integration—connote sets of attributes that are conducive to the smooth functioning of society and, at the same time, are consistent with the optimum psychological development of the individual.[5]

*Autonomy*

Research to date has addressed several issues relevant to autonomy, defined broadly to include attributes of individuals that enable them to function effectively on their own in society. Thus, studies have provided data and raised unanswered questions about the relations between working and self-reliance; constructive work habits; knowledge of business and money concepts; experience in financial decision making; and future employment prospects. Many of these studies originate from Greenberger and Steinberg's Adolescent Work Project, which examined correlates and consequences of working in a sample of high school sophomores and juniors drawn from diverse family backgrounds in four Orange County, California high schools. The focus of the study was 212 youngsters holding their first part-time job outside the family, along with 319 comparable, nonworking students. The project had both cross-sectional and longitudinal research components.[6]

Longitudinal data from this project showed that scores on a self-report measure of self-reliance from Greenberger's Psychosocial Maturity Inventory (Greenberger, Josselson, Knerr, & Knerr, 1975; Greenberger & Bond, 1976) increased slightly but significantly among girls who worked, but did not increase among working boys. More specifically, gains in self-reliance were a positive function of time spent in the work place, with girls who had had more total hours of job experience showing greater gains (Steinberg, Greenberger, Garduque, Ruggiero, & Vaux, 1982). Attempting to explain the sex difference in effects of working on self-reliance, Steinberg et al. discounted differences in *opportunities* of boys and girls to exercise autonomy on the job—there were none, according to youngsters' self-reports—and focused on possible differences in the meaning of the work to the two sexes. Because employment is strongly expected of men, but less consistent with social expectations of women, the authors suggested, girls may be more disposed to see entry into the labor force as an act of independence and to draw from ongoing participation in the work place an increased sense of initiative and self-direction (compare Bronfenbrenner, 1961; Elder, 1974).

Several findings from the same study suggest that working has a number of positive effects on work habits. First, youngsters themselves believe that working has taught them to be more dependable and punctual. Indeed, if they do not have or acquire these traits, they may lose their jobs: The existence of a large supply of youngsters who can potentially replace them no doubt serves as a vivid reminder of the importance of these basic workers' virtues. Second, working youngsters showed small but significant gains in scores on the work orientation scale of the Psychosocial Maturity Inventory. This self-report scale measures the ability to work with persistence and to obtain satisfaction from completing tasks competently. As before, gains were positively associated with youngsters' time commitment to working.

*Ability* to take a constructive work orientation and *actual performance* on the job are, of course, two different matters. It is probably not the case that working transforms youngsters (or adults, for that matter) into paragons of the Protestant ethic. About half of a subsample of youngsters who were interviewed indicated that they performed assigned tasks conscientiously, but about half of the sample (often the same youngsters) described neglecting duties or "goofing off." Hardly any youngsters spontaneously described incidents of going beyond the call of duty on the job (Greenberger & Steinberg, 1981).

It also appears that working may increase adolescents' practical knowledge in areas such as economic and business concepts (e.g., the meaning of "overhead" and "interest"); consumer arithmetic; and informed consumer practices. Knowledge of this kind has clear implications for functioning adequately on one's own. In cross-sectional analyses of workers' and nonworkers' scores on a timed test of practical knowledge, with controls for grade-point average and social class background, working adolescents scored higher than their nonworking peers. However, longitudinal analyses left some doubt as to whether the observed difference was actually caused by working, or was attributable to factors related to initial selection into the labor force (Steinberg, Greenberger, Garduque, Ruggiero & Vaux, 1982).

Perhaps the most obvious potential source of work-derived autonomy is money. Insofar as youngsters earn a significant amount of money, they may obtain a significant degree of experience in money management. That youngsters do in fact earn—and spend—a good deal of money is substantiated by national surveys. In 1981, for example, the average working sophomore earned $143 per month; the average senior, $272 (based on Lewin-Epstein, 1981). In that same year 56% of high school seniors spent between half and all of their earnings on what are described as their "own needs and activities" (Johnston et al., 1982).

Two different processes seem to be at work in the spending behavior of employed adolescents. First, they assume responsibility for buying for themselves some of the things that their parents previously had provided (e.g., items of clothing); and second, they buy things that they did not own before, and that their parents likely would not provide (e.g., an automobile—still the quintessential grand purchase of teenagers). Thus, working youngsters pay for more of their expenses of living than do nonworkers (Greenberger, Steinberg, Vaux, & McAuliffe, 1980).

Interestingly, workers' greater financial self-sufficiency is not just a matter of parental expectations, but perhaps equally or more a matter of youngsters' own choice. Many youngsters seem to take on responsibility for some of their own expenses without much explicit discussion, especially in relation to satisfying a taste for luxury commodities.

Adolescents' earnings have important implications for their day-to-day experience of autonomy. Adolescents who work report more freedom (i.e., less parental oversight) in deciding how to spend their money than do non-workers. Among other reasons, parents seem likely to view money that children earn, compared to money they are given as allowance, as youngsters' own, to do with as they want. Put differently, parents treat money that adolescents earn as their private property (compare the common law conception of parents' rights in children's earnings, defined later in this chapter). The privacy and freedom youngsters gain when they become wage-earners perhaps help to explain why three-quarters of adolescents said they would rather work than simply receive the same amount of money from their parents (Greenberger & Steinberg, in press). Although youngsters' net gain from working, in dollars, is not so great as it seems at first glance, since they give up a measure of parental support, it appears that the gain in autonomy more than balances the psychological ledgers.

One other issue, concerning children's long-range autonomy, merits attention. Inkeles (1968) has observed that a major purpose of socialization is to produce mature individuals who have the skills and information that enable them to perform the kinds of work that society needs done—i.e., work that ensures a viable economy. Greenberger, Steinberg, and Ruggiero (1982) have shown, however, that adolescents' jobs typically offer little training or instruction, suggesting that the skill and information level of adolescents is not greatly advanced by working. Nearly half of their sample reported that a grade school education or less would suffice for performing the job they held—a statistic that does not correspond well to the demands of most adult jobs, or at least, those jobs that best promote self-sufficiency in adulthood.

### Social Integration

Research from several quarters has explored the impacts of working on social integration, defined broadly to include attributes of individuals that increase their ability to participate in, and feel part of, the larger society. Thus, studies have examined the effects of adolescent work on adult careers, feelings of social participation, intergenerational contact, accumulation of earnings for future use, and deviance.

In view of the pivotal role of employment in defining adults' position in the social system and in generating feelings of social connectedness, it is important to ascertain whether working during the high school years has any impact on adult careers. Exceedingly high rates of unemployment among those 18 to 25 years old make the question, "Does employment improve the employment prospects of young adults?" particularly important and timely.[7] Numerous large-scale surveys, typically concentrating on youth who have gone directly to work upon graduation from high school, have not provided an unequivocal answer. Freeman and Wise (1982) found that the weekly number of hours worked in the senior year is strongly related to weeks of employment per year in each of the next four years, and moderately related to hourly wages over the same period. However, researchers have not been able to rule out exogenous factors that might account for both intensive employment during high school and success in the labor market. In other words, unmeasured factors such as persistence, social competence, and achievement motivation may explain both early (adolescent) and subsequent (adult) labor force behavior.

Returning to the more immediate impacts of working on social participation, evidence is mixed. On the one hand, over 80 percent of adolescents take pride in the products or services they help provide, and feel that the way they perform their job may have an effect on other people (Greenberger & Steinberg, in press). On the other hand, most workers do not feel that their work is essential to the functioning of the organization or enterprise, and most feel rather easily replaceable. As well, some youngsters who work become more cynical about the intrinsic value of work and its importance in the larger scheme of things (Ruggiero, 1980; Steinberg, Greenberger, Garduque, Ruggiero, & Vaux, 1982). Finally, expectations that the early integration of adolescents into the labor force will increase contact and understanding between the younger and older generations (President's Science Advisory Committee, 1973) have not been borne out. Adolescents work in settings characterized by a high degree of age segregation. For this and other reasons the work place is not a rich source of interaction with adults, and such interaction, when it occurs, is likely to be restricted to the work place and focused on the task at hand (Greenberger & Steinberg, 1981).

The money earned by youngsters is a potentially important asset in becoming part of the adult world. Savings can be used to offset the costs of education, to establish an independent household, and to serve other future-oriented goals. Johnston et al. (1982) found, however, that over 80 percent of a national sample of high school seniors saved "none" or only "a little" of their earnings for either their post-high-school education or for other long-range purposes.

We turn, finally, to the relations between working and deviance. Because work has been conceptualized as a vehicle for integration into the mainstream of society, it frequently has been proposed that individuals who have jobs will be more likely than the unemployed to lead law-abiding, law-respecting lives. In the context of social planning for youth, the idea that working will reduce juvenile delinquency has led a charmed life, retaining a strong body of true believers despite minimal, and sometimes contradictory, evidence. Recently, for example, Shannon's large-scale survey of youngsters who were in high school in the late 1950s and early 1960s revealed that, "'contrary to the notion that employment in high school deterred delinquency, those who were employed . . . particularly the males, had somewhat more police contacts and higher seriousness scores than did others.'" Shannon suggests that working may provide teenagers with resources (e.g., money and cars) that can be used in a "trouble-producing way" (Criminal Justice Newsletter, 1982). Although this study does not permit the conclusion that working actually caused the greater deviance of employed youngsters (there were no statistical controls for youngsters' police contacts and seriousness scores before initial employment or during periods of unemployment), it does suggest that holding a job does not prevent high school students from engaging in delinquent behavior.

Ruggiero (1980, in progress) has suggested that the work place itself may become the arena for deviant behavior. Sixty-two percent of youngsters in the Adolescent Work Project sample reported having committed at least one act of theft or nontheft deviance on their first job. The most common acts were giving away goods and services for less than their market price, taking things from the employer or employees, and working while under the influence of drugs or alcohol (Ruggiero, Greenberger, & Steinberg, 1982). On a related theme, Morgan (1981b) reported a study showing that the use of alcohol, marijuana, and cocaine increased with longer hours of work (which, of course, means greater earnings); and Greenberger, Steinberg, and Vaux, (1981) found that youngsters who worked longer hours under more stressful job conditions reported higher frequencies of using cigarettes, alcohol, and marijuana.[8]

Data about deviance among young workers, in combination with other findings we have discussed, raise interesting questions about the role of work in promoting integration into the larger society. Specifically, into which "larger society" are young workers being integrated? Insofar as youngsters interact mainly with other young people at work, "donate" goods and services to their friends, and spend their earnings chiefly on consumer goods that are highly salient in the peer culture, it may be that working does more to enhance solidarity with the society of their peers than to build bridges to adulthood (Ruggiero, Greenberger, & Steinberg, 1982).

## Work and Family Relations

Research on the consequences of adolescent employment for families is sparse. Issues of interest include possible changes in the family economy and in family relations and responsibilities.

Although over 90 percent of high school seniors report that they give "none" or only "a little" of their earnings to their family to meet expenses, youth from poor families contribute appreciably more (Johnston et al.,

1982). Most of the financial benefits to families come in the form of an indirect, rather than direct, income transfer. As noted earlier, working youngsters take over responsibility for many purchases that once came out of the family purse. Since they also buy luxury items that their families would not have bought for them, however, there is no easy way to calculate the actual savings to parents that result from their youngsters' work.

The changes that working introduces into the psychosocial economy of the family are even more complex. A teenager's success in getting and keeping a steady paid job has the earmarks of an important step toward maturity. It is plausible, therefore, that parents of working teenagers allow them more self-direction. This does not seem to be the case, however. Parents of workers have as many rules as parents of nonworkers about matters such as doing homework and not socializing with certain youngsters; and parents of working adolescents do not give their youngsters a larger role in decisions that affect the family (Greenberger, Steinberg, Vaux & McAuliffe, 1980). Another "plausible" impact of adolescents' work also is not clearly confirmed by data. Results are contradictory on the question of whether adolescents who work spend less time at home, engaged in family activities. These are, in fact, two questions. It seems likely that the former, at least, is true for youngsters who spend long hours in the work place.

Evidence does quite clearly suggests that the *quality* of parent-child relations is affected by working. As boys spend more time at work, feelings of closeness to parents increase; in contrast, girls' feelings of closeness decline (Steinberg, Greenberger, Garduque, Ruggiero, & Vaux, 1982). Although this sex difference cannot be firmly pinned down, it is amenable to interpretation.

For example, it has been suggested that working may lead adolescents to develop greater empathy with their parents, based on common experience of the demands encountered in the workplace (Steinberg, Greenberger, Jacobi, & Garduque, 1981). It is possible, however, that increased empathy particularly enhances sons' closeness to their fathers, since "worker" is a more central component of the adult male role than of the adult female role. It is also plausible that increases and decreases in closeness to family members have different implications for the development of adolescent boys and girls. Adolescent girls generally report much greater closeness (and self-disclosure) to family members than same-age boys (Greenberger, in press); therefore, the apparent decrease in closeness between working girls and their parents may not indicate a worsening of relations, but merely a moderation of their earlier dependency. The increased self-reliance of girls who spend considerable time at work already has been noted and discussed.

In any case, the discrepant directions of change in family closeness for adolescent boys and girls who work may be constructive for both sexes, in view of the different developmental tasks they face. It is widely held that the greatest problem for adolescent girls is individuation or autonomy; for boys, intimacy and social integration (Douvan & Adelson, 1966; Greenberger, in press).

We know least about changes in the services that adolescents perform for their families that may follow from adolescents' employment. The modal young worker reports no change in the extent to which he or she helps out around the house. However, one in three report doing "a little less than before," and another 14 percent, "a lot less than before" (Greenberger & Steinberg, in press). A question that needs further research is whether the departure of adolescents for the work place has contributed to the growing number of younger children who are left in what has been called, euphemistically, "self-care." In view of the dramatic increase in employment of women with young children over the past several decades, and the concommitant increase in part-time employment of teenagers, it may be that families are forgoing a service of older children that was once highly valued: the care of their younger siblings.

## Summary

We began with the premise that healthy development during adolescence means growth in the directions of autonomy and social integration. That is, if youngsters are to achieve both psychological and social maturity, they must gain a variety of dispositions and competencies that enhance their ability to function on their own and that increase their ability to participate in, and contribute to, the survival of the social system.

In general, research suggests that working during high school has more demonstrable positive effects on autonomy than on social integration. In neither of these two domains, however, are the positive effects of working truly striking, either in number or degree; and in the domain of social integration, working may exact some costs.

Briefly, the most clear-cut consequences of working for the development of autonomy are the strengthening of effective work habits and, for girls, of self-reliance. Youngsters who work also become more financially autonomous in a number of ways, but this fact should be interpreted with caution. Most youngsters do not have to confront hard decisions about housing and food, because these are provided by their parents. Although it is true, moreover, that adolescent workers exercise considerable autonomy over the money they earn, the way they actually deploy their earnings does not clearly support the goal of moving toward adult self-sufficiency—i.e., autonomy in the sense intended by our model of constructive development during the transition from adolescence to adulthood.

The most clear-cut positive effect of working on social integration has to do with encouraging youngsters' sense that the way they perform their work has real consequences for other people. It is possible, but not firmly established, that working puts non-college-bound youngsters at an advantage in the first years of post-high-school employment. On the other side of the ledger, we note increased marijuana and alcohol use, and increased cynicism, under certain conditions, about the intrinsic value of working; and we observe the initiation of adolescents into occupational deviance. Working, in fact, may do more to promote solidarity with the peer culture than to facilitate integration into the broader adult social world.

Research on adolescent work and family relations does not lend itself readily to description in terms of positive and negative consequences. It is clear that most youngsters do not work, as they once did, for the economic benefit of their family. Nonetheless, some financial responsibility shifts from parents to adolescents when the latter earn a substantial paycheck. Working youngsters spend less time at home, and many spend less time helping out with household tasks. The impact of adolescents' time budgets on parents, and on younger children at home, is not known.

## Children's Work in the Current Legal and Social Context

I have shown in previous sections that children's work has been emancipated, to a considerable degree, from the family functions it once served and has become embedded in a new, more individualistic context. In order to appreciate the nature and extent of this shift, it is instructive to review briefly the legal status of children's work and to contextualize recent debate on the merits of continued regulation of children's labor.

### Legal Status

The place of children's work in the family is well established in common law: The father is entitled to both the services and the earnings of his minor children, in return for the duty of support.[9] In other words, children's paid work was construed primarily as an activity of potential benefit to the family—and not, primarily, as an activity for the child's psychosocial or financial benefit.

As Americans moved from the farmlands to the cities, the nature and location of children's work changed dramatically, and an equally dramatic change took place in the legal framework underlying children's employment. In an effort to eliminate widespread abuses of child labor, and for other reasons noted earlier, legislation was enacted that vested in the state the formerly parental rights of control over children's work. To bring us up to date quickly, the federal Fair Labor Standards Act of 1938 (FLSA), amended numerous times since its enactment, now sets age standards for various forms of employment; establishes wage minima; and grants authority to the Secretary of Labor to designate hazardous occupations and permissible hours of work. State laws, which vary considerably among themselves, further specify conditions under which children may work.[10,11]

Despite the increased dominance of the state vis à vis the family in the regulation of children's work, important elements of parental control remain intact. For example, state labor laws typically require parental consent (or at least the employer's statement of belief that parental consent has been given) before a work certificate for a minor is issued to an employer. Moreover, all work of children for their parents, or persons standing in the place of parents, is exempted from the provisions of the child labor laws, except for those pertaining to the exclusion of children from hazardous occupations. (Even the usual proscriptions on hazardous occupations do not apply in agricultural work, which enjoys broader exemptions than other forms of work.) Finally, parents are still entitled to the earnings of their minor children. I will comment briefly on the latter two issues.

The exemption from child labor regulations of work that children perform for their parents seems to preclude the possibility that parents' expectations may be excessive, i.e., may constitute the kind of "oppressive child labor" that the FLSA sought to eliminate. It is not inconceivable, for example, that the conditions and hours of employment of children who work in family enterprises may pose threats to their health and well-being, the bonds of kinship notwithstanding.

Whereas some parents do, in fact, employ their own children, free from the restrictions generally imposed on children's work, few parents seem to exercise, or exercise fully, their rights in their children's earnings. This conclusion is consistent with national data, described earlier, that demonstrate the minimal amount of their earnings youngsters contribute to the family, and the contrasting large amount they devote to personal spending (and to a lesser extent, personal savings). Just as the trend toward smaller families and the invention of labor-saving devices for the household have resulted in less need for children's services at home, the rise in the standard of living has resulted in less need for their earnings. Because children's work is now more often voluntary than obligatory for the family's survival, the financial fruits of children's labor are treated, in practice, as private property.

## The Current Debate

The central question under discussion today is whether child labor legislation, in whole or in part, has outlived its usefulness. Paraphrasing Mnookin (1978, p. 646), the regulation of child labor presents a fascinating context to explore the question of whether reform legislation enacted in an earlier period, under very different conditions, may now produce undesirable consequences. On one side of the debate are critics who claim that child labor laws, initially intended to protect youngsters from the harmful effects of employment, currently restrict them from reaping the benefits of safe and useful work experience ("Fair Labor Standards Act," 1982; Mnookin, 1978; "Child Labor Laws—Time to Grow Up," 1975); on the other side of the debate are observers who assert that protection—at least, protection from excessive employment—is still appropriate. These commentators cite possible costs to adolescents' well-being and family functioning, and to society, associated with long hours of work (Greenberger, 1982; Greenberger & Steinberg, in press).

Proponents of the deregulation of child labor, or of liberalizing current restraints, argue that earlier concerns that working would imperil children's health, interfere with their education, lead to juvenile delinquency, and create competition with adult labor, are no longer valid. They claim that the facts today are, if anything, exactly the reverse (Mnookin, 1978; "Child Labor Laws—Time to Grow Up," 1975). They argue that work-place safety has been greatly enhanced by federal regulations that cover individuals of all ages; and that working provides education for adult roles, prevents delinquency, and combats youth employment—now a more pressing problem than interference with adult unemployment.

All of these points deserve careful consideration and analysis, but can receive only brief comment here. Suffice it to say that many of these assertions or assumptions, have been discussed herein, and that the evidence does not, in all cases, justify such optimistic conclusions. For example, the correlation between rates of youth unemployment and frequency of property crimes by juveniles does not justify the inference that the one causes the other ("Child Labor Laws—Time to Grow Up," 1975). Care needs to be exercised in suggesting that fewer restraints on child labor—restraints that affect 14- and 15-year-olds more than older students—will help to solve the massive problem of youth unemployment. "Youth unemployment"—a term used by labor specialists to describe facts that pertain to the 18 to 25 age group—is cited inappropriately in many treatises as evidence for the need to broaden opportunities for minor children to work.

In my view, research indicates that review and possible revision of the Hazardous Occupations Orders is clearly in order (compare National Child Labor Committee, 1980); but continued efforts to prevent the *overworking* of children during "prime time" for their socialization and development is still warranted, and is in the best interests of both children and society. The latter issue recently emerged in the public arena, when congressional hearings were held on a Labor Department proposal to weaken restraints on the hours/time provisions that regulate employment of 14- and 15-year-olds during the school year (Greenberger, 1982). Although the proposal was withdrawn, the issue promises to be of continued interest to professionals concerned with children's welfare and children's rights.

My concern about overworking children is based both on empirical findings and on consideration of alternatives to working that may be useful in promoting the transition to adulthood. The latter subject would take us too far afield, but is discussed fully elsewhere (Greenberger & Steinberg, in press). Earlier in this chapter, however, I summarized data that indicate that working long hours increase the frequency of use of alcohol and other illegal drugs and may have problematic impacts on family functioning. Other studies, not included in the review above, put an additional spotlight on long hours of work. Intensive employment (generally, more than 15 hours per week for high school sophomores and more than 20 hours for seniors) leads youngsters to spend less time on homework and may lead to declining grades among academically less able students (Steinberg, Greenberger, Garduque, & McAuliffe, 1982; Greenberger & Steinberg, in press).

These lines of evidence coincide with several issues that are matters of serious national concern. Substance use is, of course, a major health problem. The quality and quantity of family life are also much lamented ("Our Neglected Kids," 1982), and deficiencies of the educational system are legendary.

Regulatory changes that would permit young teenagers longer hours of work likely would further decrease the amount of time youngsters and their parents spend with each other; and it appears that such time already is very limited (Medrich, Roizen, Rubin, & Buckley, 1982; Robinson, 1977). Medrich and his colleagues, based on a study of children between the ages of 10 and 11 in Oakland, California, put the figure at less than 1½ hours per day, including time spent "together" watching television. Time that adolescents spend at work, moreover, tends to be "taken out of" time spent at home (Greenberger, Steinberg, Vaux, & McAuliffe, 1980). Early adolescents who work long hours may lose out on needed parental nurturance and guidance, for which they are not being compensated by social relations in the work place.

Moreover, permitting longer hours of work during the school year may compound serious educational deficits of the younger generation. The educational achievement of American students, compared to their counterparts in several other countries, has been declining for some time. Poor educational achievement during the high school years may compromise youngsters' individual attainments as adults; as well, suboptimal educational achievement of the younger generation poses a threat to the future well-being of society. Although it is true that restricting hours of employment when school is in session does not oblige youngsters to spend time on their studies, it is unlikely that relaxing such restrictions will lead to increased time on, or devotion to, schoolwork. (High school students can hardly spend less time than they now do on homework: under one hour per day, on the average, according to a recent survey [Lewin-Epstein, 1981].)

It is important to remember that child labor historically has been a target of exploitation. Despite current sentiment about a wide range of social issues, favoring deregulation and/or expansion of children's rights to participate in decisions that affect their lives, it may be a mistake to remove *all* restrictions on adolescents' work. Definition of what constitutes "overworking" during adolescence probably will remain somewhat elusive and require complex judgments about the long-run interests of society, as well as adolescents. Several social indicators—among them, the increasing investment of parental time in work, rising numbers of children with no adult supervision for substantial portions of the day, climbing rates of child abuse and neglect, and declining aid to families with dependent children, have led to a troubling conjecture: "There is an anti-child spirit loose in the land" ("Our Neglected Kids," 1982, p. 54). In this social environment, it would be wise to tread slowly, and with deliberation, in debating how much employment is good for young people and who should make that decision.

## Notes

1. Research concerning the effects of working has taken somewhat different points of departure, depending on whether it focuses on men or women. Studies of men tend to emphasize the consequences of *unemployment* for family income. Studies of women, on the other hand, tend to focus on the consequences of *employment* for children's psychological well-being. The differential attention to male unemployment and female employment and to economic issues versus child development no doubt reflects past history and present reality. Despite the dramatic increase in women's labor force participation since 1940, men still are more likely than women to work; men's earnings still make a greater contribution to household income; and women still have the major responsibility for child rearing.

2. The initial source of legislative reform was the states. By 1860 eight states had laws that restricted the number of hours per day that children could work. By 1930 most states had set minimum age requirements for employment and had reduced permissible working hours to eight per day. Federal legislation, first attempted in 1916 (but declared unconstitutional) came to fruition in 1938, when Congress enacted the Fair Labor Standards Act of 1938 (Mnookin, 1978).

3. In 1900, for example, 60.1 percent of all white males between 14 and 19 were employed, or had tried unsuccessfully to find employment, in comparison to 39.5 percent of similar youngsters fifty years later. Figures for other population groups showed the same trend (Lewin-Epstein, 1981).

4. Common job titles are counter worker (food service), box boy/bagger, sales clerk, busboy, cashier, assembler, waitress, cleaner (janitor), vehicle washer, typist, and service station attendant.

5. The related terms—agency and communion—were introduced into the social science literature by Bakan (1966) and subsequently elaborated and operationalized by Baumrind and

Black (1967) and Baumrind (1982). "Agency" refers to a domain of personality characterized by individuation and self-assertion; "communion" refers to a domain characterized by feelings of social dependence and unity.

6. For more complete details on sampling and procedures, see Steinberg, Greenberger, Garduque, Ruggiero, and Vaux (1982), and other publications of which Greenberger and Steinberg together are authors.

7. The decision to consider adult employment as a socially integrative consequence of early work experience is arbitrary, since adult employment is also an important aspect of autonomy. For heuristic purposes, *training* for potential future jobs was considered in the discussion of autonomy, and *actual* post-high-school employment is treated in the present section.

8. The association between substance use and working brings to mind our earlier discussion of youngsters' autonomy over the use of their earnings. It is important to emphasize, however, that substance use is not simply attributable to the income provided by jobs, but increases with duration of job stress.

9. The inference that fathers and mothers in fact have equal rights in their childrens' services and earnings can be drawn from broad statutes giving parents equal powers and rights with respect to their children (Vernier, 1936).

10. See the report of the National Child Labor Committee (1980) for a state-by-state compendium of child labor laws. This report also contains recommendations for regulatory changes.

11. A thumbnail sketch of current regulations that are common to most states looks something like the following: The minimum age for formal employment is 14, although permissible occupations for youngsters this age are quite restricted. At age 16 many but not all of these restraints are lifted. The child labor laws also regulate children's work through hours and time provisions. These provisions differentiate among youngsters by age and as a function of whether school is in session. For example, 14- and 15-year-olds have curfews on night-time employment, but youngsters 16 and older do not; and 14- and 15-year-olds can work only 18 hours per week when school is in session, whereas the work of 16- and 17-year-olds enrolled in school is not restricted.

## References

Bakan, D. *The duality of existence: Isolation and communion in western man.* Boston: Beacon Press, 1966.

Baumrind, D. *Familial antecedents of adolescent adjustment: Stress reactivity in adolescence.* Grant application submitted to DHHS. Berkeley: University of California, 1982.

Baumrind, D., & Black A. Socialization practices associated with dimensions of competence in preschool boys and girls. *Child Development,* 1967, *38,* 291-327.

Bronfenbrenner, U. Some familial antecedents of responsibility and leadership in adolescents. In L. Petrullo & B. Bass (Eds.), *Leadership and interpersonal behavior.* New York: Holt, Rinehart & Winston, 1961.

Catalano, R., & Dooley, D. Environmental factors in primary prevention: The case of economic change. In R.H. Price, J. Monahan, B.C. Baker, & R.F. Ketterer (Eds.), *Prevention in community mental health: Research, policy and practice.* Beverly Hills, CA: Sage, 1980.

Child labor laws—time to grow up. *Minnesota Law Review,* 1975, *59,* part 1, 575-608.

Cobb, S., & Kasl, S.V. *Termination: The consequences of job loss* (Report No. 76-1261). Cincinnati: Ohio National Institute for Occupational Safety & Health, Behavioral & Motivational Factors Research, June 1977.

Criminal Justice Newsletter, 1982, *18*, 1-3.

Dooley, D., & Catalano, R. Economic change as a cause of behavioral disorder. *Psychological Bulletin*, 1980, *87*, 450-468.

Douvan, E., & Adelson, J. *The adolescent experience.* New York: Wiley, 1966.

Durkheim, E. *Suicide: A study in sociology.* Glencoe, IL: Free Press, 1951.

Elder, G. *Children of the Great Depression.* Chicago: University of Chicago Press, 1974.

Fair Labor Standards Act: Child labor regulation number 3; employment of 14- and 15-year-olds. *Federal Register*, 1982, *47*, 3125-3129.

Ferber, M., & Birnbaum, B. The impact of mother's work on the family as an economic system. In S. Kamerman & C. Hayes (Eds.), *Families that work: Children in a changing world.* Washington, DC: National Academy Press, 1982.

Freeman, R., & Wise, D. *The youth labor market problem: Its nature, causes, and consequences.* Chicago: University of Chicago Press, 1982.

Ginzberg, E. The job problem. *Scientific American*, 1977, *237*, 43-51.

Greenberger, E. A researcher in the policy arena: The case of child labor. *American Psychologist*, 1982, *38*, 104-111.

Greenberger, E. Defining psychosocial maturity in adolescence. In P. Karoly & J. Steffen (Eds.), *Adolescent behavior disorders: Current perspectives.* Lexington, MA: D.C. Heath, in press.

Greenberger, E., & Bond, L. User's manual for the Psychological Maturity Inventory (mimeo). Irvine: University of California, 1976.

Greenberger, E., Josselson, R., Knerr, C., & Knerr, B. The measurement and structure of psychosocial maturity. *Journal of Youth and Adolescence*, 1975, *4*, 127-143.

Greenberger, E., and Sorensen, A. Toward a concept of psychosocial maturity. *Journal of Youth and Adolescence*, 1974, *3*, 329-358.

Greenberger, E., & Steinberg, L. Part-time employment of in-school youth: A preliminary assessment of costs and benefits. In R. Taggart & B. Linder (Eds.), *A review of youth employment problems, programs, and policies: Vol. 1. The youth employment problem: Causes and dimensions.* Washington, DC: Vice President's Task Force on Youth Employment, U.S. Department of Labor, 1980.

Greenberger, E., & Steinberg, L. The workplace as a context for the socialization of youth. *Journal of Youth and Adolescence*, 1981, *10*, 185-210.

Greenberger, E., & Steinberg, L. *Teenage work in America* (tentative title). Cambridge: Harvard University Press, in press.

Greenberger, E., Steinberg, L., & Ruggiero, M. A job is a job is a job . . . or is it? Behavioral observations in the adolescent workplace. *Work and Occupations*, 1982, *9*, 79-96.

Greenberger, E., Steinberg, L., & Vaux, A. Adolescents in the workplace: Health and behavioral consequences of job stress. *Developmental Psychology*, 1981, *17*, 691-703.

Greenberger, E., Steinberg, L., Vaux, A., & McAuliffe, S. Adolescents who work: Effects of part-time employment on family and peer relations. *Journal of Youth and Adolescence*, 1980, *9*, 189-202.

Inkeles, A. Society, social structure and child socialization. In J. Clausen (Ed.), *Socialization and society.* Boston: Little, Brown, 1968.

Jahoda, M., Lazarsfeld, P.F., & Zeisel, H. *Marienthal: The sociography of an unemployed community.* Chicago: Aldin-Atherton, 1971.

Johnson, B., & Waldman, E. Marital and family patterns of the labor force. *Monthly Labor Review*, 1981, *194*(10), 36-38.

Johnston, L., Bachman, J., & O'Malley, P. *Monitoring the future: Questionnaire responses from the nation's high school seniors, 1981.* Ann Arbor: Institute for Social Research, University of Michigan, 1982.

Kamerman, S.B., & Hayes, C.D. (Eds.). *Families that work: Children in a changing world.* Washington, DC: National Academy Press, 1982.

Levitan, S., & Belous, R. Working wives and mothers: What happens to family life? *Monthly Labor Review,* 1981, *104*(9), 26-30.

Lewin-Epstein, N. *Youth employment during high school.* Washington, DC: National Center for Education Statistics, 1981.

Medrich, E., Roizen, J., Rubin, V., & Buckley, S. *The serious business of growing up.* Berkeley: University of California Press, 1982.

Mnookin, R. *Child, family and state: Cases and materials on children and the law.* Boston: Little, Brown, 1978.

Morgan, D. Coming of age in the '80s. Part 2. Security versus fulfillment: Caught in conflicting values. *Washington Post,* December 28, 1981. (a)

Morgan, D. Coming of age in the 80's. Part 3. Growing up bored: There's nothing to do so you get high. *Washington Post,* December 29, 1981. (b)

National Child Labor Committee. Child labor laws and youth employment: A compendium, an analysis, and a design for change. New York: Author, 1980.

Our neglected kids. *U.S. News and World Report,* August 9, 1982, pp. 54-58.

President's Science Advisory Committee. *Youth: Transition to adulthood.* Chicago: University of Chicago Press, 1973.

Robinson, J. *How Americans use time.* Ann Arbor: Institute for Social Research, University of Michigan, 1977.

Ruggiero, M. Adolescent occupational crime: A psychosocial analysis. Paper presented at the annual meeting of the Western Psychological Association. Irvine: University of California, 1980.

Ruggiero, M. *Work as an impetus to delinquency: An examination of the theoretical and empirical connections.* Doctoral dissertation, Irvine, University of California, in progress.

Ruggiero, M., Greenberger, E., & Steinberg, L. Occupational deviance among first-time workers. *Youth and Society,* 1982, *13,* 423-448.

Special Task Force to the Secretary of Health, Education, & Welfare. *Work in America.* Cambridge, MA: MIT Press, 1979.

Steinberg, L., Catalano, R., & Dooley, D. Economic antecedents of child abuse and neglect. *Child Development,* 1981, *52,* 975-985.

Steinberg, L., & Greenberger, E. The part-time employment of high school students: A research agenda. *Children and Youth Services Review,* 1980, *2,* 161-185.

Steinberg, L., Greenberger, E., Garduque, L., & McAuliffe, S. High school students in the labor force: Some costs and benefits to schooling and learning. *Educational Evaluation and Policy Analysis,* 1982, *4,* 363-372.

Steinberg, L., Greenberger, E., Garduque, L., Ruggiero, M., & Vaux, A. Effects of early work experience on adolescent development. *Developmental Psychology,* 1982, *18,* 385-395.

Steinberg, L., Greenberger, E., Jacobi, M., & Garduque, L. Working: A partial antidote for adolescent egocentrism. *Journal of Youth and Adolescence,* 1981, *10,* 141-157.

U.S. Department of Commerce, Bureau of the Census. Characteristics of the population, 1940, Vol. 14, Part I, pp. 94. Washington, DC: U.S. Government Printing Office, 1943.

U.S. Department of Labor, Bureau of Labor Statistics. Bulletin 2070, pp. 125-131. Washington, DC: U.S. Government Printing Office, 1980.

Vernier, C.G. *American family laws.* Stanford: Stanford University Press, 1936 (reprinted in 1971 by Greenwood Press, Westport, CT).

Winn, M. The loss of childhood. *New York Times Magazine,* May 3, 1983, pp. 18ff.

# PART III

# CHILDREN IN THE HEALTH CARE SYSTEM

# 6

# Adolescents' Reproductive Rights

## Abortion, Contraception, and Sterilization

**Elizabeth Scott**

*University of Virginia*

Mental health professionals who treat adolescents may frequently see clients struggling with decisions relating to sexual behavior, pregnancy, and abortion. Unlike most problems that arise in a therapy context, these issues may have complex legal as well as psychological dimensions. Twenty years ago the assertion that an adolescent has a constitutional right to make independent reproductive decisions would have seemed absurd to many people. Today it is clear that teenagers do, in fact, have some legal rights to make abortion and contraception decisions. The constitutional contours of these rights remain unclear, however, and the extent to which adolescent autonomy on these issues is recognized varies widely from state to state.

One reason that there is substantial uncertainty is that the U.S. Supreme Court, in a series of opinions on adolescents' reproductive rights since 1976, has been divided, and has not offered a clear, consistent position. While the Court initially seemed to support a right of reproductive privacy for adolescents similar to that enjoyed by adults,[1] later cases have emphasized the importance of parental involvement in decisions regarding their children.[2] Thus, while the Court has made clear that certain legal restrictions would be unconstitutional—such as denying the mature minor the right to make her own abortion decision[3]—it is also clear that there is considerably more latitude to legally restrict minors' reproductive rights than would be acceptable for adults.

Federal and state responses to the uncertain guidance of the Supreme Court have varied. Not surprisingly, political resolution of what are extremely controversial philosophical and moral issues have been subject to heated debate and reflect a range of concerns. Some states[4] and (at least until recently) the federal government[5] give minors virtually the same autonomy as adults, providing easy access to contraception and abortion. This approach reflects both support for the autonomy and privacy of adolescents and a more pragmatic concern about the enormous personal, social, and economic cost of teenage pregnancy (Zimring, 1982). Other states adopt a more restrictive approach,[6] giving adolescents only as much autonomy as the Supreme Court has found to be constitutionally required. This response suggests, in part, attitudes supporting the traditional view of the legal status of minors as incompetent to make decisions and as subject to their parents' and the state's authority. Philosophical political, and moral considerations are also important (Tribe 1978). Support for a restrictive stance may be most intense among those who oppose abortion and modern adolescent sexual mores in general (Rosoff, 1982).

A different type of reproductive decision recently examined by courts and legislatures involves the sterilization of retarded individuals. Since 1980 courts in several states have determined that a judge may authorize sterilization where parents or guardians seek the operation for their retarded child.[7] In contrast to the questionable practice of eugenic sterilization of the "defective" in the interest of society—popular earlier in the century (Ferster, 1966)—the recent trend has been to authorize sterilization only when it is in the interest of the retarded person (Burnett, 1981; Melton & Scott, in press).

Sterilization of retarded minors arises in a very different context and raises somewhat different issues from abortion and contraception sought by normal minors. It does not involve an affirmative exercise by the minor of her [8] reproductive rights. Nonetheless, these rights are implicated in sterilization, as they are in abortion and contraception.

Mental health professionals who deal with teenagers may more effectively assist their clients if they understand the basic legal context of reproductive decision making for the adolescent. This chapter will examine the recent constitutional and legal developments with the objective of clarifying that context. It will also focus on the direct implications of these legal developments for the mental health professional, whose expertise may be sought to assist in the determination of such legal criteria as competency. Other issues of professional role and ethics will be explored.

## The Law and Minors' Reproductive Choices

The idea that minors may have a constitutionally protected interest in making independent choices about contraception and abortion is an extension of a line of Supreme Court cases that established the right of reproductive privacy for adults. In 1965 the Supreme Court [9] struck down a Connecticut law that prohibited the use of contraceptives. Emphasizing the sanctity of marriage and the intimate and private nature of the decision of whether or not to have a child, the Court recognized for the first time a constitutional right of reproductive privacy. In *Eisenstadt v. Baird*,[10] several years later, the Court declared that a Massachusetts law restricting the sale of contraceptives to married couples was unconstitutional. The right or reproductive privacy, the Court asserted, is the right of the individual, married or single, to make the decision of whether or not to have a child, free from state intrusion. In the 1973 landmark case of *Roe v. Wade*,[11] the Supreme Court determined that the constitutional right of reproductive privacy extended to a woman's decision to have an abortion. During the first trimester, at least, this decision should be left to the woman and her doctor; the state's interest in her health or in the developing fetus are not sufficient to outweigh the woman's right to decide independently whether or not to bear a child.

## Minors' Abortion Rights

### Constitutional Developments

The Supreme Court first addressed the question of whether minors have a right to make reproductive decisions in *Planned Parenthood of Central Missouri v. Danforth*[12] in 1976. *Danforth* involved a Missouri law that required unmarried minors to have their parents' consent to obtain an abortion. The Court held that minors, like adults, have a constitutional interest in reproductive privacy and, thus, the Missouri law was unconstitutional.

The Court rejected the traditional presumption of the law that parents have authority to make important decisions affecting their children's lives, and that children themselves are not competent to make decisions, medical or otherwise (Wadlington, 1983). While acknowledging the state's obligation to protect the welfare of minors and the traditional importance of parental authority, the Court found these interests to be outweighed by the minor's constitutional interest in making an independent, private abortion decision. The Court reasoned that since, under *Roe v. Wade*, the state itself cannot prohibit abortion in the first trimester, it cannot, by requiring parental consent, delegate to the parents an "absolute and possibly arbitrary veto"[13] over the minor's decision. Further, Justice Blackmun, writing for the Court, questioned whether requiring parental consent to abortion could serve the otherwise legitimate purpose of strengthening the family unit "where the minor and the non-consenting parent are so fundamentally in conflict and the very existence of the pregnancy already has fractured the family structure."[14]

The Supreme Court had on several occasions in the past fifty years confirmed that minors as well as adults have constitutional rights. The landmark case of *In re Gault*[15] in 1967 and later cases extended to minors many of the procedural rights accorded adults in criminal proceedings. Minors also have a First Amendment right of free speech, although it may be narrower than the right of adults (Dembitz, 1980). *Danforth* and later reproductive rights cases represent a departure from existing law in finding that minors have constitutional rights to make autonomous decisions that may not be infringed upon by *parents* as well as by the state (Garvey, 1978; Keiter, 1982).

While *Danforth* established that adolescents have a constitutional right to reproductive privacy, it also suggested that it may be restricted with less justification than adults. Although Justice Blackmun, writing for the Court, described the right as extending to the "competent minor, mature enough to have become pregnant,"[16] he shortly thereafter noted that "not every minor regardless of age or maturity may give effective consent for the termination of her pregnancy."[17] This observation takes on significance in light of the later cases that focus on the minor's maturity as a critical factor in determining the extent of her right to reproductive privacy.

*Danforth* left unsettled the extent to which a state may involve parents in their child's reproductive decision, short of a blanket-consent requirement. In cases following *Danforth*, the Court has repeatedly shown deference toward the importance of the role of parents in guiding their children and balanced this interest against that of the adolescent in making an independent decision, and the state's interest in protecting her welfare. *Bellotti v. Baird (II)*,[18] decided by a divided Court in 1979, illustrates this balancing act. In striking down the Massachusetts statute, the Court, in an opinion by Justice Powell, held that the state must allow the mature minor to make the abortion decision herself. While the state may require parents' consent as one form of access to abortion, an alternative, either a judicial or administrative proceeding, must be available to the girl who is reluctant to approach her parents. If she demonstrates that she is "mature and competent to make the abortion decision"[19] to the satisfaction of the judge or other state decision maker, she must be allowed to act independently. Even if she fails to establish her capacity to make a mature decision, the abortion should be authorized if it is in her best interest.

In acknowledging the parents' and the state's interest in the minor's abortion decision, the Court in *Bellotti* allowed the state to place a burden on the adolescent's rights which would be unconstitutional if applied to adults. Adults are assumed to be competent to make medical decisions; only in extraordinary circumstances is this capacity scrutinized (Meisel, 1979). Although the proceeding proposed in *Bellotti* is presented as an avenue to abortion for the girl who does not want to get parental permission, it may seem like a forbidding path to a teenager who is likely to lack experience in or knowledge about legal procedures. A requirement that minors pursue a legal remedy to prove their ability to make an abortion decision may potentially lead to delayed decisions (and hence more risky abortion), illegal abortion, and increased incidence of unwanted childbirth (Torres, Forrest, & Eisman, 1980). The effect of requiring an official recognition of the minor's maturity before she can make the decision has not been studied. That there may be negative implications is ignored by the Court.

The problem is compounded by the fact that the Supreme Court offered no guidelines in *Bellotti* for determining which minors have the capacity to make the abortion decision independently. It is unclear whether the finding required is the intellectual capacity to give informed consent to the specific medical treatment or a more general maturity. The former alternative avoids placing burdens on the minor that would not apply to adults, and reduces the risk of bias of the decision maker. Some commentators have challenged whether it makes sense to question at all the competency of the minor who, learning of her pregnancy, has taken the initiative to obtain an abortion (Dembitz, 1980).

*Bellotti* also proposed no guidelines for the determination of whether or not abortion is in the best interest of the immature minor. It is left to the discretion of the decision maker to determine whether the girl's well-being is best served by allowing the abortion or by refusing permission unless the girl consults her parents. Again the values of the decision maker may enter. It would seem an unlikely case in which a girl too immature to make the abortion decision is better served by being forced to bear a child against her wishes—unless abortion is viewed as abhorrent on ethical grounds.

While *Danforth* and *Bellotti* established that states may not require that teens must have parental consent to obtain an abortion, notice to parents of the abortion may be an acceptable restriction. In 1981 the Supreme Court in *H.L. v. Matheson*[20] upheld a Utah law requiring the physician to give notice to parents when performing an abortion on a minor. This case emphasized the importance of parental consultation in a "decision that has potentially traumatic and permanent consequences," particularly if the "patient is immature."[21] Chief Justice Burger also asserted that "if the pregnant girl elects to carry her child to term, the *medical* decisions to be made entail few—perhaps none—of the potentially grave emotional and psychological consequences of the decision to abort."[22] The Court viewed adolescents as of questionable competency to make informed abortion decisions and assumed that parental involvement would lead to better decisions for minors than would otherwise result. The Court specifically declined to address whether notice could be required where a mature minor is involved.

There is little empirical support for the assumptions on which the Court based its conclusion that notice to parents is a legitimate infringement on adolescents' privacy rights (Melton, in press). In examining the studies of negative psychological effects of abortion, Osofsky and her colleagues conclude that "a surprisingly low number of complications can be found" (Osofsky, Osofsky, Rajan, & Fox, 1971). Cates (1981) reports finding little evidence that adolescents suffer greater psychological or physical effects of abortion than do adult women. As Melton noted, one of the two studies cited by the Court to support a contrary assertion involved pregnant teenagers who did *not* abort (Melton, in press). Bracken, Hachamovitch, and Grossman (1974) found a more negative response to abortion among young women whose parents disapprove of abortion. However, knowledge of the abortion by parents was not independently linked to abortion response. No studies to date support the notion that teenage abortion is psychologically more damaging than childbirth. David, Rasmussen, and Holst (1981) report a Danish study finding comparable numbers of admissions to psychiatric hospitals following abortion and childbirth for age groups including 15-19 year-olds.

The Court's suggestion that abortion is a more serious medical decision than any *associated* with childbirth is also without empirical basis and somewhat disingenuous, as it seems to exclude childbirth itself from the relevant "decisions," perhaps because the minor has no choice at that point but to bear the child. Childbirth for an adolescent patient has five times the morbidity/mortality rate of a first-trimester abortion (Cates, 1981). While second-trimester abortions do involve comparable risks to childbirth (Cates, 1981; Tietze, 1978), this does not support requiring parental notice, since the requirement itself may lead girls who are reluctant to consult with their parents to postpone their decision, thereby contributing to an increase in the number of more risky and traumatic second-trimester abortions (Rooks and Cates, 1977; Bracken and Kasl, 1975).

The Court's assumption that a better decision will be made if the pregnant girl consults with her parents suggests both that she is unlikely to make a competent decision herself and that her parents will act in her interest. Weithorn's research suggests, however, that by age fourteen, adolescents may be as intellectually competent to make treatment decision as adults (Weithorn & Campbell, 1982). The ethical, moral, and social dimensions of the abortion decision may distinguish it from other types of medical decisions and suggest that further study of decision making in the abortion context is needed (Melton, in press). It should be noted, however, that adults are not required to exhibit comprehension of these dimensions of the decision. The only existing study suggests that minors do not differ significantly from adults in their decision-making process on this issue (Lewis, 1980).

The assumption that parents informed of their daughters abortion without her consent will respond in a way that is beneficial to her interests has not been examined empirically. One study indicated that pregnant teenagers overestimated the negativity of their parents' reactions (Furstenburg,

1976a). However, while many parents may respond supportively, as *H.L. v. Matheson* suggests, it seems equally plausible that others will respond negatively.

The teenager's fears may affect her behavior, regardless of her parents' actual response. The Court does not examine the effect of a parental notice requirement on the pregnant minor who does not want her parents to know of her pregnancy or planned abortion. While some girls may reluctantly tell their parents of their abortion, others may feel unable to do so. In 1979-1980, the Alan Guttmacher Institute conducted a national survey of 3000 teenagers to determine the effect of notice requirements on contraception and abortion practices. Of 1170 unmarried teenagers obtaining abortions through family planning clinics and hospitals, 55 percent reported that their parents knew about their proposed abortion (54 percent of girls in clinics *without* notice requirements had this response); 21 percent said that while their parents did not know about the abortion, a notice requirement would not have deterred them from seeking the operation. However, 23 percent of the sample reported that they would not have sought the operation if notification of parents had been required. Of these, 9 percent stated they would procure illegal or self-induced abortions, 9 percent would have had the baby, 2 percent said they would leave home, and 3 percent did not know what they would do. The authors concluded that a large percentage of girls would be in a desperate situation with a parental notice requirement (Torres, et al. 1980).

In its most recent decision, *City of Akron v. Akron Center for Reproductive Health*,[23] the Court has reaffirmed its support of reproductive privacy for the mature minor. This 1983 opinion struck down an Akron ordinance requiring parental consent before a minor under 15 could obtain an abortion. The Court emphasized the requirement, first announced in Belotti, that each minor must be allowed to demonstrate that she is mature enough to make an independent abortion decision. The Akron ordinance denied this opportunity to younger minors.

### State Law

Several states have responded to the Supreme Court abortion cases by passing laws modeled on those approved by the Court. Some states have adopted the *Bellotti* guidelines, allowing abortion on parental consent or upon a judicial determination that the minor has the maturity to make an independent decision or that the abortion is in her best interest.[24] Several other states have parental notice provisions similar to the Utah statute upheld in *Matheson*.[25] Notice requirements may become more common, since they have been declared constitutional by the Supreme Court[26] (Donovan, 1981).

Some states allow minors to obtain abortions without restrictions other than those that would be applicable to adults. Wyoming, for example, defines "woman" in its abortion statute as "any female person whether an adult or minor."[27] The Virginia statute provides that the woman's informed written consent for abortion must be obtained without reference to the age of the woman.[28] States providing general access to medical treatment to mature or emancipated minors may authorize these minors to obtain abortions independently.[29]

### Minors' Contraception Rights

#### Constitutional Developments

Only one Supreme Court opinion—*Carey v. Population Services International* [30]—has specifically addressed the issue of minors' right of access to contraceptives. In this 1977 opinion the Supreme Court struck down as unconstitutional a New York law that made illegal the distribution of all contraceptives to any minor under the age of sixteen. Since minors under the New York statute were denied access to contraceptives even where parents approved, *Carey* did not directly raise the controversial issue of the permissible involvement of parents in their children's decisions, which has been at the center of the constitutional struggle over abortion. In fact Justice Powell, in concurrence, found the New York statute unconstitutional partly because it denied parents the right to buy contraceptives for their children.

The Supreme Court rejected the state's argument that banning minors' access to contraceptives was a legitimate means of furthering the state's interest in discouraging sexual activity among teenagers. While the state may regulate minors' sexual behavior [31] (as well as that of unmarried adults), no evidence was presented that sexual activity would be reduced among teens if contraceptives were not available. In fact, there was substantial evidence that such a law would have no deterrent effect on sexual behavior.[32] The effect of the New York law was to "prescribe pregnancy . . . as the punishment for fornication."[33] As Justice Stevens pointed out in his concurring opinion, "it is as though the state decided to dramatize its disapproval of motorcycles by forbidding the use of safety helmets."[34]

It is unclear after *Carey* whether the Supreme Court would find any basis for distinguishing permissible restrictions on contraception from those found acceptable for abortion. Justice Brennan, in *Carey*, suggested that the state has even less basis for interfering with minors' privacy where the interest in fetal life and the mother's health are not at stake. However, it is unclear that the rest of the Court would share his view.

#### State Law

In most states minors have relatively free access to contraceptives. No state specifically requires parental consent or notice as a condition for minors' procuring contraceptives. A majority of states specifically affirm by statute, court decision, or attorney general's opinion, the right of persons under eighteen to consent to contraceptive services (Kenney, Forrest, & Torres, 1982). One form of access is the minors' consent statute, which generally authorizes minors to privately obtain contraceptive services as well as treatment for venereal disease and substance abuse. These are all treatments that minors may hesitate to seek if they must notify their parents, but that are deemed of critical importance to their welfare, and the welfare of society (Wadlington, 1983). Many states have passed these statutes in recent years.[35]

The mature-minor doctrine has been utilized in some states to make contraceptive services available to adolescents. This doctrine is premised on the view that older minors may be as capable as adults of making informed treatment decisions (Wadlington, 1973, 1983). As noted previously, the psychological research supports this premise (Weithorn, 1982; Weithorn and Campbell, 1982). Some states make contraceptive services available through general statutory provisions allowing competent minors to consent to medical treatment.[36] Unlike the minor consent statutes, which presume competency, mature-minor statutes may put a burden on the individual to demonstrate competency. Legally endorsed scrutiny of an adolescent's capacity to give consent may deter her from seeking contraception.

A few states authorize minors to obtain contraceptive treatment where they are referred by designated sources, such as schools, ministers, state agencies, or the family planning agencies, or where they have their parents' consent.[37] This does not impose much of a burden on access where there are family planning agencies, since presumably these agencies will provide ready referral.

The social policy goal of preventing teenage pregnancy has not influenced the law in all states. While no state forbids minors access to contraceptives outright (a position that would be clearly unconstitutional), several impose substantial barriers, which may discourage minors from seeking the services. Several states allow parental notice when a teen seeks contraception,[38] a requirement that may be constitutional after Matheson, except possibly as applied to mature teens. Others have requirements that, if applied strictly as written, would be of questionable constitutionality. These include laws that imply that only married, pregnant, or emancipated minors may obtain contraceptives.[39]

### Federal Family Planning Policy

The federal government has provided substantial funding for family planning services in recent years (Isaacs, 1980). State or private agencies receiving federal funds must follow federal law and regulations. Federal policy until recently has been to make services available to adolescents without requiring parental involvement (Alan Guttmacher Institute, 1982). Any agency receiving funds under Titles XIX and XX of the Social Security Act (Medicaid funds) must make family planning services available "without regard to age or marital status."[40] Title X of the Public Health Services Act, passed in 1970, was designed to implement a policy of making family planning services available "to all persons desiring such services."[41] Several efforts to require parental consent or notice as a condition for the receipt of these services have been defeated in Congress over the years (Alan Guttmacher Institute, 1982). In 1975 a federal district court in Utah held that the state administrative requirement of parent's consent before minors could obtain family planning services under Aid to Families with Dependent Children and Medicaid programs violated federal law. The court found the consent requirement to be a violation of the minor's right to confidentiality, which interfered with Congress's purpose of making family planning services generally available to sexually active minors.[42]

Very recently, federal policy toward contraceptive services for teenagers has undergone a change, reflecting largely the attitudes of the Reagan administration (Rosoff, 1982). In 1981, shortly after *Matheson* was decided, Title X was amended to require those receiving federal grants to "encourage family participation."[43] Implementation of this seemingly innocuous policy statement came in the form of a controversial regulation, which required that whenever unemancipated minors receive prescription drugs or devices from federally funded family planning programs, their parents must be notified, unless notice would result in physical harm to the child. Another provision requires that adolescents be charged for services based on their family's and not their own income.[44]

This regulation (the "squeal" rule), like other legal restrictions on minors' access to contraception and abortion, was justified as a means of promoting parental participation in decisions of critical importance to the teenager, of protecting the health of the teenager, and of discouraging sexual experimentation (Kenney, et al., 1982). There is little empirical basis for assuming that parental notice will have the effects desired by its supporters. A large percentage of adolescents already discuss their use of contraceptives with their parents and many family planning clinics encourage parental involvement by providing family counseling (Kenney et al., 1982). Of those girls who have not informed their parents, it is questionable whether a requirement of parental notice would promote the desired consultation (Torres, 1978; Torres et al., 1980). A recent study indicated that confidentiality (i.e., no parental notice) is the most important concern of many adolescents in choosing a family planning clinic (Zabin & Clark, 1983). Parental notice requirements would also seem to have little impact on teenagers' decision to become sexually active. There is evidence that many teenagers seek contraception a significant period of time after they first become sexually active (Settlage, Baroff, & Cooper, 1973). The proponents of mandatory parental involvement assume that adolescent response will be to consult with parents or, if parental involvement is intolerable, to forgo both contraception and sexual activity. The Alan Guttmacher Institute survey suggests a third possibility, which will be the choice of a sizable group: to engage in sex without contraception or to use less effective nonprescription contraceptives (Torres et al., 1980). Unless pregnancy is proposed as an acceptable punishment for premarital sexual activity—a notion rejected by the Supreme Court in *Carey*—this approach cannot be justified.

It is not surprising that there was substantial opposition to this regulation, which would affect hundreds of family planning clinics and an estimated 500,000 teenagers receiving prescription contraceptives (Kenney et al., 1982). More than 75 percent of the states expressed opposition to the proposed regulation, as did numerous groups, including the American Academy of Pediatrics and the American Bar Association (Kenney et al., 1982). Several groups, including Planned Parenthood Association, challenged the regulation in two federal circuit courts. In 1983 both courts struck down the squeal rule as inconsistent with the federal family planning law that it purported to implement.[45] The Reagan administration decided not to appeal these rulings.

### Sterilization of Retarded Minors

#### Constitutional Doctrine

The Supreme Court has never examined the question of whether the right of reproductive privacy includes the right to be sterilized. Several lower courts have found such a right for normal adults.[46] Very few states, however, permit normal minors to consent to sterilization (Isaacs, 1980). This limitation on reproductive choice is justified as a small infringement that preserves the minor's right to make a choice at a time when it is more likely to be maturely weighed (Melton & Scott, in press). Thus, sterilization of retarded minors has somewhat different constitutional dimensions from those involved in the normal minor's right to abortion or contraception. However, all of these issues implicate the right of reproductive privacy of individuals who may have a questionable capacity to exercise their right autonomously (Garvey, 1981). In the sterilization context the issue is whether parents or a court may decide to sterilize a retarded individual, thus permanently foreclosing her opportunity to make an independent decision in the future.

Historically, involuntary sterilization of the retarded was justified as a constitutional infringement on the individual's rights because it promoted the

legitimate state purpose of preventing the birth of defective individuals (Ferster, 1966). In 1927 the Supreme Court upheld Virginia's eugenic sterilization law against a challenge that it violated the equal protection rights of the
retarded and other "defectives."[47] Justice Holmes's notorious proclamation,
"Three generations of imbeciles is enough,"[48] reflects the Court's implicit
acceptance of the genetic theory underlying these statutes. As this theory
has been discredited scientifically, it no longer legitimately can serve as a
justification for involuntary sterilization laws (Burgdorf and Burgdorf,
1977).

The recent approach to sterilization initiatives of parents or guardians of
retarded individuals begins with the assumption that the retarded individual,
like everyone else, has a constitutionally protected interest in reproductive
privacy, which may be threatened by the sterilization petition (Ross, 1981).
This interest involves both the right to make independent private reproductive choices (including a choice for or against sterilization) and an interest in
having and caring for children. The trend toward normalization of the
retarded has created skepticism about the presumed incapacity of all retarded
individuals to make important decisions affecting their lives (Neuwirth,
Heisler, & Goldrich, 1974-1975), to marry (Perske, 1973), and to care for
children (Hertz, 1979; Shaman, 1978).[49] Only when the person is so disabled that she is incapable of making her own decision and of filling the role
of parent may nonconsensual sterilization be authorized. The right of the
competent retarded individual to make an independent choice is analogous
to the mature minor's right to make an abortion decision. The incompetent
individual's constitutional rights are further protected by requiring that sterilization be authorized only if it is in her best interest, rather than the interest
of society or the petitioners[50] (Burnett, 1981). An important consideration
here is the individual's constitutional interests in bodily privacy, i.e., in
avoiding nonconsensual bodily intrusions (Sherlock & Sherlock, 1982).

### State Law

Sterilization law is currently in a state of transition. Several states maintain laws authorizing compulsory sterilization of the retarded, which are
based on a eugenic rationale or which are justified by the burden placed on
the state by the care of children of retarded parents (Sales, 1982; Sherlock &
Sherlock, 1982). Despite the severe criticism of compulsory sterilization
statutes on both scientific and constitutional grounds, (Burgdorf and
Burgdorf, 1977; Haavik and Menninger, 1982) and a trend in recent years to
repeal these statutes, more than a dozen remain (Sales, 1982).

Much of the recent development in sterilization law has been through
judicial opinions[51] in several states. *In re Hayes*,[52] a 1980 Washington

Supreme Court case, was one of the first opinions to propose standards, and it has been a model for later case law and statutes adopting a *parens patriae* approach (Melton & Scott, in press). Under the Hayes approach, the threshold determination is the individual's capacity to make an independent decision (Burnett, 1981). Only where the individual is permanently incompetent (i.e., her incompetency is not due to immaturity or lack of information), to make an informed decision, may the judge examine whether sterilization is in her best interest. In making this determination most standards require the judge to consider a number of criteria—the individual's lack of capacity (present and potential) to care for a child, "unworkability" of less drastic means of contraception, the need for contraception (i.e., the probability of sexual activity), and her physical capacity for reproduction.[53] Some laws have required the judge to examine other factors, such as the "medical necessity of the sterilization,"[54] and the psychological impact of sterilization as well as childbirth.[55]

The purpose of the criteria is to assure that there is a real need for sterilization and that it does not represent an infringement on fundamental constitutional rights. While this general goal is desirable, it would seem that some criteria, such as medical necessity, would severely limit, in a way that is of questionable benefit, the availability of the sterilization for contraceptive purposes.

States vary in the weight given the criteria. Some state laws require very specific findings that each criterion has been proved before sterilization can be ordered.[56] Others allow judicial discretion, presenting the criteria for consideration, but directing that the decision be made in the interest of the retarded person.[57]

The new laws all provide procedural protections for the retarded person. A formal judicial proceeding is generally required and an attorney is appointed for the retarded person to present evidence and cross-examine witnesses (Melton & Scott, in press). Most laws require the judge to speak with the individual to attempt to discern her preferences; the individual's desires are not binding, however, unless she is competent.[58] A requirement of medical and psychological evaluation is required in many states.[59]

### Minors' Reproductive Rights: The Empirical Basis for "Liberal" Policies

Many states have chosen to allow minors to freely obtain abortions and contraceptives even though the Supreme Court has found certain restrictions to be constitutionally permissible. There are sound reasons for such a policy besides a concern for the minor's constitutional right of privacy. A large percentage of adolescents are sexually active (Zelnick and Kantner, 1980). Each year more than one million teenagers become pregnant in the United States. It has been estimated that more than two-thirds of these pregnancies are unplanned and unwanted (Zelnick and Kantner, 1978; Tietze, 1978). Approximately 40 percent result in abortion (Jaffe & Dryfoos, 1976). Where legal abortion services are not readily available, teenagers may turn to illegal abortion, which is associated with higher morbidity (Kahan, Baker, & Freeman, 1975). These statistics reflect a social problem of significant proportions not only for the teenage parents, but also for their children and for society.

Several studies have indicated convincingly that teenagers who become parents are detrimentally affected in many ways. Compared to women who give birth in their twenties, teenagers suffer greater medical problems and a higher mortality rate. This is often attributed to the fact that teens are less likely to have adequate prenatal care (Zackler, 1969).

Adolescent parents, both mothers and fathers, generally have a lower level of educational achievement than their peers (Trussell, 1976; Furstenburg, 1976a; Card and Wise, 1978). Only 18 percent of young women who bear children when they are under 18 complete high school, compared to 55 percent of those who postpone childbirth until after 18 (Trussell, 1976). Although pregnant students and teenage mothers can no longer be excluded from public school classes as they once were, many are unable to handle the substantial difficulties of caring for a child and going to school (Card and Wise, 1978).

Not surprisingly, teenage parents have fewer employment opportunities compared to their peers. Card and Wise (1978) studied adolescent parents through age 29 and found that both parents, but particularly mothers, were overrepresented in lower-paying unskilled jobs and underrepresented in the professions. Some of the discrepancy between teenage parents and their peers is correlated with prepregnancy socioeconomic status, academic aptitude, and educational expectations. However, even when compared to peers with similar aptitudes and expectations, those who become parents as teens had fewer years of education and subsequently lower-paying and lower-prestige jobs.

The personal lives of teenage parents is also disrupted. While only 3 percent of adolescents who become pregnant are married at conception, almost one-half eventually marry the father of the child (Furstenburg, 1976a). It is not surprising that a high proportion of these marriages end in divorce. One study found that 60 percent of teenage marriages involving a premarital pregnancy ended within six years (Furstenburg, 1976b).

The adverse effects of adolescent parenthood are not limited to the teenage parents. Their children may alsò suffer consequences of being born to very young parents, who often lack marital and economic stability. Children of teenage mothers have more health problems in infancy and exhibit cognitive deficits compared to other children (Baldwin and Cain, 1980; Furstenburg, 1976a). Some observers believe these deficits result from the deprived educational and economic situation of their parent (Baldwin and Cain, 1980). Finally, the economic cost to society of teenage pregnancy is great. Teenage mothers are significantly more likely to require public assistance than older mothers (Trussell, 1976).

The enormous social cost of teenage pregnancy and parenthood is, in itself, the basis of legal policy in many states facilitating minors' access to contraception and abortion. The Alan Guttmacher Institute surveys described earlier give substantial support to the concerns about the negative effects of restrictive laws. Notice and consent requirements may influence many teenagers to forego contraceptives, use less effective nonprescription contraceptives, have illegal or self-induced abortions, or to have unwanted children (Torres, 1978; Torres et al., 1980). Thus, there is widespread support for liberal laws among professional groups and others who have little concern for expanding the "rights" of adolescents to make autonomous decisions, but rather are concerned to protect teens from the high cost of predictable sexual experimentation (Alan Guttmacher Institute, 1981). Zimring (1982) observed aptly that where the issue is whether or not a sexually active teenager should use contraceptives, "there is only one preferred public choice."

## Mental Health Professionals and
## Adolescent Reproductive Rights

The recent legal developments concerning adolescent reproductive rights are important to mental health professionals in two ways. Where minors seek contraception or abortion or where parents seek sterilization of their child, clinicians may be asked to assume evaluative roles, assessing the minor's capacities or best interest for the judge or physician. Mental health professionals may also serve as counselors and therapists to adolescents making decisions about contraception and abortion. Difficult issues of professional role may arise for the clinician attempting to assist a client struggling with these decisions. The legal dimensions of these issues may make the mental health professional uncertain about her role.

## The Clinician as Evaluator

### Evaluations of Minors in Abortion
### and Contraception Cases

The issue on which mental health expertise will be most frequently sought where minors seek abortion and, less frequently, contraception is the girl's *competency* to give informed consent to treatment. This requirement will exist either implicitly or explicitly wherever a minor makes an independent medical decision. Consent to any medical procedure must be competent, voluntary, and knowledgeable (based on adequate information) for the decision to constitute legal authorization (Weithorn, 1982). Depending on state law, the doctor may informally decide that the minor has adequate understanding (as would be typical for adult patients), while in other states she may have to affirmatively prove competency in a judicial proceeding. In the latter situation, clinical input may be sought. States following *Bellotti* authorize an independent abortion decision by the minor where she can demonstrate that she is "mature and well enough informed" to make an intelligent decision.[60] As described earlier, most commentators advocate that competency to make the specific medical decision rather than general competency or maturity be the focus where a question is raised about an individual's competency to give informed consent (Meisel, 1979; Weithorn, 1982). However, at least one state requires that the court making the abortion decision receive evidence on the minor's "emotional development, maturity, intellect and understanding."[61]

Several standards have been proposed (and used) for competency to give informed consent to medical procedures, ranging from a standard finding competency where the individual evidences any choice regarding the treatment, to a standard requiring a "reasonable outcome of choice," to one that involves scrutiny of the reasoning process (Weithorn, 1982; Roth, Meisel, and Lidz, 1977; Meisel, 1979). The standard of competency that is most appropriate in the present context would find the minor competent who is capable of appreciating the basic "elements of disclosure" (Meisel, 1979) of the treatment decision, including the nature and purpose of the treatment, potential consequences, alternatives available to the patient, and risks and benefits. Competency under this standard would involve recall and factual understanding as well as some ability to think inferentially and apply the disclosed information to one's own situation (Weithorn, 1982; Applebaum and Roth, 1981). Under these standards, a minor who understands the relevant elements of the decision would not be rendered incompetent by basing her decision on a variable that most would not weigh heavily. For example, the decision to abort because of a horror of fatness may be distasteful but is not necessarily incompetent.

A minor's competency should not be judged by a standard that would not be required of an adult. A sophisticated understanding of the medical procedure is not required, nor is a comprehension of every conceivable risk or possible alternative. Where the individual's capacity to give informed consent is the subject of scrutiny, one may unknowingly apply a stricter standard for comprehension than would actually be required in most medical settings.

The clinician assessing competency should ascertain what information the adolescent has been given and not judge the minor incompetent who is merely uninformed. Although capacity is at issue and not factual understanding, competency to make an informed decision can be assessed with greater accuracy if the individual has been given the relevant information about the medical procedure (Appelbaum & Roth, 1981).

Where the minor seeks abortion, a number of inquiries are relevant. The minor must understand the purpose and result of the procedure. She must know that it will end the pregnancy. She should have some rudimentary understanding of the medical procedure itself—that an anesthetic will be administered, and so on. She should be aware of any significant complications that may arise, such as infection and hemorrhaging, and their probability, as well as significant normal postoperative symptoms. She should understand significant implications of not having the abortion.

Medical consent must also be voluntary to be valid (Weithorn, 1982). Thus, a minor's serious ambivalence about the decision (Friedman, 1973) or the observation that she is subject to pressure should be explored by the clinician.

The inquiry regarding competence is similar when the minor obtains contraceptives. She should indicate an understanding of the purpose of the pill or device and of its effect of preventing pregnancy. Where the minor is seeking to obtain oral contraceptives, she should understand requirements of use and possible effects of not using as prescribed. She should understand any significant risks associated with the form of birth control chosen. Finally, she should have some very basic understanding of alternative forms of contraception.

In states that allow the immature minor to obtain an abortion if she shows that it is in her *best interest,* mental health opinion may be sought on this issue. Clinical opinion on the potential psychological effect of abortion or of continued pregnancy on the girl may be of some use to the judge in determining whether to authorize the abortion. A number of variables may be significant: the intensity of the girl's desire for the abortion; ambivalence concerning the decision; her capacity for coping with pregnancy and childbirth; the effect of continued pregnancy on her future plans and expectations; the impact of parental knowledge about the pregnancy and the potential psychological impact of the abortion.

Clinical opinion on this issue is very problematic. As Zimring (1982) observed, the decision of whether abortion is in a minor's best interest is a determination made more appropriately by a theologian than by a judge (or, one might add, by a mental health professional). Where professional input is sought, the clinician will do well to adopt a restrained stance on this value-laden issue, withholding opinion on the "ultimate issue" of whether the abortion is in the minor's best interest—and simply giving clinical observations about positive and negative effects of one course or the other, given the girl's preferences, emotional maturity, and psychological, social, and familial functioning.

### Sterilization Evaluation

Given the recent legal trend, mental health professionals may have a central role in the legal determination of whether mentally retarded minors may be sterilized. The standards that have been recently adopted typically call for the court to make rulings concerning the retarded individual's capacity—present and potential—to make an independent decision about sterilization, her ability to care for a child, the suitability of less restrictive forms of contraception, and in some cases her ability to master the task of menstrual hygiene. Some of the criteria for making the sterilization decision are simply factual or medical determinations, not within the scope of mental health expertise. These include whether the individual is sexually active and whether she is capable of reproduction. However, the critical assessments of competency should involve mental health professionals with an expertise in mental retardation.

Evaluation of adolescents whose parents seek sterilization is complicated by the need to determine the individual's future as well as present competency. If the adolescent lacks competency to make an autonomous decision or to act as a parent because of immaturity, and is potentially competent, sterilization without her consent should not be authorized, as her opportunity for making an independent decision would be forever foreclosed. Thus, the clinician must attempt to discern whether the person's intellectual limitations render her permanently incompetent. This type of assessment is necessarily somewhat speculative. Caution should be exercised in finding incompetency in minors; in marginal cases, the possibility of future competency should be emphasized (Melton & Scott, in press).

The determination of the individual's competency to make the sterilization decision should be based on her ability to comprehend the purpose, nature, and consequences of the procedure, as well as risks and alternatives. Given the threat to autonomy that nonconsensual sterilization represents, only a basic level of understanding should be required. The clinical inquiry should focus on the individual's understanding of the procedure (an operation with anesthetic), its contraceptive purpose and irreversible nature, significant risks and the availability of alternative forms of contraception (Melton & Scott, in press). As in the abortion situation, the clinician must ascertain that the individual has received all appropriate medical information and that incapacity is not merely ignorance.

The retarded individual's competency to care for a child is another focus of the clinical assessment. Melton and Scott (in press) have argued that the level of incompetency that should be required to support nonconsensual sterilization is that which would result in such inadequate care that the state would be justified in removing the child from the care of the individual and terminating parental rights. Only by adopting such a relatively low standard is discrimination against the mentally retarded avoided. Thus, the clinical assessment should focus on the individual's ability to meet a child's basic needs. Is she capable of providing adequate care—of clothing and bathing a child, protecting her from harm and seeking medical assistance when it is needed? The capacity of the parent to provide cognitive stimulation and emotional support—while important to healthy child development—are probably beyond the scope of inquiry about minimal competency. The retarded individual cannot be required to function at higher levels than would be generally required of parents. Parents who are providing basic care and are not psychologically abusive should not lose their children because of limitations in psychological or cognitive stimulation. The clinician may need to guard against a bias against retarded individuals as parents—a bias that is commonly shared by clinicians and judges (Hertz, 1979; Shaman, 1978).

The assessment of minimal parental competency is complicated by its predictive and speculative nature. The primary means of assessment may be through verbal problem solving and examination of the individual's self-care skills. These are at best an inexact measure of the individual's actual child-care competency (Melton & Scott, in press).

Whether the retarded individual can use alternative forms of contraception is dependent on both her ability to participate in the requirements of use and to discern problems that require attention. There has been no research on the trainability of mentally retarded individuals in the use of contraceptives (Melton & Scott, in press). The ability to use oral contraceptives would seem to require a higher functional level than an intrauterine device (IUD), as the individual must be capable of following a regime requiring significant motivation or supervision (LaVeck & de la Cruz, 1973). It would be helpful if the IUD user could discuss and report expulsion of the device, which occurs in about 10 percent of the cases. However, this risk alone may not justify sterilization. The individual should also be capable of tolerating the insertion of the IUD without resistance, to avoid perforation of the uterus (Melton & Scott, in press). Otherwise, a general anesthetic may be required.

Whether alternatives to sterilization are in fact "less drastic" may depend in some cases on medical risks—the risk of long-term use of oral contraceptives, and the risk of general anesthetic if this is required to insert an IUD. Where the individual is incompetent to make her own decision and to care for a child, these medical considerations may be relevant in weighing alternatives.

Since sterilization of moderately and severely retarded individuals is sometimes sought not only for contraceptive purposes, but because the girl has been unable to learn to handle her menstrual hygiene needs, the individual's capacity in this regard is sometimes the focus of clinical inquiry. Existing research indicates that, through a combination of positive reinforcement and aversive conditioning, most moderately retarded women can learn to manage menstrual hygiene needs and severely retarded women can be trained in all steps except initiation (Hamilton, Allen, Stephans, & Davall, 1969).

Where sterilization of minors is sought, the role of the mental health professional may well be one of consultation to parents and the court. Often the pressing concerns that drive parents to seek sterilization may be dealt with through alternative means. Mental health professionals may assist in providing information to parents about menstrual hygiene training, availability of alternative forms of contraception, and sex education for retarded adolescents. They may also help parents to accept their child's emerging sexuality (Melton and Scott, in press).

## Issue of Professional Role

Mental health professionals in schools, outpatient mental health clinics, health care facilities, and family planning clinics face issues involving their professional role dealing with teenagers making decisions about contraception and abortion. Often the therapist may be the only adult adviser consulted by the teenager. In providing assistance with problems that may have complex legal as well as psychological dimensions, it is important that the mental health professional have some understanding of the legal issues at stake and sensitivity to the problems of professional ethics that may be raised.

The options available to adolescents considering contraception or abortion may, depending on state law, be accessible and well defined, or they may be unclear, or burdensome. In some states school personnel and therapists are among the authorized referring parties for contraception. Counselors may better assist their teenage clients if they are familiar with their state's law and are able to explain the options. While mental health professionals should not give legal advice, they may provide valuable assistance just by having needed information. In states where minors must approach a court if they do not want to inform their parents of their desire for an abortion, the clinician may want to be familiar with the procedures and have the information to direct the client to legal counsel.

State laws regarding confidentiality of mental health and medical records are also important in this context. Parents often have a right of access to their minor children's records, even in some states where the minor has the right to independently seek mental health, contraception, or abortion treatment.[62] It may be useful for mental health professionals counseling minors who are making contraception and abortion decisions to be aware of state law regarding confidentiality and be able to advise their clients about limitations that may exist. Where parental notice is required, the clinician may inform the teenager of this requirement and assist her in exploring its likely implications.

There are issues of professional ethics inherent in this therapy context. The therapist who opposes abortion may feel obligated to make her views known to her teenage client considering this option, and to offer to refer her to another therapist. A similar course may be followed by the clinician who views abortion as the only viable course for the pregnant adolescent. Clinicians may also have strong views on the desirability of parental consultation. There are probably few other issues that create such a substantial risk that the clinician's subjective values may merge with her professional role.

Issues of shifting professional role may arise where the treating therapist is asked to assume an evaluation role and render an expert opinion on the client's capacity to give informed consent to treatment or on her best interest. Many clinicians believe that mixing roles in this way is detrimental to the therapeautic relationship. Although the treating clinician may be in a good position to assess the adolescent's competency, the prior relationship with the client may also contribute a bias to the clinical opinion that would be absent with a neutral evaluator. Further, the mental health professional called as an expert may be questioned about issues that were discussed as part of a confidential therapeutic relationship. Most clinicians will wish to discuss with the client any decision to provide expert opinion on issues related to abortion or contraception, and to explore the implications and risks.

## Notes

1. Planned Parenthood of Central Missouri v. Danforth, 428 U.S. 52 (1976).

2. H.L. v. Matheson, 450 U.S. 398 (1981).

3. Bellotti v. Baird (II), 443 U.S. 622 (1979).

4. See Calif. Welf. & Instit. Code Sect. 14503 (1980).

5. Title X Public Health Service Act (42 U.S.C. Sect. 300 et seq., 1970); Titles XIX and XX Social Security Act. (42 U.S.C. 1396 et seq., 42 U.S.C. 1901). In 1982 a federal regulation was proposed that would require parental notice when minors obtain contraceptives.

6. See Mass. Gen. Laws Ann. Ch. 112, Sect. 125 (1981 Cum. Supp.).

7. See In re Hayes, 93 Wash. 2d 228, 608 P2d 635 (1980).

8. The feminine pronoun will be used throughout this chapter in referring to the minor involved in reproductive decisions, and for simplicity, to clinicians.

9. Griswold v. Connecticut, 381 U.S. 479 (1965).

10. 405 U.S. 438 (1972).

11. 410 U.S. 113 (1973).

12. 428 U.S. 52 (1976).

13. Id. at 74.

14. Id. at 75.

15. 387 U.S. 1 (1967).

16. 428 U.S. at 75.

17. Id. at 75.

18. 443 U.S. 622 (1979).

19. Id. at 647.

20. H.L. v. Matheson, 450 U.S. 398 (1981).

21. Id. at 411.

22. Id. at 412-413.

23. 51 U.S.L.W. 4767 (6/14/83).

24. Minn. Stat. Sect. 525.56 (Cum. Supp. 1982).

25. Md. Ann, Code Art. 43 Sect. 135(1) (1980).

26. Before Matheson, several lower courts had found notice statutes to be unconstitutional. See Woman's Community Health Center, Inc. v. Cohen, 477 F. Supp. 542 (D. Me 1979).

27. Wy. Stat. Sect. 35-6-101(a) (viii) (1977).

28. Va. Code Ann. Sect. 18.2-72 (1979).

29. Miss. Code Ann. Sect. 41-41-3 (1973).

30. 431. U.S. 678 (1977).

31. However ill-defined minors' constitutional reproductive rights may be, they do not include a right to engage in sexual activity. Thus, many commentators have observed that minor's reproductive rights are better described as the right *not* to reproduce (Hafen, 1983).

32. The Court cited several studies, including Settlage, Baroff, and Cooper (1973). 431 U.S. at 695-696.

33. Quoting Eisenstadt v. Baird, 405 U.S. at 448 (431 U.S. at 695).

34. 431 U.S. at 715 (Stevens, J., concurring opinion).

35. See Ky. Rev. Stat. Ann. Sect. 214.185 (1977).

36. See Nev. Rev. Stat. Sect. 129.030 (1979).

37. Tenn. Code Ann. Sect. 68-34-107 (1971).

38. Ore. Rev. Stat. Sect. 109.640 (1979).

39. Mass. Gen. Laws, Ch. 112 Sect. 12F (Supp. 1982).

40. 45 C.F.R., Sect. 1392.21 (1980).

41. P.L. 91-572, Sec. 2(1) (1970).

42. T.H. v. Jones, 425 F. Supp. 873 (D. Utah, 1975).

43. P.L. 97-35, Sec. 931(b)(1).

44. Fed. Register, Vol. 47, No. 35, February 22, 1982.

45. Planned Parenthood Federation of America, Inc. v. Schweiker, 712 F2d 650 (DC Cir. 1983); New York v. Heckler, 10 FLR 1024 (2d Cir. 1983).

46. Hathaway v. Worcester City Hospital, 475 F.2d. 701 (1973).

47. Buck v. Bell, 274 U.S. 200 (1977).

48. Idem at 207.

49. "Normalization" is based on an increasingly accepted view that, to the extent possible, retarded individuals should be encouraged to develop skills and to live like other people. Deinstitutionalization and mainstreaming in education exemplify this trend (Nirje, 1969).

50. The early sterilization laws were grounded in the state's *police power* authority to protect society. Authority for the recent laws is based on the parens patriae power of the state to take care of those members of society who are unable to care for themselves, such as children and incompetents.

51. Courts in New York, Washington, New Jersey, Alaska, Colorado, Maryland, Massachusetts, New Hampshire, and South Carolina have found judicial authority to order sterilization in the interest of the retarded person. Parens patriae statutes have been passed in several states, including Maine, Vermont, Virginia, and Connecticut (Scott & Melton, Note 1).

52. See Note 7, supra.

53. These criteria are included in the standards proposed by Hayes and have been adopted by most later cases and statutes.

54. Matter of A.W., _____ Colo. _____ 637 P2d. 366 (1981).

55. See Note 7, supra.

56. Va. Code Ann. Sect. 54.1-325.12 (1981).

57. In re Penny N, 120 N.H. 269, 414 A2d. 541 (1980).

58. See In re Grady 85 N.J. 235, 426 A2d. 467 (1981).

59. See Note 53, supra.

60. See Note 18, supra.

61. Mo. Rev. Stat. Sect. 188.02862(3) (Supp. 1982). The Supreme Court, in Planned Parenthood Ann. of Kansas City v. Ashcroft, decided with City of Akron (see Note 23), did not question this provision. See U.S.L.W. 4783 (6/14/83).

62. Va. Code Ann. Sect. 2.1-342(b) (3) (1968).

## References

Alan Guttmacher Institute. Family planning and teens: Perspective. *Public Policy Issues in Brief*, 1981, *1*(4), 1-4.

Alan Guttmacher Institute. Family planning teenagers and government. *Public Policy Issues in Brief*,1982, *2*(2), 1-5.

Appelbaum, P., & Roth L. Clinical issues in the assessment of competency. *American Journal of Psychiatry*, 1981, *138*(11), 1462-1467.

Baldwin, W., & Cain, V. The children of teenage parents. *Family Planning Perspectives*, 1980, *12*(1), 34-43.

Bracken, M., Hachamovitch, M., & Grossman, G. The decision to abort and psychological sequelae. *Journal of Nervous and Mental Disease*, 1974, *158*, 154-162.

Bracken, M., & Kasl, S. Delay in seeking induced abortion: A review and theoretical analysis. *American Journal of Obstetrics and Gynecology*, 1975, *121*(7), 1008-1019.

Burgdorf, R., & Burgdorf, M. The wicked witch is almost dead. *Buck v. Bell* and the sterilization of handicapped persons. *Temple Law Quarterly*, 1977, *50*, 995-1034.

Burnett, B.A. Voluntary sterilization for persons with mental disabilities: The need for legislation. *Syracuse Law Review*, 1981, *32*, 913-955.

Card, J., & Wise, L. Teenage mothers and teenage fathers: the impact of early childbearing on the parents' personal and professional lives. *Family Planning Perspectives*, 1978, *10*(4), 199-205.

Cates, W., Jr. Abortion for teenagers. In J.E. Hodgson (Ed.), *Abortion and sterilization: Medical and social aspects*. London: Academic Press, 1981.

David, K., Rasmussen, N., & Holst, E. Postpartum and postabortion psychotic reactions. *Family Planning Perspectives*, 1981, *13*(2), 88-92.

Dembitz, N. The supreme court and a minor's abortion decision. *Columbia Law Review*, 1980, *80*, 1251-1263.

Donovan, P. Parental notification: is it settled? *Family Planning Perspectives*, 1981, *13*.

Ferster, E. Eliminating the unfit—is sterilization the answer? *Ohio State Law Journal*, 1966, *27*, 591-633.

Friedman, C. Making abortion counseling therapeutic. *American Journal of Psychiatry*, 1973, *130*, 1257-1261.

Furstenburg, F., Jr. The social consequences of teenage parenthood. *Family Planning Perspectives*, 1976, *8*(4), 148-164.(a)

Furstenburg, F., Jr. *Unplanned parenthood: The social consequences of teenage childbearing*. New York: MacMillan, 1976.(b)

Garvey, J. Child, parent, state and the due process clause: An essay on the Supreme Court's recent work. *Southern California Law Review*, 1978, *51*, 769-822.

Garvey, J. Freedom and choice in constitutional law. *Harvard Law Review*, 1981, *94*, 1756-1794.

Haavik, S., and Menninger, Ken II. *Sexuality, law, and the Developmentally disabled person.* Baltimore: Paul Brookes, 1981.

Hafen, B. The constitutional status of marriage, kinship and sexual privacy—balancing the individual and social interests. *Michigan Law Review,* 1983, *81*(3), 463-574.

Hamilton, J., Allen, P., Stephens, L., & Davall, E. Training mentally retarded females to use sanitary napkins. *Mental Retardation,* 1969, *7*(1), 40-43.

Hertz, R. Retarded parents in neglect proceedings: The erroneous assumption of parental inadequacy. *Stanford Law Review,* 1979, *31*, 785-805.

Isaacs, S. The law of fertility regulation in the United States: a 1980 review. *Journal of Family Law,* 1980, *19*, 65-96.

Jaffe, F., & Dryfoos, J. Fertility control services for adolescents: Access and utilization. *Family Planning Perspectives,* 1976, *8*(4), 167-175.

Kahan, R., Baker, L., & Freeman, M. The effects of legalized abortion on morbidity resulting from criminal abortion. *American Journal of Obstetrical Gynecology,* 1975, *121*(1), 114-116.

Keiter, R. Privacy, children and their parents. On and beyond the Supreme Court's approach. *Minnesota Law Review,* 1982, *66*, 459-518.

Kenney, A., Forrest, J., & Torres, A. Storm over Washington: the parental notification proposal. *Family Planning Perspectives* 1982, *14*(4), 185-197.

LaVeck, G.C. and de la Cruz, F.F. Contraception for the mentally retarded: Current methods and future promise. In G.C. LaVeck and F.F. de la Cruz (Eds.), *Human sexuality and the mentally retarded.* New York: Brunner/Mazel, 1973.

Lewis, C. A comparison of minors' and adults' pregnancy decisions. *American Journal of Orthopsychiatry,* 1980, *50*, 446-453.

Meisel, A. The "exceptions" to the informed consent doctrine: Striking a balance between competing values in medical decision-making. *Wisconsin Law Review,* 1979, 413-488.

Melton, G. Minors and privacy: Are legal and psychological concepts compatible? *Nebraska Law Review,* 1983, *62*, 455-493.

Melton, G., & Scott, E. Evaluation of mentally retarded persons for sterilization: contributions and limits of psychological consultation. *Professional Psychology,* in press.

Murdock, C. Sterilization of the retarded: A problem or a solution? *California Law Review,* 1974, *62*, 917-935.

Neuwirth, G., Heisler, P., & Goldrich, K. Capacity, competence, consent: Voluntary sterilization of the mentally retarded. *Columbia Human Rights Law Review,* 1974-1975, *6*, 447-472.

Nirje, R. The normalization principle and its human management implications. In R. Kugel & W. Wolfenberger (Eds.), *Changing patterns in residential services for the mentally retarded,* 1969.

Osofsky, J., Osofsky, H., Rajan, R., & Fox, M. Psychologic effects of legal abortion. *Clinical Obstetrics and Gynecology,* 1971, *14*, 215-234.

Perske, R. About sexual development: An attempt to be human with the mentally retarded. *Mental Retardation,* February 1973, 6-10.

Rooks, J., & Cates, W., Jr. Emotional impact of D&E vs. instillation. *Family Planning Perspectives,* 1977, *9*(b), 276-277.

Rosoff, J. Why now? *Family Planning Perspectives, 1982, 14*(4), 180.

Ross, D. "Sterilization of the developmentally disabled: shedding some myth conceptions." *Florida State Law Review,* 1981, *9*, 599-643.

Roth, L., Meisel, A., & Lidz, C. Tests of competency to consent to treatment. *American Journal of Psychiatry,* 1977, *134*, 279-284.

Sales, B., Powell, D., & Van Duizand, R. *Disabled persons and the law.* New York: Plenum, 1982.

Settlage, D., Baroff, S., & Cooper, D. Sexual experience of younger girls seeking contraceptive assistance for the first time. *Family Planning Perspectives*, 1973, *5*(4), 223-226.

Shaman, J. Persons who are mentally retarded: Their right to marry and have children. *Family Law Quarterly*, 1978, *12*, 61-84.

Sherlock, R.K., & Sherlock, R.D. Sterilizing the retarded: constitutional, statutory and policy alternatives. *North Carolina Law Review*, 1982, *60*, 943-983.

Tietze, C. Teenage pregnancies: Looking ahead to 1984. *Family Planning Perspectives*, 1978, *10*(4), 205-207.

Torres, A. Does your mother know? *Family Planning Perspectives*, September 1978, *10*, 280-282.

Torres, A., Forrest, J., & Eisman, S. Telling parents: Clinic policies and adolescents' use of family planning and abortion services. *Family Planning Perspectives*, 1980, *12*(6), 284-292.

Tribe, L. *American constitutional law*. Mineola, NY: Foundation Press, 1978.

Trussell, T. Economic consequences of teenage childbearing. *Family Planning Perspectives*, 1976, *8*(4), 184-190.

Wadlington, W. Minors and health care: The age of consent. *Osgoode Hall Law Journal*, 1973, *11*, 115-125.

Wadlington, W. Consent to medical care for minors. In G. Melton, G. Koocher, & M. Saks (Eds.), *Children's competence to consent*. New York: Plenum, 1983.

Weithorn, L. Developmental factors and competence to make informed treatment decisions. In G. Melton (Ed.), *Legal reforms affecting child and youth services*. New York: Haworth Press, 1982.

Weithorn, L., & Campbell, S. The competency of children and adolescents to make informed treatment decisions. *Child Development*, 1982, *53*, 1589-1598.

Zabin, L., & Clark, S., Jr. Institutional factors affecting teenagers' choice and reasons for delay in attending a family planning clinic. *Family Planning Perspectives*, 1983, *15*(1), 25-29.

Zackler, J., Andelman, S., & Bauer, F. The young adolescent as an obstetric risk. *American Journal of Obstetrics and Gynecology*, February 1969, *103*, 305-312.

Zelnick, M., & Kanter, J. Contraceptive patterns and premarital pregnancy among women aged fifteen through nineteen in 1976. *Family Planning Perspectives*, 1978, *10*(3), 135-142.

Zelnick, M., & Kanter, J. Sexual activity, contraceptive use and pregnancy among metropolitan area teenagers, 1971-1979. *Family Planning Perspectives*, 1980, *12*(5), 231-237.

Zimring, F. *The changing legal world of adolescence*. New York: Free Press, 1982.

# 7

# Family and Mental Hospital as Myths

## Civil Commitment of Minors

### Gary B. Melton
*University of Nebraska—Lincoln*

In 1979, in *Parham v. J. R.*, the Supreme Court ruled that parents may "voluntarily" commit their children to mental hospitals without a formal due-process hearing.[1] The Court unanimously held that all that was constitutionally required prior to admission was an informal review of the child's need for treatment by a physician[2] acting as "neutral factfinder." To avoid hospitalization for longer than necessary, the Court did find some form of postadmission review to be constitutionally required. The Court declined to specify the nature of the requisite postadmission review, but did suggest (with Justices Brennan, Marshall, and Stevens dissenting) that a formal adversary hearing was unnecessary. Indeed, Chief Justice Burger, writing for the majority, disparaged such formal procedures as "time-consuming procedural minuets" (p. 605) which take professional staff away from their care-giving activities and frustrate parents in their efforts to maintain family integrity and to fulfill their duty of providing needed treatment for their children.

*Parham* represented a remarkable shift from trends toward judicial recognition of independent civil rights of children and provision of both substantive and procedural due process protections for persons threatened with the "massive curtailment of liberty"[3] that psychiatric hospitalization brings. While not without qualification (see generally Melton, 1983b), the Supreme Court had within the previous twelve years held that minors had constitutionally protected rights to due process in delinquency proceedings,[4] freedom of political expression in public schools,[5] and privacy in abortion[6] and contraception[7] decisions. The abortion cases appeared to provide considerable impetus toward recognition of due process rights for minors independent of their parents, because they rested explicitly on an assumption of inherent conflict between parents and child in abortion decisions.[8] Surely there was no less potential for conflict in parents' decisions to "put away" their minor child. Arguably the child's alleged need for hospitalization ipso facto signaled a fractionation of the family and a breakdown in the unity of interests between parents and child, a unity that may not exist to the extent assumed by the Court, even for "normal" families (Melton, 1982). To hold otherwise would clearly require a conceptualization of the balance of power among parents, child, and state decidedly different from the Supreme Court's analysis in the preceding abortion cases (Annas, 1979).

The preceding decade also had brought dramatic changes in the rights accorded persons facing civil commitment. Following both a landmark federal district court case in Wisconsin,[9] which specified constitutional protections due respondents in civil commitment proceedings and statutory enactment of detailed procedures and standards for civil commitment in California,[10] there had been a virtual revolution in state mental health statutes to provide due process in commitment proceedings—albeit a "moderate" revolution in which civil commitment was "legalized" but not abolished ("Developments in the Law," 1974; Morse, 1982). While these statutory revisions seldom resulted in the adversary proceedings the reformers intended (see, e.g., Hiday, 1977, 1981; Luckey & Berman, 1979; Poythress, 1978; Stier & Stoebe, 1979), there can be little doubt that there was widespread recognition by courts and legislatures that involuntary mental hospitalization is often not a benign exercise of state power. The Supreme Court itself had just four years earlier noted the fallibility of psychiatric diagnosis and the profound harm that may result from unnecessary hospitalization.[11] In the face of such precedent, to rely on medical or psychological decision makers without judicial review for civil commitment of minors would require a denial of the risks of unnecessary and erroneous curtailment of liberty, unless diagnosis could be shown to be substantially more reliable and valid for minors than for adults, or the stigma and deprivation of liberty could be shown to be substantially less harmful.

Given the clarity of the trends with respect to the rights of both children and mental patients, it is hardly surprising that several states, in apparent anticipation of a child-libertarian decision in *Parham*, adopted procedures for judicial review of "voluntary" admissions of minors to psychiatric facilities in the four years that elapsed between the time when the Supreme Court first heard the issue and its decision in *Parham*.[12] In fact, about half of the states provide greater procedural due process than *Parham* ultimately required (Knitzer, Note 1; Perlin, 1981). Significantly, there has been no movement to repeal these statutes despite the Chief Justice's dire predictions of the effects of adversary hearings on family life and the progress of treatment, predictions echoed by the American Psychiatric Association (Note 2).

**TABLE 7.1** Psychological Assumptions in *Parham*

(1) There is no evidence of the use of mental hospitals as a "dumping ground." (pp. 597-598)

(2) "The state through its voluntary commitment procedures does not 'label' the child." Rather, stigma results primarily from the "symptomatology of a mental or emotional illness." (pp. 601-602)

(3) "The las's concept of the family rests on a presumption that parents possess what a child lacks in maturity, experience, and capacity for judgment required for making life's difficult decisions. Most important, historically it has recognized that natural bonds of affection lead parents to act in the best interests of their children." (p. 602)

(4) "Most children, even in adolescence, simply are not able to make sound judgments concerning many decisions, including their need for medical care or treatment." (p. 603)

(5) The state restricts use of "its costly mental health facilities" to persons in "genuine need." (pp. 604-605)

(6) Adversary proceedings will deter parents from seeking needed treatment for their children. (p. 605)

(7) "Time-consuming minuets" (i.e., due process hearings) take mental health professionals away from patient care. (pp. 605-606)

(8) Provision of a "neutral factfinder" adequately protects against erroneous admissions. (pp. 606-607)

(9) "Here the questions are essentially medical in character." The opinions of mental health professionals are necessary to determine "the *meaning* of the facts" in a determination of whether an individual meets legal requirements for admission. (p. 609)

(10) Judicial review does not heighten the reliability and validity of psychiatric diagnosis. "Common human experience and scholarly opinions suggest that the supposed protections of an adversary proceeding to determine the appropriateness of medical decisions for the commitment and treatment of mental and emotional illness may well be more illusory than real." (p. 609)

(11) Adversary proceedings will exacerbate preexisting familial conflicts. (p. 610)

(12) "It is unrealistic to believe that trained psychiatrists, skilled in eliciting responses, sorting medically relevant facts and sensitive to motivational nuances will often be deceived about the family situation surrounding a child's emotional disturbance." (pp. 611-612)

(13) The state's mental health professionals are competent, conscientious, and dedicated. (pp. 615-616)

(14) There is no evidence that the state acts differently from parents in committing its wards. (p. 618)

*Parham* marked then a pronounced turnabout in the assumptions believed to underlie juvenile mental health law. In engineering this reversal, Chief Justice Burger relied on a panoply of psychological assumptions (see Table 7.1) without supporting evidence. Indeed, it is the contention here that the majority opinion in *Parham* represents a construction of the supposed reality of how hospitalization occurs, derived from idyllic notions of how the family and the mental health professions should be. As such, this opinion reflects both a representation of myths (of wishes for a world that isn't and perhaps never was) as facts and an antiempiricist bias among the Court's conservative members.

## The Case Facts

It is useful before proceeding to a more detailed analysis of the majority's assumptions in *Parham* to examine the facts presented at trial, case facts that stood in sharp contrast to the sociai facts asserted by the chief justice. The suit in *Parham* was brought by two boys (J.R., age 12, and J.L., age 13)—both of whom had been patients at Georgia state hospitals for more than five years—on behalf of themselves and the class of approximately 200 minors in Georgia's mental hospitals. They contended that they had been deprived of liberty without procedural due process or attention to whether the hospital was the "least drastic environment" for their treatment.

J.R. had been removed from his natural parents at age three months because of severe neglect.[13] He lived in a succession of seven foster homes before being placed by welfare authorities at age 8 in Milledgeville State Hospital after the authorities had failed to find an adoptive home. Initial diagnoses were borderline mental retardation and unsocialized aggressive reaction of childhood. After hospitalization for about 2½ years, hospital personnel began requesting long-term foster care or an adoptive home for J.R. because they felt that he "will only regress if he does not get a suitable home placement, and as soon as possible." Three years later, he was still in the hospital.

J.L.'s young life was equally tragic:

J.L. at birth on October 1, 1963, was adopted. His parents divorced when he was three, and he went to live with his mother. She remarried and soon gave birth to a child. On May 15, 1970, his mother and step-father . . . applied for his admission to what is now Central State Hospital; he was admitted. Hospital personnel found that J.L. was mentally ill and diagnosed his illness as "Hyperkinetic Reaction of Childhood 308.00." On September 8, 1972, he was discharged to his mother, but she brought him back to the hospital and readmitted him ten days later. He then remained in confinement and at the time this lawsuit commenced had been in confinement for five years and five months of his twelve years, one month life. In 1973 hospital personnel indicated to the Department of Family and Children Services that J.L. needed to be removed from hospital confinement and placed in specialized foster care. His records show that the Department of Family and Children Services indicated that the department could not pay for institutionalized (private) foster care unless J.L. was eligible for such care to be paid for by A.F.D.C. or Social Security funds. He was not an A.F.D.C. eligible child . . .[14]

J.L. and J.R. were not unusual cases. The state had stipulated that at least one-fourth of the hospitalized children in Georgia could be cared for in less restrictive settings. The majority of the institutionalized children were said to be wards of the state and not psychotic. In short, the picture emerging from a review of the *Parham* facts was that many, perhaps most, of the hospitalized children in Georgia, a state with a relatively well-developed community mental health system, were in the institution because their families were unable or unwilling to care for them and the state had not developed alternative residential services.

## The Parham Assumptions

The scenario developed by the Chief Justice seems almost totally divorced from the record developed at trial. Drawing from the "pages of human experience" (p. 602), i.e., his own intuition, Burger established a series of social "facts" by judicial notice (see Table 1). Specifically, the Court generated particular concepts of the family, the mental health system, and the effects of various procedural forms on both of these institutions.

### The Family[15]

The Court's view of the family may be summarized as follows:

*Parents, including the state acting in loco parentis, almost never "dump" children into mental hospitals. Rather, children are placed there because their parents (unlike the children themselves) have the wisdom to judge the children's need for treatment accurately. Parents' and children's interests are coextensive, because parents can be validly assumed to act in their children's best interests.*

Several of the assumptions underlying this idyllic view of the family—specifically, of parental authority—are of questionable validity. Most basically, the deference to parental authority in *Parham* was at least ostensibly based on minors' incompetence and the potential harm of badly reasoned decisions. However, there is ample evidence that adolescents are generally indistinguishable from adults in their reasoning about treatment decisions

(Grisso & Vierling, 1978; Koocher, 1983; Melton, 1981; Weithorn, 1982; Weithorn & Campbell, 1982). It should be noted, however, that no study of minors' treatment decisions has used inpatient samples, although some of the relevant studies have used outpatient clinical samples (e.g., Day & Reznikoff, 1980). There is a need for research to determine the generalizability of the existing studies of children's competence to consent to mental health treatment to samples at risk for hospitalization. Ideally, such research would tap seriously disturbed adolescents' *capacities* for reasonable decision making about mental health treatment e.g., (through, responses to hypothetical situations presented in laboratory interviews) as well as their in vivo *performance* when given options during admissions interviews, when level of stress is probably high and pressures for "voluntary" admissions may be great (Gilboy & Schmidt, 1971). Obviously in such circumstances decisional competence (i.e., the "intelligence" of the decision) may be compromised by stress, or the adolescent may perceive no real choice, even if the decision is theoretically the prospective patient's to make. Nonetheless, the existing literature gives good reason to doubt that adolescents' decisions under such circumstances would be any less competent than those of similarly situated adults.

Even assuming that minors lack competence to make reasonable decisions concerning admissions to mental hospitals and need someone's help in that regard, the Chief Justice exaggerated the salutary aspects of relationships between parents and disturbed children and adolescents. The Court's faith in caseworkers to act as concerned parents was particularly circuitous: Georgia expects social workers to act in their wards' best interests; therefore, they obviously must do so. The empirical invalidity of such an assumption is well demonstrated by one study of children in foster care in Illinois (Bush & Gordon, 1978), which found that only 60 percent even knew who their caseworker was. Of these, about 25 percent had not seen the caseworker for at least six months. Fifty percent of the sample had lived in at least four homes since entering foster care. The general lack of continuity for children who are wards of the state is well documented (Mnookin, 1973). There essentially is no basis for believing that caseworkers can be expected to act as "real" parents for all of their children or that children will come to perceive their caseworkers as surrogate parents.

When one abandons a *de jure* conception of "parents" as inclusive of guardians of state wards, the picture is not as bleak. Nonetheless, the Court's view of typical parent-child relationships was certainly through rose-colored glasses. First, it must be acknowledged that, although most parents probably do strive to guard their children's best interests, the family as an institution has been under considerable stress. Single-parent families are common, and traditional extended-family supports are no longer modal (Conger, 1981; Keniston, 1977; National Academy of Sciences, 1976). In such circumstances, there may be a need to reevaluate common-law presumptions concerning the sanctity of the family and its privacy (Garbarino, Gaboury, Long, Grandjean, & Asp, 1982).

Second, it is probably fallacious to assume that general expectations of parental concern can be applied uncritically to parents of children being considered for admission to mental hospitals. It is well established that dynamics of families of seriously disturbed children vary in important ways from those of normal families, although the specific deviations may vary with the nature of the child's condition (Hetherington & Martin, 1979). Certainly conventional clinical wisdom suggests that parents' perceptions of their disturbed children's needs are frequently distorted by their own needs (Quay, Note 3). Moreover, as the *Parham* dissenters argued, the mere fact of an attempt at hospitalization suggests a fractionation of parental and child interests. Family integrity is effectively diminished by the attempt to institutionalize a child, particularly for the relatively lengthy periods characteristic of placements for juveniles. Unity of interests is particularly questionable when the bases for institutionalization are misbehavior (i.e., conduct disorders) and lack of another place to go, rather than "mental illness" (i.e., psychosis). As noted in the description of the case facts, Georgia stipulated that such bases frequently characterized hospitalization of minors in that state. Warren (1981) has indicated that such use of the mental health system is common elsewhere and apparently increasing as a result of policy changes making the juvenile justice system less accessible as a remedy for "incorrigibility" and extreme family discord.

In short, while the purpose here is not to render a blanket indictment of parents' intentions in attempting to hospitalize their children, it is clear that the simple picture of parents seeking treatment for their children as they would for a child in need of a tonsillectomy or an appendectomy is naive. Moreover, where the "parent" is the state, such a perception is plainly erroneous, given the lack of accountability in the foster care system in most states.

## Mental Hospitals

The Court's view of state mental hospitals was almost as positive as its concept of the family. The picture the majority painted of state institutions was almost free of blemish. It could be summarized as follows:

*State mental hospitals work well without external judicial review. Staff are competent, and physicians almost always evaluate families and children val-*

*idly. Civil commitment is, after all, a "medical" issue, and physicians will of course not allow a child to be admitted to, or remain in, the hospital unless medically necessary.*

### Quality of Care

Compare the Court's assumptions with the summary of the literature about state hospitals by Morse (1982), an articulate critic of involuntary hospitalization:

The inadequate conditions of public mental hospitals have been a feature of state mental health care for over a century. Many of the psychiatrists are poorly qualified, if "qualified" at all; physical conditions and staffing are inadequate; and satisfactory treatment is a myth. Periodic exposes and calls for reform have not yet led to acceptable improvement. Although courts have shown a willingness to supervise public mental hospitals when the level of care provided drops beneath a minimally humane level of decency, there is still no evidence that legislatures are willing to allocate the money necessary to ensure optimum care and treatment. Indeed, states faced with right to treatment decrees that force them to expend far greater resources on their patients have responded by "dumping" the patients into the community instead of treating them with the degree of care and expertise dictated by decency and medical ethics. This is not to say that there have not been improvements in state hospital care; it is simply to underscore the reality of inadequate care and treatment nearly everywhere. Arguments that what is available is better than nothing are unacceptable. People who are locked up because they are allegedly disordered must be treated properly. If they are not, we should admit that the major goals of involuntary hospitalization are preventive detention and warehousing and proceed to analyze the system on that basis. (pp. 81-83; footnotes omitted)

Even the psychiatric establishment itself (e.g., Stone, 1982) has recognized the dismal conditions present in many state hospitals. Besides inadequacy of basic "custodial care,"[16] attracting qualified staff has been nearly impossible for many state hospitals, even when special inducements are provided under court order (see, e.g., Stickney, 1976). The result has been a reliance in many states on foreign-born, foreign-trained physicians, who may have difficulty in speaking and understanding English and accordingly may lack the communication skills necessary in psychiatry (Torrey & Taylor, 1973). Even with the use of such "cheap labor," patient contact with professional staff is likely to be minimal (Rosenhan, 1973).

The problems may not be merely ones of inadequate financing and difficulty recruiting high-quality professionals to work with patients who are chronically and severely disordered or simply hard to manage. Rather, the hospital model of treatment may be inherently ineffective for many patients. The debilitating effect of "total institutions" has long been documented in the sociology of deviance (Goffman, 1961; Goldstein, 1979; McEwen, 1980). At least with adults, patients may eventually become "institutionalized" to the point at which it is so much easier to "cope" in the institution than in the community that they actively avoid discharge through presentation of themselves as "sick" (Braginsky, Braginsky, & Ring, 1969). Such problems may be particularly acute for minors in view of the relatively long hospital stays common for that age group.

Most basically, there simply is not empirical evidence to support the efficacy of hospital treatment. In arguing for a national policy of "noninstitutionalization," Kiesler (1982) reviewed ten studies in which seriously disordered patients were randomly assigned to inpatient care or some alternative mode of outpatient treatment. In no instance was inpatient care superior, and in most studies the alternative programs were more effective in fostering adaptation in the community (e.g., maintaining employment or staying in school) and substantially less expensive. Comparable studies of hospital care versus alternative care are not available for children and adolescents (Quay, 1979b). There is, however, particular reason for doubting the efficacy of hospital treatment for the conduct-disordered adolescents who are being increasingly admitted to mental hospitals (Miller & Kenney, 1966). Medically oriented hospitals are unlikely to provide the comprehensive educational/vocational/psychological approach that is most likely to give "difficult" juveniles the skills necessary to adapt in a positive manner (Goldenberg, 1971; Melton, 1983a; Sechrest, White, & Brown, 1979; Shore & Massimo, 1979).

## Reliability and Validity of Diagnosis

Even if one does assume that psychiatric hospitalization is beneficial for some children and adolescents, there still remains a substantial liberty interest in avoiding erroneous commitment, an interest that even the Supreme Court recognized,[17] but underemphasized.[18] The underemphasis seemed to stem from two primary factors: a characterization of the commitment decision as a "medical" decision, and a denial of risks of error in the admitting physician's assessment of the situation. Secondarily, the Court assumed that whatever minimal risk of error existed would not be reduced by the provision of judicial review.

The Court's concept of the commitment decision seems at its root fallacious. The decision to deprive an individual of liberty is an ethical/legal determination, not a medical one (Morse, 1978). Line-drawing as to the limits of "mental illness" for legal purposes is a legal determination about which mental health professionals have no expertise.

Moreover, the Court ignored the fact that decisions to institutionalize a child are often based on considerations other than the child's so-called objective illness. For example, Warren (1981) has found that "delinquents" and "status offenders" have frequently been "transinstitutionalized" into the mental health system as the gates have closed to the juvenile justice system. A recent survey of administrators of residential treatment programs (Quay, Note 3) has starkly documented these extraneous pressures. About half of the respondents expressed agreement with a statement that "agencies often accept and discharge clients based on agency need or convenience rather than the needs of the child." About two-fifths of the respondents admitted that "treatment decisions are more often influenced by agency policy than by a child's needs," and a majority acknowledged that professionals often increase the severity of a child's "label" to ensure that the child will receive services. A survey of social-welfare caseworkers (Billingsley, 1964) indicated similar supremacy of bureaucratic pressures over client needs in many cases.

Assuming for argument, though, that legal concepts of mental illness are interchangeable with clinical concepts and that diagnosis is free of political and social distortions, there is no reason to believe that problems of diagnostic reliability and validity endemic to psychological/psychiatric assessment of adults (Ennis & Litwack, 1974; Morse, 1978) are any less profound for assessment of children and adolescents. Existing clinical diagnostic systems for children are poorly conceptualized, largely unrelated to the empirical literature on symptom clusters, and subject to mediocre reliability across raters and settings (Achenbach & Edelbrock, 1978). There are, however, some syndromes empirically derived via factor analyses of behavior ratings, which do seem to generate acceptable agreement between raters and across time, but only mediocre reliability across situations (Achenbach & Edelbrock, 1978; Quay, 1979a). These research-based taxonomies have seldom found their way into clinical practice, however.[19] Moreover, this body of research is not yet clearly translatable into prescription of services for children matching a particular classification or syndrome (Achenbach & Edelbrock, 1978).

There is even less reason to believe that family assessments will be largely error-free, notwithstanding the Court's assurances that mental health professionals are unlikely to be fooled by the picture the parents initially present. There has been little effort to validate techniques for assessing family interaction (Achenbach, 1974). Most commonly in fact, clinicians rely on parental reports as the principal bases for judging the child's behavior

(McCoy, 1976). While there is some reason for doing so (i.e., parents are likely to have the most cross-situational knowledge of the child), the clinician has little basis in an admission interview for determining points of distortion or "scapegoating" in the parent's report (compare Simmonds, 1976). It is interesting in that regard to note that there is some evidence suggesting that children are more likely than parents (in cases presented to a child guidance center) to identify problems as family issues rather than problems of an "identified patient" (Small & Teagno, Note 4).

### Adversary Procedures

Besides underestimating the risk of error in commitment of children, the Court assumed that whatever error does occur would not be reduced by judicial review, and indeed that formal hearings would create substantial harm:

> Adversary proceedings disrupt both the family (including presumably the "family" of the state welfare worker; see American Psychiatric Association, 1982) and the hospital, without benefit to the child.

The notion of the lack of effectiveness of adversary procedures was based on two assumptions. First, it was argued that the decision to commit is a medical decision; therefore, lawyers will add little to the process. As already noted, this construction of the commitment decision seems plainly wrong. Second, the Court referred to several articles suggesting that the "legalization" of commitment had had minimal effect on what actually happens in commitment hearings. Interestingly, the authorities cited used such evidence to argue that more, rather than less, stringent procedures were needed. In fairness, there is an argument to be made from such data that civil commitment proceedings carry an inherent high risk of error and that moderate reforms will not work (Morse, 1982). It does not follow, however, that risks of error should be passively accepted when deprivation of liberty is at stake. Moreover, there is evidence from some jurisdictions (e.g., Zander, 1976) that adversary procedures and clear standards do have an impact on commitment proceedings when judges take the due process provisions seriously. While pressures to hospitalize crazy people may reduce the probability of courts' adopting such a stance (Morse, 1982) even when the bar receives special training in the examination of mental health professionals (Poythress, 1978), it is ironic that, while bemoaning the ineffectiveness of formal civil commitment procedures, the Court suggests deference to mental health professionals in commitment decisions.[20] When such a position is taken, commitment proceedings will of course be simply hollow rituals.

Data regarding the actual psychosocial effects of juvenile commitment hearings are practically nonexistent. One is left to speculate on the bases of anecdotal reports and of laboratory experiments testing the effects of various procedural forms on adults' perceptions of justice (see Thibaut & Walker, 1975, 1978).

The most systematic collection of outcome data from juvenile commitment hearings, was conducted by the New Jersey Division of Mental Health Advocacy, which examined the cases of the 213 minors it had represented over the period 1975-1977 (Perlin, 1981). There were a variety of individual dispositions. Sixty-five of the juveniles were released at or prior to a hearing. Hospitalization in psychiatric facilities occurred in 90 cases (38 cases, voluntary admission; 22 cases, commitment; 30 cases, confinement continued). In the remainder of cases, an alternative placement (e.g., residential school) was arranged. Thus, the role of counsel was not limited to "a finite commit/release paradigm" (Perlin, 1981, p. 157); formal advocacy by counsel also extended to investigation and negotiation concerning other possibilities (compare Wexler, 1981, pp. 98-101). Without independent representation for the child, such exploration of alternatives with less devastating effects on liberty might not have occurred.

Moreover, the dire consequences the Court posited for families did not occur. While the data presented in Perlin's article were unsystematically gathered by trial counsel themselves (and perhaps, therefore, subject to bias), the interview material presented suggests that parents generally welcomed the "pushing" for the child, which adversary counsel undertook. Even well-intentioned parents' knowledge of resources potentially available to the child is likely to be limited, and the child's counsel may actually be helpful to the parents in attempts to obtain relatively unrestrictive treatment.

Finally, existing social psychological research and theory suggest that there may be positive psychological benefits for the child. Having had some control over the process (a form of control inherent in a truly adversarial system) is likely to enhance sense of perceived justice and perhaps to decrease resistance to treatment, where it is ultimately ordered (compare Melton, 1983c; Melton & Lind, 1982).

## Conclusions

It is clear from a review of the extant research that the majority's assumptions about social facts in *Parham* are largely incongruent both with the case facts developed at trial and with what we now about the functioning of families of disturbed youngsters and of the mental health system. It appears that the assumptions that ostensibly formed the foundation for the Supreme Court's analysis were derived from a desire to support particular mythical concepts of the family and the mental health system as social institutions. Attention by the Court to the relevant social science research might have led to a different result (if the social-fact assumptions were really the basis of the analysis) or at least to more honesty about the constitutional values the decision was intended to support.

At the same time, it should be noted that the door is not closed to future consideration of this evidence. States are free to establish more stringent due process protections, and the form of constitutionally necessary postadmission review has yet to be specified by the Supreme Court. Furthermore, the Chief Justice's assumptions that were most directly contrary to existing research (e.g., incompetence of adolescents as decision makers) have received few subsequent citations in judicial opinions (Perry & Melton, Note 5), suggesting that their precedential value may be limited. Given potential policy relevance, psychologists would be well advised to begin to address some of the unanswered questions with respect to the generalizability of existing research on minors' competence to make treatment decisions, and on effects of various procedural forms to the population of minors at risk for "voluntary" commitment.

## Notes

1. Parham v. J.R., 442 U.S. 584.

2. While Chief Justice Burger speaks throughout the majority opinion of "physicians," it is likely that he would consider psychologists as expert evaluators. See Jenkins v. United States, 307 F.2d 637, 647 (D.C. Cir. 1962)—concurring opinion.

3. Humphrey v. Cady, 405 U.S. 504 (1972).

4. In re Gault, 387 U.S. 1 (1967).

5. Tinker v. Des Moines Independent School District, 393 U.S. 503 (1969).

6. Planned Parenthood of Central Missouri v. Danforth, 428 U.S. 52 (1976).

7. 431 U.S. 678 (1977).

8. Justice Blackmun's remarks in *Planned Parenthood* are particularly noteworthy. Writing for the Court, he argued that parental veto power over minors' abortion decisions would be unlikely to foster family integrity "where the minor and the nonconsenting parent are so fundamentally in conflict and the very existence of the pregnancy already has fractured the family structure." 428 U.S. at 75.

9. Lessard v. Schmidt, 349 F. Supp. 1078 (E.D. Wis. 1972).

10. Lanterman-Petris-Short Act, Cal. Welfare and Institutions Code §§ 5000 et seq.

11. O'Connor v. Donaldson, 422 U.S. 563 (1975). Ironically, Chief Justice Burger's concurring opinion in *Donaldson* is particularly pointed in its notation of the uncertainties of psychiatric diagnosis; id. at 584.

12. The issue of whether parents may admit their children to mental hospitals first reached the Supreme Court in 1975 after a federal district court declared Pennsylvania's procedures

unconstitutional. Bartley v. Kremens, 402 F. Supp. 1039 (E.D. Pa. 1975). Subsequently, Pennsylvania revised its statute to treat adolescents over the age of 14 as adults for the purpose of a voluntary admission. Because the named plaintiffs in the *Bartley* class action suit were over 14, the Supreme Court remanded the case for exclusion from the class of those whose claims were moot. Kremens v. Bartley, 431 U.S. 119 (1975).

    *Parham* was argued initially in December 1977. The Pennsylvania case, sub nom. Secretary of Public Welfare v. Institutionalized Juveniles, reached the Supreme Court once again before a decision was reached in *Parham*. The cases were consolidated for argument in October 1978. Decisions in both cases were finally announced in June 1979. See Secretary of Public Welfare, 442 U.S. 640 (1979).

    13. J.R.'s case is described at J.L. v. Parham, 412 F. Supp. 112, 116-117 (M.D. Ga. 1976).

    14. Id. at 117.

    15. That this section may be appropriately entitled "*The* Family" is indicative of the single-minded, mythical approach that the Court took. Little attention was given to the range of motivations and competence of parents admitting their children to mental hospitals.

    16. Right-to-treatment suits have often been based on the lack even of humane care and adequate physical facilities. See, e.g., Wyatt v. Stickney, 324 F. Supp. 781 (M.D. Ala. 1971), enforced, 344 F. Supp. 373 (M.D. Ala. 1972) and 344 F. Supp. 387 (M.D. Ala. 1972), modified sub nom. Wyatt v. Aderholt, 503 F.2d 1305 (5th Cir. 1974).; N.Y.S. Ass'n for Retarded Children, Inc. v. Rockefeller, 357 F. Supp. 752 (E.D.N.Y. 1973), enforced sub nom. N.Y.S. Ass'n for Retarded Children, Inc. v. Carey, 393 F. Supp. 715 (E.D.N.Y. 1975) and 409 F. Supp. 606 (E.D.N.Y. 1976), aff'd, 596 F.2d 27 (2d Cir. 1979), enforced, 492 F. Supp. 1099 (E.D.N.Y. 1980).

    17. 442 U.S. at 601.

    18. E.g., id. at 601-602.

    19. In response to the inadequacy of child diagnoses in the DSM-III (the current diagnostic system of the American Psychiatric Association), the American Psychological Association has commissioned a task force to develop a research-based behavioral taxonomy for children. The task force consists of three of the leading researchers in this area: Thomas Achenbach (chair), Keith Conners, and Herbert Quay.

    20. 442 U.S. at 609.

## Reference Notes

1. Knitzer, J. Personal communication, July 19, 1982.
2. American Psychiatric Association. *Guidelines for psychiatric hospitalization of minors: Commentary.* Revised and approved by the Assembly, New Orleans, May 1981.
3. Quay, H. Personal communication, August 26, 1982.
4. Small, A.C., & Teagno, L. *A comparative study of children's and their parents' expectations of psychotherapy.* Paper presented at the meeting of the American Association of Psychiatric Services for Children, Chicago, November 1979.
5. Perry, G.S., & Melton, G.B. *Precedential value of judicial notice of social facts:* Parham *as an example.* Manuscript in preparation.

## References

Achenbach, T.M. *Developmental psychopathology.* New York: Ronald Press, 1974.
Achenbach, T.M., & Edelbrock, C.S. The classification of child psychopathology: A review and analysis of empirical efforts. *Psychological Bulletin,* 1978, *85,* 1275-1301.

American Psychiatric Association. Guidelines for the psychiatric hospitalization of minors. *American Journal of Psychiatry*, 1982, *139*, 971-975.

Annas, G. Law and the life sciences: Parents, children, and the Supreme Court. *Hastings Center Report*, October 1979, *9*, 21-41.

Billingsley, A. Bureaucratic and professional orientation patterns in casework. *Social Service Review*, 1964, *38*, 400-407.

Braginsky, B.M., Braginsky, D.D., & Ring, K. *Methods of madness: The mental hospital as a last resort.* New York: Holt, Rinehart & Winston, 1969.

Bush, M., & Gordon, A.C. Client choice and bureaucratic accountability: Possibilities for responsiveness in a social welfare bureaucracy. *Journal of Social Issues*, 1978, *34*(2), 22-43.

Conger, J.J. Freedom and commitment: Families, youth, and social change. *American Psychologist*, 1981, *36*, 1475-1484.

Day, L., & Reznikoff, M. Social class, the treatment process, and parents and children's expectations about child psychotherapy. *Journal of Clinical Child Psychology*, 1980, *9*, 195-198.

Developments in the Law. Civil commitment of the mentally ill. *Harvard Law Review*, 1974, *87*, 1190.

Ennis, B.J., & Litwack, T.R. Psychiatry and the presumption of expertise: Flipping coins in the courtroom. *California Law Review*, 1974, *62*, 693-752.

Garbarino, J., Gaboury, M.T., Long, F., Grandjean, P., & Asp, E. Who owns the children? An ecological perspective on public policy affecting children. In G.B. Melton (Ed.), *Legal reforms affecting child and youth services.* New York: Haworth, 1982.

Gilboy, J.A., & Schmidt, J.R. "Voluntary" hospitalization of the mentally ill. *Northwestern University Law Review*, 1971, *66*, 429-453.

Goffman, E. *Asylums.* New York: Doubleday, 1961.

Goldenberg, I.I. *Build me a mountain: Youth, poverty, and the creation of new settings.* Cambridge, MA: MIT Press, 1971.

Goldstein, M.S. The sociology of mental health and illness. *Annual Review of Sociology*, 1979, *5*, 381-409.

Grisso, T., & Vierling, L. Minors' consent to treatment: A developmental perspective. *Professional Psychology*, 1978, *9*, 412-427.

Hetherington, E.M., & Martin, B. Family interaction. In H.C. Quay & J.S. Werry (Eds.), *Psychopathological disorders of childhood* (2nd ed.). New York: Wiley, 1979.

Hiday, V.A. Reformed commitment procedures: An empirical study in the courtroom. *Law and Society Review*, 1977, *11*, 651-666.

Hiday, V.A. Court discretion: Application of the dangerousness standard in civil commitment. *Law and Human Behavior*, 1981, *5*, 275-289.

Keniston, K. *All our children: The American family under pressure.* New York: Harcourt Brace Jovanovich, 1977.

Kiesler, C.A. Mental hospitals and alternative care: Noninstitutionalization as potential public policy for mental patients. *American Psychologist*, 1982, *37*, 349-360.

Koocher, G.P. Competence to consent: Psychotherapy. In G.B. Melton, G.P. Koocher, & M.J. Saks (Eds.), *Children's competence to consent.* New York: Plenum, 1983.

Luckey, J.W., & Berman, J.J. Effects of a new commitment law on involuntary admissions and service utilization patterns. *Law and Human Behavior*, 1979, *3*, 149-161.

McCoy, S.A. Clinical judgments of normal childhood behavior. *Journal of Consulting and Clinical Psychology*, 1976, *44*, 710-714.

McEwen, C.A. Continuities in the study of total and nontotal institutions. *Annual Review of Sociology*, 1980, *6*, 143-185.

Melton, G.B. Children's participation in treatment planning: Psychological and legal issues. *Professional Psychology,* 1981, *12,* 246-252.

Melton, G.B. Children's rights: Where are the children? *American Journal of Orthopsychiatry,* 1982, *52,* 530-538.

Melton, G.B. *Child advocacy: Psychological issues and interventions.* New York: Plenum, 1983. (a)

Melton, G.B. Children's competence to consent: A problem in law and social science. In G.B. Melton, G.P. Koocher, & M.J. Saks (Eds.), *Children's competence to consent.* New York: Plenum, 1983. (b)

Melton, G.B. Decision making by children: Psychological risks and benefits. In G.B. Melton, G.P. Koocher, & M.J. Saks (Eds.), *Children's competence to consent.* New York: Plenum, 1983. (c)

Melton, G.B., & Lind, E.A. Procedural justice in family court: Does the adversary system make sense? In G.B. Melton (Ed.), *Legal reforms affecting child and youth services.* New York: Haworth, 1982.

Miller, R.B., & Kenney, E. Adolescent delinquency and the myth of hospital treatment. *Crime and Delinquency,* 1966, *12,* 38-48.

Mnookin, R.H. Foster care: In whose best interest? *Harvard Educational Review,* 1973, *43,* 599-638.

Morse, S.J. Crazy behavior, morals, and science: An analysis of mental health law. *Southern California Law Review,* 1978, *51,* 527-653.

Morse, S.J. A preference for liberty: The case against involuntary commitment of the mentally disordered. *California Law Review,* 1982, *70,* 54-106.

National Academy of Sciences. *Toward a national policy for children and families.* Washington, DC: Author, 1976.

Perlin, M. An invitation to the dance: An empirical response to Chief Justice Warren Burger's "time-consuming procedural minuets" theory in Parham v. J.R. *Bulletin of the American Academy of Psychiatry and Law,* 1981, *9,* 149-164.

Poythress, N.G., Jr. Psychiatric expertise in civil commitment: Training attorneys to cope with expert testimony. *Law and Human Behavior,* 1978, *2,* 1-24.

Quay, H.C. Classification. In H.C. Quay & J.S. Werry (Eds.), *Psychopathological disorders of childhood* (2nd ed.). New York: Wiley, 1979. (a)

Quay, H.C. Residential treatment. In H.C. Quay & J.S. Werry (Eds.), *Psychopathological disorders of childhood* (2nd ed.). New York: Wiley, 1979. (b)

Rosenhan, D.L. On being sane in insane places. *Science,* 1973, *179,* 250-258.

Sechrest, L., White, S.O., & Brown, E.D. (Eds.). *The rehabilitation of criminal offenders: Problems and prospects.* Washington, DC: National Academy of Sciences, 1979.

Shore, M.F., & Massimo, J. Fifteen years after treatment: A follow-up study of comprehensive vocationally oriented psychotherapy. *American Journal of Orthopsychiatry,* 1979, *49,* 240-245.

Simmonds, D.W. Children's rights and family dysfunction: "Daddy, why do I have to be the crazy one?" In G.P. Koocher (Ed.), *Children's rights and the mental health professions.* New York: Wiley, 1976.

Stickney, S.S. *Wyatt v. Stickney:* Background and postscript. In S. Golann & W.J. Fremouw (Eds.), *The right to treatment for mental patients.* New York: Irvington, 1976.

Stier, S.D., & Stoebe, K.J. Involuntary hospitalization of the mentally ill in Iowa: The failure of the 1975 legislation. *Iowa Law Review,* 1979, *64,* 1284-1458.

Stone, A. Psychiatric abuse and legal reform: Two ways to make a bad situation worse. *International Journal of Law and Psychiatry,* 1982, *5,* 9-28.

Thibaut, J., & Walker, L. *Procedural justice*. Hillsdale, NJ: Erlbaum, 1975.

Thibaut, J., & Walker, L. A theory of procedure. *California Law Review*, 1978, *66*, 541-566.

Torrey, E. F., & Taylor, R.L. Cheap labor from foreign nations. *American Journal of Psychiatry*, 1973, *130*, 428-433.

Warren, C.A.B. New forms of social control: The myth of deinstitutionalization. *American Behavioral Scientist*, 1981, *24*, 724-740.

Weithorn, L.A. Developmental factors and competence to make informed treatment decisions. In G.B. Melton (Ed.), *Legal reforms affecting child and youth services*. New York: Haworth, 1982.

Weithorn, L.A., & Campbell, S.B. The competency of children and adolescents to make informed treatment decisions. *Child Development*, 1982, *53*, 1589-1598.

Wexler, D.B. *Mental health law: Major issues*. New York: Plenum, 1981.

Zander, T.K. Civil commitment in Wisconsin: The impact of *Lessard v. Schmidet. Wisconsin Law Review*, 1976, 503-562.

# PART IV

## CHILDREN IN THE JUVENILE JUSTICE SYSTEM

# 8

# Procedural Issues in the Juvenile Justice System

## Thomas Grisso
*St. Louis University*

## Marcia Conlin
*National Juvenile Law Center*

The purpose of this chapter is to review procedural issues at four critical stages in the processing of delinquency cases in the juvenile justice system. An "issue" is defined as any concern for a juvenile's psychological well-being when it is placed at risk by some codified procedure in the juvenile justice system's management of a delinquency case.[1] The four stages are pretrial interrogation, pretrial detention, transfer of juveniles to criminal court jurisdiction, and postadjudication disposition. For each stage, we will briefly examine (a) the procedures that generally are followed by juvenile courts;[2] (b) the risks that certain procedures pose for the psychological development or mental health of some juveniles; and (c) ways to address the problem through legal reform. The chapter will conclude with suggestions for social science research that would assist in making decisions about legal reforms in these areas of juvenile justice.

Before proceeding to the four reviews, three types of procedural rules are defined in order to provide the structure for each of the subsequent analyses.

Authors' Note: Material for this chapter was collected with the assistance of National Institute of Mental Health Research Grants MH-27849 and MH-35090 (NIMH, Center for Studies of Crime and Delinquency) to the first author. The opinions and viewpoints stated in this chapter do not necessarily represent those of the National Institute of Mental Health or the National Juvenile Law Center, Inc.

## Discretion and Procedural Rules

Juvenile justice personnel are allowed considerable discretion when making decisions about juveniles who have been charged with delinquent conduct. Traditionally, the law has allowed juvenile courts considerable freedom from rigid rules and procedures for decision making, so that the legal system could make decisions that would meet the individualized needs of juveniles for rehabilitation and correction (Davis, 1983).

Meeting the needs of juveniles has been a primary objective of the juvenile justice system since its beginning early in this century. This is, however, only one of the juvenile system's goals. Another goal is the protection of the community from certain juveniles whose habitual behaviors are assaultive or destructive of property. Further, juvenile courts must meet certain objectives, typical of any organization, concerning efficiency, management, and budget constraints.

All of these goals have their influence upon juvenile courts' decisions about juveniles. Further, when decisions consistently are dominated by the objectives of community protection and system management, there is a greater risk that decisions will not be tailored to the well-being or mental health of juveniles themselves. For example, a community may seem more safe if all juveniles are held in secure detention facilities while their delinquency cases are being decided. Such use of detention, however, disregards the fact that not all juveniles present equivalent risks to the community, and it ignores the negative effects of detention on juveniles due to separation from family and school.

In this light, the broad discretion that traditionally has been allowed in juvenile court decision making is a two-edged sword. When working at its best, the system has allowed juvenile courts to meet juveniles' individual needs while giving proper attention to the courts' other goals. At its worst, however, discretionary power has been abused; there is ample evidence that at various times in its history, the juvenile justice system's discretionary powers have resulted in decisions that ignore the welfare of the juveniles for whom the system was created (Institute of Judicial Administration/American Bar Association, 1980).

Therefore, in recent years the legal system has developed complex rules that constrain the justice system's process for making decisions about juveniles. These rules—provided variously by state juvenile codes (statutes), case precedent ("case law"), and special administrative policies—set certain limits and requirements that significantly reduce discretion by the decision maker and simultaneously seek to allow enough flexibility to deal with the wide variety of needs among juveniles about whom the courts must make decisions. These procedural rules are the focus of the present chapter.

Many readers will have seen one of those bewildering diagrams, or "decision trees," that describe the complex, branching paths that delinquency cases may take through the juvenile justice system. Wilkins (1979) has likened these networks of case options to a railroad switchyard. The pattern of tracks describes the optional routes that the cars may take, each alternative branching several times into other alternatives. The switches at each branching point represent decisions that must be made regarding which route will be taken.

Procedural rules in the juvenile justice system regulate the flow of cases through this network by (a) prescribing the available options at various stages; (b) describing the types of cases that justifiably may be "switched" into any of the optional pathways; and (c) regulating the ways in which the system decides that a given case is of the type described by law. The relevance of each of these three types of rules warrants explanation.

First, one type of rule prescribes optional outcomes; we will call these rules *procedural options.* For example, juvenile courts may consider several options for the placement of a juvenile while the case is awaiting a hearing on the delinquency charge. Among these options are temporary placement in a secure detention facility, placement in an open shelter care facility, temporary foster care, or placement in the juvenile's own home. Laws may specifically exclude other options, such as holding juveniles in adult jails. Some procedural options during case processing in the juvenile justice system are inherently risky, in the sense of increasing the possibility of psychologically deleterious effects for juveniles: for example, the option to transfer a juvenile to an adult criminal court, where he or she may be tried and imprisoned with adult criminals. Other options represent a significant risk to psychological development or mental health only for some types of juveniles. In the following analyses, the risks inherent in various procedural options will be discussed.

Second, other rules, which we will call *decision standards,* describe what types of juveniles legally may be processed along particular optional routes. For example, in many states, only juveniles of a particular age (often 14) or who have been arrested for a particular level of offense are "eligible" for consideration for transfer to an adult criminal court for trial. Most often, though, the descriptions in statute or case law are vague or abstract. For example, many states require that only juveniles who are "unamenable to treatment" in the juvenile justice system (often no further elaboration is offered) may be transferred to an adult criminal court. The latter type of decision standard allows a considerably greater degree of discretion in decision making than the former.

A third type of rule regulates the ways in which a court must decide whether or not a juvenile case meets the decision standard that justifies a particular optional outcome. These rules we will call *decision procedures*. One example of a decision procedure is the requirement that a defense attorney be present at a hearing at which a judicial decision will be made. Other rules about decision procedures require that particular kinds of information about a juvenile must be considered when an abstract, discretionary decision standard is involved. For example, some states require a judge to consider the juvenile's responses to each past rehabilitation attempt of the juvenile system, when deciding whether or not the juvenile is unamenable to treatment in relation to a decision about transferring the juvenile to an adult criminal court.

These three types of procedural rules suggest three different ways for reforming law, when it can be demonstrated that the risk of psychological damage that is inherent in present procedures outweighs the benefit of the procedures to society, law enforcement, or juveniles themselves. Depending upon the nature of the risk and the procedures involved, one might consider any of three alternatives, or "strategies":

Strategy A: Delete or increase certain *procedural options* in the system.

Strategy B: Increase the specificity of a *decision standard* (i.e., reduce discretion), or narrow the types of juveniles who are "eligible" for particular options.

Strategy C: Develop *decision procedures* that promote greater care in evaluating the potential psychological risks of an option for certain juveniles.

At the end of each of the following four sections, these three strategies will be used to structure consideration of legal reforms that may be needed regarding the procedural issues in question.

### Pretrial Interrogation[3]

#### Procedures

Police have the procedural option to attempt to obtain a confession or other useful, offense-related statement from a juvenile soon after arrest.[4] If they hope to use the confession in later court proceedings in the case, police must apply a decision standard prior to questioning: The juvenile must be capable of making a "knowing, intelligent and voluntary" waiver of rights to silence and legal counsel. This is an abstract rather than specific decision standard; the law describes no specific characteristics of juveniles (e.g., no particular age) that automatically exclude the procedural option of interrogation.

Statutes and case law have provided a variety of decision procedures in this area, that is, conditions that are required when one applies the decision standard. For example, police must inform juveniles of their rights to silence and legal counsel, as well as the use of confessions in court and the availability of free legal counsel.[5] In many states, police are required to unite juveniles and their parents prior to questioning, so that the juveniles might have the advice of their parents when considering waiver of rights.

Further, various courts have provided lists of variables—for example, age, educational level, and intelligence—that are to be considered when addressing the abstract decision standard.[6] Such lists do not, however, specify any particular age or educational level to be used in making the decision concerning the juvenile's ability to make a knowing, intelligent, and voluntary waiver. Failure to have read rights to the juvenile or to have obtained the presence of parents usually (but not always) makes the results of the interrogation option invalid and, thus, not usable in later court proceedings. Courts have been quite clear, however, that a reading of the rights and parental advice do not alone signify that the decision standard has been met.

## Psychological Concerns

Third-degree tactics in the interrogation of juveniles have not been a problem in recent decades (President's Commission on Law Enforcement and Administration of Justice, 1967). Police officers have found that a friendly stance, coupled with their authority and recognized power, is far more effective in securing confessions than were the overtly threatening tactics of earlier years (Inbau & Reid, 1967; Kenney & Pursuit, 1970). This more subtle approach is especially effective with suspects who are powerless and vulnerable.

Courts have questioned whether juveniles' confessions are likely to be reliable under these conditions.[7] Indeed, there have been reports of juveniles whose fear and confusion, together with "fatherly" questioning by police, have resulted in confessions to serious offenses that they never committed (Barthel, 1977). In situations such as these, juveniles may be processed, adjudicated, and sent to juvenile correctional settings without reason and to their psychological detriment. Short of such extreme circumstances, extensive investigations and court proceedings following from unreliable confessions can be traumatic and stigmatizing in themselves.

Although a variety of types of juveniles (and adults) might be at risk of such consequences, one would expect that these risks are greatest among very young suspects. Grisso (1981) has produced considerable empirical evidence to show that, as a group, juveniles below age fourteen are likely to be confused about their rights in interrogation and about the meaning and importance of the interrogation itself. Equally confused were older adolescents with markedly inferior intellectual abilities.

## Procedural Remedies

The three strategies for procedural reform can now be examined for their potential to reduce risk to juveniles during pretrial interrogations.

*Strategy A.* To rule out the procedural option of interrogation in all juveniles' cases would seriously hamper the work of law enforcement officers, conceivably endangering the lives of other juveniles and of adults in some cases.

*Strategy B.* Based on the above description of data obtained by Grisso (1981), one might consider the development of a specific decision standard that would automatically exclude certain juveniles from the interrogation option. "Below age fourteen" might be a rational rule. Grisso's data suggested that these juveniles, as a group, have very poor comprehension of Miranda warnings and can be expected to be more confused and deferential in the context of interrogations. Thus, there is an empirical rationale for expecting that they are psychologically at risk and in need of special procedural considerations. The age standard can easily be ascertained by police prior to interrogation procedures, and the rule would not unduly frustrate the work of police or the administration of justice. In one metropolitan jurisdiction, for example, less than 13 percent of juvenile interrogations involved children who were below age fourteen (Grisso & Pomicter, 1977). Further, juveniles at these younger ages tend not to commit the most serious felonies in most jurisdictions. Thus, a specific decision rule excluding interrogation with younger juveniles would not interfere with police efforts to deal with "hardcore delinquency." While the rule would not protect all juveniles who might be at risk (e.g., older juveniles with serious developmental deficiencies), it would at least serve to exclude one identifiable class of juveniles who are especially at risk of psychological harm.

*Strategy C.* The development of precautionary decision procedures during pretrial interrogation raises several problems. For example, requiring the presence of an attorney to advise juveniles probably would have the same effect as removing the interrogation option altogether, since attorneys would almost always advise against waiver. Requiring more extensive attempts by police to explain or to teach the rights to juveniles prior to interrogation would be of questionable benefit, since neither the situation nor the participants would be likely to enter into the activity in a manner conducive to learning. Further, there is evidence that requiring the presence of parents during a juvenile's decision about waiver of rights does not provide the necessary protections (Grisso & Ring, 1979).[8] On balance, then, Strategy B offers the greatest potential for reform in this area of juvenile justice procedure.

### Pretrial Detention[9]

#### Procedures

When police take a juvenile into custody on a delinquency charge, they are allowed several procedural options in many states. One of these options is to deliver the juvenile to his or her home, a relative, or a guardian. Various circumstances might preclude this option, in which case the juvenile can be placed in the temporary custody of an authorized facility. Among these legally sanctioned facilities in many states are shelter care facilities, where basic needs are provided in a nonsecure setting. The need for more secure detention is most likely to be provided by a special juvenile detention facility, although some states still allow detention of juveniles in municipal jails with adult offenders.[10] Police also are authorized to deliver a juvenile directly to a psychiatric facility when the juvenile's demeanor suggests to them that this temporary placement would be more appropriate than the aforementioned options. Once the juvenile is detained in any of these settings, continued residence there or transfer to any of the other types of facilities may occur under certain circumstances.[11]

The decision standards for detention of juveniles in many states are patterned after the Uniform Juvenile Court Act of 1968 and the Model Family Court Act of 1974. In general, a juvenile may be detained on a delinquency charge (a) to protect the person or property of others; (b) to protect the juvenile if substantial harm would come otherwise; (c) to secure the juvenile's presence at subsequent court hearings (i.e., if the juvenile is thought likely to flee prior to a court hearing); or (4) to provide care for juveniles who lack adequate supervision at home or in the home of relatives or guardians. Some states provide, in addition, that juveniles may be detained for a variety of other reasons: e.g., to hold juveniles who are fugitives from other jurisdictions, or upon a juvenile's request for protection.[12]

The decision procedures of most states require that a detention hearing be held within two working days after the juvenile's admission to detention. This is to determine whether there is sufficient reason (as provided by the state's decision standards) to continue the juvenile's detention pending further court proceedings. A judge or hearing officer presides at the detention hearing and makes the ultimate decision regarding the legal merits of continued detention. Police or juvenile officers are required to show probable cause regarding the charges in about one-half of the states, and every state's juvenile code provides that the juvenile is entitled to legal counsel during the detention hearing.

Most state statutes offer no guidance to judges in deciding when a juvenile meets one of the decision standards. A few states require that certain factors be considered (nature of the offense charged, prior record, mental condition, family ties, and school record), but how these factors will apply to decision making is left to judicial discretion.[13] Four states require that the court's decision must represent the least restrictive alternative that will meet the needs of the juvenile and the safety of the community.

### Psychological Concerns

During the mid-1970s over 520,000 juveniles were admitted annually to detention centers, and over 120,000 juveniles were admitted to adult jails during the same period (National Juvenile Justice Assessment Center, 1980). Clearly the most serious concern for the mental health of juveniles is raised by the practice of jailing them with adult offenders, where rape and physical abuse of children are common, and where the suicide rate for juveniles is eight times higher than in juvenile detention centers (Community Research Forum, 1980).

Significant reforms in juvenile detention centers in the past decade have greatly reduced the physical hazards of earlier years. The mere fact of detention, however, has certain important consequences for a juvenile, regardless of the degree of safety provided. Detention means separation from parents, uncertainty and anxiety, little access to emotional supports, and impersonal treatment that may involve strip searchers, institutional clothing, and routinized programs (Kihm, 1980). Many juveniles refer to their experiences in juvenile detention centers as among the worst episodes in their lives and the places that they most want to avoid in the future (Sarri, 1974).

The fear and lack of emotional support experienced by juveniles in detention centers may have more far-reaching effects. For example, the risk of serious psychological reactions of a psychotic or depressive nature may be increased for some juveniles. In addition, the detention experience may increase the likelihood of damage to self-esteem or of increased identification with delinquent subgroups. Currently there are no definitive research results to tell us the extent of risk of such consequences in the practice of detention. They would seem to be unavoidable, however, for at least some detained juveniles.

## Procedural Remedies

There is considerable evidence to support the opinion of the President's Commission on Law Enforcement and Administration of Justice (1967) that juveniles are placed in secure detention in numbers far greater than necessary for their own welfare or the safety of the community. For example, it is known that the vast majority of juveniles are detained simply because of their parents' unwillingness to take them home (Guggenheim, 1977), a consequence that, arguably, does not require high-security detention in most cases. Further, a recent study examined the effects in two counties of new detention standards that greatly restricted the types of juveniles who could be detained (Kihm, 1980). Compared to matched counties without these restrictions, the two counties eventually detained far fewer juveniles, yet manifested similar or lower rearrest rates than did the less restricted jurisdictions. Results such as these have supported conclusions that "the danger of too much detention . . . currently outweighs the danger—both for juveniles and society—of too much release" (Institute of Judicial Administration/ American Bar Association, 1980, p. 3). Mental health risks associated with detention could be reduced by merely reducing the number of juveniles who are detained unnecessarily. The frequent overuse of the secure detention option can be laid to a combination of factors, ranging from the availability of the option to vagueness in the decision standards applied to judicial discretion in the assignment of juveniles to detention.

*Strategy A.* Secure detention undoubtedly serves a necessary purpose in some juvenile cases. Elimination of this option could produce an increased risk of danger to the community. In contrast, there would seem to be no justification for the option of detaining juveniles in adult jails, and the federal government is committed to a policy of eliminating this practice, which is still all too frequent, by 1985.[14] The construction of more juvenile detention facilities, of course, would reduce the need to use adult jails. On the other hand, there is evidence that the likelihood that detention will be selected as an option in juvenile cases is in direct proportion to the availability of detention facilities (Kramer & Steffensmeier, 1978). Ironically, then, policy reformers who press for construction of more juvenile detention facilities may be contributing to one ill (the overuse of detention) in their attempts to deal with another (jailing juveniles with adults). In jurisdictions where no juvenile detention facilities exist, this approach may be warranted, nevertheless. The better strategy for many jurisdictions, though, would be to increase shelter care options (nonsecure facilities) and to maintain only modest secure detention facilities for those few juveniles who may require them. Such redistribution of availability of options could exert considerable influence upon judicial decisions themselves, at least partially correcting current overuse of secure detention.

*Strategy B.* The overuse of detention is made possible in part by the broad, largely undefined decision standards in virtually all states. Clarity in decision standards regarding specifically who may be detained might reduce the less discriminant use of current decision standards, thereby reducing the number of unnecessarily detained juveniles. The Juvenile Justice Standards Project (Institute of Judicial Administration/American Bar Association, 1980) has proposed standards that, in effect, require certain felony charges and evidence of certain past behaviors (e.g., past failure to appear at court proceedings) as decision standards for detention, replacing the current standards that call for highly discretionary "predictions" about behavior (e.g., dangerousness).[15] Similarly, Mulvey and Saunders (1982) conclude their review of detention decision standards with three recommendations for new standards: (a) creating standards consistent with the short-term use of detention; (b) eliminating standards that call for predictions of juveniles' behavior; and (c) emphasizing standards that refer to specific past events or behaviors, as opposed to inferred traits or personality characteristics.

*Strategy C.* Several decision procedures recommended by national advisory groups have yet to be implemented by most states. For example, several advisory bodies (e.g., National Advisory Committee, 1980) have called for the requirement that a judge produce written reasons for his or her belief that a juvenile did or did not meet the applicable decision standard for detention. In addition to current requirements for a court hearing within 48 hours after admission, periodic review of each detention decision (e.g., every 7-10 days) has been recommended. Finally, routine evaluation of juveniles by mental health professionals prior to detention hearings may be of value, in order to screen those juveniles who might be at greater risk of psychological harm by detention placement.

## Transfer to Criminal Jurisdiction[16]

### Procedures

Juvenile courts have available the procedural option to transfer jurisdiction of certain juveniles from the juvenile justice system to the criminal court, where they may be tried according to procedures for adults.

This option is one among several alternatives for handling juvenile cases at the pretrial level. Other options include dismissal of charges, "informal adjustment" of the case, or commitment to a psychiatric facility. Informal adjustment may occur by any of several arrangements between the juvenile court officer, the juvenile, and the parent. For example, they may informally agree that the juvenile will seek community services voluntarily, or they may form a consent decree (often a "contract" sanctioned by a hearing officer of the court) that the juvenile and parent accept certain conditions (e.g., acceptance of treatment services or probation) without the need for a formal hearing on the delinquency charges. The psychiatric commitment option often arises prior to trial if a juvenile's behavior in detention suggests the need for intensive inpatient mental health services, for evaluation, or for emergency psychiatric care.[17] In cases in which none of these options is appropriate, the two primary options remaining are to hold an adjudication hearing (i.e., to establish whether the juvenile is delinquent regarding the alleged offense) or to hold a hearing to decide whether the juvenile's case should be transferred and tried in criminal court.[18]

The decision standards for transfer of jurisdiction are of two types. First, most statutes specify age and/or offense criteria. Various states specify a minimum allowable age of 14, 15, or 16; some states, though, set the age limit as low as 10 years and 7 states specify no minimum age. The most common offense criteria allow transfer for alleged felonies and misdemeanors, alleged felonies only, or only for particular categories of alleged felonies. A showing of probable cause is required in some states, and 11 states require a finding that the juvenile is not commitable to an institution for the mentally ill or mentally retarded. If these criteria are met, a second type of more discretionary standard applies to the ultimate decision to transfer. Most states require a finding that (a) the juvenile is "not amenable to treatment" or is "not a fit and proper subject" for rehabilitation services within the control of the juvenile justice system; or (b) that the safety of the public requires that the juvenile be transferred to criminal court jurisdiction. Some statutes provide only one or the other of these standards, while others allow transfer for either reason.

The initial step in the decision procedure is the decision of a prosecutor or juvenile officer to petition the court for transfer. The court must respond with a formal hearing, including legal counsel for the juvenile, counsel's access to social records considered by the court, and a written reason for the ultimate decision reached by the court.[19] The hearing must be made prior to an adjudicatory hearing[20] and does not result in a finding concerning delinquency or the veracity of the allegations.

Thirty-seven states list factors that are to be considered by courts when applying the decision standards for transfer (amenability to treatment, danger to community). Those factors that appear with greatest frequency include the nature of the alleged offense (specifically, the degree of violence and premeditation, and whether against person or property), the previous social and offense record (especially repetitive patterns of offenses), educational background, the sophistication and maturity of the juvenile, and the nature of past rehabilitation efforts and the juvenile's responses to them.[21] No guidelines are offered regarding how to employ these factors, and the law gives no special weight to any particular factor.[22] The transfer decision, then, is highly discretionary after the case has met the threshold requirements of age and type of offense.

## Psychological Concerns

A juvenile's transfer to an adult criminal court for trial brings with it several risks concerning the juvenile's mental health and welfare. The juvenile's record becomes public, no longer protected by the confidentiality surrounding juvenile cases. Thus, the juvenile may be barred from later military service or public employment. Public trial may be stigmatizing, and the consequences of a guilty verdict may mean harsher confinement with older and more sophisticated offenders. Generally the juvenile will not have the benefit of treatment, rehabilitation, or educational services that are more prevalent in the juvenile justice system than in adult correctional settings.[23]

One's concern regarding these consequences is increased by the fact that, as noted earlier, several states allow the transfer of very young juveniles. Further, the stereotype of the transferred juvenile as a hardened, violent offender who threatens the lives of citizens is questioned by recent findings regarding more than 7000 juveniles nationwide who were transferred in 1978: (a) Only about 20 percent of the transfer cases were for violent offense charges; (b) 45 percent were for crimes involving property, not assaults or other offenses involving personal harm; (c) 17 percent (and in some states, as high as 46 percent) of transfers were for alcohol, drug, and other public order charges (Academy of Contemporary Problems, 1982).

The wide range of nonviolent offenses and types of juveniles that are involved in transfers, together with the extreme discretion allowed to courts by decision standards, presents the considerable possibility of exposing some juveniles unnecessarily to the troubling psychological and physical consequences of transfer noted earlier.

## Procedural Remedies

*Strategy A.* If the consequence of abolition of the transfer option were the construction of high-security institutions for truly habitual violent juvenile offenders, then it would probably be preferable to retain the transfer option, rather than create yet another and easier way to lock up juveniles.

Strict application of the "amenability to treatment" standard requires a showing that no facilities available to the juvenile justice system offer a prospect of treatment, given the juvenile's character. Therefore, any development of new treatment resources in the community increases the chances that defense attorneys can argue effectively against transfer for some types of juveniles. Augmentation of treatment resources might focus especially on very young, violent juveniles (for whom transfer represents the greatest mental health risk) and on resources for older but nonviolent juveniles (whose behaviors do not represent a serious threat of personal harm). Efforts to increase treatment options for these types of juveniles are frustrated, of course, by financial cost and probable lack of public support.

*Strategy B.* Setting a high threshold age for transfer in all states (e.g., age fifteen, as recommended by various national advisory groups)[24] would at least reduce the risk of psychological harm to younger juveniles, who are the most vulnerable to transfer's negative consequences. Similarly, limiting transfer in all states to charges of certain violent offenses, or a certain prior number of sustained and serious felony offenses, would reduce the wide range of types of juveniles who are transferred, while still protecting the public. Current trends, however, suggest a greater tendency for states to *ease* restrictions on juvenile transfer rather than to narrow juveniles' eligibility for transfer.[25]

*Strategy C.* Decision procedures might be improved somewhat in their consistency by clarifying the factors to be considered when meeting discretionary decision standards for transfer. Instructing courts to consider a juvenile's sophistication and maturity, for example, is of little value unless some more ascertainable signs of these characteristics are provided in decision-making guidelines. In addition, a state might require that each treatment resource available to the juvenile justice system be reviewed specifically and openly in each transfer case, with reasons given by the court for rejecting each option in cases in which a decision to transfer is made. This procedure could protect against hasty or unjustified exclusion of some juveniles from services within which there might be some chance of rehabilitation without transfer.

### *Postadjudication Disposition*[26]

**Procedures**

After a juvenile has been adjudicated delinquent in a juvenile court hearing, the court must decide whether or not the juvenile is in need of care or rehabilitation and, if so, what disposition or treatment is appropriate for the juvenile. Procedural options for dispositions are as varied as the range of mental health services, educational and social services, and correctional settings within the court's jurisdiction. A representative list of options might include probation with neither services nor special limitations on the juvenile; probation with supervision by a juvenile court officer; special curfew or other restrictive requirements; restitution; placement in foster or group home; placement in a residential setting in the community, for special education and rehabilitation; and placement in a more restrictive training school or

other correctional facility, often under the control of the state's youth authority or commission.

Most states provide no more specific decision standard than that the decision regarding any disposition must be in the best interests of the child and
the state. Eleven states narrow judicial discretion somewhat by requiring
that the disposition selected must be the least restrictive alternative appropriate to the circumstances. In addition, some state statutes set a minimum age
at which juveniles may be committed to a state agency and a maximum period of time during which they may be held in a state training school.

The decision procedures of all states require (by statute or case law) that
a formal disposition hearing must be held, and that it must be separate from
the adjudication hearing. All state codes either permit or require the preparation of a social history report for court use at the disposition hearing, in
order to assist in decision making about needed treatment and rehabilitation.
Court orders for psychological or psychiatric evaluations are permitted in all
states and are frequently implemented in many juvenile courts. Juveniles
have the right to counsel, the right to cross-examine and full access to
records and reports, and the right to present information to the court relevant
to the question of need for treatment and the appropriate type of treatment.

### Psychological Concerns

The intent of disposition statutes is to place before the judge the task of
making decisions that are not unlike those faced by mental health professionals in many psychiatric settings. The juvenile's character, personality,
conflicts, and emotional needs must be "diagnosed," and a suitable treatment, if necessary, must be determined. In the courtroom and in the clinic,
the mental health professional is concerned about several circumstances of
treatment decisions that may be detrimental to the mental health of
juveniles.

First, there is the risk of deciding that no intervention is needed, when in
fact it is. Most disposition hearings, though, apparently result in a determination that some intervention is necessary.

Second, some juveniles might be considered to be in need of treatment
when in fact they are not. This error may be of little consequence if the dispositional option is relatively nonintrusive. On the other hand, it may result
in various detrimental consequences if, for example, the disposition
involves residential placement. Removal from home and community for
some significant period of time may increase unnecessarily the stress and
burden of readjustment and stigmatization that may be associated with the
intervention.

Third, a juvenile in need of treatment may be assigned a dispositional
alternative different from the one that might fit the juvenile's needs more

closely. Similarly, a juvenile in need might be provided a disposition that, in effect, offers little or no potential for treatment or positive change. The latter is a distinct possibility in some jurisdictions, where training schools offer mere custodial care and little that would promote rehabilitation. In such circumstances the negative effects of the disposition (association with delinquent peers and deterioration of family and community ties) may well outweigh any minimal benefit of removing the juvenile from home and neighborhood.

Finally, a juvenile may be ordered to one of two equally viable disposition options, but to the one that is the more restrictive of the two. For reasons noted in the previous example, the risks associated with the more restrictive and isolative disposition may deter the treatment process, thus detracting from the extent of gain that might otherwise have been possible in the less restrictive option.

The literature contains virtually no reliable information with which one could estimate the prevalence of these possible types of "diagnostic error" in juvenile court disposition proceedings. It is difficult to imagine that their frequency is negligible, however, given the complexity of the diagnostic process in both legal and clinical situations.

## Procedural Remedies

*Strategy A.* There would seem to be no reason to decrease procedural options, other than to dismantle those training schools that can provide little beyond custodial care. Even this action, however, must be considered cautiously, since the lack of any secure facilities for juveniles might increase the court's use of the option to transfer juveniles to criminal court jurisdiction in cases where community safety is a major concern.

*Strategy B.* Among changes in decision standards that might offer some protection against undue risk to juveniles would be legislation of the rule of least restrictive alternative, which currently exists in a minority of states.

*Strategy C.* Changes in decision procedures are more feasible, perhaps, than the above-mentioned strategies. Many courts make use of mental health and social work professionals to assess the juvenile and describe to the court the juvenile's character and needs. A far greater problem in many courts is maintaining an accurate and informed perspective on the range of available treatment options, the nature and quality of treatment programs within each option, and the programs' perceived or empirical effectiveness with juveniles of various types. This has led three national advisory panels[27] to recommend certain schemes for decision making; their intent has been to structure and clarify the disposition process, to reduce discretion, and thereby to reduce the potential for bias, confusion, and error in disposition judgments.

For example, recommendations have urged that the full range of procedural options in a jurisdiction be classified into three categories: (a) nominal (e.g., reprimand); (b) conditional (e.g., probation while at home); and (c) custodial (e.g., removal from home). The decision process would first involve selecting and justifying one of these categories in a specific case, based on the seriousness of offense, culpability, age, and prior record. Once chosen, the category's available treatment options would then be matched (in a discretionary manner) with the juvenile's needs.

For a system of this type to be most effective, one might consider mandating a court's periodic collection and review of basic information about each procedural option (e.g., a treatment center's current physical, staffing, and administrative operations, treatment programs available, and information on effectiveness). This data base, to which the court and defense attorney alike could refer, might promote clarity and rationality in the disposition decision process.

## Research to Guide
## Procedural Changes

We have examined procedural rules in four areas of decision making in the juvenile justice system, as well as reasons for concern about the psychological well-being of juveniles to whom these procedures are applied. We have also examined potential revisions of rules in light of those concerns. Looking across this four-part discussion, it is apparent that many of the observations and recommendations do not rest firmly upon empirical ground, but instead are based on a variety of untested assumptions. One of the social sciences' primary roles in the legal reform process, then, would be to produce more reliable information with which to consider procedural changes in juvenile justice.

Research on procedural issues in juvenile justice must consider that the justice system has many goals. One of these goals is to promote the welfare of juveniles, providing needed rehabilitation and doing so in a manner that minimizes risk to their mental health and development. This goal is the main focus of the present chapter. The system, however, has several other goals, as noted earlier in this chapter. It is charged also with protecting the public, reducing the incidence of juvenile offenses, and in other ways considering the interests of the community. It is required to administer justice by procedures that meet statutory standards and to do so with greatest efficiency. It must also meet fiscal obligations. These several goals frequently are in conflict in juvenile court practices, with an increase in the attainment of any one of them almost always being at the cost of another. Despite policy statements that elevate the treatment goal above all others, the various other goals cannot be ignored in social science research and in recommendations for procedural change.

The most valuable research, then, would produce information that can be applied to address as many of these goals as possible: that is, juveniles' mental health and welfare, society's concerns for protection, efficient and careful due process, and economic considerations. We can recommend three types of research, based on these criteria and on current scarcity of information across all areas of procedure discussed in this chapter. These three research recommendations correspond to the three types of procedural rules that have been the structure of analysis for this chapter.

First, there is a critical need for research that documents the consequences of various procedural options within each of the decision making areas that we have reviewed. There are many procedural options (for example, pretrial detention, transfer to criminal court jurisdiction, and various treatment dispositional alternatives) for which we simply have very little reliable information concerning the possible negative consequences for the self-esteem, identity, and mental health of juveniles. Anecdotal information has told us that such consequences do occur; but anecdote teaches us neither the extent of problems nor the types of juveniles who are more likely to be at risk of these consequences. Similarly, many courts do not have reliable information on the benefits of various dispositional options or concerning the types of juveniles for whom particular options have been more or less beneficial. Comprehensive outcome studies of "match and mismatch" between juveniles and treatment programs, such as that of Jesness (1975) in California, are costly in time and money; but evaluation studies with more modest criteria can serve limited yet useful purposes for local jurisdictions.

Research of that type addresses not only the mental health needs of juveniles, but also the juvenile justice system's other goals. Inefficient or inappropriate use of procedural options certainly cannot promote the community's interest in protecting its citizens, the court's interest in a substantive and procedural due process that will promote respect for the law, or the responsible and prudent use of public finances.

A second type of needed research would focus on the content of juvenile justice decision making: that is, the case variables that are employed, or that could be profitably employed, when addressing decision standards. This general topic can be approached from many different directions. The most common approach has been to determine the characteristics of juveniles that differentiate those whom the court found to meet a legal decision standard from those whom it believed did not: for example, differences between juveniles who have or have not been perceived by courts as capable of participating in various legal processes (Grisso, 1981), juveniles who have or have not been detained (Dungworth, 1977; Cohen, 1975a; Sarri, 1974;

Sumner, 1971; Lawlak, 1977), juveniles who have or have not been transferred to criminal courts (Keiter, 1973; Solway & Hays, 1978; Hays, Solway, & Schreiner, 1978; Hays & Solway, 1979; Feld, 1978; Lovinguth,
1981), and juveniles for whom various dispositional alternatives have been
decided (Cohen, 1975b; Cohen & Kluegel, 1978; Thornberry, 1973;
Thomas & Cage, 1977; Scarpetti & Stephenson, 1971; Bailey & Peterson,
1981; Barton, 1976; Carter, 1979; Horwitz & Wasserman, 1980; Mann,
1980). This body of research has exhibited many methodological shortcomings, yet it is a start. It cannot go far by itself, however, because there is no
assurance in such studies that the discriminating variables that they discover
are the ones that influence judicial decisions. More critically, perhaps, the
case variables discovered in these studies have never been able to account
for more than a very small amount of the variance in the judicial decision
outcomes.

The above approach must be accompanied by others. For example, one
may attempt to determine more directly which case variables the decision
makers claim to use in making various decisions according to particular
legal standards (Grisso, 1980). One may then use these or other variables in
studies to determine whether they have validity as predictors of the behaviors and eventualities to which decision standards refer: for example, ability
to participate meaningfully in legal proceedings (Grisso & Lovinguth, 1982;
Grisso, 1981), the likelihood of fleeing prior to trial, intractability to treatment, or failure in particular community dispositional placements. One may
also use external criteria to form groups of particular relevance to decision
standards (e.g., "dangerous" and "nondangerous" juveniles) in order to
search for variables that reliably discriminate between them and therefore
might be of use to juvenile justice decision makers.

We need these kinds of investigations into the validity of case variables
for decision making; yet the complexity of the problem makes this a less
feasible type of research than the former (consequences of procedural
options) or the third type to be proposed. One of the major complicating factors is the tremendous diversity across juvenile courts, and across decision
makers within specific systems, in their use of decision variables. Thus,
generalization from particular study samples to other jurisdictions frequently
is questionable. Further, decisions undoubtedly rest on many variables that
are not case variables as such: for example, community attitudes that influence judicial decisions, political and financial constraints, other system variables, and even the personalities of decision makers themselves (Mulvey &
Saunders, 1982). Our potential to find characteristics of juveniles that will
account for, or could be used to assist, judicial decisions must therefore be
viewed realistically regarding its limitations.

Third, researchers may study processes with which juvenile justice decisions are made. Can decision procedures be developed to improve the con-

sistency and inherent fairness of decisions affecting the psychological well-being of juveniles?

This question, too, can be approached in several ways. One may study whether certain forms of information or the participation of various actors in the decision process contribute to more or less consistent decisions across cases. In contrast, one can employ psychology's sophisticated advances in decision-making theory and research method (Hammond, McClelland, & Mumpower, 1980; Carroll & Payne, 1977; Gottfredson & Gottfredson, 1980; Konecni & Ebbesen, 1982; Lamiell, 1979) to study the decision process at the level of the decision maker's attributions, assumptions, logical processes and uses of information. The payoff for this type of research would occur if we could provide decision makers not with formulae for decisions, but with schemas and structures that would assist them to process available information more reliably. If these schemas could also contribute to more efficient decision making, and if they could incorporate in their structure the principles of due process (see, for example, the final recommendation in the section on dispositions), then we could provide assistance relevant to all of the various goals of the juvenile justice system.

There was a time when psychology's research contributions to the mental health of delinquent juveniles was confined primarily to studies of the etiology of delinquency, or to the development of methods for delinquents' rehabilitation. These are still important research objectives. Yet, by broadening our perspective to examine the effects of procedural rules in legal responses to delinquent youths, we have an opportunity to make use of the wider range of psychology's research methods to promote the psychological well-being of juveniles.

## Notes

1. We have chosen to use juveniles' psychological well-being and mental health as the object of concern because of the expected readership of this book. One could select other objects for concern regarding court procedures—e.g., their compliance with constitutional rights and protections for juveniles, or the extent to which procedural rules are effective in governing the actual practice of juvenile justice personnel.

2. We describe only the most common procedural rules and ignore the considerable diversity of rules across states or local jurisdictions for any given stage of delinquency case processing. Sources of information regarding the states' variations in rules at each stage are cited at various points in the chapter.

3. Information on pretrial interrogation procedures with juveniles has been drawn from Grisso (1981).

4. Grisso and Pomicter (1977) found that in one jurisdiction police attempted interrogations for about three-quarters of all juvenile felony charges.

5. Miranda v. Arizona, 384 U.S. 436 (1966).

6. See, for example, Fare v. Michael C., 442 U.S. 707, 725 (1979), in which the court considered "age, experience, education, background and intelligence."

7. In re Gault, 387 U.S. 1 (1967).

8. For a review of other less fruitful options for reform, see Grisso (1981, Chap. 9).

9. Information about the law in this procedural area, as well as in the subsequent transfer and disposition sections, has been extracted from three unpublished working reports by the second author of this chapter. These reports are comprehensive legal reviews and syntheses of the relevant statutes for all fifty states and the District of Columbia, complete to December 1, 1982 and with statute citations. The working papers were prepared by the second author and the National Juvenile Law Center, Inc., on contract from NIMH Research Grant MH-35090 (Psychological Definitions of Concepts in Juvenile Law) to the first author. Copies of working reports 10 (Detention), 11 (Transfer), and 12 (Disposition) are available upon inquiry to the first author.

10. Currently only nine states specifically prohibit the jailing of juveniles under any circumstances, and thirteen other states prohibit the jailing of status offenders.

11. Only four states appear to grant an absolute right for juveniles to be released on bail.

12. Somewhat looser standards apply in most states to police decisions regarding short-term detention of juveniles immediately after they are taken into custody by police. As will be noted under "Decision Procedures," however, greater accountability is required at a detention court hearing, which must occur generally within two days after the juvenile's admission to a detention facility.

13. For an excellent review of factors related to detention decisions, see Mulvey and Saunders (1982).

14. See, for example, report of the National Advisory Committee (1980).

15. Social scientists employing the best statistical methods and vast amounts of data on offender populations have accumulated an impressive body of literature on the prediction of dangerousness. They have concluded (see, generally, Monahan, 1981) that currently there is no way to make such predictions at even modest levels of acceptability. A person's past behavior, however, is among the more fruitful predictors of a person's future behavior, a principle that the IJA/ABA proposed standards take into account.

16. See Note 9, supra. Note, also, that transfer of jurisdiction in some states is called "certification" or "waiver of jurisdiction."

17. We intended to include a section in this chapter on commitment to mental hospitals from juvenile courts. All states provide this option, and many juveniles become involved in a "revolving door" between the mental health and juvenile justice systems. The current lack of reliable information about practices and procedures in this area, however, caused us to forgo its review.

18. In addition to these options, some jurisdictions allow plea bargaining between prosecutors and the attorneys of juveniles.

19. These basic provisions were decided in Kent v. United States, 383 U.S. 541 (1966).

20. Breed v. Jones, 421 U.S. 519 (1975).

21. Many states have taken these and other factors from the Appendix to the U.S. Supreme Court decision in Kent v. United States, 383 U.S. 541, at 565-568 (1966).

22. A few statutes are exceptions to this general rule. For example, Colorado permits transfer automatically on the basis of a record of two or more previously sustained petitions for felony offenses.

23. One should note, however, that sometimes the criminal court trial outcomes of transferred juveniles are *less* severe than the dispositional treatment that might have been provided, had the case been heard in a juvenile court. For example, about one-half of juveniles in the United States who were transferred and found guilty in 1978 received probation or fines, rather than confinement (Academy for Contemporary Problems, 1982), although almost all of them probably would have been confined if adjudicated by juvenile courts. On the other hand, those who were transferred, found guilty, and confined received sentences that promised longer confinement than would have occurred in the juvenile system (Academy of Contemporary Problems, 1982).

24. For example, juvenile justice standards recommended by the IJA/ABA joint commission (1980).

25. For example, the Vermont legislature in 1981 lowered the age of eligibility for transfer from the previous limit of age sixteen to a new limit of age ten. Vt. Stat. Ann. tit. 33, 635a (1981).

26. See Note 9, supra.

27. President's Commission on Law Enforcement and Administration of Justice (1967); National Advisory Committee on Criminal Justice Standards (1976); IJA/ABA (1980).

## *References*

Academy for Contemporary Problems. *Youth in adult courts: Between two worlds.* Washington, DC: U.S. Department of Justice, 1982.

Bailey, W., & Peterson, R. Legal versus extra-legal determinants of juvenile court dispositions. *Juvenile and Family Court Journal,* 1981, *32,* 41-59.

Barthel, J. *A death in Canaan.* New York: Dell, 1977.

Barton, W. Discretionary decision making in juvenile justice. *Crime and Delinquency,* 1976, *22,* 470-480.

Carroll, J., & Payne, J. Judgments about crime and the criminal: A model and a method for investigating parole decisions. In B.D. Sales (Ed.), *Perspectives in law and psychology, V.1: The criminal justice system.* New York: Plenum, 1977.

Carter, J. Juvenile court dispositions: A comparison of status and nonstatus offenders. *Criminology,* 1979, *17,* 341-359.

Cohen, L. *An empirical analysis of the pre-adjudicatory detention of juveniles in Denver.* Washington, DC: U.S. Department of Justice, 1975. (a)

Cohen, L. *Juvenile dispositions.* Washington, DC: Department of Justice, 1975. (b)

Cohen, L. *Pre-adjudicatory detention in three juvenile courts: An empirical analysis of the factors related to detention decision outcomes.* Washington, DC: U.S. Government Printing Office, 1975. (c)

Cohen, L., & Kluegel, J. Determinants of juvenile court dispositions: Ascriptive and achieved factors in two metropolitan courts. *American Sociological Review,* 1978, *43,* 162-176.

Community Research Forum. *An assessment of the national incidence of juvenile suicide in adult jails, lockups, and juvenile detention centers.* Champaign: University of Illinois Press, 1980.

Davis, S. *Rights of juveniles: The juvenile justice system.* New York: Clark Boardman, 1983.

Dungworth, T. Discretion in the juvenile justice system: the impact of case characteristics on prehearing detention. In J.T. Ferdinand (Ed.), *Juvenile delinquency.* Beverly Hills, CA: Sage, 1977.

Feld, B. Reference of juvenile offenders for adult prosecution: The legislative alternative to asking unanswerable questions. *Minnesota Law Review,* 1978. *62,* 515-618.

Gottfredson, J., & Gottfredson, D. *Decision making in criminal justice: Toward the rational exercise of discretion.* Cambridge, MA: Ballinger, 1980.

Grisso, T. *Psychological definitions of concepts in juvenile law.* Research Grant R01-MH35090, National Institute of Mental Health, Rockville, MD: Center for Studies of Crime and Delinquency, 1980.

Grisso, T. *Juveniles' waiver of rights: Legal and psychological competence.* New York: Plenum, 1981.

Grisso, T., & Lovinguth, T. Lawyers and child clients: A call for research. In J. Henning (Ed.), *The rights of children: Legal and psychological perspectives.* Springfield, IL: C.C. Thomas, 1982.

Grisso, T., & Pomicter, C. Interrogation of juveniles: An empirical study of procedures, safeguards, and rights waiver. *Law and Human Behavior,* 1977, *1,* 321-342.

Grisso, T., & Ring, M. Parents' attitudes toward juveniles' rights in interrogation. *Criminal Justice and Behavior,* 1979, *6,* 211-226.

Guggenheim, M. Paternalism, prevention, and punishment: Pretrial detention of juveniles. *New York University Law Review,* 1977, *52,* 1064-1092.

Hammond, K., McClelland, G., & Mumpower, J. *Human judgment and decision making: Theories, methods, and procedures.* New York: Praeger, 1980.

Hays, J., & Solway, K. Psychological characteristics of juveniles against whom waiver of juvenile jurisdiction is considered. *Journal of Forensic Psychology,* 1979, *7,* 55-62.

Hays, J., Solway, J., & Schreiner, D. Intellectual characteristics of juvenile murderers versus status offenders. *Psychological Reports,* 1978, *43,* 80-82.

Horwitz, A., & Wasserman, M. Formal rationality, substantive justice, and discrimination: A study of a juvenile court. *Law and Human Behavior,* 1980, *4,* 103-115.

Inbau, F., & Reid, J. *Criminal interrogation and confessions.* Baltimore, MD: Williams & Wilkins, 1967.

Institute of Judicial Administration/American Bar Association (IJA/ABA). *Juvenile justice standards project.* Cambridge, MA: Ballinger, 1980.

Jesness, C. Comparative effectiveness of behavior modification and transactional analysis programs for delinquents. *Journal of Consulting and Clinical Psychology,* 1975, *43,* 758-779.

Keiter, R. Criminal or delinquent? A study of juvenile cases transferred to the criminal court. *Crime and Delinquency,* 1973, *19,* 528-538.

Kenney, J., & Pursuit, D. *Police work with juveniles and the administration of juvenile justice.* Springfield, IL: C.C. Thomas, 1970.

Kihm, R. Prohibiting secure juvenile detention: Assessing the effectiveness of national standards detention criteria. *Juvenile and Family Court Journal,* 1980, *31,* 3-17.

Konecni, V., & Ebbesen, E. *The criminal justice system: A social-psychological analysis.* San Francisco: Freeman, 1982.

Kramer, J., & Steffensmeier, D. The differential detention/jailing of juveniles: A comparison of detention and non-detention courts. *Pepperdine Law Review,* 1978, *5,* 795-807.

Lamiell, J. Discretion in juvenile justice: A framework for systematic study. *Criminal Justice and Behavior,* 1979, *6,* 76-101.

Lawlak, E. Differential selection of juveniles for detention. *Journal of Research in Crime and Delinquency,* 1977, *14,* 152-165.

Lovinguth, T. *Discriminatory variables in certification of juvenile offenders.* Unpublished doctoral thesis, St. Louis University, St. Louis, MO, 1981.

Mann, C. Courtroom observations of extra-legal factors in the juvenile court dispositions of runaway boys: A field study. *Juvenile and Family Court Journal,* 1980, *31,* 43-52.

Monahan, J. *The clinical prediction of violent behavior.* Rockville, MD: National Institute of Mental Health, 1981.

Mulvey, E., & Saunders, J. Juvenile detention criteria: State of the art and guidelines for change. *Criminal Justice Abstracts,* 1982, *2,* 261-289.

National Advisory Committee on Criminal Justice Standards. *Report of the National Advisory Committee for Juvenile Justice and Delinquency Prevention: Standards for the administration of juvenile justice.* Washington, DC: U.S. Department of Justice, 1980.

National Juvenile Justice Assessment Center. *Reports of the National Juvenile Justice Assessment Center: Juveniles in detention centers and jails (An analysis of state variations during the mid-1970's).* Washington, DC: U.S. Department of Justice, 1980.

President's Commission on Law Enforcement and Administration of Justice. *Task force report: Juvenile delinquency and youth crime.* Washington, DC: U.S. Government Printing Office, 1967.

Sarri, R. *Under lock and key: Juveniles in jails and detentions.* Ann Arbor: National Assessment of Juvenile Corrections, University of Michigan, 1974.

Scarpetti, R., & Stephenson, R. Juvenile court dispositions: Factors in the decision-making process. *Crime and Delinquency,* 1971, *17,* 142-151.

Solway, K., & Hays, J. An intellectual and personality study of juveniles who are petitioned for waiver of juvenile jurisdiction. *Journal of Adolescence,* 1978, *7,* 319-325.

Sumner, H. Locking them up. *Crime and Delinquency,* 1971, *17,* 168-179.

Thomas, C., & Cage, R. The effect of social characteristics on juvenile court dispositions. *Sociological Quarterly,* 1977, *18,* 237-252.

Thornberry, T. Race, socioeconomic status and sentencing in the juvenile justice system. *Journal of Criminal Law and Criminology,* 1973, *64,* 90-98.

Wilkins, L. Policy control, information, ethics, and discretion. In L. Abt & I. Stuart (Eds.), *Social psychology and discretionary law.* New York: VanNostrand Reinhold, 1979.

# 9

# Judging Amenability to Treatment in Juvenile Offenders

## Theory and Practice

**Edward P. Mulvey**
*Western Psychiatric Institute and Clinic*
*University of Pittsburgh*

Amenability to treatment, or likelihood of rehabilitation, is a determination clinicians are often asked to make regarding juvenile offenders. This clinical judgment is a difficult one, however, since it requires a technical expertise that is often sorely lacking. Little is really known about what will work with a given juvenile offender. Moreover, deciding about a youth's treatment often entails deciding about the setting to which the youth will be sent (e.g., institution or community), and ethical considerations regarding community safety and juvenile rights cannot be ignored. Clinicians are placed in the role of "expert," knowing all too well that their expertise is frequently based more on intuitive hunch and personal values than on empirical evidence.

Developing theory and designing research to help the clinician out of this dilemma is a complex task. Judgments about juvenile offenders are made in a context in which social control is intertwined, and often confused, with treatment. Rarely is a decision about services merely a rational matching of the youth and a treatment modality. As a result, understanding amenability determinations and trying to improve their validity requires understanding the process of this decision making as well as the content of the decision itself.

This chapter examines the amenability determination in both theory and practice. It is argued that an integration of these two pictures is necessary in order to construct usable research on this topic. Clinicians are caught in a

Author's Note: This chapter was prepared while the author was supported by a grant from the National Institute of Mental Health (MH 15201-04) at the Urban Systems Institute, Carnegie-Mellon University. J. Fialkov and N.D. Reppucci offered helpful criticism of earlier drafts.

difficult situation, and the hope of being helped by research results rests on the sensitivity of researchers to the phenomenon as it really exists and the self-awareness of clinicians regarding the implications of their status as experts.

## Overview

One of the most basic, long-standing issues in both criminal and civil law is the appropriate balance to be struck between reliance on the rule of law and reliance on individual discretion. As Roscoe Pound noted,

> Almost all of the problems of jurisprudence come down to a fundamental one of rule and discretion, of administration of justice by law and by the more or less trained intuition of experienced magistrates . . . both are necessary elements in the administration of justice, and . . . instead of eliminating either we must partition the field between them. (Pound, 1954, p. 54)

Many actions in both civil and criminal law call for specific discretionary judgments (Shah, 1977; Monahan & Loftus, 1982), but the weight given discretion varies with the particular action in question and the historical period. In general, discretion checks the potential for arbitrary, rule-based decisions, and the rules of legal process limit the idiosyncratic application of the law. In particular cases an observed imbalance of these two forces fosters the evolution of legal standards.

The delicate balance between discretion and the rule of law is particularly important to keep in mind when considering juvenile justice, since probably no other part of the justice system relies as heavily on discretion. Since its inception, the hallmark·of the juvenile court has been its attempt to provide individualized justice by focusing on the characteristics of the individual rather than the offense (Fox, 1970). In addition, rehabilitation has always been the primary aim of the juvenile system (Zimring, 1978; Comment, 1976); and the other commonly recognized crime control methods of deterrence, retribution, and incapacitation (Gibbs, 1975) have been deemed generally inappropriate tactics for juveniles. The mission of the juvenile court, and more recently of the family court, has been to arrive at dispositions providing support and services for a youth and his or her family (Mulvey, 1982). Given this focus, it is not surprising that juvenile court action has been based more on intuition than legal procedure.

This heavy emphasis on "individualized justice" (Pound, 1947) and treatment has spawned an interdependent relationship between the juvenile justice system and mental health practitioners. From the first "court clinics" to the present "assessment centers," social workers, psychiatrists, and psychologists have played a major role in helping the juvenile court assess and treat problem youth (Levine & Levine, 1970; Rothman, 1980). Clinical assessments by professionals have been embraced as a refined tool for accomplishing the primary aim of juvenile justice, since a clear understanding of the particular qualities and needs of a youth has been considered a necessity for successful intervention by the court. Ideally, a mixture of professional expertise and judicial wisdom provide individualized dispositions in the child's best interest.

In addition to assisting in deciding the best course to take with a youth, mental health professionals have also been involved in ensuring that alternatives exist to serve these youths' needs. A service network has arisen, directed primarily toward providing services for problem youth coming before the court (Handler & Zatz, 1982). Mental health professionals assist the court in recommending and providing appropriate services, and the court assists mental health professionals in requiring and funding various treatment options. In a symbiotic fashion, mental health and juvenile justice professionals have forged an individually focused, discretion-based treatment system for problem youth.

However, concerns regarding the ineffectiveness of the present juvenile system for controlling youth crime and for protecting the rights of juveniles have forced reappraisal of the heavy reliance on clinical and judicial discretion. The large number of youthful offenders arrested every year has provided a consistent, disturbing reminder of the present system's inadequacies for preventing crime (Zimring, 1978). Moreover, the nagging issue of just how much a court could do "to" a child in order to do something "for" a child (Allen, 1964) precipitated a string of judicial decisions expanding juvenile rights and calling for greater procedural fairness when a juvenile's loss of liberty is at stake.[1] This redirection toward adversariness was necessary because juveniles were receiving what Justice Fortas (in *Kent v. U.S.*) termed the "worse of two possible worlds"; no due process safeguards against incarceration and no guarantee of effective treatment. Finally, two influential task forces on juvenile justice (Institute for Judicial Administration/American Bar Association, 1980; Twentieth Century Fund, 1978) have openly acknowledged the potentially punitive nature of the juvenile system and called for proportional sentencing rather than individualized programming. The efficacy and fairness of a rehabilitative juvenile system based on individualized treatment are presently open questions.

Informed juvenile justice policy debate has been limited, however, by the surprisingly small amount of empirical data on the operation of the present "rehabilitative" juvenile system. The voluminous juvenile justice literature has provided observational studies of the court process (e.g., Cicourel, 1968; Emerson, 1969; Silberman, 1978, Chap. 9), but little quantifiable data on the exact factors that affect court action. Quantitative data can be obtained from retrospective studies examining the characteristics of juveniles receiving one disposition or decision in comparison to those receiving another outcome (see Barton, 1976, for a general review; Mulvey & Saunders, 1982, for a review of detention decisions; IJA/ABA, 1980, for a review of court dispositions), but these data have significant limitations. Many of the characteristics of the juveniles appear to be chosen for their accessibility in juvenile records, rather than their demonstrated salience to the decision maker, and the high correlation that often exists between many of the factors (such as offense type and sex) often leads to guarded conclusions. The only solid conclusions would seem to be that the juvenile, system is highly variable and that actuarial factors (e.g., number of offenses and age at first offense) are more powerful than clinical factors for explaining offense incidence (Monahan, 1981; Bookin, 1979; Strasburg, 1978; Wolfgang, Figlio, & Sellin, 1972). Moreover, it is safe to say that only limited descriptive and minimal solid empirical data exist regarding the matching of juvenile offenders and treatment alternatives (Sechrest, White, & Brown, 1979).

Perhaps the lack of powerful data on juvenile justice processing is understandable, however, given this system's reliance on discretion over procedure. As emphasized earlier, the avowed primary mission of juvenile justice is one of individualized treatment planning, and case decisions often rest on inferences about the underlying process bringing the youth before the court as much (or more) as on the notion of consistent retribution or deterrence for the acts committed. While social control or punishment motivations do contribute somewhat to decisions in the juvenile system (Malmquist, 1979), these factors are tempered by the primary motive of individualized justice. The result is a highly variable system oriented more toward a belief in the offender's potential for change and less toward "just deserts" (von Hirsch, 1976) or consistency of outcome. Given this heavy reliance on inference and idiographic judgment, it may be inappropriate to expect consistency along legal or sociological dimensions. The juvenile system may be more understandable heuristically as a hybrid of the clinical diagnostic process and the "systems" models associated with adult criminal justice.

A number of researchers have conceptualized juvenile justice as a series of interdependent clinical judgments made by a variety of actors regarding the appropriate course of action to be taken with a particular juvenile (Gottfredson & Gottfredson, 1980; Lamiell, 1979; Blomberg, 1977). Understandably, this conceptualization has led to a different research emphasis than that of previous studies. In this approach, the relationship between juvenile justice outcomes and case characteristics is less important than the factors that consistently affect the judgment process of the professionals in the system. In other words, the content of the decision is less important than the process of the decision. In terms of outcomes of like cases, juvenile justice may not be a terribly consistent "system" across locales (Rubin, 1976), but factors affecting decision making at different points in the processing of juveniles may be consistent. The hope is that understanding the rules governing the interactions between the case, the decision makers, and the conditions in particular locales will help explain the widely observed variance in the juvenile justice system.

Translating this general approach to useful research is obviously an involved task. Potential judgments requiring consideration are numerous. Also, judgments can be amorphous but critical to the mission of juvenile justice (e.g., "the child's best interest") or circumscribed and specific (e.g., the decision to place in a detention facility). Some judgments may be made by one individual (e.g., arrest), while others may be the result of a group process (e.g., institutional release). In general, case characteristics, decision maker characteristics, and organizational pressures will all be necessary considerations, but the weights and forms of these factors will vary considerably with the decision examined. Obviously, no one model will apply across all juvenile justice judgments; separate ones will have to be formulated with careful consideration for the ecological validity (Bronfenbrenner, 1977) of the model used for analysis.

## The Amenability Judgment

Amenability to treatment, or likelihood of rehabilitation, is one of the most basic and pervasive judgments made in the processing of juveniles. Viewed broadly, this judgment reflects the core issue plaguing juvenile justice policy, i.e., the appropriate tension to be maintained between rehabilitation and community safety. Both general policy and individual discretion in juvenile justice must balance treatment and security, and each amenability judgment is really a microcosm of this issue. More important, however, judged amenability is the pragmatic issue upon which an individual juvenile's fate often rests. Responsiveness to certain treatment approaches underpins individual decisions to divert, transfer, or institutionalize (Whitebread & Paulsen, 1974; Sechrest, White, & Brown, 1979). Thus, the amenability judgment has both a symbolic and operational importance. It reflects a larger social debate and at the same time holds very real consequence for youth.

Besides underpinning the logic of the juvenile system, this judgment is also of timely importance, and several recent developments in criminal justice policy and research should keep it as such. First, current diversion and deinstitutionalization policies rely heavily on determinations of amenability to treatment, since both rest on the ability of professionals to distinguish those youth most likely to benefit from community-based alternative treatment from those for whom juvenile justice processing (and possible institutionalization) is appropriate. Much of the political consensus between liberals and conservatives on the issue of diversion assumed the ability of the system to make this distinction (Miller, 1978), and evaluation of this policy will eventually have to address how realistic this hope was and is. Also, diversion "from" the juvenile justice system has become largely diversion "to" alternative services (Carter & Klein, 1976), and the amenability consideration has taken on more direct operational significance in the informal decisions of intake and probation personnel. Second, primarily as a result of reservations about the adequacies of dangerousness predictions, and individual's "need for treatment" has resurfaced as a potentially valid consideration in judging the appropriateness of state intervention with various populations, including juveniles (Cohen, Groth, & Siegel, 1978). This attempt to skirt the problems of dangerousness predictions will probably only bring increased scrutiny of treatment decisions. Finally, the recent focus by criminologists on "career criminals" should fuel the search for discriminators of hard core youth versus malleable youth. Since Wolfgang, Figlio, and Sellin's (1972) finding that a large proportion of crimes were committed by a small number of offenders in a cohort, a major thrust of criminological research has been identification of these "career criminals," with an eye toward maximizing the incapacitation effect associated with imprisonment (Petersilia, 1980). Searching for predictive factors related to juvenile records is considered a potentially fruitful approach to this task (Greenwood, 1982), and early intervention is a desirable policy goal associated with the development of this knowledge (Estrich, Moore, McGillis, & Spelman, 1983).

In sum, the identification of juvenile offenders likely to benefit from treatment is basic to juvenile justice and serves a number of purposes. It is an attractive philosophical compromise between retribution and rehabilitation, and it offers the promise of a more efficient use of limited juvenile justice resources. As we move away from the "state as parent" (Rothman, 1974) and into an era of retributive justice (compare von Hirsch, 1976), the questions about matching youth to treatment or punishment strategies are likely to remain focal.

### The Amenability Judgment in Practice

Although central to juvenile justice, the amenability determination is difficult to isolate in operational terms. It seems to be everywhere in juvenile justice, but nowhere in particular. The amenability judgment is made by varied professionals with varied preconceptions about a broad range of cases under a broad range of circumstances.

A number of different mental health and court personnel can all make judgments regarding a youth's amenability to treatment. A psychiatric referral is not uncommon in many jurisdictions, especially for more serious offenses where incarceration is likely (Ferster & Courtless, 1972). Psychologists regularly perform evaluations of juveniles for dispositions, foster care placement, or community diversion (Rappaport, Lamiell, & Seidman, 1980). Social workers make judgments regarding amenability in court reports for delinquency, protective service, or temporary foster care. Court personnel (mainly probation officers) make recommendations in social histories regarding a juvenile's probable success given various treatment options. Finally, dispositive judgments are rendered by judges after receipt of clinical input and related testimony.

Amenability judgments are also made at a number of different points in juvenile processing, such as diversion, transfer, and disposition. Each different proceeding presents potentially different factors weighing on the amenability judgment, and no single decision equation applies to all hearings where amenability is at issue. In the transfer decision, for example, the consideration of amenability is explicit (usually defined by statute), and must be documented in the judge's written decision. Also, the consequences of a judgment of nonamenability in this hearing is that the juvenile is processed through the adult system. For transfer, the question for the clinical profession is, thus, usually one of whether the youth is treatable at all. In contrast, the diversion and disposition decisions present a much more implicit amenability question, often framed by its interaction with several unstated but influential variables (e.g., concern for public safety and court philosophy). Clinical information in these situations is deemed valuable for matching a juvenile with an appropriate service. The point is that, while pervasive, the amenability determination and the clinical question related to it are far from uniform. Different court proceedings frame the decision differently.

In addition to the wide range of decision makers and proceedings, a further obstacle to isolating the amenability judgment for study arises from the varying definitions of what could constitute "treatment." Obviously, a broad range of services could come under this rubric, and there exists little guidance for limiting the definition of the term. Statutory language appears to assume that professionals have a shared definition of treatment, with provisions regarding treatment usually defining it as "accepted or recognized practice," but rarely listing the specific services. The Virginia statute regarding amenability determinations, for example, merely states that treatment is not limited to psychotherapy or mental health interventions. A partial list of the disparate approaches qualifying as treatment available to juvenile court would thus have to include individual psychotherapy, group therapy, family therapy, advocacy, residential treatment, alternative education, and vocational training. The range is broad.

However, more important than statutory language (although probably equally encompassing) is what professionals making these judgments consider to qualify as treatment. A professional's judgment of the likelihood of success with a particular youth would seem to be inextricably linked to the type of treatment considered. The definition of treatment adopted at the outset places a limit on any judgment of the probability of success. For example, if treatment is considered to be exclusively verbal therapy, the amenability of a youth with low intelligence and limited affect with necessarily be judged as low. Preferred treatment is a filter for professional judgment.

Tangentially, it is also important to remember that the relationship between treatment (the solution) and delinquency (the problem) is an interdependent one (Rappaport, 1977, Chap. 2). Each helps to define the other operationally. Not only does a choice of treatment structure the way a youth's problems will be evaluated, but the general conception of professionals about the causes of delinquency will exert influence over the range of treatments considered in the first place. If delinquency is viewed as arising from enmeshed or diffuse family structures, for example, preferred treatment will probably focus on involving a youth's family members in any program aimed at lasting change. Thus, information about a professional's view of appropriate treatment reflects not only the mediating factors in the amenability judgment, but also indirectly reflects the guiding theory of delinquency adopted by that professional.

It is reasonable to hypothesize that professional judgments regarding appropriate treatment strategies for delinquency are not formed haphazardly or idiosyncratically. Systematic variation probably exists. However, as the partial consideration above shows, the operational factors which may affect this variation are numerous and complex. The judgment of amenability to treatment, so basic to the processing of juvenile offenders, takes on a number of forms; each ostensibly driven by the same ideal, but each involving different actors in different settings.

### The Amenability Judgment in Theory

As a theoretical issue, amenability to treatment is becoming an increasingly important part of the reframing of present research on the efficacy of treatment. Recent reviews of evaluation studies have reported discouraging results concerning the ability of any particular therapeutic approach to change either youthful or adult correctional populations (see, for example, Wright & Dixon, 1977; Lipton, Martinson, & Wilks, 1975; Resmovic, 1979). Overall, treatment efforts have been found to be narrowly conceived, inconsistently implemented, and limited in effect. The result of this wholesale indictment has been a call for more careful, systematic research on the programmatic factors related to the (admittedly few) successful programs

(Wilson, 1980; Sechrest, West, Redner, Phillips, & Yeaton, 1979). The general assumption is that, although the search for any treatment panacea has been a largely misdirected effort, "something" must be working for "someone" under "some conditions." As a result, the task before the field is now considered to be one of specifying and testing conditions of individual predilection and program operation which combine to produce favorable outcomes.

Although a great amount of "normal science" (Kuhn, 1970) is obviously necessary to accomplish this task, the eventual benefits of such an approach would be considerable. Rather than being bogged down in theoretical assumptions about the crime cause that needs remediation, treatment recommendations could be based more on the proven validity of a particular approach with a particular type of client (Glaser, 1975; Palmer, 1975). A treatment's track record, rather than its theoretical popularity, would be the issue determining its use. Before this reliance on proven validity can occur, however, more detailed program descriptions, more valid individual assessments, and more comprehensive interventions are necessary (Sechrest, White, & Brown, 1979). Thus, while direct "template matching" (Bem & Funder, 1978) between offenders and interventions is not presently possible, there is the hope that more rigorous reporting and more sophisticated methodology could eventually lead to treatment recommendations based on such an approach.

The basic premise of the matching approach is not revolutionary. It is important to note that, at present, judgments regarding a youth's amenability to treatment are assumed to be made in light of the match of clients to services, although a solid empirical foundation for these judgments is not available. Clinical practice instead makes its best guess, relying on theory, experience or intuition to match clients with a particular treatment approach. When detailing a treatment plan, it is certainly common to consider a youth's need for such factors as a "supportive environment," "a role model," or "structure." Programs are considered better or worse alternatives based on how much of the dimension needed by the youth will be provided. The push for more predictively valid measures upon which to base matching is largely an attempt to "empiricize" an existing system.

Work on typologies for delinquents has produced an array of both empirically and theoretically derived categorization schemes (see Smiley, 1977, for a review), but the amount of information regarding the matching of these delinquency subtypes to programs is limited. The fact that this line of research is in its infancy is understandable, however, given that classification of general child psychopathology is a relatively recent development in clinical research (Achenbach & Edelbrock, 1978). Moreover, research on delinquents is particularly complicated. Because delinquency is a sociolegal (as opposed to a strictly behavioral) phenomenon, the designation of "delin-quent" depends on a variety of political and social factors beyond those commonly encountered in other investigations of child psychopathology. As a result, increased caution must be exercised regarding such issues as meas-urement validity and sampling strategies (Reppucci & Clingempeel, 1978). Any typological characterization of delinquency runs the risk of portraying the naturally occurring sampling bias of the juvenile justice system as well as characteristics distinctive in the youth observed.

The most widely known theoretically derived typology is that used in the California Treatment Project by Warren and her associates (see Warren, 1971, 1976, 1977). This approach to classification is based on an assess-ment of a juvenile's I-level, or Interpersonal Level of Maturity (Sullivan, Grant, & Grant, 1957), using seven levels that reflect successive stages of general personality development. This classification method was used to assign juveniles to particular treatment options by the California Youth Authority, and follow-up studies have reported differing levels of success with particular I-level to treatment matches. However, a critical reappraisal of these findings (Lerman, 1975) has cast doubt on the validity of the out-come measures, positing that differential processing of the experimental group youth may have produced many of the observed findings.

Other researchers have presented empirically derived typologies, with delinquency subtypes based on groupings of subjects who respond similarly to particular measures (usually behavior checklists or rating scales). This technique is avowedly atheoretical, but potentially valuable to the larger process of theory development. When the empirical solutions obtained make sense in terms of theoretical constructs under consideration, more focused, hypothesis-based research is possible. In general, four empirically derived delinquent subtypes have emerged (under slightly different names) across several studies: unsocialized aggressive, neurotic disturbed, immature-inadequate, and subcultural socialized (Smiley, 1977). Quay and his associ-ates (see Quay, 1975, 1979; Quay & Love, 1977) have presented results about the potential for certain treatment approaches with different subtypes derived using their classification scheme. These results appear promising, but are limited in their applicability by the complexity of the factors in addi-tion to the youth's characteristics that may affect outcome (Quay, 1977).

Unfortunately, theory regarding categorization of treatment strategies for youth is even less developed than that regarding typologies for delinquents. It is generally recognized that the present taxonomy for treatment settings tells us little about the actual operation of a program or the salient dimen-sions related to program effectiveness (Street, Vinter, & Perrow, 1966; Frank & Atkins, 1981). "Group home," for example, may be used to describe treatment settings of different sizes with different philosophies operating under very different rules (Linney, 1982). Appropriate methods for describing and assessing treatment strength and integrity are relatively new challenges for researchers (Sechrest, West, Redner, Phillips, & Yeaton, 1979). More detailed program descriptions coupled with investigations of relevant dimensions that exist across programs (e.g., staff/client ratio, access to community resources) are presently being done, but theory development in this area is currently at the descriptive level.

What we are left with regarding the amenability judgment in theory, therefore, is a framework in its early stages of development. Matching youth to services is accepted as a theoretical refinement to the fruitless task of saying what works universally. Getting a clear picture of what is working for whom under what conditions, however, is just beginning.

## Toward a Practical Theory of Amenability

The discrepancy between the two characterizations of the amenability to treatment judgment given above is striking. In practice, this judgment is a diffuse process, taking on a number of possibly distinct forms. In theory, it is a potentially manageable, but complex, problem of matching characteristics of juveniles with characteristics of programs.

The apparent complexity of the amenability judgment in practice, however, cannot be divorced from the development of theory aimed at guiding these judgments. Remembering Lewin's adage that "theory and facts must be closely related" (Marrow, 1977), consideration of the real world context in which amenability judgments are made would appear to be a necessary step in refining theory and research regarding the matching of youth to treatment services. Considering the real-world dimensions of this judgment process is particularly important, given that research is still at such a descriptive level regarding this question. What one chooses to look at can greatly affect the theories developed subsequently. Moreover, failure to consider the real-world context of these judgments increases the risk of producing a set of interesting, but unusable, social science findings.

There is no doubt that the present theoretical approach to research could provide a valuable part of the information necessary to improve the matching of juveniles and services. As already emphasized, present research tackles the psychometric challenge of enumerating the case and program characteristics that combine to produce success. In essence, this approach is trying to establish the objective, "true" base rates of success for certain services with certain types of cases. Over time, this effort could produce useful, objective information that could result in guidelines for decision making about the placement of youth. In a best-case analysis, implementation of these guidelines could reduce some of the variance now present in juvenile justice processing (see Konecni & Ebbeson, 1982).

Careful consideration of the real-world context surrounding amenability judgments is necessary, however, to guarantee that any information obtained with the present theoretical approach will actually lead to better matching of youth with services. There is considerable evidence that demonstrates that base rate information may be subject to distortion or may be of low priority in judgments about individual cases (Nisbett & Ross, 1980). Given this, it is clear that research about the actual use of this type of information in juvenile justice decision making will be needed to complement any data obtained within the present theoretical framework. In short, data regarding ideal matching will be only as useful as our understanding of actual juvenile justice decision making allows. A useful, full model can emerge only from an integration of the judgment content and the judgment context.

Presently, however, we are only at the preliminary stages of developing any integrated theory of juvenile justice judgments. For example, the predominant underlying assumption of current legal and psychological investigations is that clinical judgments in juvenile justice are rational, "optimization" judgments. It is assumed that decision makers search for the best solution to the problem presented by the case, basing that solution on a fund of clinical knowledge. An alternative hypothesis, however, could be that decision makers really make "satisficing" (Simon, 1976), rather than optimizing, judgments, acting much more like administrative personnel than totally rational problem-solving computers. Thus, instead of formulating the best possible solution, the decision maker may be providing the best compromise answer that balances the many organizational and role pressures of the setting, interpreting the characteristics of the case to conform to these contextual factors. While it is far from clear which of these two possible models best characterizes different judgments in juvenile justice processing, resolution of such a basic applied issue would appear important. The use of base rate information would depend considerably on which of these models of decision making applies at different points in juvenile justice processing, since base rate information should be more influential in an optimization judgment than a satisficing judgment.

## Conclusion

The major purpose of this presentation has been to present a picture of the amenability judgment in practice and theory, and to emphasize that empirical information on the matching of youth to services is necessary, but not sufficient, to effect change in services for problem youth. Short of perfect discrimination using objective measures, the amenability judgment in individual cases will still be discretionary, relying partially on objective base rate information and partially on contextual factors. Some have even commented that, at present, the needs of the youth are relatively minor considerations in the choice of treatment services in juvenile justice (Handler & Zatz, 1982). Yet, the influence of the real-world context on treatment decisions has been given minimal research attention and little theoretical consideration. To assume that this means it is unimportant, however, would be a mistake.

Finally, it should be noted that the fact that firm guidelines for deciding about juvenile treatment are not forthcoming should not be too disturbing. In the larger picture, social science cannot be expected to resolve issues for the legal system. Instead, it can only test the paradigmatic assumptions that guide the law (Friedman & Macauley, 1977). Regarding treatment for juveniles, discretion has been assumed to provide optimal, individualized answers. Social science can perform a valuable service by providing information about the actual and potential operation of this discretion—not with the idea of eliminating discretion from juvenile justice in favor of rules, but to help in (as Pound noted) "partitioning the field between them."

## Note

1. Kent v. United States, 383 U.S. 541, 86 S.Ct. 1045, 16 L.Ed.2d 84 1966; In re Gault, 387 U.S. 1, 87 S.Ct. 1428, 18 L.Ed.2d 527 1967; In re Winship, 397 U.S. 358, 90 S.Ct. 1068, 25 L.Ed.2d 368 1970; and Breed v. Jones, 95 Sup.Ct. 1779 1975.

## References

Achenbach, T., & Edelbrock, C. Classification of child psychopathology: A review and analysis of empirical efforts. *Psychological Bulletin*, 1978, *85(6)*, 1275-1301.

Allen, F.A. *The borderland of criminal justice*. Chicago: University of Chicago Press, 1964.

Barton, W. Discretionary decision making in juvenile justice. *Crime and Delinquency*, 1976, *22*, 470-480.

Bem, D., & Funder, D. Predicting more of the people more of the time: Assessing the personality of situations. *Psychological Review*, 1978, *85*, 485-501.

Blomberg, T. The juvenile court as an organization and decision making system. *International Journal of Comparative and Applied Criminal Justice*, 1977, *1(2)*, 135-145.

Bookin, H. Detention in context: Decisions to detain juveniles in three Massachusetts courts. Unpublished doctoral dissertation, Department of Sociology, Harvard University, 1979.

Brennan, T. *Multivariate taxonomic techniques in criminal justice research*. Washington, DC: National Criminal Justice Reference Service, 1980.

Bronfenbrenner, U. *The ecology of human development*. Cambridge, MA: Harvard University Press, 1977.

Carter, R., & Klein, M.W. (Eds.). *Back on the streets: The diversion of juvenile offenders*. Englewood Cliffs, NJ: Prentice-Hall, 1976.

Cicourel, A.V. *The social organization of juvenile justice.* New York: Wiley, 1968.

Cohen, M., Groth, A., & Siegel, R. The clinical prediction of dangerousness. *Crime and Delinquency,* 1978, *24,* 29-39.

Comment: Rehabilitation as the justification of a separate juvenile justice system. *California Law Review,* 1976, *32,* 805-821.

Emerson, R.A. *Judging delinquents.* Chicago: Aldine, 1969.

Estrich, S., Moore, M.H., McGillis, D., & Spelman, W. *Dealing with dangerous offenders: Executive summary.* Washington, DC: U.S. Government Printing Office, 1983.

Ferster, E.Z., & Courtless, T.F. Juvenile detention in an affluent community. *Family Law Quarterly,* 1972, *6,* 21-32.

Fox, S. Juvenile justice reform: An historical perspective. *Stanford Law Review,* 1970, *22,* 1187-1239.

Frank, S.J., & Atkins, D.M. Policy is one thing; implementation is another: A comparison of community agencies in a juvenile justice referral network. *American Journal of Community Psychology,* 1981, *9*(5), 581-604.

Friedman, L., & Macauley, S. *Law and the behavioral sciences.* Indianapolis: Bobbs-Merrill, 1977.

Gibbs, J.P. *Crime, punishment, and deterrence.* New York: Elsevier, 1975.

Glaser, D. Achieving better questions: A half century's program in correctional research. *Federal Probation,* 1975, *39,* 3-9.

Gottfredson, M.R., & Gottfredson, D.M. *Decision making in criminal justice: Toward the rational exercise of discretion.* Cambridge, MA: Ballinger, 1980.

Greenwood, P. *Selective incapacitation.* Santa Monica, CA: Rand Corporation, 1982.

Handler, J., & Zatz, J. (Eds.). *Neither angels nor thieves: Studies in deinstitutionalization of status offenders.* Washington, DC: National Academy of Sciences, 1982.

Hirsch, A. von. *Doing justice: The choice of punishments.* New York: Hill and Wang, 1976.

Institute for Judicial Administration/American Bar Association (IJA/ABA). *Juvenile justice standards project. Standards relating to court disposition.* Cambridge, MA: Ballinger, 1980.

Konecni, V.J., & Ebbeson, E.B. (Eds.). *The criminal justice system: A social-psychological analysis.* San Francisco: Freeman, 1982.

Kuhn, T. *The structure of scientific revolutions.* Chicago: University of Chicago Press, 1970.

Lamiell, J.T. Discretion in juvenile justice: A framework for systematic study. *Criminal Justice and Behavior,* 1979, *6*(1), 76-101.

Lerman, P. *Community treatment and social control.* Chiciago: University of Chicago Press, 1975.

Levine, M., & Levine, A. *A social history of helping services: Clinic, court, school and community.* New York: Appleton-Century-Crofts, 1970.

Linney, J.A. Alternative facilities for youth in trouble: A descriptive analysis of a strategically selected sample. In J. Handler & J. Zatz (Eds.), *Neither angels nor thieves: Studies in deinstitutionalization of status offenders.* Washington, DC: National Academy of Sciences, 1982.

Lipton, D., Martinson, R., & Wilks, J. *The effectiveness of correctional treatment.* New York: Praeger, 1975.

Malmquist, C.P. Juveniles in adult courts: Unresolved ambivalence. In S. Feinstein & P.L. Giovaccchini (Eds.), *Adolescent psychiatry: Developmental and clinical studies (Vol. 7).* Chicago: University of Chicago Press, 1979.

Marrow, A. *The practical theorist: The life and work of Kurt Lewin.* New York: Teachers College Press, 1977.

Miller, J. The revolution in juvenile justice (from rhetoric to rhetoric). Manuscript published by Kenyon Public Affairs Forum, 1978.

Monahan, J. *Predicting violent behavior: An assessment of clinical techniques.* Beverly Hills, CA: Sage, 1981.

Monahan, J., & Loftus, E. The psychology of law. *Annual Review of Psychology, 1982, 33,* 441-475.

Mulvey, E.P. Family courts: The issue of reasonable goals. *Law and Human Behavior, 1982, 6*(1), 49-64.

Mulvey, E.P., & Saunders, J.T. Juvenile detention criteria: State of the art and guidelines for change. *Criminal Justice Abstracts, 1982, 14,*1.

Nisbett, R., & Ross, L. *Human inference: Strategies and shortcomings of social judgment.* Englewood Cliffs, NJ: Prentice-Hall, 1980.

Palmer, T. Martinson revisited. *Journal of Research in Crime and Delinquency, 1975, 12,* 133-152.

Petersilia, J. Criminal career research: A review of recent evidence. In N. Morris & M. Tonry (Eds.), *Crime and justice: An annual review of research (Vol. 2).* Chicago: University of Chicago Press, 1980.

Pound, R. The future of socialized justice. In National Probation Association (Ed.), *Society's stake in the offender. 1946 yearbook.* New York: National Probation Association, 1947.

Pound, R. *An introduction to the philosophy of law.* New Haven, CT: Yale University Press, 1954.

Quay, H. Typologies and treatment for juvenile delinquency. In N. Hobbs (Ed.), *Issues in the classification of children.* San Francisco: Jossey-Bass, 1975.

Quay, H. The three faces of evaluation: What can be expected to work. *Criminal Justice and Behavior, 1977, 4*(4), 341-354.

Quay, H. Classification. In H.C. Quay & J.S. Werry (Eds.), *Psychopathological disorders of childhood (2nd ed.).* New York: Wiley, 1979.

Quay, H., & Love, C.T. The effect of a juvenile diversion program on rearrests. *Criminal Justice and Behavior, 1977, 4,* 377-396.

Rappaport, J. *Community psychology.* New York: Holt, Rinehart and Winston, 1977.

Rapport, J., Lamiell, J., & Seidman, E. Ethical issues for psychologists in the juvenile justice system: Know and tell. In J. Monahan (Ed.), *Who is the client? The ethics of psychological intervention in the criminal justice system.* Washington, DC: American Psychological Association, 1980.

Reppucci, N.D., & Clingempeel, W.G. Methodological issues in research with correctional populations. *Journal of Consulting and Clinical Psychology, 1978, 46*(4), 727-746.

Resmovic, E.L. Methodological considerations in evaluating correctional effectiveness: Issues and chronic problems. In L. Sechrest, S.O. White, & E.D. Brown (Eds.), *The rehabilitation of criminal offenders: Problems and prospects.* Washington, DC: National Academy of Sciences, 1979.

Rothman, D. The state as parent: Social policy in the progressive era. In Q. Gaylin, I. Glasser, S. Marcus, & D. Rothman, *Doing good.* New York: Pantheon, 1974.

Rothman, D. *Conscience and Convenience.* Boston: Little, Brown, 1980.

Rubin, T. The eye of the juvenile court judge: A one-step-up view of the juvenile justice system. In M.W. Klein (Ed.), *The Juvenile justice system.* Beverly Hills, CA: Sage, 1976.

Sechrest, L., West, S.G., Redner, R., Phillips, M.A. & Yeaton, W. Introduction. In L. Sechrest et al. (Eds.), *Evaluation studies review annual (Vol. 4).* Beverly Hills, CA: Sage, 1979.

Sechrest, L., White, S.O., & Brown, E. (Eds.). *The rehabilitation of criminal offenders: Problems and prospects.* Washington, DC: National Academy of Sciences, 1979.

Shah, S. Dangerousness: Some definitional, conceptual, and public policy issues. In B. Sales (Ed.), *Perspectives in law and psychology: The criminal justice system.* New York: Plenum, 1977.

Silberman, C. *Criminal violence, criminal justice.* New York: Random House, 1978.

Simon, H. *Administrative behavior (3rd ed.).* New York: Free Press, 1976.

Smiley, W.C. Classification and delinquency: A review. *Behavioral Disorders,* 1977, *2*(4), 184-200.

Strasburg, P. *Violent delinquents.* New York: Monarch, 1978.

Street, D., Vinter, R., & Perrow, C. *Organization for treatment: A comparative study of institutions for delinquents.* New York: Free Press, 1966.

Sullivan, C.E., Grant, M.Q., & Grant, J.D. The development of interpersonal maturity: Applications to delinquency. *Psychiatry,* 1957, *20,* 373-385.

Twentieth Century Fund. *Confronting youth crime: Report of the Twentieth Century Fund Task Force on Sentencing of Young Offenders.* New York: Holmes & Meier, 1978.

Warren, M.Q. Classification of offenders as an aid to efficient management and effective treatment. *Journal of Criminal Law, Criminology and Police Science,* 1971, *62,*(2).

Warren, M.Q. Intervention with juvenile delinquents. In M. Rosenheim, (Ed.), *Pursuing justice for the child.* Chicago: University of Chicago Press, 1976.

Warren, M.Q. Correctional treatment and coercion: The differential effectiveness perspective, *Criminal Justice and Behavior,* 1977, *4*(4), 355-376.

Whitebread, C., & Paulsen, M. *Juvenile law and procedure.* Reno, NV: National Association of Juvenile Court Judges, 1974.

Wilson, J.Q. "What works?" revisited: New findings on criminal rehabilitation. *The Public Interest,* 1980, *61,* 3-17.

Wolfgang, M.E., Figlio, R.M., & Sellin, T. *Delinquency in a birth cohort.* Chicago: University of Chicago Press, 1972.

Wright, W.E., & Dixon, M.C. Community prevention and treatment of juvenile delinquency: A review of evaluation studies. *Journal of Research in Crime and Delinquency,* 1977, *14*(11), 35-62.

Zimring, F.E. Background paper. In *Confronting youth Crime: Report of the Twentieth Century Fund Task Force on Sentencing Policy Toward Young Offenders.* New York: Holmes & Meier, 1978.

# 10

# Deinstitutionalization in the Juvenile Justice System

## Jean Ann Linney
### University of South Carolina

In 1972 the Massachusetts juvenile correctional system closed the doors to its state training schools. Residents were either sent home or placed in other nonsecure programs. To date this has been the most dramatic action to deinstitutionalize the juvenile justice system. In 1974 Congress endorsed a policy of deinstitutionalization for the juvenile justice system with passage of the Juvenile Justice and Delinquency Prevention Act, "an act to provide a comprehensive, coordinated approach to the problems of juvenile delinquency." This policy spearheaded federal initiative to stimulate reform of disposition procedures for juvenile offenders and the development of alternative placements (Handler & Zatz, 1982).

This chapter examines the impact of the deinstitutionalization policy with a primary focus on the use of residential alternatives for disposition. It begins with a brief overview of the historical foundations of the juvenile justice system and the conditions that precipitated deinstitutionalization policy. The major goals of deinstitutionalization and the federal legislation supporting it are highlighted, followed by a review of what is known about the impact of these policies on the service system. The last section considers the legal implications of these systemic changes for youth in the system.

Deinstitutionalization and related reform in the juvenile justice system (e.g., procedural standards, decarceration, and diversion) reflect a changing focus from the historical tradition of *parens patriae* as legal ideology to a more civil liberties/children's rights model. During the last fifteen years there have been some far reaching changes in the legal proceedings for juvenile offenders, which reflect this changing ideology. Each reform has been directed primarily at one component of the juvenile justice system but each change has also had repercussions for the other parts of the system. Hence, it is almost impossible to isolate the effects on the system that are attributable to deinstitutionalization alone. The discussion here focuses more on what patterns of change have been observed in the use of the service system rather than identification of causal relationships between specific policy change and systemic outcomes. It is important to note at the outset that the reforms of interest here have had the most notable impact on minor offenders and "problem youth" rather than the serious or repeat offender. Changes in the service system, apart from the use of institutions, have generally involved the nonserious, nonviolent offender.

## Conceptual and Historical Underpinnings of the Juvenile Justice System

The juvenile justice system is rooted in the legal doctrine of parens patriae, which makes it the state's responsibility to intervene in the lives of wayward youth. Acting as concerned parent, the court has developed a treatment rather than exclusively punitive model of intervention. As a result, discretion in the handling of cases has been the system's hallmark—discretion that was intended to enhance the system's flexibility in providing individualized justice in the best interests of the child (Rothman, 1980), in the same manner that a wise parent would handle misbehavior from his/her own child.

For over 300 years the state's authority to intervene in the lives of juveniles has gone essentially unchallenged in the courts, with one notable exception. In 1875 the Illinois Supreme Court ruled in O'Connell v. Turner[1] that a child's right to liberty could not be infringed for any reason without due process of the law. The court held that deprivation of liberty for a wayward child was equally as heinous as such deprivation for an adult. Despite this rhetoric, the court did not obviate the parens patriae doctrine substantiating state intervention, nor did it suggest that parents have complete authority to handle their children as they see fit. Rather, the court focused on the form of state intervention and called for methods and placements that minimized the restraint of liberty. The form and process of intervention, rather than the question of whether state intervention in the lives of juveniles is warranted and beneficial, has remained the focus of debate for the last century.

For the first sixty years of the juvenile court system, intervention by the state was portrayed as almost a privilege, or perhaps a stroke of good fortune for wayward, delinquent, or neglected youth. Judge Julian Mack of the juvenile court in Chicago reflects this perspective.

> Why is it not the duty of the state, instead of asking merely whether a boy or girl has committed a specific offense, to find out what he is, physically, mentally, and morally, and then if it learns that he is treading the path that leads to criminality, to take him in charge, not so much to punish as to reform, not to degrade but to uplift, not to crush but to develop, not to make him a criminal but a worthy citizen. (Mack, 1909, p. 107)

Youth in trouble were seen as needing individualized intervention to deter them from a life of social decline. The particular form of deviance, whether it be minor crime or disobedience, was viewed as a sign of more serious problems if no intervention was forthcoming. These early notions of intervention as prevention broadened the scope of concern of the juvenile court system and resulted in a blurring of the categories of youth to be handled by the legal system—a trend that continued into the 1960s.

Framing intervention as beneficial, rehabilitative, potentially preventive treatment obviated the need for consideration of due process in disposition. This position was clearly supported in *Commonwealth of Pennsylvania v. Fisher*, when the court held that

> (1) When the state's purpose is to rescue and rehabilitate the child, whatever means it must use to do so are justified; and (2) inasmuch as punishment is not the *object* of state action, procedural guarantees are both unnecessary and inappropriate. (Zatz, 1982, p. 22)

Changing conceptions of deviance and social reforms during the Progressive Era, 1840-1920 (Levine & Levine, 1970; Rothman, 1971), led to more widespread use of residential treatment facilities (houses of refuge and asylums) and foster family placement (Garlock, 1979) for wayward and neglected youth. These out-of-home placements were based on the logic that

> by removing minor offenders—that is, idle, vagrant, deserted or wayward children—from the setting that nurtured their depravity and by placing them in surroundings that would instill the values of hard work, self-discipline, and obedience, the public safety as well as the best interests of such children would be served. (Zatz, 1982, p. 16-17).

At the turn of the century, the juvenile court became the center of this rehabilitative child saving effort (Platt, 1971). It provided the forum for coordination of services to youth and a mechanism for multiple groups to collaborate in this effort (social workers, teachers, psychologists). The court drew support from public and private helping professionals who advocated treatment, child welfare advocates interested in protection, and institution administrators who provided residential placements. The court as broker of services offered legal legitimacy to a variety of rehabilitative activities with youth.

The history of this child-caring structure rooted in the doctrine of parens patriae and the moral philosophy of "child saving" resulted in a system in which the state had broad jurisdiction to intervene and the right to exercise wide judgment regarding the intervention. The court was mandated to maintain moral as well as legal order, and to implement treatment procedures to correct both social and emotional problems (Empey, 1973). Individualized treatment for each offender was introduced during the Progressive Era (Rothman, 1980). The degree of individualization proposed required a system with broad discretion and flexibility. The system was based on the prevalent assumption that intervention is at worst benign, and as such there was little concern with the potential problem of overidentification of youth, intervening with "false positives," or protection of liberty and due process.

This rationale for involvement with youth was generally accepted for the first fifty years following the development of the juvenile court. During the 1960s, however—in the context of social reform, institutional scrutiny, and rising juvenile crime rates (Empey, 1973)—attention was drawn to the juvenile court system and its effectiveness in handling the problems of youth. The zeitgeist enveloping the civil rights movement raised consciousness about the protection of civil liberties, due process, and equal protection under the law. In the mental health and treatment realm this movement focused on confinement in the name of treatment,[2] the right to refuse and consent to treatment,[3] and commitment proceedings.[4] Each of these had relevance for proceedings in the juvenile court and corrections system as well.

The 1960s witnessed a series of horrifying exposes on the conditions of the society's asylums and "total institutions" (Goffman, 1961), including the plight of youth in correctional institutions (euphemistically named "learning centers," "training schools," "forestry camps," and "youth homes;" Dean & Reppucci, 1974). Lemert (1951) argued that the juvenile justice system was creating and compounding the problems of youth by labeling and stigmatizing those who became enmeshed in the system. Schur (1973) proposed that no intervention ought to be the method of choice. Studies of "hidden" delinquency (Gold, 1966, 1970) indicated that delinquent activity was far more prevalent than anyone imagined, and that delinquent activity might be a normal part of adolescent rebellion and the process of maturation.

By the late 1960s there was general agreement that the juvenile justice system needed change. The justifications for change and the locus of change were numerous, e.g., humaneness required the creation of minimum standards and protection of the youths incarcerated; due process required protection of civil liberties; the need for effective treatment required alternative dispositions, a greater number of options, and diversion away from the system or into another service system; and, finally, a need for efficiency called for less emphasis on minor offenders and nonoffenders who might best be excluded from the system altogether. In addition, there were supporters among fiscal conservatives who believed that dismantling the institutional system and narrowing the jurisdiction of the juvenile court would result in substantial monetary savings. Testa (1982) suggests that these multiple forces can be clustered into two predominant camps: (1) moderates who advocated curtailment of the punitive aspects of the system in support of treatment in more benign institutions, and (2) radicals who advocated curtailment of intervention altogether. The outcomes of this general reform activity reflect both of these positions—the moderates achieving reform in the nature of placements and the humaneness of intervention, and the radicals succeeding in limiting the degree of penetration into the system for status offenders and the establishment of procedural safeguards for court proceedings.

## Reforms to the
## Juvenile Justice System

### Protection of Due Process and Liberty Rights

A handful of landmark Supreme Court decisions have created substantial change in juvenile justice procedures. The most significant of these cases was *In re Gault*.[5] *Gault* established the liberty interests of juveniles as legitimate, as separate from their parents, and of higher priority than custody interests. This decision guaranteed the juvenile's right to due process in adjudication proceedings. The Supreme Court's opinion in *Gault* stated that unbridled discretion was potentially dangerous and in so doing raised questions about one of the primary characteristics of the juvenile justice system. Further, and of great importance to disposition proceedings, *Gault* distinguished punishment from treatment.

Horowitz (1977) has suggested that the deinstitutionalization and diversion movements were motivated by anticipation of the implications of *Gault* for the disposition and corrections components of the juvenile justice system. The affirmation of liberty rights as paramount over custody rights implies that the restrictiveness and therapeutic value of placement options should be considered. The due process protections of *Gault* restricted the discretion characteristic of the parens patriae court. In addition, the Court's opinion suggested that the treatment offered to youth so cavalierly may be punitive and damaging. In essence, *Gault* said that youth needed to be protected from the juvenile justice system.

The concerns of *Gault* are reflected in the disposition philosophy of diversion and deinstitutionalization, i.e., removing youth from the correctional system. The tensions between treatment and punishment, and between liberty rights and custody rights, appear to have been balanced in a disposition philosophy of the "least restrictive alternative." Theoretically, in the least restrictive placement both punishment and restraint of liberty are minimized.

### The Limits of Treatment and Rehabilitation

Several "blue ribbon" panels (e.g., President's Commission on Law Enforcement and Administration of Justice, 1967) and standard setting groups (e.g., Institute of Judicial Administration/American Bar Association, 1977) called for changes in the form and philosophy of intervention with juveniles. These groups specifically called for diversion of youth away from the juvenile justice system, decarceration of status offenders and nonoffenders (i.e., dependent and neglected children), and deinstitutionalization of youth in the corrections system. Morse and Whitebread (1982) suggest that these panel reports and standards resulted in a conceptual reform of the medical model of intervention into a "just-deserts" model of juvenile justice.

> The older medical model viewed the juvenile as the relatively helpless victim of psychosocial forces over which he or she had little control, so the system prescribed discretionary therapeutic justice. The newer view considers older juveniles—say those over fourteen years— reasonably autonomous and capable of controlling their antisocial behaviors so the sanction should be proportionate to the gravity of the offense and discretion should be substantially reduced. (Morse & Whitebread, 1982, p. 7)

This conceptual reform was concomitant with an erosion of confidence in the treatment system's potential to rehabilitate or reform anyone (Morse & Whitebread, 1982). The negative aspects of the correctional setting began to outweigh any potential positive outcome, and the correctional setting was increasingly viewed as a last resort.

### Distinguishing Status Offenders
### from Delinquent Youth

The just-deserts model of justice and the recognition that rehabilitation might be more punishment than treatment contributed to growing concern about the inappropriateness of placements for some types of youth (see Handler & Zatz, 1982). Attention was drawn specifically to status offenders and other nonoffenders handled by the juvenile court. Reformers held that these youth had not committed crimes and therefore should not be punished or processed in the same manner as delinquent youth. The historical trend of blurring categories of youth was reversed somewhat, and sharper distinctions were made regarding the adjudication and disposition of status offenders and delinquents. For example, in 1971 Wisconsin passed legislation that prohibited truants, runaways, and incorrigible youth from being sent directly to correctional institutions and, in 1973, legislation prohibiting commitment of status offenders to state institutions. Pennsylvania legislation in 1972 separated delinquent from "deprived" children and placed restrictions on the placement options for deprived children. Utah began the process of deinstitutionalization with legislation in 1971 removing certain types of youthful offenses from juvenile court jurisdiction.

### Landmark Legislative Action

Decarceration, diversion, and deinstitutionalization policies were legislated in the Juvenile Justice and Delinquency Prevention Act (JJDPA) of 1974 as amended. The policy goals of the JJDPA reaffirm the state's responsibility to intervene on behalf of troublesome youth. The act distinguishes among minor offenders, status offenders, and delinquent youth; however, it presumes that status offenses (e.g., truancy and incorrigibility), school problems, and abandonment or parental neglect may lead to more serious delinquency. The act finds that

> understaffed, overcrowded juvenile courts; probation services, and correctional facilities are not able to provide individualized justice or effective help; present juvenile courts, foster and protective care programs, and shelter facilities are inadequate to meet the needs of the countless abandoned and dependent children, who because of this failure to provide effective services may become delinquent. (P.L. 93-415, JJDPA, Title I, Sec. 101 (2)(3))

Although it acknowledges differences between types of offenses and nonoffenses, the language of the act affirms the predelinquency model and calls for intervention with nondelinquent youth. It continues to support the individualized model of intervention.

The major service-related policy goals of JJDPA are to reduce or limit penetration into the correctional system for status offender and nonoffender youth and to redirect the form of treatment for youth served by the juvenile justice system. More specifically, the act intends (1) to restrict placement of status offenders and nonoffender youth in secure detention or other secure correctional settings (decarceration); (2) to discourage comingling of status offender and delinquent youth in residential placement and comingling of youth and adults in any correctional or detention facility; (3) to encourage diversion of status offenders from the juvenile justice system wherever possible; and (4) to encourage the use of alternative community-based treatment settings rather than institutional correctional facilities (deinstitutionalization). This federal action regarding disposition options reflected the growing concern for the liberty rights of juveniles affirmed by the Supreme Court in *Gault*, and increasing recognition of the iatrogenic effects of involvement in correctional settings. It does not, however, advocate nonintervention, but rather intervention in a different form or in alternative settings. Reduction in the census of state training schools is an implied goal of the policy, although funds to the states were dependent on reduction in the census of nonoffender youth only, along with concomitant changes in the state code.

## Systemic Impact of Reform: Direct Effects

It is almost impossible to isolate the unique contribution of deinstitutionalization to changes affecting youth in the system or the workings of the service system. The simultaneous movements toward diversion and procedural reform have developed interdependently, e.g., youth deinstitutionalized may be placed in a program developed as part of a diversion effort; changing adjudication procedures may have resulted in alternative pathways through the juvenile justice system or out of it altogether for minor offenders or nonoffenders. There is no doubt that changes in other juvenile justice procedures have had effects on the desired outcomes of deinstitutionalization.

The implementation of deinstitutionalization has varied by locality and has been accomplished via changing definitions of who is eligible for institutional placement, changing the nature of the institutional settings, creating or utilizing alternative settings, or (as in the case of Massachusetts) closing the institutions by administrative order. Individual states and localities have proceeded at their own pace in changing their codes and developing alternatives. However, there are some important changes in the functioning of the service system that have implications for broad deinstitutionalization goals, specifically the use of institutional placements and the development of alternative methods or procedures for disposition.

### The Use of Institutions

Most analysts conclude that (with the exception of Massachusetts) there has been no significant decline in the use of secure facilities for youth

(Coates, Miller, & Ohlin, 1978; Hylton, 1982). Like deinstitutionalization in the mental health system, the institutional settings still take the lion's share of the corrections budget, and as such remain a priority in the treatment system (Hylton, 1982; Wolfle, 1980). A report in *The Economist* in September 1978 indicates that, for the nation as a whole, only 17 percent of juvenile lawbreakers are treated outside of institutions ("Out with Institution," 1978). Massachusetts boasts an 89 percent noninstitutionalized rate, but the next highest state is South Dakota with 59 percent. Vinter, Downs, and Hall (1975) concluded from their national evaluation:

> Despite the much heralded movement toward handling adjudicated delinquents within communities where they live, the traditional training school or public institution continues to be the dominant choice for incarcerating juvenile offenders in the care and custody of state agencies. (p. 9)

Lerman (1980) examined change in institutional use by type of secure placement. He concluded that "the overall trend (since 1950) is increased use of jails and detention and private correctional facilities" (p. 290). He does not find an increase in the use of public training schools. His analysis indicates that the total rate of confinement per 100,000 youths has increased since 1950, implying that any reduction in one type of institutional setting (e.g., public training schools) has been more than compensated by increases in other types of secure residential placements.

The conclusions on institutional use are based on data up to 1975. Given the incentive and impetus of compliance with JJDPA by 1980, there may be some changes in these patterns of institutional use post-1975. Those analyses remain to be done. The parallels between deinstitutionlization in juvenile justice and mental health and mental retardation offer only minimal promise of alteration in this pattern, however. The difficulties of dismantling the institutional settings are parallel (see Levine, 1981; Wolfle, 1980; Miller & Ohlin, 1976), and the two systems have faced similar resistance in developing alternatives (Klein, 1979; Linney, 1982).

## Community-Based Alternatives

The JJDPA identifies the community-based program as the treatment of choice for adjudicated youth. The act defines community-based facility, program, or service as

> a small, open group home or other suitable place located near the juvenile's home or family and programs of community supervision and service which maintain community and consumer participation in the planning, operation, and evaluation of their programs which may include, but are not limited to, medical, educational, vocational, social, and psychological guidance, training, counseling, alcoholism treatment, drug treatment, and other rehabilitative services. (JJDPA, Title I, Sec. 103(1))

In the enthusiasm to eliminate the ills of the institutional settings, reformers have embraced the notion of community-based facilities. The degrading and unjust conditions of correctional facilities prior to the 1960s were believed to be endemic in the institutional setting. Thus, more humane conditions conducive to rehabilitation were sought in noninstitutional settings.

Little is known about the nature or effectiveness of these community-based alternatives for youth (Coates, 1981) or how they differ from the institutions they were intended to replace. There is also little conceptual agreement on what constitutes being "community-based" and the degree to which such a notion can be accomplished or is consistent with societal notions about delinquents and troublesome youth.

There are many forms of community-based facilities and great diversity among them (Coates et al., 1978; Linney, 1982; McEwen, 1978). Localities include foster care, group homes, and other residential treatment facilities in their roster of community-based alternatives. The hope of reformers was that the alternatives developed would be smaller, more humane, provide more treatment and offer a more normalizing experience for the youth (Rosenheim, 1976), involving both the youth's family and community in an integrated program. Overall, the alternatives appear to be more humane than the pre-reform era institutions (Linney, 1982; McEwen, 1978). They are generally smaller than the state correctional facilities. In terms of treatment and normalization, there is so much diversity that generalizations are difficult. Without a conceptual model of the quantitative and qualitative dimensions of the concept "community-based," the programs have developed in diverse ways. Coates et al. (1978) observe,

> Much of what has heretofore passed as community-based must be recognized for what it is—the establishment of small institutions that nevertheless remain just as isolated as the larger institutions they were designed to augment or replace. (Coates et al., 1978, p. 20)

It is clear that being smaller, nonsecure, and located in the middle of a city does not necessarily constitute being noninstitutional or normalizing.

> The extent to which the out-of-home experience parallels that of home-living is more formally restricted by (a) the degree of supervision of resident activity afforded by program rules, (b) the limits on the youth's freedom to leave the facility premises, and (c) the availability of opportunities to become involved

in nonprogram activities. Most facilities maintain a "structured" program that has limitations on the youth's choice of activity and companions. The very existence of a program (i.e., rather than a family-living environment) renders these facilities at least marginally institutional, even though they do not have the blatantly depersonalizing and controlling features of the stereotypic institutional setting. (Linney, 1982, p. 173)

CHINS (child in need of service) and delinquent youth are served by these programs with little distinction between legally defined categories. With the increasing use of the term "emotionally disturbed" to describe youth in trouble, behavior, attitude, and disposition history—rather than legal status—seem to correlate with placement. This is more consistent with the parens patriae traditions of the juvenile justice system than with the just-deserts model described by Morse and Whitebread (1982). The programs function as alternatives to the institutional setting in that a youth is likely to be placed in the less restrictive community setting before going to the institutional facility. If the youth completes the program and remains out of trouble, the facility has served its alternative function; however, for those youth who fail to complete the community-based program or who return to court, commitment to the correctional facility remains an option.

### Systemic Impact of Reform:
### Indirect Effects and Unintended Outcomes

#### Recategorization and Relabeling

The data consistently show that status offenders and nonoffender youth have been removed from the institutional correctional facilities (Handler & Zatz, 1982; Hylton, 1982) and in large part from secure detention. What is apparent is that few or no youths are placed in these facilities on a charge that is considered a status offense. Many have speculated, however, that relabeling or recategorization of youth may be occurring (Mulvey & Hicks, 1982; Spergel, Lynch, & Korbelik, 1980). For example, a young girl who takes $20 from her father's wallet before she runs away from home could be charged with the delinquent offense of petty larceny or the status offense of runaway. These charges lead to different outcomes within the juvenile justice system. They potentially open different treatment doors. It is not clear to what extent those in institutions now are the same types of youth who would have been there ten years ago as status offenders, or to what extent the delinquent or CHINS petition is used as a tool to acquire services. Spergel and colleagues (1980) suggest that these kinds of relabeling occur more as a result of organizational resources and for instrumental purposes than on ideological grounds. As the state codes regarding juvenile adjudication and disposition have changed, decision makers may be practicing some kinds of relabeling in order to acquire the service or disposition they believe to be necessary for a youth.

## Growth of Alternatives

Alternatives to the "red brick training schools" have developed in many places. Both state and federal monies have been directed to this purpose, along with efforts in the private child-caring system. Increased use of alternatives, however, has not paralleled declining use of institutions. Vinter, Newcomb, and Kish (1976) found that states with the highest per capita use of alternatives also had greater than average use of institutions. Rutherford and Bengur (1976) concluded that the development of community-based alternatives was not associated with decreased rates of incarceration. On the contrary, community-based services "reflect a supplementation of other correctional programs and not a substitute for institutionalization" (Pabon, 1978, p. 493). Wolfle (1980) has suggested that states operate a dual system, one institutional and one community-based. She asserts that the amount and type of money available through the JJDPA was hardly an incentive for states to develop alternatives. New York, for example, had one of the largest state grants in 1979, and it totaled only $5 million. Furthermore, there was no requirement that the money be spent developing alternatives (Wolfle, 1980).

## An Alternative Youth-in-Trouble System

Lerman (1980) proposes that a new treatment network for correctional youth has become established. The new network seems to be the result of a blending of service systems (including mental health, special education, and welfare) and increased permeability in service system boundaries. Lerman (1980, p. 292) observes that

> there appear to be significant shifts in auspices, legal accountability, ease of crossing system boundaries, emphasis on psychological treatment, and modes

of funding. The evidence is quite persuasive that the private sector (publicly subsidized by welfare via purchase of custody, care and treatment arrangements) is now a significant factor in long-term corrections, continues to be the dominant institutional resource in child welfare, and even plays a significant role in private and general hospitals, as well as community mental health center inpatient units.

Parallel trends in other service systems—e.g., deinstitutionalization in mental health, growth of foster care placements, and placements for special education—have provided alternatives for problem youth and contributed to this blended system. Single facilities may provide service to multiple service systems; for instance, a single provider agency received similar dollar amounts in the same year for purchase of service from the Massachusetts Division of Youth Services and the state child welfare agency for residential custody, care, and treatment (Lerman, 1980). Multiple sources of payment for residential care—e.g., Social Security Act Titles IV and XX, OJJDP, Runaway Youth Programs, AFDC-foster care, Medicaid, and various special education placement monies—have not only provided several avenues for accomplishing out-of-home placements, but have further contributed to permeability in service system boundaries. These varying sources of money may have also stimulated development of placement options from the private sector. There has been a sizable shift from public to private care in handling juveniles from the correctional system. In 1950, 21 percent of youths in nondetention correctional facilities were in private agencies. By 1974 this proportion had more than doubled to 48 percent (Lerman, 1980).

### Increase in Voluntary Placement and Widening the Net

The generally insignificant declines in institutional use and notable increases in the number of alternatives (both within and outside of the juvenile justice system) have prompted some scholars to propose that a "widening of the net" has occurred. Rather than fewer youth involved in the juvenile justice treatment system, as implied by the goals of deinstitutionalization and diversion, more youth may have become involved in various alternative programs. Blomberg (1980) has shown that greater numbers of individuals (both youth and adults) have been drawn into the service system as a result of diversion and deinstitutionalization programs. These individuals are generally not involved in the correctional system per se but, rather, in other counseling or mental health agencies by referral from the court or under the auspices of the court.

For the total "youth-in-trouble system," there have been two significant shifts: (1) an increase in the number of voluntary placements and (2) a trend toward identifying youth in trouble as emotionally disturbed (Lerman, 1980). These two shifts have gone hand-in-hand with the blending of service systems and increases in total out-of-home placements. Reforms in the juvenile justice system have made it more difficult to commit a youth to a state correctional institution, but creation of the CHINS category has made it easier to acquire services for these youth. Linney's (1982) study of alternative facilities in Massachusetts, for example, found that many youth were adjudicated CHINS because more money was available for services, there were more services for CHINS, and it was easier to get them. In many states CHINS are considered dependent and neglected, hence they are under the umbrella of the Department of Social Services as well. It is ironic that the procedural reforms and policy priorities of the juvenile justice system may have contributed to greater social control and more penetration into other service systems for nonoffending and nondelinquent youth. While the correctional system may debase treatment and its prospects (Morse & Whitebread, 1982), it seems apparent that the system has curtailed provision of these services within its own institutional jurisdiction, and instead referred youth to other service systems, e.g., mental health, education, and social welfare.

## Institutional Placement as the Last Resort

It appears that deinstitutionalization policy in juvenile justice has been more a policy of noninstitutionalization (Kiesler, 1982). Rather than efforts to empty the institutions (as in Massachusetts or in the mental health system), deinstitutionalization in juvenile justice has been operationalized as a reprioritization of disposition options (Testa, 1982). The policies discourage immediate placement in an institutional setting even for serious offenses, instead emphasizing the least restrictive alternative as a first option and the institution as a last resort when all else has failed. As Testa (1982) has indicated, the radical argument for nonintervention and the moderate argument for benign intervention have resulted in less punitive settings and the creation of settings differing in the degree of restrictiveness and intrusiveness in the youth's life. To the extent that these less restrictive alternatives are operated by systems other than juvenile corrections, adjudicated youths become involved in those treatment systems as well.

## Legal Implications for Youth

The blending of service systems, increases in voluntary placements outside the clear jurisdiction of the juvenile court, and increasing numbers of youth enmeshed in this alternative youth-in-trouble system have important implications for due process and liberty concerns of juveniles and the nature of treatment versus punishment. These were important issues leading to deinstitutionalization policy.

### Liberty Rights and Due Process

The due process protections affirmed in *Gault* apply to adjudication proceedings. Due process protections have been affirmed for commitment proceedings in particular,[6] but have not generally been extended to disposition decisions. There are not guidelines or rules regarding the use of information contributing to disposition decisions, or safeguards or third parties to ensure that the least restrictive alternative is proposed and that the disposition is appropriate to the youth's needs. These decisions rest with the judge and the probation staff in much the same way as prior to *Gault*.

The Supreme Court and legislative policy have held that youth may not be deprived of liberty without due process, and that certain kinds of youthful behavior (e.g., status offenses) do not warrant deprivation of liberty. The adaptations observed in the youth-in-trouble service system (i.e., blending of systems, fluidity and permeability among system boundaries, diversion and referral to other non-juvenile justice services, voluntary placement increases) appear to have bypassed these legal protections for a large number of youth. CHINS cases handled informally by the court or outside of the court altogether do not have formal protection of liberty interests through due process. These protections may be of particular concern because with the blending of service systems youths may be referred outside of the court system, yet receive the very same services as an adjudicated delinquent, although not directly sponsored by the juvenile justice system. For example, the court may transfer custody of a youth to the social welfare department, whereupon the youth is placed in a residential treatment facility serving delinquent youth and CHINS. These adaptations may result in replication of the degree of discretion in handling cases that were identified as problematic for the court pre-*Gault*.

The issues for due process and liberty deal with the extent to which these placements provide treatment or restrict liberty. Without due process the state may not confine an individual except to protect the community. If due process is defined, the *quid pro quo* to justify confinement is provision of treatment; however, the state may not confine an individual solely for the purposes of treatment (Waddlington, Whitebread, & Davis, 1983). These issues are particularly salient for the broad category of "problem youth" handled outside the court by referral for these less restrictive alternatives. It is clear that juvenile justice system placements serve more purposes than just punishment or treatment (Spergel et al., 1980). For example, placement may provide time-out for an overstressed family or a transitional home for a youth seeking emancipation. These types of placements may not need to be covered by due process concerns, but the specific placements are not different from those for adjudicated delinquents presumed to be in need of treatment and/or punishment. Does a youth need due process protections to be placed in a facility that deals with delinquents and other types of youth, or is the due process protection linked with the particular status of the youth? Currently it seems that the due process protection is associated with the service system and the type of offense (i.e., delinquent).

Voluntary placement may be one system adaptation to these uncertainties. With voluntary admission due process is a moot point. It is not known how many voluntary placements are covertly coerced for youths seen to be particularly at risk by the gatekeepers of this youth-in-trouble care system. The rise in so-called voluntary placements suggests that such practices may be widespread. Here also those youth considered diverted, or CHINS receiving services outside of the correctional system may be most affected.

Although large numbers of youth are on voluntary placement (in Linney's sample [1982] all facilities except detention required the youth's voluntary admission), once admitted to a program, youth are hardly free to leave. Leaving a program before completion is tantamount to failure and evidence of more serious problems. Legal status (i.e., delinquent commitment, voluntary placement, status offense) does not appear to be relevant in the care and handling of a youth once they are involved in a program. Such differential treatment by legal status may not be consistent with the treatment methods of group placements. In some community-based programs residents have the illusion of freedom in that they attend public school and may leave the premises for activities and approved periods of time; however, in reality, they are only "slightly free" (Hylton, 1982). Do community-based alternatives provide enough treatment to balance the lack of due process protection for nonvoluntary placements? Do these placements sufficiently limit liberty to necessitate more attention to due process?

## Right to Treatment

The Supreme Court has not definitively ruled that a juvenile confined by the juvenile court has a right to treatment, but it has assumed that right in other decisions.[7] Waddlington, Whitebread, and Davis (1983, p. 579) conclude that

> the "right to treatment" includes the right to minimum acceptable standards of care and treatment for juveniles and the right to *individualized* care and treatment. Because children differ in their need for rehabilitation, individual need for treatment will differ. When a state assumes the place of a juvenile's parents, it assumes as well the parental duties, and its treatment of its juveniles should, so far as can be reasonably required, be what proper parental care would provide. Without a program of individual treatment the result may be that juveniles will not be rehabilitated, but warehoused, and that at the termination of detention they will likely be incapable of taking their proper places in free society; their interests and those of the state and the school thereby being defeated.

This interpretation asserts that minimum standards be defined, individualized treatment provided, and a normalization model adopted. What constitutes minimal treatment? What constitutes individualized treatment and "what proper parental care would provide?" What constitutes a normalizing environment for adolescence, and can that be reconciled with the restraint and punishment purposes of correctional facilities? With the blending of service systems that has been identified, does a right to individualized treatment prevail across services?

The legal issues related to treatment rights for juveniles are similar to those in the mental health area. In the case of juveniles, however, there is little agreement among experts regarding what constitutes the "treatment of choice" (even in a generic sense), and some degree of pessimism on the efficacy of treatment in general. In some programs, placement outside the home constitutes the treatment (Linney, 1982; Rosenberg, 1983). Conclusions drawn from programs that have reported success (Ross & Gendreau, 1980) indicate that a broad definition of care givers and treatment settings is necessary. The state of the art in treatment needs to be more adequately delineated to inform the law in establishing definitions of minimum standards and individualized treatment. The developmental characteristics of adolescence as a stage may have important implications for what constitutes an environment that is normalizing. Hylton (1982) has suggested that the condition of being "slightly free" in residential treatment alternatives may actually trigger the independence seeking and rebellion of teens, ultimately serving counterproductive purposes.

There appears to be a trend to increasingly consider youth as more like adults than children (Melton, 1983). This direction has serious implications for the efficacy of disposition options and the establishment of standards of care. Legal thinking distinguishes between a child and an adult; however, developmentally the adolescent is neither, but has characteristics in common with both. This unique developmental stage needs to be more thoughtfully incorporated into the design of treatment and punishment alternatives and procedures for decision making within the court system. We tend to see delinquent behavior as immature and lacking responsibility. Hence, our treatments provide structure, and few or no opportunities for responsibility (Linney, 1982). However, some of the early programs for delinquent youth that were relatively successful—e.g., the Residential Youth Center (Goldenberg, 1971)—did just the opposite. Adolescents were given autonomy and responsibility in a structured way that perhaps better facilitated the desired individual changes. Designing programs that provide an ecology matched to the developmental status of adolescence may yield more productive outcomes both for the juveniles affected and for the definition of standards within the law.

## Conclusions

In the last fifteen years there have been some sweeping changes in the adjudication of youth and conceptions of the legal status of adolescents vis a vis the law. These changes seem to have had spillover effects for other service systems that deal with troublesome youth as well. Many of the problems precipitating change remain (e.g., high juvenile crime rates and recidivism), suggesting that rather than second-order change (Watzlawick, Weakland, & Fisch, 1974) the larger child-caring system has adapted.

Morse and Whitebread (1982) have argued that the conceptual shift to the just-deserts model of juvenile justice reflects a reappraisal of treatment as a realistic goal for corrections. As the juvenile justice system functions now, there does seem to be greater appreciation of the limits of rehabilitation, but a simultaneous faith in the treatment powers of other systems, most notably mental health. The deinstitutionalization policy may have reduced use of the correctional facility in the name of treatment, yet there now appears to be more psychological treatment and psychological explanation for wayward behavior being supported via referral to other agencies. Corrections may be dispensing less treatment, but it seems to be prescribing more of it. These reforms may have increased both treatment and discretion through the extensive use of referrals and diversion programs. Procedural and policy change in the juvenile justice system has been based on protection of due process concerns; however, adaptations in the larger service system suggest that there has been significant shift in service system jurisdiction for troublesome youth. These adaptations raise new questions regarding the due process protections of problem youth, and regarding clarification of what constitutes treatment and distinguishes it from punishment. It is proposed here that a developmental focus be taken in consideration of these issues, and that the multiple functions of out-of-home placement be recognized. Second, efforts must continue to reduce the negative effects of the institutional setting and reduce its prominence in the correctional system. Third, there is a tremendous need for methodologically adequate research on the effects of community-based alternatives and definition of the parameters that contribute to desirable outcomes (Sechrest, White, & Brown, 1979). Without such evidence, we face the risk of a return to the secure institution as the only form of treatment.

## Notes

1. O'Connell v. Turner, 55 Ill. 280 (1875).
2. Wyatt v. Stickney, 325 F. Supp. 781 (1971).
3. Kaimowitz v. Department of Mental Health, 13 Crim. L. Rep. 2452 (1973).
4. Jackson v. Indiana, 406 U.S. 715 (1972).
5. In re Gault, 387 U.S. 1 (1967).
6. Morales v. Turman, 364 F. Supp. 166 (E.D. Tex. 1973).
7. Kent v. United States, 383 U.S. 541 (1966); Martarella v. Kelley, 349 F. Supp. 575 (S.D. N.Y. 1972).

## References

Blomberg, T.G. Widening the net: An anomaly in the evaluation of diversion programs. In M.W. Klein & K.S. Teilmann (Eds.), *Handbook of criminal justice evaluation*. Beverly Hills, CA: Sage, 1980.

Coates, R.B. Community-based services for juvenile delinquents: Concept and implications for practice. *Journal of Social Issues*, 1981, *37*,(3), 87-101.

Coates, R.B., Miller, A.D., & Ohlin, L.E. *Diversity in a youth correctional system. Handling delinquents in Massachusetts*. Cambridge, MA: Ballinger, 1978.

Dean, C.W., & Reppucci, N.D. Juvenile correctional institutions. In D. Glaser (Ed.), *Handbook of criminology*. Chicago: Rand-McNally, 1974.

Empey, L.T. Juvenile justice reform: Diversion, due process, and deinstitutionalization. In L.E. Ohlin (Ed.), *Prisoners in America*. Englewood Cliffs, NJ: Prentice-Hall, 1973.

Garlock, P.D. Wayward children and the law, 1820-1900: The genesis of the status offense jurisdiction of the juvenile court. *Georgia Law Review*, 1979, *13*, 341-447.

Goffman, E. *Asylums: Essays on the social situation of mental patients and other inmates.* Garden City, NY: Anchor Books, 1961.

Gold, M. Undetected delinquent behavior. *Journal of Research in Crime and Delinquency*, 1966, *3*, 27-46.

Gold, M. *Delinquent behavior in an American city*. Belmont, CA: Brooks/Cole, 1970.

Goldenberg. I.I. *Build me a mountain: Youth, poverty and the creation of new settings.* Cambridge, MA: MIT Press, 1971.

Handler, J., & Zatz, J. (Eds.). *Neither angels nor thieves: Studies in deinstitutionalization of status offenders*. Washington, DC: National Academy Press, 1982.

Horowitz, D.L. *The courts and social policy.* Washington, DC: Brookings Institution, 1977.

Hylton, J.H. Rhetoric and reality: A critical appraisal of community correctional programs. *Crime and Delinquency*, 1982, *28*, 341-373.

Institute of Judicial Administration/American Bar Association. Standards for Juvenile Justice, Juvenile Justice Standards Project. Washington, DC: Author, 1977.

Kiesler, C.A. Mental hospitals and alternative care: Noninstitutionalization as potential public policy for mental patients. *American Psychologist*, 1982, *37*, 349-360.

Klein, M. Deinstitutionalization and diversion of juvenile offenders: A litany of impediments. In N. Morris & M. Tonry (Eds.), *Crime and justice: An annual review of research (Vol. 1)*. Chicago: University of Chicago Press, 1979.

Lemert, E.M. *Social pathology.* New York: McGraw-Hill, 1951.

Lerman, P. Trends and issues in the deinstitutionalization of youths in trouble. *Crime and Delinquency*, 1980, *26*, 281-298.

Levine, M. *The history and politics of community mental health.* New York: Oxford University Press, 1981.

Levine, M., & Levine, A. *A social history of the helping services: Clinic, court, school and community.* New York: Appleton-Century-Crofts, 1970.

Linney, J.A. Alternative facilities for youth in trouble: Descriptive analyses of a strategically selected sample. In J. Handler & J. Zatz (Eds.), *Neither angels nor thieves: Studies in deinstitutionalization of status offenders*. Washington, DC: National Academy Press, 1982.

Mack, J.W. The juvenile court. *Harvard Law Review*, 1909, *23*, 104-122.

McEwen, C.A. *Designing correctional organizations for youths: Dilemmas of subcultural development.* Cambridge, MA: Ballinger, 1978.

Melton, G.B. Toward "personhood" for adolescents: Autonomy and privacy as values in public policy. *American Psychologist*, 1983, *38*, 99-103.

Miller, J., & Ohlin, L.E. The new corrections: The case of Massachusetts. In M.K. Rosenheim (Ed.), *Pursuing justice for the child*. Chicago: University of Chicago Press, 1976.

Morse, S.J., & Whitebread, C.H. Mental health implications of the juvenile justice standards. *Child and Youth Services*, 1982, *5*,(1/2), 5-28.

Mulvey, E.P., & Hicks, A. The paradoxical effect of a juvenile code change in Virginia. *American Journal of Community Psychology*, 1982, *10*, 705-722.

Out with institution. *The Economist*, September 16, 1978, *268*,(7064), 53.

Pabon, E. Changes in juvenile justice: Evolution or reform. *Social Work*, 1978, *23*, 492-497.

Platt, A. *The child savers: The invention of delinquency.* Chicago: University of Chicago Press, 1971.

President's Commission on Law Enforcement and Administration of Justice *Task force report: Corrections*. Washington, DC: U.S. Government Printing Office, 1967.

Rosenberg, M.S. Treatment and normalization in alternative settings. Paper presented at the annual meeting of the American Psychological Association, Anaheim, CA, 1983.

Rosenheim, M.K. Notes on helping juvenile nuisances. In M.K. Rosenheim (Ed.), *Pursuing justice for the child*. Chicago: University of Chicago Press, 1976.

Ross, R.R., & Gendreau, P. (Eds.). *Effective correctional treatment*. Toronto: Butterworth, 1980.

Rothman, D. *The discovery of the asylum: Social order and disorder in the new republic*. Boston: Little, Brown, 1971.

Rothman, D.J. *Conscience and convenience. The asylum and its alternatives in Progressive America*. Boston: Little, Brown, 1980.

Rutherford, A., & Bengur, O. *Community-based alternatives to juvenile incarceration*. Washington, DC: National Institute of Law Enforcement and Criminal Justice, 1976.

Schur, E.M. *Radical non-intervention: Rethinking the delinquency problem*. Englewood Cliffs, NJ: Prentice-Hall, 1973.

Sechrest, L., White, S.O., & Brown, E.O. *Rehabilitation of criminal offenders: Problems and prospects*. Washington, DC: National Academy of Sciences, 1979.

Spergel, I., Lynch, J.P., & Korbelik, J. *Deinstitutionalization in Illinois: The case for removal of status offenses from court processing*. Unpublished paper prepared for the Panel on Deinstitutionalization of Children and Youth, National Academy of Sciences, Washington, DC, 1980.

Testa, M. Child placement and deinstitutionalization: A case study of social reform in Illinois. In J. Handler & J. Zatz (Eds.), *Neither angels nor thieves: Studies in deinstitutionalization of status offenders*. Washington, DC: National Academy Press, 1982.

Vinter, R.D., Downs, G., & Hall, J. *Juvenile corrections in the states: Residential programs and deinstitutionalization*. Ann Arbor: University of Michigan, 1975.

Vinter, R.D., Newcomb, T.M., & Kish, R. (Eds.). *Time out: A national study of juvenile correctional programs*. Ann Arbor: National Assessment of Juvenile Corrections, University of Michigan, 1976.

Waddlington, W., Whitebread, C.H., & Davis, S.M. *Cases and materials on children in the legal system*. Mineola, NY: Foundation Press, 1983.

Watzlawick, P., Weakland, J.H., & Fisch, R. *Change: Principles of problem formation and problem resolution*. New York: Norton, 1974.

Wolfle, J. *Deinstitutionalization of mental health patients and non-offender youth in New York state*. Unpublished paper prepared for the Panel on Deinstitutionalization of Children and Youth, National Academy of Sciences, Washington, DC, 1980.

Zatz, J. Problems and issues in deinstitutionalization: Historical overview and current attitudes. In J. Handler & J. Zatz (Eds.), *Neither angels nor thieves: Studies in deinstitutionalization of status offenders*. Washington, DC: National Academy Press, 1982.

# 11

# The Adolescent Passage and Entry into the Juvenile Justice System

**Edward Seidman**

*University of Illinois at Urbana-Champaign*

Adolescence is a phase of human development that is replete with hurdles. Some are biological and onotogenetic in origin, while others are influenced by sociocultural forces. As each youth progresses through adolescence, the origin, nature, and significance of some of these hurdles become phenomenologically more understandable, others remain partially or totally inexplicable. Each individual negotiates some hurdles successfully, others partially, and some only minimally. Undoubtedly, a certain amount of what society views as deviant behavior occurs for most youth. Nevertheless, in varying ways and to varying degrees, most youth eventually negotiate the passage to adulthood. Very few attain the status of an adult criminal or permanent psychological casualty.

Much of what is labeled social deviance may simply be a natural concomitant of the adolescent passage in Western society. Our reactions to this "deviance," as well as the nature of our juvenile justice system, are structured in ways that seek out and overidentify youthful misbehavior. Consequently, our societal constructions and their reflection, the law, are prone to enjoin each other in an overextension of both the law and human services. Here, exercising the law or administering human services often has an iatrogenic effect; paradoxically, in the process of trying to resolve the difficulty a larger problem is created. In order to counter this tendency a greater understanding of the normative nature of adolescent passage is required. That understanding can lead to a restructuring and delimitation of the scope of our

Author's Note: I would like to thank Barton Hirsch, Julian Rappaport, and N. Dickon Reppucci for their helpful comments on an earlier draft of this chapter.

juvenile justice and related human service systems. This chapter proposes that increased attention to the development of social structures focusing on the normative and positive characteristics of the adolescent passage can reduce the incidence of serious forms of deviant behavior.

## The Adolescent Passage

In reviewing the nature of the adolescent passage, I briefly portray both its normative characteristics and developmental tasks as well as the variety of deviant outcroppings and their future consequences.

### Normative Characteristics and Developmental Tasks

There are a number of inherent biological and maturational processes that transpire during adolescence. They include the acceleration of physical growth, changing bodily dimensions, hormonal changes, development of primary and secondary sex characteristics, increased sexual drive, and further growth and differentiation of cognitive abilities. Not surprisingly many youth are initially caught off guard by these changes. Feelings of confusion and distress are commonplace, even if not articulated. They have entered a passage that is both qualitatively and quantitatively distinct from their earlier experiences (Conger, 1977).

Culture influences the nature, quality, form, and duration of the adolescent passage, but not its occurrence. Contemporary Western cultures are characterized by longer periods of adolescence than earlier or less-developed cultures, where youth become a part of the working society with well-defined and responsible roles at much younger ages (Kett, 1977). Nevertheless, adolescents must commence the task of individuation from their family without losing their sense of community. Moreover, individuation is not easy to negotiate. At the same time, adolescents are subjected to a variety of peer pressures, and for most, their social status and reflected appraisals of their peers take on increased meaning in their own self-definition. This too proves to be a difficult transition to negotiate.

Another major task of adolescence comes in the form of increasing demands and expectations for achievement. The duration of schooling continues to lengthen, while for many education remains irrelevant. For the latter group of individuals, the world of work takes on increased significance.

As a youth enters the adolescent passage, older, more familiar ways of responding tend to lose their adaptational value. New and still untried responses must be sought and learned (Conger, 1977). To integrate the expanding biological, hormonal, cognitive, affective, and social awarenesses with the changing pressures of parents, peers, schools, and the larger society with as little conflict and disruption as possible is a task of major proportions. To negotiate these dilemmas without at least some conflict and behavioral deviance is almost unheard of and, undoubtedly, an unrealistic expectation. The policies and programs of the juvenile justice system must be informed by these normative characteristics and developmental tasks.

## Deviant Occurrences and Future Consequences

Before turning to deviant behavior more commonly associated with adolescent development, let us take a brief look at the incidence of other forms of serious psychological deviance. As Weiner (1980, p. 449) has summarized:

1. *Schizophrenia* . . . is more likely to make its first appearance during the adolescent and early adult years than at any other time of life.

2. *Depression.* In its mild and transient forms, depression is probably the most commonly experienced type of psychological distress among adolescents.

3. *Suicidal behavior.* The frequency of suicide attempts is disproportionately high among adolescents as compared to other age groups.

Thus, it can be seen that the turbulence of adolescence is characterized by higher rates of several forms of emotional disturbance. High-quality longitudinal data attempting to discern the adult consequences of adolescent emotional disturbance is scant. Weiner and DelGaudio (1976) followed a group of adolescents appearing in a countywide psychiatric registry for ten years. Almost half the identified population had no further contact during the follow-up period, as indicated in the case registry. Yet, even this investigation provides only minimal information concerning the long-term consequences of such disturbances into adulthood. It is not unlikely that for most adolescents their experience of emotional difficulty eventually takes its place in their personal history as a developmental crisis that they either outgrow or master.

Turning to delinquent behavior, a meaningful discussion needs to be preceded by noting two issues. First, delinquency is a global category that often includes a wide array of acts, ranging from truancy and incorrigibility to robbery and assault and battery. A meaningful discussion of the significance, as well as the methods of dealing with, delinquent behaviors requires more discriminating referents. Second, official delinquency records underreport occurrences and are also biased. In particular, official delinquency records consistently demonstrate a strong inverse association to youths' socioeconomic status, while adolescent self-report data fail to demonstrate such an association (Gold & Petronio, 1980). Consequently, the bulk of the discussion in this section on rates refer primarily to the probably more veridical self-report data.

In a recent review, Strasburg (1978) indicated that delinquent behavior is a widespread phenomenon, and in fact, self-report studies demonstrate that most if not all juveniles commit illegal acts. However, violent acts are much less frequent, representing from 4 to 12 percent of all juvenile arrests, depending on the study. A surprisingly high percentage of arrested delinquents have engaged in violent acts at least once, though repeated violence is not a common phenomenon.

As summarized by Gold and Petronio (1980), the National Survey of Youth 1972 (Gold & Reimer, 1975) demonstrates an increase in both frequency and seriousness of nontrivial delinquent behavior during the adolescent years. While the acceleration of frequency is most marked at age 15, the acceleration continues throughout adolescence. On the other hand, the seriousness of offenses peaks at 15, then levels off. Boys consistently confess to more delinquent acts than girls. The Youth in Transition study (O'Malley, Bachman, & Johnston, 1977) tracked self-reported delinquent behavior, weighted by seriousness, in a representative sample of tenth grade boys, into their twenty-third year, demonstrating a decline from age 16 to 18, with a rise at 19, then a decline through age 23. While the Youth in Transition study (Johnston, O'Malley, & Eveland, 1978) suggests a relationship between delinquent behavior in adolescence and criminal behavior in adulthood, it is quite small. For example, a correlation of .21 was found for theft and vandalism measured at ages 15-16 and then again at ages 22-23, and only .17 for interpersonal aggression at 15-16 correlated with later criminal behavior. In summary,

> Delinquent behavior is surely one component of the reputed adolescent turmoil, and we have seen that it is indeed more prevalent in adolescence, especially in more serious forms. (We hasten to say that the data show *most adolescents are not very delinquent.*) (Gold & Petronio, 1980, p. 513; italics added)

Consistent with these self-reported data is the fact that official rates of criminal behavior begin to decline after age 16, and violent behavior after age 18 (Strasburg, 1978). In a reanalysis of the data on the Philadelphia cohort of 9945 boys tracked through school, police and court records from age seven until eighteen (Wolfgang, Figlio & Sellin, 1972), Clarke (1975) fails to find any evidence for "escalation" theory—that undesirable behavior in juveniles tends to increase in dangerousness with age, on a continuum from trivial status offenses to nontrivial delinquent offenses. First-time status offenders infrequently have multiple offenses or offenses of greater seriousness. They rarely reach the status of a "chronic" offender (at least five recorded offenses). While initial offenses involving personal injury, theft, and/or damage to property are related to both second and more serious offenses, only 15 to 34 percent eventually become "chronic" offenders.

For those adolescents who engage in nontrivial delinquent behavior, few lead careers as adult criminals. Even in serious cases of delinquency, the normal and gradual process of maturation appears to be a major curative factor. Many youngsters simply abandon their participation in delinquent activities as they grow up, join the Army, get married, or obtain a job (President's Commission on Law Enforcement and Administration of Justice, 1967). Hickey (1977, pp. 121-122) has made the same point from a somewhat different vantage point. "It should be recognized that juvenile misbehavior is often completely normal; the United States is full of mature responsible adults who passed through a period of juvenile misbehavior without the assistance of the juvenile court." This realization also needs to inform the policies and programs of the juvenile justice system.

## The Juvenile Justice System

Before discussing entry into the juvenile justice system, the evolving historical context is presented and analyzed. The focus is on both the changing social values and their reflection in legal statutes. Early entrance into the juvenile justice system appears to be a critical point at which decisions about the disposition and/or treatment of alleged adolescent offenders are made. A referral schema is explicated along with a guiding philosophy and an exemplification.

### Changing Values and Statutes

Since the seventeenth century there have been laws in this country to punish children for wayward and disobedient behavior (Lerman, 1977; Zatz, 1982). The root causes of such deviance were perceived as residing in the individual; while these deviants could never be eradicated, they were viewed as controllable.

By the nineteenth century, poverty and a life of crime were seen to go hand in hand; deviance was no longer an isolated phenomenon. It was believed that children of the poor could be saved from the cycle of poverty and crime by removal from their families. Many of these youth were simply vagrant or wayward and were placed in "houses of refuge" for rehabilitation. Treatment was often harsh.

The spread of juvenile institutions and wayward-child laws, and the passage of various types of protectionist legislation (e.g., child labor laws, compulsory school attendance laws, the exclusion of children from particular types of settings and occupations) signaled a fundamental change in the status of children. Although this change was by no means complete until the early twentieth century, nineteenth century child advocates were bent on differentiating childhood as a distinct developmental stage and on influencing its progression. (Zatz, 1982, p. 17).

Concurrently, the doctrine of *parens patriae* was steadily expanded, justifying the power of the state to institutionalize a wide array of noncriminal youth.

In the late nineteenth century, the law became increasingly concerned with the protection of children from a life of misfortune, regardless of whether state incarceration was aimed at punishment for a crime or rehabilitation for a life of misfortune. Not surprisingly there was a statutory emphasis on child welfare issues. These events, along with the influences and activities of scholars and professionals, became part of the child reform movement, culminating in the establishment of the Illinois Juvenile Court in 1899. Its guiding value was to differentiate among problem youth and provide preventive care, as opposed to viewing youth as homogeneous and providing rehabilitative care; "children who appeared before the court were not inherently bad, but were in need of educative and purposeful activity" (Zatz, 1982, p. 21).

While juveniles were separated from adult proceedings and provided with individual therapeutic rather than exclusively punitive dispositions and remedies, wayward behavior continued to be viewed as a precursor to criminality. Consequently, state intervention into the lives of such children and an expanding range of other nonoffender youth, continued under the principle of parens patriae. This movement was supported by court decisions, such as *Commonwealth of Pennsylvania v. Fisher* (1905).

In the 1960s several states modified their juvenile statutes to differentiate between status offenders and delinquents, variously referring to them as children, persons, juveniles, or minors in need of supervision (CHINS, PINS, JINS, MINS). It was expected that community-based programs would play a greater role in the rehabilitation of status offenders than they had previously done.

Several landmark federal court decisions in the 1960s and 1970s[1] served as precedents to

> (1) attack the extent of the juvenile court's jurisdiction over status offenders on grounds of vagueness and overbreadth; (2) insist on a juvenile's right to appropriate services in the least restrictive setting and to nonpunitive treatment; and (3) argue for procedural protections in status offense as well as delinquency proceedings. (Zatz, 1982, p. 28)

In addition, the 1974 Juvenile Justice and Delinquency Prevention Act called for further discrimination among status and delinquent offenders, and between deinstitutionalization, decriminalization, and diversion of status offenders from the juvenile justice system whenever possible. This act also served as a model for state legislation.

These changing values led a few states to pass legislation decriminalizing status offenses, with the goal of keeping these youth out of the juvenile justice system. While such a statute in a Virginia county led to their decreased numbers in the juvenile justice system, paradoxically, the rate of labeled delinquent offenders climbed (Mulvey and Hicks, 1982). It appeared that many of those previously labeled as status offenders were relabeled, thus subverting the statute's intent. The discretionary powers of juvenile justice system personnel remains large.

In summary, the history of juvenile justice has been characterized by a kaleidoscope of incompatible goals (Hazard, 1976). The juvenile court occupies a sort of conceptual no man's land lying vaguely between the models of criminal and civil commitment law applicable to the mentally ill, and some others "in need of treatment." Juvenile court law has some characteristics of each but also possesses unique attributes. The juvenile courts have oscillated between (1) concern for violations of the criminal law, (2) the amelioration of supposed harmful conditions, such as waywardness, and (3) the rescue of the child as victim, while simultaneously, professing therapeutic objectives for any official intervention (Schultz & Cohen, 1976). At the practical level they continue to possess and exercise considerable *de facto* and *de jure* discretion. Moreover, emphases of the juvenile justice system are continually changing from a protection-of-society rationale to one concerned with the needs and rights of the client (Rappaport, 1981).

## Analysis

Historically the dominant mindscape, or world view, characterizing many Western societies has been imbued with the premise of individualism—that is, the bias of attributing personal responsibility to individuals (Seidman, 1983a, 1983b). The premise of individualism continues to characterize the changing nature of the juvenile justice system too. Functionally, for the most part, institutional and systemic causes and solutions are given only fleeting attention. When the focus of concern is some form of behavioral deviance, the premise of individualism is rapidly transformed into what has come to be known as "blaming the victim" (Ryan, 1971). In other words, the individual or family afflicted by institutional or systemic problems is viewed and treated as the causal agent in their resulting plight.

Another characteristic mode of thinking in our society is the conceptualization of a large class of often loosely related problems and solutions based on extreme deviant and atypical examples. Much of our thinking about the causes of, and solutions to, the "delinquency problem" stems from our images of the rare youth who repeatedly commits the most heinous crimes. This social construction is reified by the mass media, which give such events extensive and sensationalistic coverage. All of us, including juvenile justice system personnel and legislators, come to view these extreme examples as characteristic of youth who are labeled delinquent. We come to believe that if they have not yet performed such acts, they eventually will.

The entire process becomes even more problematic because of the ever-expanding boundaries of delinquency. Given this mind set, low-level deviance among children (e.g., disrespect for authority) comes to be viewed as a problem in need of intervention. A phenomenon that Rosenheim (1976) has referred to as "problemization" ensues naturally. "Problemization refers to the activity of individuals and agencies in organizing and applying their particular apparatus of classification and cure." (Rosenheim, 1976, p. 52). Watzlawick, Weakland, and Fisch (1974), Rappaport and Seidman (1983), among others, have discussed a similar process of transforming difficulties into problems. This process runs counter to a normalization perspective, in which the normative information, presented briefly in the first part of this chapter, would inform the nature of our response to youth with difficulties. Normalization need not require that we ignore rare and truly extreme forms of behavior among youth; indeed, it would help us to understand such behavior.

The history of the juvenile justice system operating under the parens patriae principle, is characterized by an expanding definition of the category "delinquency." There have been efforts to restrict the definition, but functionally such efforts have not been successful. This has led to an overextension of the juvenile justice system (Blomberg, 1980), often by integrating components of human service systems, (e.g., mental health, child welfare), which have also overextended their reach. Such overextension is in part a function of definitional vagueness. The effort to help is often based on the assumption of continuity of behavior from early instances of low-level deviance. It is functionally aided by the wide latitude of discretion available to juvenile justice system personnel. Normative data on the adolescent passage has played, and continues to play, an insignificant role in this process.

Despite the ostensible search for novel solutions to adolescent problems, there is a remarkable consistency to the enacted interventions. The nature of the solutions result in part from generalizing from solutions more suited to extreme and atypical forms of deviance. Thus, uniform solutions to particular problems appear to be the norm, not the exception (Seidman, 1983a, 1983b).

These social constructions and processes (i.e., premise of individualism, generalization from extreme examples, problemizing, overextension, discretion, uniform solution to particular problems) interact and co-mingle in complex ways. The result is a juvenile justice system that has neither been informed by the normative characteristics and developmental tasks of the adolescent passage, nor by the data on genuine deviant outcroppings during adolescence and their manifestations into adulthood. Using this information to inform the juvenile justice system could lead to a very different system and very different outcomes.

### Entry into the Juvenile Justice System

> The findings from numerous evaluations establish that there are more negative consequences for youth who are committed to institutional rather than community-based programs. Moreover, safety of the public is not enhanced by institutional placement except in the short period of incarceration. (Sarri, 1981, pp. 46-47).

In addition to the failure of institutional placement, normalization of such treatment environments is clearly less rational than using normative developmental data to inform the nature and form of dispositions prior to such deep penetration into the juvenile justice system—the earlier the better. Consequently, here I will focus on the current status and efficacy of early dispositions and interventions in the juvenile justice system and how they might be improved.

Given the large number of youth who still find themselves in institutional placement, deinstitutionalization continues to present a set of issues of considerable importance; these are thoroughly discussed by Linney (Chapter 10 of this volume). The focus of the balance of this chapter is on the alternative referred to as juvenile diversion. Our own intervention research will be used to highlight a number of relevant issues and points (Davidson, Seidman, Rappaport, Berck, Rapp, Rhodes, & Herring, 1977; Rappaport, Seidman & Davidson, 1979; Seidman, 1981).

### Juvenile Diversion

#### What Is It?

In practice, diversion takes many forms, such that it might be unrecognizable to the uninitiated. The term "diversion," made popular by the recommendations of the President's Commission on Law Enforcement and Administration of Justice (1967), simply means the turning or redirection of something from its normal path. Diversion not only takes many forms, but occurs at several decision/discretion points in the juvenile justice system, e.g., at the time of apprehension, police hearing, preadjudication, or formal court hearing. While it can occur early in a youth's penetration into the system, it often does not take place until considerable penetration has occurred. Sometimes it simply entails outright release; at other times it requires treatment or the receipt of some form of service. The treatment/service may either be voluntarily administered or mandated, and it is often voluntary in name only.

### Who Falls in the Diversion Net?

The range of offenses that can get a youth snagged in the diversion net is quite large. The largest group is composed of status offenders, those in trouble for committing an act that would not be illegal if they were adults, such as running away, curfew violation(s), truancy, disrespect for authority, and the like. Many of these status offenders are variously referred to as children, persons, juveniles, or minors in need of supervision. The next largest group consists of those who have committed minor or trivial offenses or engaged in nuisance behaviors, e.g., petty thieves, playground assailants, and raucous loiterers. The last group to be differentiated have committed more serious offenses, such as robbery and assault. All three groups are often considered delinquent. However, they are not equally likely to be diverted.

### Current Status and
### Efficacy of Diversion

Because of the wide variety of definitions and programs that fall under the rubric of diversion and the poor methodological quality of research overall, firm conclusions regarding its efficacy are difficult to reach (Gibbons & Blake, 1976; Klein, 1979; Rutherford & McDermott, 1976). As Davidson, Snellman, and Koch (1981, pp. 112-113) have pointed out, the effectiveness of diversion

> actually consists of at least three questions: (1) Is diversion without services more effective than traditional court processing? (2) Is diversion with services more effective than traditional processing? (3) What is the relative effectiveness of diversion with services as compared to diversion without services?

The nature and quality of the empirical data are too equivocal to answer these questions with a high degree of scientific certainty. Nevertheless, close scrutiny of the well-conducted diversion research programs, particularly the successes and failures, provides considerable information regarding the necessary, but not sufficient, factors and considerations needed to make diversion work. A brief look at these issues is in order.

One must avoid net-widening, that is, the tendency to divert youth to a service-based alternative when they would normally be released outright. Such individuals are not a true test of diversion. In fact, they bring more youth into the net (Blomberg, 1980; Klein, 1983). This raises issues of who is to be diverted and when, i.e., timing (Rappaport, Lamiell, & Seidman, 1980).

Given our society-based premise of individualism, a treatment philosophy of individual responsibility follows naturally. Not surprisingly, individually oriented counseling characterizes most diversion programs (Klein, 1983). Institutional or system-oriented change programs are rare. Even working with the youth's social network of family and peers is unusual.

Rosenheim (1976) has formulated several tactics for normalizing delinquency interventions, including immediacy and authenticity of response, and respect for the help-seeker's problem formulation. Also, involvement of the client in the decision-making process (Coates, 1981) might serve as a critical part of the developing adolescent's individuation process and assumption of personal responsibility.

Community agency priorities are another set of considerations (Klein, 1983; Seidman, 1981). These relate in part to net-widening. Seldom does an agency reduce its size or go out of business when a problem has been substantially reduced or solved. For example, a dramatic reduction in the number of serious offenders dealt with by a local service agency that was developed specifically to serve youth is not likely to reduce its overall size. Instead, it begins to accept other referrals initially excluded as targets, e.g., status offenders. This process feeds into the ever-expanding juvenile justice system and the overextension of human services. It is also partly a function of most professionals' tendency to conceptualize problems in a manner consistent with their own training and skills (Rappaport & Seidman, 1983). Problemization is a frequent outcome, whether needed or not. Consequently, the agency's needs often come to have greater priority than its clients' needs (Klein, 1983).

This brief review of considerations necessary for successful diversion indicates that we need to be concerned with factors at the level of the individual offender, aspects of his/her social network, community agency priorities, and the larger juvenile justice system. Who gets referred, treated, and the nature, quality, and timing of service also remain of central importance.

### Diversion as It Might Be

*Guiding philosophy: toward the normalization of diversion.* Taking seriously the plethora of hurdles and developmental task demands, as well as the normative occurrence of some form of deviant behavior among most youth in transit through the adolescent passage, we are inevitably led to conclude that a normalization, in contrast to a problemization perspective, is the optimal form of diversion. Diversion needs to be structured and informed by knowledge of the normative characteristics of the adolescent passage. We need to treat deviant outcroppings, with the exception of those that are quite serious and repeated, as typical and transitory. Thus, we should not overinterpret and overreact to juvenile misbehaviors. Not all such misbehaviors should be viewed as early indicants of criminal careers. Similarly, the responses of helping systems should be structured so as to minimize the criminogenic meaning of such misbehaviors; labeling, stigmatization, and penetration into the juvenile justice system should be minimized. Youth should be released outright or diverted to alternatives with the least possible intrusiveness into their lives, and the intervention itself should attempt to minimize the extent to which it creates the view that the youth is the problem.

*When and for whom should diversion and other juvenile justice system responses occur?* Recently Palmer and Lewis (1980) have presented a comprehensive and differentiated plan to address these questions. They describe five different youth groups based on referral source and prior arrest record. Two non-justice system referral groups are delineated—self and parent/school referrals—and three justice system referral groups with zero, one, and two or more prior arrests. Five different alternative dispositions are defined. These are (1) outright release, that is, diversion without any programming; (2) non-justice system (e.g., private agency-operated) program on a voluntary basis; (3) non-justice system program on a nonvoluntary basis; (4) justice system (e.g., police- or probation-operated) program on a voluntary basis; and (5) justice system program on a nonvoluntary basis. Table 11.1 clearly illustrates the Palmer and Lewis (1980) suggested priority schema for matching these five youth groups and alternative dispositions.

Obviously, the Palmer and Lewis (1980) schema is not congruent with the analysis of the juvenile justice system, and the issues and considerations discussed above. First, it is questionable whether any nonvoluntary, that is, police- or court-mandated program, housed either in or outside the justice system, is a genuine diversion alternative; there should be little question that a nonvoluntary justice system program is, at best, a feeble diversion alternative. The frequent second-choice priority status accorded to this latter "alternative" by Palmer and Lewis (1980) continues to overextend the reach of the juvenile justice and human service systems. Second, the first-choice recommended alternative for parent and school referred status and trivial offenders is non-justice system programs; these too tend to expand the net.

TABLE 11.1 Palmer and Lewis's (1980) Schema of Recommended Diversion Alternatives

| Youth Group | Outright Release | Non-Justice System Voluntary Program | Non-Justice System Nonvoluntary Program | Justice System Voluntary Program | Justice System Nonvoluntary Program |
|---|---|---|---|---|---|
| | | Diversion Alternatives | | | |
| 1. Non-justice system (self-) referrals | − | 1st choice | − | 2nd choice | − |
| 2. Non-justice system (parent, school) referrals | −[a] | 1st choice | − | 2nd choice | − |
| 3. Justice system referrals with no prior arrests | 1st, 2nd or 3rd choice[b] | 1st, 2nd, or 3rd choice[b] | 1st, 2nd, or 3rd choice[b] | −[a] | − |
| 4. Justice system referrals with 1 prior arrest | − | 1st choice | 3rd choice | 2nd choice | 4th choice[c] |
| 5. Justice system referrals with 2 or more prior arrests | − | 3rd choice | 1st choice | 4th choice | 2nd choice |

SOURCE: T. B. Palmer and R. V. Lewis, "A differentiated approach to juvenile diversion," Journal of Research in Crime and Delinquency, Vol. 17, pp. 209-229. Copyright ©1980 by the National Council on Crime and Delinquency. Reprinted by permission of authors and publisher.

NOTE: Diversion alternatives under which a dash appears are not recommended for the given referral group. Youths might be recommended for short- or longer-term programs depending largely on how much service and/or external control they appear to need.

a. May be recommended under specified conditions.

b. First choice among the alternatives in question depends on (1) whether there is an apparent need for service and/or external control; and, if there is such a need, (2) the extent to which either service or control appears to be the principal concern.

c. Recommended only if there is an apparent need for external control.

Correlated with such net-widening is the exacerbation of individual stigmatization and labeling, increased penetration of the juvenile justice system, increased conceptualization of youthful behavior from a problemization perspective, and minimal likelihood that the nature of the alternatives will be informed by a normative understanding of the adolescent passage.

Taking these issues into consideration, Table 11.2 presents a set of recommendations for matching youth with diversion alternatives more consistent with the analyses and values explicated in this chapter. The reader can see that nonvoluntary alternatives, in or out of the justice system, are given very low priority or excluded as a viable option. It is difficult to envision a coercive alternative as a genuine diversionary endeavor. A problemization perspective is inherent in the selection of such an alternative, as well as increased labeling, stigmatization, and—when within the justice system—penetration. For status, trivial, and serious offenders with one or fewer prior arrests, outright release is the consistently recommended first-choice alternative. This is the ultimate form of diversionary alternative; it achieves all the critical objectives described above. Consistent with these objectives, if outright release is not possible or deemed unwise or unethical, referral to a nonjustice system voluntary program may be indicated. For status and trivial offenders, involuntary or justice system alternatives are excluded as potential referrals because of the noncriminal and normative nature of the "offenses." In unusual circumstances, serious offenders with one or fewer prior arrests may need a nonvoluntary, nonjustice system program, though justice-system-based programs remain unacceptable. On the other hand, for serious offenders with two or more prior arrests some active intervention is required, since they account for a large majority of juvenile crime, particularly violent crime (Strasburg, 1978). However, voluntary alternatives external to the justice system remain the preferred dispositions.

*An exemplification and its undoing.* Below, I briefly review our own experiences in juvenile diversion to highlight the rationality and appropriateness of this referral schema (Davidson et al., 1977; Rappaport et al., 1979; Seidman et al., 1980; Seidman, 1981). Based on our experiences over the course of several years in a local juvenile justice system, we realized that it was necessary for us to intervene prior to the probation phase of adolescent penetration into the legal system. Equally important, we learned that there was a real danger in overidentifying so-called predelinquent youth. In general, police were often willing to use their discretionary powers to warn and release status offenders and, to a slightly lesser extent, trivial and first offenders. Consequently, our intentions were to aim our interventions at a very narrow set of children; those for whom the police had already used a warn-and-release option and for whom the juvenile officer now felt that there was no choice but to file a petition with the state's attorney's office. If that petition were filed, it would have meant

TABLE 11.2    Revised Schema of Recommended
              Diversion Alternatives

| | | Diversion Alternatives | | | |
|---|---|---|---|---|---|
| Youth Group | Outright Release | Non-Justice System Voluntary Program | Non-Justice System Nonvoluntary Program | Justice System Voluntary Program | Justice System Nonvoluntary Program |
| 1. Status offenders (primarily non-justice system referrals–self, parent, school) | 1st choice | 2nd choice | – | – | – |
| 2. Trivial offenders (includes minor legal offenses and nuisance behaviors; both non-justice and justice system referrals) | 1st choice | 2nd choice | – | – | – |
| 3. Serious offenders with one or fewer prior arrests | 1st choice | 2nd choice | 3rd choice | – | – |
| 4. Serious offenders with 2 or more prior arrests | – | 1st choice | 3rd choice | 2nd choice | 4th choice |

NOTE: Diversion alternatives under which a dash appears are not recommended for the given referral group.

the formal engagement of the youth in the court system, complete with a formal trial, in which the child would almost always be represented by a public defender and in most cases be placed on probation. He or she would then be officially labeled as delinquent. Our first and foremost aim was to prevent this from happening, because from our experience, values, and reading (e.g., Gold, 1970; Schur, 1973), we were convinced that it made things worse rather than better for the youth.

The program to be described pertains entirely to youth for whom the police were about to file a petition for court action (essentially serious offenders with two or more prior arrests) but referred to our voluntary program instead. The program provided a true alternative to adjudication. If the children were to be warned and released, we did not take them in the program.

In addition to aiming our intervention at this specific group of children, we targeted our goals for each youngster around a uniform aim: to keep them out of legal entanglements. Our values also brought to bear a number of other considerations. We were committed to the notion that not only does labeling a child as delinquent create more harm than good, but also that the sensible way to approach such problems is by focusing intervention efforts on resource stimulation and generation rather than on individual repair. This approach has been referred to as an environmental resources social advocacy point of view (Davidson & Rapp, 1976; Davidson & Rappaport, 1978). This conception, together with the sense that the youth with whom we were dealing often had a variety of strengths and competencies that needed encouragement and development rather than therapy (Rappaport, 1977), led us to emphasize an intervention based on social advocacy and behavioral contracting with significant others. Both of these approaches required that youth be regarded as full-fledged active participants in planning for, and carrying out needed change, rather than children whose "best interests" needed to be protected by the independent planning of professional helpers, authorities, and/or parents. Although not neglecting the individual adolescent, the relationships within a youth's mini-social network (e.g., parental, peer, or schoolmates) were the prime target of intervention.

Apprehended youth were randomly assigned to either a college student who worked with them on a one-to-one basis or a "treatment as usual" condition in lieu of juvenile court referral. Examination of archival data at several intervals (one year prior to project, eighteen weeks during, and both one and two years after the program conclusion) indicated highly significant decrements in police contact, seriousness of offense, and juvenile court referral for experimental as opposed to control group children. We also found that the diversion project reduced the proportion of all youth petitioned to court by the cooperating police departments during the time of the project's operation.

Despite the powerful effects of the major outcome data, standard self-report questionnaire measures, like locus of control and self-reported delinquency, failed to yield any trends or statistically significant main or interaction effects. These same measures were completed from the perspective of the parents and nominated peers of each targeted youth. Again, no effects occurred.

In the following year, the behavioral contracting and advocacy training and supervisory orientations were separated to ascertain the relative efficacy of each. A new group of youth who were about to be petitioned to juvenile court were referred to the program and randomly assigned to either a behavioral contracting, a child advocacy, or a control condition. An additional research design component involved the administration of process interviews at six-week intervals with the target youth, their parents, the volunteer student, and the student's supervisors, aimed at ascertaining critical life events, intervention components, and performance in training and supervision (Davidson, 1976).

As in the previous year, police-court data indicated significantly less delinquent behavior for each of the experimental groups in contrast to controls. In addition, analyses of school data indicated that the experimental youth were more likely to continue attending school, whereas the control youth decreased their school attendance dramatically. Analyses of questionnaire data again failed to yield changes from the perspective of the youth, parent, or nominated peer.

The relationship between process dimensions and outcome was also examined. Successful cases were much more likely to maintain positive interactions with significant social systems (family, school), less likely to report deterioration on change dimensions, more likely to successfully initiate their respective intervention package (advocacy or contracting), and more likely to receive a broad band intervention (focusing on more than one social system). Those youth who became reinvolved in the justice system did so almost immediately after referral to the project and were unable to extricate themselves from the system. This led to relatively narrow interventions focused on the youth's continued involvement in the justice system.

Based on this research, we felt justified in concluding that our alternative to the traditional juvenile justice system had demonstrated efficacy in reducing the rates and severity of official delinquency in two successful years with two independent groups of youngsters. These changes endured through a two-year and one-year follow-up period for the first and second set of participants, respectively. What seemed most critical was keeping the youth involved with normalizing social systems—family and/or school—and not any intrapsychic, personality, or behavioral changes.

The success of this diversion project highlights the utility of the referral schema presented in Table 11.2. After development and evaluation of this demonstration project, we arranged for its takeover by a county-based youth service agency. In our role as consultants we continued to observe the project unfold. What we saw was instructive regarding both the impact of the community context and agency priorities, as well as the utility of the referral schema.

Officially, the program functioned very well for seven years after the end of the demonstration research project. The local agency continued to operate the program at full capacity and was supported by county funds, the police cooperated and expressed pride in it, and undergraduate students continued to wait in line to sign up for participation. But we also saw several things change.

One overt change was in the nature of the referred population. Despite the fact that this aspect had always been a key element in written as well as verbal agreements, over the years the police, under pressure from a newly elected judge, tended to refer fewer and fewer youths for whom they were actually about to file a court petition. Instead, they became increasingly willing to refer adolescents for whom they would normally have used a warn-and-release procedure. This occurred during a rapidly changing socio-political zeitgeist characterized by a "get tough on crime attitude." Spear-headed by the newly elected judge and considerable media attention, the most trivial juvenile misbehaviors were viewed as having criminogenic meaning and the response was to "snuff them out" early by dealing with them in the most stringent fashion.

At the same time, the county agency, under pressure to show a significant number of cases, tended increasingly to accept referrals from the State Department of Children and Family Services and from mental health agencies, school counselors, and social workers. The problems handled were more and more problems of mental health adjustment rather than legal problems. It was not so much that the youths were intrinsically different, but rather that a program with a reputation for success among the social service and school community was expected to solve all sorts of problems for which it was neither designed nor had any empirical evidence of success.

The county agency was willing to accept referrals wherever it could get them. It had to show a caseload. The university had a similar problem. To operate the program, students had to register for a course in August for an entire year. If the police were not referring appropriate cases, then the students would have no work to do. At some point in the school year the university, like the service agency, was willing to accept referrals from anywhere, so that it could keep its obligation to the students.

The crux of the matter is this: The successful adolescent diversion demonstration project failed to continue to be a diversion project. The net was widened, and youth who should have been released outright were being served; youth with more serious criminal entanglements and for whom the project was originally designed were much less likely to be referred, but instead penetrated further into the juvenile justice system. The project became a place for referral of children who would ordinarily have been left alone, as Schur (1973), and others (Institute of Judicial Administration/ American Bar Association, 1977) have suggested they should be. The impact of the community context and community agency priorities on altering the idealized referral schema should be apparent. Unfortunately, the cost has been the dimunition or elimination of most of the diversion project's achievements and goals.

## Beyond the Juvenile Justice System

Though the prior discussion of referral patterns and intervention methods was informed by the normative aspects and developmental task demands characteristic of the adolescent passage, the focus was primarily upon individual targets, and occasionally included their mini-social network. Consequently, our discussion of solutions to juvenile misbehavior has been restricted to individually oriented and reactive secondary prevention strategies. Yet, full comprehension of the nature and meaning of the adolescent passage could equally as compellingly lead to a search for non-individually oriented, proactive primary prevention strategies. Our search now takes us beyond both individuals and the juvenile justice system.

There are at least two general types of primary prevention strategies. The first concerns the development or alteration of socioenvironmental structures and settings that not only take account of, but also expand and build upon the normative and positive characteristics of the adolescent passage. The second type of primary prevention strategy focuses upon influencing societal reactions to manifestations of adolescent social deviance.

The lengthy adolescent passage in Western culture along with the lack of meaningful roles and responsibilities dictate the need to create social structures that provide such opportunities in ways that start from the youth's psychological and social frame of reference. Here we may profit by applying Barker's (1960, 1968) concept of undermanning, as O'Donnell (1980) has done. Undermanned settings provide individuals with the opportunity and organizational requirement of assuming more roles and responsibilities. The outcomes are increased participation, satisfaction, and psychosocial well-being. This concept can be usefully applied in school settings, since the duration of schooling encompasses the entire adolescent period. Several programs of this nature indicating positive outcomes have been reviewed by O'Donnell (1980).

In a related, but different vein, Felner, Ginter, and Primavera (1982) report on an innovative school-based primary prevention program for youth making the transition to high school. This project restructured the role of homeroom teachers to serve as the primary administrative-counseling link between students, their parents, and the rest of the school, and reorganized the school environment to reduce the flux of the social setting confronting the student. By the end of the year, project students compared to controls had better academic performance and attendance records, "more positive self-concepts, and saw the school environment as having clearer expectations and organizational structure and higher levels of teacher support" (pp. 286-287). Actually, the differences were accounted for primarily by the deterioration of control students as opposed to the improvement of the project students. Indeed, while this transition is a difficult period for youth, this project suggests that non-individually oriented, proactive primary prevention projects can facilitate smoother transitions.

Another approach would be to capitalize on adolescent need and desire to achieve economic independence in conjunction with a focus on the strength of their peer culture, by stimulating efforts of adolescents to create and manage businesses to serve other adolescents. For instance, teenagers created and still maintain a natural science museum for themselves, younger children, and the rest of the community in Cornwall, New York; adolescents operate their own youth employment agency to help others find and keep jobs in Gary, Indiana (Resources for Youth, 1980). Such achievements appear to hold considerable promise and would accomplish numerous socially and psychologically desirable goals.

The other set of primary prevention goals has to do with the reduction of society's proclivity, including members of the juvenile justice and human service delivery systems, to interpret most instances of juvenile misbehavior with regard to its criminogenic meaning. As we have seen, not only is this unwarranted but it creates difficulty in its own right. There is a great need for public education programs to inform the public's understanding about the turbulence of adolescence and the unlikelihood that instances of juvenile misbehavior actually lead to careers as either a criminal or long-term psychological casualty. Success in this venture could help facilitate both the juvenile justice and human service delivery systems in delimiting their reach.

By and large, the presentation of these primary prevention strategies are undeveloped and undocumented suggestions requiring considerable thought, experimentation, and evaluation. Nevertheless, the time has come to move beyond short-sighted, reactive solutions. As we have seen, the results of these solutions have often been paradoxical. We must experiment with innovative, sociostructural, proactive primary prevention strategies if we are to make progress in facilitating a smoother and more productive course through the adolescent passage. This will necessitate change in the business-as-usual stance of juvenile justice and human service delivery professionals.

## Note

1. In re Gault (1967) 387 U.S. 1; Kent v. United States (1966) 383 U.S. 541; Wyatt v. Stickney (1971) 325 F. Supp. 781.

## References

Barker, R.G. Ecology and motivation. In M.R. Jones (Ed.), *Nebraska Symposium on Motivation*. Lincoln: University of Nebraska Press, 1960.

Barker, R.G. *Ecological psychology*. Stanford: Stanford University Press, 1968.

Blomberg, T.G. Widening the net: An anomaly in the evaluation of diversion programs. In M.W. Klein & K.S. Teilmann (Eds.), *Handbook of Criminal Justice Evaluation*. Beverly Hills, CA: Sage, 1980.

Clarke, S.H. Some implications for North Carolina of recent research in juvenile delinquency. *Journal of Research in Crime and Delinquency*, 1975, *12*, 51-60.

Coates, R.B. Community-based services for juvenile delinquents: Concept and implications for practice. *Journal of Social Issues*, 1981, *37*, 87-101.

Conger, J.J. *Adolescence and youth: Psychological development in a changing world* (2nd ed.). New York: Harper & Row, 1977.

Davidson, W.S. *The diversion of juvenile delinquents: An examination of the processes and relative efficacy of child advocacy and behavioral contracting*. Unpublished doctoral dissertation, University of Illinois at Urbana-Champaign, 1976.

Davidson, W.S., & Rapp, C. "Child advocacy in the justice system." *Social Work*, 1976, *21*, 225-232.

Davidson, W.S., & Rappaport, J. Toward a model for advocacy: Values, roles, and conceptions from community psychology. In G.H. Weber and G.J. McCall (Eds.), *Social scientists as advocates: Viewed from applied disciplines*. Beverly Hills, CA: Sage, 1978.

Davidson, W.S., Seidman, E., Rappaport, J., Berck, P.L., Rapp, N., Rhodes, W., & Herring, J. "The diversion of juvenile offenders: Some empirical light on the subject." *Social Work Research and Abstract*, 1977, *14*, 313-338.

Davidson, W.S., Snellman, L., & Koch, J.R. Current status of diversion research: Implications for policy and programming. In R. Roesch & R.R. Corrado (Eds.), *Evaluation and criminal justice policy*. Beverly Hills, CA: Sage, 1981.

Felner, R.D., Ginter, G., & Primavera, J. Primary prevention during school transitions: Social support and environmental structure." *American Journal of Community Psychology*, 1982, *10*, 277-290.

Gibbons, D.C., & Blake, G.F. Evaluating the impact of juvenile diversion programs. *Crime and Delinquency*, 1976, *22*, 411-427.

Gold, M. *Delinquent behavior in an American city*. Belmont, CA: Brooks Cole, 1970.

Gold, M. & Petronio, R.J. Delinquent behavior in adolescence. In J. Adelson (Ed.), *Handbook of adolescent psychology*. New York: Wiley, 1980.

Gold, M., & Reimer, D.J. Changing patterns of delinquent behavior among Americans 13 through 16 years old: 1967-72. *Crime and Delinquency Literature*, 1975, *7*, 483-517.

Hazard, G.C. The jurisprudence of juvenile deviance. In M.K. Rosenheim (Ed.), *Pursuing justice for the child*. Chicago: University of Chicago Press, 1976.

Hickey, W.L. Status offense and the juvenile court. *Criminal Justice Abstracts*, 1977, *9*, 91-122.

Institute of Judicial Administration/American Bar Association Standards for Juvenile Justice, Juvenile Justice Standards Project. Washington, DC: Author, 1977.

Johnston, L.D., O'Malley, P.M., & Eveland, L.K. Drugs and delinquency: A search for causal connections. In D.G. Kandel (Ed.), *Longitudinal research on drug use: Empirical findings and methodological issues*. Washington, DC: Hemisphere, 1978.

Kett, J.F. *Rites of passage: Adolescence in America 1790 to the present.* New York: Basic Books, 1977.

Klein, M.W. Deinstitutionalization and diversion of juvenile offenders: A litany of impediments. In N. Morris & M. Tony (Eds.), *Crime and justice.* Chicago: University of Chicago Press, 1979.

Klein, M.W. Where juvenile justice meets social service: Social intervention with troubled youth. In E. Seidman (Ed.), *Handbook of social intervention.* Beverly Hills, CA: Sage, 1983.

Lerman, P. Delinquency and social policy: A historical perspective. *Crime and Delinquency,* 1977, *23,* 383-393.

Mulvey, E.P., & Hicks, A. The paradoxical effect of a juvenile code change in Virginia. *American Journal of Community Psychology,* 1982. *10,* 705-721.

O'Donnell, C.R. Environmental design and the prevention of psychological problems. In P. Feldman & J. Orford (Eds.), *Psychological problems: The social context.* London: Wiley, 1980.

O'Malley, P.M., Bachman, J.G., & Johnston, L.D. *Youth in transition. Final report: Five years beyond high school: Causes and consequences of educational attainment.* Ann Arbor: Institute for Social Research, University of Michigan, 1977.

Palmer, T.B., & Lewis, R.V. A differentiated approach to juvenile diversion. *Journal of Research in Crime and Delinquency,* 1980, *17,* 209-229.

President's Commission on Law Enforcement and Administration of Justice. *Task force report: Corrections.* Washington, DC: U.S. Government Printing Office, 1967.

Rappaport, J. *Community psychology: Values, research and action.* New York: Holt, Rinehart & Winston, 1977.

Rappaport, J. In praise of paradox: A social policy of empowerment over prevention. *American Journal of Community Psychology,* 1981, *9,* 1-15.

Rappaport, J., Lamiell, J.T., & Seidman, E. Ethical issues for psychologists in the juvenile justice system: Know and tell. In J. Monahan (Ed.), *Who is the client: The ethics of psychological intervention in the criminal justice system.* Washington, DC: American Psychological Association, 1980.

Rappaport, J., & Seidman, E. Social and community intervention. In C.E. Walker (Ed.), *Handbook of clinical psychology.* Homewood, IL: Dow-Jones-Irwin, 1983.

Rappaport, J., Seidman, E. & Davidson, W.S. Demonstration research and manifest versus true adoption: The natural history of a research project to divert adolescents from the legal system. In R.F. Munoz, L.R. Snowden, J.C. Kelly (Eds.), *Social and psychological research in community settings.* San Francisco: Jossey-Bass, 1979.

Resources for Youth 10 (1, 2), 1980.

Rosenheim, M.K. Notes on helping juvenile nuisances. In M.K. Rosenheim (Ed.), *Pursuing justice for the child.* Chicago: University of Chicago, 1976.

Rutherford, A., & McDermott, R. *Juvenile diversion.* Washington, DC: National Institute of Law Enforcement and Criminal Justice, 1976.

Ryan, W. *Blaming the victim.* New York: Vintage, 1971.

Sarri, R. The effectiveness paradox: Institutional versus community placement of offenders. *Journal of Social Issues,* 1981, *37,* 34-50.

Schultz, J.L., & Cohen, F. Isolationism in juvenile court jurisprudence. In M.K. Rosenheim (Ed.), *Pursuing justice for the child.* Chicago: University of Chicago, 1976.

Schur, E.W. *Radical non-intervention: Rethinking the delinquency problem.* Englewood Cliffs, NJ: Prentice-Hall, 1973.

Seidman, E. The route from the successful experiment to policy formation: Falling rocks, bumps and dangerous curves. In R. Roesch & R.R. Corrado (Eds.), *Evaluation and criminal justice policy.* Beverly Hills, CA: Sage, 1981.

Seidman, E. Introduction. In E. Seidman (Ed.), *Handbook of social intervention.* Beverly Hills, CA: Sage, 1983.(a)

Seidman, E. Unexamined premises of social problem-solving. In E. Seidman (Ed.), *Handbook of social intervention.* Beverly Hills, CA: Sage, 1983.(b)

Seidman, E., Rappaport, J., & Davidson, W.S. Adolescents in legal jeopardy: Initial success and replication of an alternative to the criminal justice system. In R. Ross & P. Gendreau (Eds.), *Effective correctional treatment.* Toronto: Butterworth, 1980.

Strasburg, P.A. *Violent delinquents: A report to the Ford Foundation from the Vera Institute of Justice.* New York: Sovereign, 1978.

Watzlawick, P., Weakland, J.H., & Fisch, R. *Change: Principles of problem formation and problem resolution.* New York: W.W. Norton, 1974.

Weiner, I.B. Psychopathology in adolescence. In Adelson, J. (Ed.), *Handbook of adolescent psychology.* New York: Wiley, 1980.

Weiner, I.B. & DelGaudio, A.C. Psychopathology in adolescence: An epidemiological study. *Archives of General Psychiatry,* 1976, *33,* 187-193.

Wolfgang, M.E., Figlio, R.M., & Sellin, T. *Delinquency in a birth cohort.* Chicago: University of Chicago Press, 1972.

Zatz, J. Problems and issues in deinstitutionalization: Historical overview and current attitudes. In J.F. Handler & J. Zatz (Eds.), *Neither angels nor thieves: Studies in deinstitutionalization of status offenders.* Washington, DC: National Academy Press, 1982.

# PART V

# CHILDREN IN THE EDUCATIONAL SYSTEM

# 12

# Psychological Assessment in the Schools

**Donald N. Bersoff**
*Ennis, Friedman, Bersoff & Ewing*
*Washington, DC*
*University of Maryland*
*Johns Hopkins University*

It has been estimated that more than 250 million standardized tests of academic ability, perceptual and motor skills, emotional and social characteristics, and vocational interests and talent are administered by school systems each year (Brim, Glass, Neulinger, Firestone, & Lerner, 1969; Holman & Docter, 1972). The use of tests has been so widespread that it is likely that every person in the United States has been affected in some way by their results (Haney, 1981). Tests are used in conjunction with almost every major educational practice, e.g., screening, placement, program planning, program evaluation, and assessment of individual progress. It is because they have such a significant impact on children's futures that they have come under increasing legal scrutiny (Bersoff, 1979, 1982). This is especially so in two major kinds of cases: (1) where it is alleged that the tests are discriminatory tools denying minority and handicapped children the full realization of their civil and constitutional rights; (2) where it is generally asserted that tests serve as devices fostering impermissible intrusion by the government into the private lives of its citizens.

Author's Note: This chapter is a revised and updated version of materials appearing in the following work. Donald N. Bersoff, "Children as Participants in Psychoeducational Assessment," in *Children's Competence to Consent,* G. Melton, G. Koocher, and M. Saks (eds.). Copyright ©1983 by Plenum Publishing Corp. Reprinted by permission.

## Legal Underpinnings

Although criticism of testing from social, political, and psychological commentators spans more than six decades, only in the last fifteen years have legal scholars, the legislature, and the courts begun to examine their use. This recent activity, in turn, has generated intense reexamination by behavioral scientists. In the past two years, for example, the American Psychological Association (APA) devoted an entire issue of the *American Psychologist* (Glaser & Bond, 1981) and a full day at its 1981 convention to testing; the National Academy of Sciences financed three extended examinations by blue ribbon committees (Heller, Holtzman, & Messick, 1982; Sherman & Robinson, 1982; Wigdor & Garner, 1982) of the topic; and a joint committee of the APA, the American Educational Research Association, and the National Council on Measurement in Education (1974) began revising the *Standards for Psychological & Educational Tests* to be published in 1985.

The courts are traditionally wary of interfering with the discretion of trained experts, especially in those areas in which they concede lack of specialized knowledge. And, there are few fields of endeavor that are more arcane and unknowable than measurement and evaluation. However, when the activities of psychologists directly and sharply implicate fundamental values protected by the Constitution, the courts, as ultimate interpreters of its content, have found it appropriate to intervene.

Two basic constitutional values relevant to those who construct, use, interpret, and take tests appear in the Fifth and Fourteenth Amendments. Generally, those amendments serve as barriers to thoughtless and arbitrary actions by local, county, state, and federal officials (the Fifth Amendment pertains to the federal government; the Fourteenth to other governmental entities). The two most important concepts embodied in those amendments are equal protection and due process. Under the equal protection clause, governments are forbidden to give differential treatment to persons who are similarly situated, unless there is a supportable reason for so doing. And, when special groups of persons are affected by the state's action, the courts will scrutinize that action even more closely. For example, while the battle for the Equal Rights Amendment has been lost (at least for the time being), the Supreme Court has held that governmental bodies must produce substantial and legitimate reasons for detrimental gender-based actions. With regard to racial and ethnic minorities, the test is even more difficult. When the state has deliberately acted to the disadvantage of one of those groups, it must prove that it has a compelling or overriding need to do so. This is because these groups have been

> saddled with such disabilities or (have been) subjected to such a history of purposeful unequal treatment, or relegated to such a position of political powerlessness as to command extraordinary protection from the majoritarian political process.[1]

The result, when courts apply this "strict scrutiny" test, is almost invariably against the government.

The due process clause forbids the government from denying persons life, liberty, or property without a legitimate reason and without providing some meaningful and impartial forum to prevent abitrary deprivations of those protected interests. Both property and liberty interests have been broadly defined by the Supreme Court. Property interests include any government-created entitlements, such as tenure, licensure to practice one's profession, or access to public education. Liberty includes not only freedom from involuntary incarceration in a prison or commitment to a mental institution. It also encompasses the right to privacy, personal security, and reputation. Thus, for example, the Constitution prevents governmental institutions from unilateral, unsupportable, and stigmatizing labeling—"official branding" Justice Douglas once called it—of persons as handicapped or mentally ill. What procedures due process may require under any given set of circumstances begins with a determination of the precise nature of the government function as well as the potential entitlement that will be lost as the result of the governmental action. While the precise contours of due process change with the nature of the interest at stake, at bottom the clause requires fundamental fairness when the government deals with persons within its jurisdiction.

In addition to these constitutional guarantees, there is a whole litany of federal and state statutory protections that may be invoked to challenge the inappropriate use of tests, not only in the public sector, but in private industry as well. Together, these enactments provide extensive armamentaria for potential plaintiffs.

With this background, let us now turn to some of the most important examples of challenges to tests in education.

## Early History

The Supreme Court's ringing declarations in *Brown v. Board of Education*[2] ended state-imposed segregation in the public schools. But in the decade after *Brown*, many southern school systems refused to accept the Court's decision as final. They interpreted the Court's assertion that separation of black children from white "solely because of their race generates a feeling of inferiority . . . that may affect their hearts and minds in a way unlikely ever to be undone" (p. 494) as an empirically testable hypothesis, not a normative legal principle. Thus, in the early 1960s one of Georgia's school systems sought to disprove what it believed to be an erroneous factual premise. They attempted to show that differences in learning rates, cognitive ability, behavioral traits, and capacity for education in general were so great that not only was it impossible for black children and white children to be educated effectively in the same room but that to "congregate children of such diverse traits in schools . . . would seriously impair the educational opportunities of both white and Negro and cause them grave psychological harm."[3]

To prove their contentions, the defendants called several expert witnesses. Based on such instruments as the California Achievement Test and the California Mental Maturity Tests, they testified that significant differences in test scores were indicative of inherent differences in the races and that only minor changes could be achieved by educational readjustment or other environmental change. While the test results that led these witnesses to conclude that black children were genetically inferior and the tests on which those conclusions were based went unchallenged by attorneys fighting to enforce desegregation, the idea that such devices could measure innate ability found its way into a 1967 decision that, at the time, became the most persuasive and widely quoted legal opinion of its kind. That case is *Hobson v. Hansen.*[4]

At issue in Hobson was not psychological testing but rather the constitutionality of disparities in the allocation of financial and educational resources in the Washington, D.C., public school system that, it was claimed, favored white children. Also at issue was the overrepresentation of black children in lower, and white children in upper, ability groups. In the course of the trial, however, it was adduced that the method by which track assignments were made depended almost entirely on such standardized group ability scales as the Metropolitan Readiness and Achievement Test and the Otis Quick-Scoring Mental Ability Test. Thus, it was disproportional placement in programs found to have a negative impact on black children, determined primarily by reliance on standardized tests, that triggered the court's intensive inquiry into the nature and limitations of standardized tests.

The court decided that classification on the basis of ability could be defended only if such judgments were based on measures that assessed children's capacity to learn, i.e., their innate endowment, not their present skill levels. The court concluded that the assessment devices upon which the classifications depend did not accurately reflect students' learning ability. The inevitable result was that ability grouping and the group tests relied upon to make tracking decisions were ruled unconstitutional. The words the court used to condemn the school system's practices were to have a profound effect on the use of psychological tests during the next decade.

> The evidence shows that the method by which track assignments are made depends essentially on standardized aptitude tests which, although given on a system-wide basis, are completely inappropriate for use with a large segment of the student body. Because these tests are standardized primarily on and are relevant to a white middle class group of students, they produce inaccurate and misleading test scores when given to lower class and Negro students . . . these students are in reality being classified . . . (on) factors which have nothing to do with innate ability.[5]

*Hobson*, when read in its entirety, represents the justified condemnation of rigid, poorly conceived classification practices that negatively affected the educational opportunities of minority children and led to permanent stigmatization of blacks as unteachable. But swept within *Hobson*'s condemnation of harmful classification practices were ability tests used as the sole or primary decision-making devices to justify placement. Tests were banned unless they could be shown to measure children's innate capacity to learn. No psychologist who has written on the subject, including Jensen (1969, 1980), believes that tests measure hereditary endowment solely (e.g., Anastasi, 1976; Cleary, Humphreys, Kendrick, & Wesman, 1975). But, if that were the criterion, no test could pass it.

The decision, however, stimulated a round of post-*Hobson* cases throughout the country. In many southern school systems during the early 1970s, any kind of ability or achievement testing for pupil assignment purposes was banned until unitary school systems were established. In the Southwest there was another group of cases with two new significant dimensions. First, the plaintiffs were Hispanics, rather than blacks. Second, the cases they brought began to attack the stately, revered, and venerated devices against which all other tests were measured—the individual intelligence scales such as the Stanford-Binet and the Wechsler Intelligence Scale for Children (WISC). The most important trio of cases, *Covarrubias v. San Diego Unified School District*,[6] *Guadalupe Organization, Inc. v. Tempe School No. 3*,[7] and *Diana v. State Board of Education*,[8] were all settled out of court by consent decree (i.e., voluntary agreement by the parties, approved by the court prior to the final judgment, in which the litigants accept findings and structure remedies), but each led to important changes in school testing policy that foretold more pervasive developments.

### Individual Intelligence Tests:
### Larry P. and PASE

The decade from 1971-1980 brought the most severe challenge to the use of individual intelligence scales, as the result of federal court decisions in San Francisco[9] and Chicago.[10] If *Hobson* was the seminal case of the 1960s, *Larry P. v. Riles* (1972, 1979) deserves similar status for the 1970s. The trial court's decision on the merits, which took eight years to reach, threatens the continued administration of individual intelligence tests and the existence of classes for the educably mentally retarded (EMR) as they involve minority children. As the rationale of the decision will almost certainly guide future litigation concerning psychological assessment generally, the case warrants detailed examination. The case has had two phases: the granting of a preliminary injunction in 1972 (*Riles I*)[11] and the decision on the merits in 1979 (*Riles II*).

In 1971 black children attending the San Francisco schools filed suit charging discrimination and misplacement in EMR classes as a result of administration of state-approved intelligence tests. The plaintiffs claimed they were not mentally retarded and that the tests used to place them were culturally biased. They requested that the court grant a preliminary injunction restraining the school system from administering IQ tests to determine EMR placement of black children until there was a full trial to decide the merits of their complaint.

The legal importance of the case in 1971 lay in the plaintiff's contention that the testing practices in San Francisco resulted in a disproportionate and harmful impact on black children in violation of the equal protection clause. Framed in that manner, a court was faced squarely for the first time with the issue of the constitutionality of individual psychological testing when used for placement in classes for the retarded in situations adversely affecting racial minorities.

The undisputed facts in the case were that, although blacks constituted only 28.5 percent of students in the San Francisco school system, 66 percent of all students in its EMR program were black. Similarly, although blacks comprised 9.1 percent of the California school population, 27 percent of all school children in the state in EMR classes were black. Thus, the contention of the plaintiffs was that, although placement in EMR classes was based on intelligence, not race, the method of classification led to a disproportionate impact on black children.

San Francisco in 1972 conceded that the tests were racially and culturally biased but justified their continued use on the fact that, in the absence of suitable alternatives, they were the best means available for the purpose of classifying students as retarded. The court retorted that

the absence of any rational means of identifying children in need of such treatment can hardly render acceptable an otherwise concededly irrational means, such as the IQ test as it is presently administered to black students. (*Riles I*, 1972, p. 1313)

Other attempts to sustain the reasonableness of their practices of to explain racial disproportionality in EMR programs also were rejected and the school system's practices were adjudged to violate the equal protection clause. The court enjoined any future placement of black children in EMR classes on the basis of criteria that relied primarily on the results of intelligence tests and led to racial imbalance in such classes. (For an empirically-based defense of the part school psychologists played in the evaluation of these children see Meyers, Macmillan, & Yoshida, [1978].)

Three events followed the court's decision. An appellate tribunal in 1974 affirmed the lower court's order holding that "the carefully limited relief granted (was) justified by the 'peculiar facts' in this case" (*Larry P. v. Riles*, 1974, p. 965). Then the trial court approved the plaintiff's motion to broaden the injunction so as to prohibit the administration of individual intelligence tests to all black children in the state. Finally, California itself decided to go beyond even that ban. In 1975 it issued a resolution stating that until further notice none of the IQ tests then on its approved list could be used to place any children, regardless of race, in EMR classes in the state.

This activity ended the first phase of the case. The second phase, the trial on the substantive issues, did not begin until October 1977 and did not end until mid-1978, producing over 10,000 pages of testimony. Only in October 1979 did the court finally publish its opinion, in which it decided whether the preliminary injunction it granted in 1972 should become permanent.

In the interim, Congress enacted a series of laws that continue to have a considerable impact on the practice of psychological assessment in the public schools. In 1975 Congress passed Public Law (P.L.) 94-142 (20 U.S.C. §§1401-1461), the Education for All Handicapped Children Act, extending legislation it had first passed in 1966 and 1974. Two years earlier it enacted section 504 of the Rehabilitation Act of 1973 (29 U.S.C. §794) and subsequently amended it in 1978. Implementing regulations for both those bills were drafted by the Department of Health, Education and Welfare (now Department of Health and Human Services and the Department of Education) which took effect in 1977.

P.L. 94-142 is essentially a grant-giving statute providing financial support to state and local education agencies for special education and related services if they meet certain detailed eligibility requirements. Earlier legislation (P.L. 93-380) had put school systems on notice that they would have to develop methods for ensuring that any assessment devices used,"for the purposes of classification and placement of handicapped children will be selected and administered so as not to be racially and culturally discriminatory." P.L. 94-142 and its implementing regulations reaffirmed this mandate concerning nondiscriminatory evaluation and fleshed out the meaning of this requirement:

(a) Tests and other evaluation materials:
> (1) Are provided and administered in the child's native language or other mode of communication . . .,
> (2) Have been validated for the specific purpose for which they are used; and
> (3) Are administered by trained personnel in conformance with instructions provided by their provided. (34 C.F.R. §300.532)

The most ambiguous of these provisions is (a)(2). The regulations, on their face, require test validation but not test validity.[12] Even if one infers that both are necessary, there is no indication as to what level of validity a test must conform. Validity coefficients that psychologists find acceptable may not pass constitutional muster. One court has ruled that "when a program talks about labeling someone as a particular type and such a label could remain with him for the remainder of his life, the margin of error must be almost nil" (*Merriken v. Cressman*, 1973, p. 920).[13] "Nil" implies nearly perfect coefficients. Few, if any, psychometric instruments yield reliability, much less validity, coefficients above .95. Until the decision in *Riles II*, as we shall see, there were few clear-cut judicial or statutory guidelines with regard to standards of validity in school testing or the general concept of nondiscriminatory assessment (see Neuberger, 1981; Smith 1980).

With regard to the Rehabilitation Act, a multipurpose law to promote the education, employment, and training of handicapped persons, Congress declared in §504,

> No otherwise qualified handicapped individual in the United States . . . shall, solely by reason of his handicap, be excluded from participation in, be denied the benefits of, or be subjected to discrimination under any program or activity receiving federal financial assistance.

This section represents the first federal civil rights law protecting the rights of handicapped persons and reflects a national commitment to end discrimination on the basis of handicap. Unlike P.L. 94-142, the requirements of §504 are not triggered by receipt of funds under a specific statue, but they protect handicapped persons in all institutions receiving federal financial assistance. Thus, any school system, public or private, receiving federal monies is bound by its mandates.

In mid-1977 the Office of Civil Rights, Department of Health, Education and Welfare (DHEW), published a lengthy set of regulations implementing the broad right-granting language of section 504. Subpart D of six subparts pertains to preschool, elementary, and secondary education. In addition to general principles already established under P.L. 94-142, they include rules for the evaluation of children suspected of being handicapped. The language of those provisions (including the requirement of validated tests) is almost identical to that which now appears in the implementing regulations to P.L. 94-142 and will not be repeated here (see 34 C.F.R. §104.35).

Judge Peckham finally published his long, controversial opinion on the merits in October 1979. The court found in favor of the plaintiffs on both statutory and constitutional grounds. It permanently enjoined the defendants

> from utilizing, permitting the use of, or approving the use of any standardized tests . . . for the identification of black EMR children or their placement into EMR classes, without first securing prior approval by this court. (*Larry P. v. Riles*, 1979, p. 989)

The court's primary focus was on the nondiscriminatory provisions of section 504 and P.L. 94-142, particularly that part of the implementing regulations requiring that the assessment instruments be "validated for the specific purpose for which they are used." The court's interpretation of these provisions, of crucial importance in its ultimate decision and the shaping of the final remedy, broke new ground, for as the court recognized, "there are no cases applying validation criteria to tests used for EMR placement" (p. 969).

The court held that defendants should bear the burden of proving that the tests used for placement had been validated for black children. However, it would not merely accept proof that the tests used were able to predict school performance. It adopted the more stringent requirement that the tests be shown valid for selecting children who would be unable to profit from instruction in regular classes with remedial instruction. The tests would have to identify accurately those children who belonged in what the court characterized as isolated, dead-end, stigmatizing EMR programs. This kind of validation, the court found, had not been done.

> Defendants must come forward and show that they (the tests) have been validated for each minority group with which they are used . . . This minimal burden has not been met for diagnosing the kind of mental retardation justifying the EMR placement. (p. 971).

The court rejected validity studies correlating IQ scores with college grades or with other achievement tests. It was satisfied only with research relating IQ scores for black children with classroom grades, although the latter were admittedly subjective. The one relevant study cited (Goldman & Hartig, 1976) yielded correlations between IQ scores and grades for white children of .25 and only .14 for blacks. On that basis, one prominent psychologist testified that the WISC had "little or no validity for predicting the scholastic performance of black or brown children" (p. 972). (For a methodological critique of this study, see Messé, Crano, Messé, & Rice, [1979].) Thus, the court concluded "the I.Q. tests are differentially valid for black and white children . . . Differential validity means that more errors will be made for black children than whites, and that is unacceptable" (p. 973).

The court continued its analysis and found that alternative mechanisms for determining placement in EMR classes did exist. Between 1975 and the resolution of this case in 1979 there had been a statewide moratorium on the use of IQ tests to place all children, regardless of race, in EMR programs. The state's own employees, called as adverse witnesses by the plaintiffs, testified that adequate assessments had been made during that period without IQ tests, and that there was no evidence to suggest that misplacements had occurred as a result. In fact, the court found that more time and care had been taken during this period in placing children in EMR classes. Nevertheless, the court warned, alternatives to IQ tests themselves had not been validated, and disproportionate placement, while less egregious than in the pre-1975 era, was still present. Continued use of tests would still be needed—not, however, for the purpose of labeling children as retarded, but for "the development of curricula that respond to specific educational needs" (p. 974).

Judge Peckham was not content to rest his decision solely on statutory grounds. Testing for EMR placement had been preliminarily enjoined in *Riles I* on the basis of equal protection claims, and the court felt bound to determine whether the plaintiffs continued to warrant relief under the Constitution "where this litigation commenced" (p. 975). But the plaintiffs' task under the Fourteenth Amendment was to show that the school system had acted with the intent to discriminate. This task was made easier when the court, in Riles II, made clear that it would not so narrowly define discriminatory purpose "to mean an intent to harm black children" (p. 979). It would suffice if plaintiffs showed an intent to segregate those children into classes for the educably retarded. In the end, the court was satisfied that the plaintiffs had met this burden.

It was the EMR program, however, that received the brunt of the court's condemnation. Throughout the opinion, Judge Peckham labeled the program "dead-end," "isolating," "inferior," and "stigmatizing." The court concluded that EMR classes were "designed to separate out children who are *incapable* of learning in regular classes" (p. 941) and were not meant to provide remedial instruction so that children could learn the skills necessary for eventual return to regular instruction. Given these characteristics, the court considered

> the decision to place children in these classes . . . a crucial one. Children wrongly placed in these classes are unlikely to escape as they inevitably lag farther and farther behind the children in regular classes. (p. 942)

Coupled with this pejorative view of the EMR program was the undeniable, substantial overrepresentation of black children in those classes—a fact essentially unchanged from *Riles I.*

The next step in the court's analysis was a review of the process by which a disproportionate number of black children were placed in EMR classes. It found that, although California had acknowledged in 1969 that minorities were overrepresented in EMR classes, it chose for the first time in that year to mandate the use of specific standardized individual intelligence tests for EMR placement. The list had been developed by a state department of education official who was not an expert in IQ testing, and was formulated primarily by surveying which tests had been most frequently used by California's school psychologists and by relying on the recommendations of test publishers. The court concluded that this "quick and unsystematic" process failed to consider "critical issues stemming from I.Q. testing" (p. 946), and its reaction was harsh: "by relying on the most commonly used tests, (the defendants) opted to perpetuate any discriminatory effects of those tests" (p. 947).

The court also found that despite California's statutory scheme that required the consideration of other pertinent and specified data, "the I.Q. score was clearly the most scrupulously kept record, and it appears to have been the most important one" (p. 950). Thus, the court hypothesized, "if the I.Q. tests are discriminatory, they inevitably must bias the entire process" (p. 950).

These initial analyses finally brought the court to the central issue: the nature of the intelligence tests themselves. Expert witnesses for both plaintiffs and defendants had agreed on two crucial facts. First, it was impossible to "truly define, much less measure, intelligence." Instead, "I.Q. tests, like other ability tests, essentially measure achievement" (p. 38), a significant departure from the assumption in *Hobson* and *Riles I* that the tests measure innate ability. Second, black children did significantly less well on intelligence tests than did their white counterparts. Only 2 percent of white students in California achieved IQ scores below 70, while 15 percent of black students did. The court then proceeded to discover if there were any acceptable explanations for the significantly disparate scores of blacks and white on IQ tests.

It confronted the most controversial explanation first—that the differences between the races were genetic in origin—but rejected any notion of inherent inferiority in black children. The defendants themselves eschewed reliance on this ground, although at least one psychological expert witness for the state did not rule out such an explanation. The court reasoned that the genetic theory overlooked the possibility of bias in the tests, and noted that believing intelligence is inherited did not lead inexorably to the conclusion that blacks were intellectually inferior.

The court gave somewhat more serious consideration to a socioeconomic theory upon which the defendants relied. The state claimed that differences in scores resulted from the rearing of poor children, both black and white, in inadequate homes and neighborhoods. But, while the court could accept the theory that poverty resulted in mental retardation, it refused to conclude that membership in the lower socioeconomic classes produced substantially more mentally retarded children.

The court then examined the hypothesis that cultural bias in the tests was the most cogent explanation for the disparities. The court noted that versions of the Stanford-Binet and Wechsler scales prior to the 1970s had been developed using only white children in the process of deriving norms against which all children would be measured. That these tests had been restandardized in the early 1970s to include a representative proportion of black children did not satisfy the court that they were valid for culturally different groups. "Mixing the populations without more does not eliminate any preexisting bias" (p. 957). The process failed to yield data that could be used to compare black and white children's performance on particular items.

In addition to standardization problems, the court identified two other indices of cultural bias. First, to the extent that black children were more likely to be exposed to nonstandard English, they would be handicapped in the verbal component of intelligence tests. Second, it averred that certain items were inherently unfair to black children from culturally different environments when viewed from the perspective of the scoring criteria offered in the examiner's manual. The court concluded that,

> to the extent that a "black culture" exists and translates the phenomenon of intelligence into skills and knowledge untested by the standardized intelligence tests, those tests cannot measure the capabilities of black children. (p. 960)

The court charged that the tests were never designed to eliminate bias against black children and blamed test developers and users for assuming "in effect that black children were less 'intelligent' than whites" (pp. 956-957).

Thus, the plaintiffs were held to have met their burden of proving discriminatory intent. The defendants could prevail only if explanations for their conduct passed muster under the most exacting of the equal protection tests. However, the court held that "defendants can establish no compelling state interest in the use of the I.Q. tests nor in the maintenance of EMR classes with overwhelming disproportions of black enrollment" (p. 985).

After finding for plaintiffs under both federal law and the Constitution (as well as the California Constitution), all that was left for the court was to forge proper remedies. In doing so, it recognized the genuine changes initiated by California during the course of litigation and the complexity and risk of judicial interference in the administration of education. It also did not want its condemnation of intelligence tests to be seen as the final judgment on the scientific validity of such devices. But these concerns did not dissuade the court from holding the state responsible for its failure to properly assess and educate black children, and from fashioning remedies to halt both test abuse and disproportionate enrollment of blacks in EMR classes.

The court permanently enjoined the state from using any standardized intelligence tests to identify black children for EMR placement without first securing approval from the court. The state board of education would have to petition the court after determining that the tests they sought to use were not racially or culturally discriminatory, that they would be administered in a nondiscriminatory manner, and that they had been validated for the purpose of placing black children in EMR classes. The petition would have to be supported by statistical evidence submitted under oath, and certification that public hearings had been held concerning the proposed tests.

With regard to disproportionate placement, the state was ordered to monitor and eliminate overrepresentation by obtaining annual data documenting enrollment in EMR classes by race and ethnicity, and by requiring each school district to prepare and adopt plans to correct significant imbalances. To remedy the harm to those children misidentified, the defendants were to reevaluate all black children then labeled as educably retarded without resort to any standardized intelligence tests that had not been approved by the court. Finally, schools would have to draft individual education plans designed to return all incorrectly identified children to regular classrooms.

The decision, over the objection of the California state board of education, has been appealed by Defendant Riles to the Ninth Circuit Court of Appeals. In November 1981 the appellate tribunal had heard the case, but its decision is not expected until late 1983.

Almost nine months to the day after Judge Peckham issued his opinion in *Riles II*, Judge Grady (a federal court judge in Illinois), rendered his decision in *PASE v. Hannon* (1980). While the facts, issues, claims, and witnesses were very similar to *Larry P.*, the analysis and outcome could not have been more different. Rather than ruling that the tests in question were culturally biased, as did Judge Peckham, Judge Grady held that the WISC, WISC-R and Stanford-Binet tests, when used in conjunction with the statutorily mandated ("other criteria") for determining an appropriate educational program for a child (under P.L. 94-142) . . . do not discriminate against black children in the Chicago public schools. Defendants are complying with the statutory mandate. (*PASE v. Hannon*, 1980, p. 883)

The case was brought on behalf of all black children who were or would in the future be placed in Chicago's EMR classes. Like the plaintiffs in *Larry P.*, they claimed that blacks were overrepresented in those programs. As in San Francisco, the EMR curriculum is limited to helping the child become economically independent. Children who graduate from EMR classes are not qualified for college entrance, nor do they receive a regular diploma. The court called inappropriate placement in EMR classes "an educational tragedy" (p. 834) and accepted as fact that even for children properly placed, EMR students "suffer from feelings of inferiority" (p. 834).

Using a strategy similar to that in *Larry P.*, the two named plaintiffs in *PASE* showed that although they were placed in EMR classes for several years, they were not genuinely retarded. Recent reevaluations indicated they were children of normal intelligence whose learning was hampered by remediable disabilities. The plaintiffs claimed that the misassessment was caused by racial bias in the individually administered IQ tests. The use of those tests, they claimed, violated the equal protection clause of the Constitution, as well as the same federal statutes at issue in *Larry P.* Unlike *Larry P.*, the trial itself lasted only three weeks. Many of the witnesses who appeared in *Riles II* also testified for the plaintiffs in *PASE* and offered similar testimony concerning the history of IQ misuse and cultural bias. The defendants conceded that the tests could be slightly biased but asserted that this did not deprive the tests of their utility; nor did the use of the tests result in misclassification. The school system reminded the court that the ultimate diagnosis of retardation was based on a combination of factors, and that the IQ score was only one of them. They were concerned that the absence of this relatively objective measure would force the school to make decisions on predominantly subjective criteria.

While Judge Peckham carefully listened to and frequently cited the opinions of the expert witnesses who testified in San Francisco, Judge Grady was significantly less influenced by those same witnesses in Chicago.

> None of the witnesses in this case has so impressed me with his or her credibility or expertise that I would feel secure in basing a decision simply upon his or her opinion. In some instances, I am satisfied that the opinions expressed are more the result of doctrinaire commitment to a preconceived idea than they are the result of scientific inquiry. I need something more than the conclusions of the witnesses in order to arrive at my own conclusion. (p. 836)

Judge Grady claimed to have considered the expert testimony, but stated that he was not bound by it. What he felt it imperative to do was to examine the tests themselves, item by item, so he could judge for himself whether the claim of cultural bias could be sustained. He concluded that he could not see how an informed decision concerning the question could be reached in any other way. He had no reservations about his competency to make those determinations. Thus, in a startling and extraordinary maneuver, Judge Grady proceeded to cite every question on the WISC, WISC-R, and Stanford-Binet and to give every acceptable response (including both the two- and one-point answers where pertinent) for the purpose of determining which items, in the court's estimation, were culturally biased against black children. This process took nearly 35 pages of the court's 52-page opinion.

The end result of this analysis was the court's conclusion that only eight items on the WISC or WISC-R and one item on the Binet were "biased or so subject to suspicion of bias that they should not be used" (p. 875). He rejected the assertions of Robert Williams, the black psychologist who had devised the BITCH test (Black Intelligence Test of Cultural Homogeneity), that many other items were unfair to blacks:

> It would be possible to devise countless esoteric tests which would be failed by persons unfamiliar with particular subject matter. Every ethnic group . . . has its own vocabulary, its own universe of information, which is not generally shared by others. The fact that it would be possible to prepare an unfair test does not prove that the Weschler or Stanford-Binet tests are unfair.

> Dr. Williams' criticism of many test items appear unrelated to the question of racial bias. In fact, of the relatively few items he did discuss, most of them were criticized as inappropriate tests of any child's intelligence, not simply a black child's intelligence. (pp. 874-875)

If the tests were not culturally biased, then, what was the explanation for the significant mean differences between white and black children's IQ scores? Like the parties in *Larry P.*, both the plaintiffs and defendants in *PASE* rejected a genetic theory: "There is no dispute . . . about the equality of innate intellectual capacity. Defendants assert no less strongly than plaintiffs that there are no genetic differences in mental capacity" (p. 877). Unlike the court in both *Riles I* and *Riles II*, where Judge Peckham had rejected a socioeconomic explanation, Judge Grady found that argument persuasive. Accepting the arguments of the school system's witnesses that the acquisition of intellectual skills is greatly affected by a child's early intellectual stimulation, the court reasoned,

> Defendant's explanation of the I.Q. difference, that it is caused by socio-economic factors . . . is consistent with other circumstances not accounted for by

plaintiff's theory of cultural bias. It is uncontradicted that most of the children in the EMH (Educably Mentally Handicapped; same as EMR) classes do in fact come from the poverty pockets of the city. This tends to suggest that what is involved is not simply race but something associated with poverty. It is also significant that many black children who take the test score at levels high enough to preclude EMH placement. Plaintiffs have not explained why the alleged cultural bias of the tests did not result in EMH level scores for these children. Plaintiffs' theory of cultural bias simply ignores the fact that black children perform differently from each other on the tests. It also fails to explain the fact that some black children perform better than most whites. (p. 878)

With that, the court concluded that the plaintiffs had failed to prove their contention that the intelligence tests were culturally unfair to black children. Even if they were, the court believed that still would not make the assessment process biased. Judge Grady read P.L. 94-142's prohibition against single measures and its requirement of nondiscriminatory assessment as meaning that the entire psychoeducational evaluation, when viewed as a whole, had to be nonbiased. A single procedure, by itself, could be discriminatory without condemning the entire system as invalid for placing minority children in EMR programs. The court reasoned that multiple procedures assured that results from the intelligence test would be interpreted in the light of other evaluation devices and information sources.

The court in *PASE*, therefore, viewed the placement process as a protective device against misclassification, in contrast to the court in *Riles II*, which concentrated on an analysis of the tests. Judge Peckham found California's system of assessment sound in theory, but condemned it in practice, finding that testing continued to loom as the most important determinant of EMR placement. Judge Grady scrutinized the process in Chicago and concluded that referral, screening, multidisciplinary evaluation, and the staff conference helped ensure that misclassification did not occur. In fact, he found that for all subranges within the EMR classification scheme, fewer children were ultimately labeled as retarded than would have been the case based on their IQ score alone. Although the court conceded that some children were misplaced, it rejected the hypothesis that erroneous placements were due to racial bias in the intelligence tests. (However, for research that casts serious doubt on this analysis and concludes that IQ is the critical causal variable in the placement, see Berk, Bridges, and Shih [1981].)

But what of Judge Peckham's decision in *Riles II*? Judge Grady's reference to *Larry P.* occupied a bit less than one page of his long opinion, and he virtually rejected its persuasiveness out of hand. He concluded that Judge Peckham's analysis never attacked what Judge Grady considered the threshold question—whether or not the tests were in fact biased. Judge Grady believed that one could not arrive at a proper decision concerning the plaintiffs' claims in either case without examining the issue of test bias in detail. As for the California court's ultimate decision, Judge Grady merely said, "the witnesses and the arguments that persuaded Judge Peckham have not persuaded me" (p. 882).

The plaintiff school children appealed Judge Grady's decision. Ironically, Chicago's new school board voluntarily decided to end individual intelligence testing for EMR placement as part of a schoolwide desegregation plan, thereby making the appeal unnecessary, from the plaintiffs' perspective. The case is currently entangled in procedural maneuvers, and an ultimate decision on appeal may never be reached.

There is no doubt that in their disparate ways, *Riles II* and *PASE* will have a significant effect on professional practice in the schools. Broadly interpreted, *Riles II* casts doubt on the continued utility of traditional psychometric evaluations using psychology's current storehouse of standardized ability tests. The court required the state to meet several validity criteria before it would approve continued administration of intelligence tests:

(1) Tests would have to yield the same pattern of scores when administered to different groups of people.
(2) Tests would have to yield approximately equal means of all subgroups included in the standardization sample.
(3) Tests would have to be correlated with relevant concurrent or predictive measures.

Regarding the third criterion, the court rejected validity studies correlating IQ scores with college grades or with other achievement tests. As all the experts agreed that intelligence tests were merely achievement tests by another name, the court in *Riles II* held that studies comparing IQ scores with scores on labeled achievement tests spuriously inflated validity coefficients because of "autocorrelation." The court would be satisfied only with research relating IQ scores of black children with classroom grades.

Given the court's definition of validity, it is unlikely that any of the currently used intelligence tests meets its criteria. In fact, it is unlikely that any psychological test, particularly the commonly used personality and projective instruments, would be acceptable to the court.

The most important disagreement between *Riles II* and *PASE* consisted of their analyses of the allegation of cultural bias in the Wechsler Scales and the Stanford-Binet. Judge Peckham found the tests to be deficient on this ground; Judge Grady did not. The permanent injunction against the administration of individual intelligence tests to place black children in EMR classes in *Riles II* was based almost entirely on the court's conclusion that the tests were culturally biased. The persuasiveness of the court's opinion, therefore, depends almost entirely on the correctness of this finding. Regardless of whether one applauds or decries the result, there are unfortunate infirmities in the court's analysis. In like manner, Judge Grady's eventual holding that the black plaintiffs in *PASE* had failed to prove that the tests were discriminatory was based on his estimation of the absence of bias. The method by which he reached that judgment was embarrassingly devoid of intellectual integrity.

Though Judge Peckam rested his decision on the finding that the tests were culturally biased, he provided little hard data to support such a conclusion, and was tentative in discussing it. In fact, in his almost 70-page printed opinion, the empirical support for the court's conclusions consumed only one page. Moreover, the court's determination that the tests contain questions biased against poor black children is not uniformly accepted, and there are some data to suggest that whatever discrimination there is in tests, lower scores in blacks are not the result of content bias.

Efforts to produce culture-free tests or to reduce content bias have met with little success. "Nonverbal or performance tests are now generally recognized as falling short of the goal of freedom from cultural influences, and attempts to develop cultural fair verbal tests . . . are recognized as failures" (Reschly, 1979, p. 231). More specifically, Anastasi (1976, p. 348) states, "On the WISC, for instance, black children usually find the Performance Tests as difficult or more difficult that the Verbal tests; this pattern is also characteristic of children from low socioeconomic levels (p. 348)." Kirp (1973) concludes that it is sobering but instructive to recognize that minority children do poorly even on so-called culture-free tests" (p. 758).

There has been relatively little research on content bias itself, particularly with regard to individual intelligence tests. What has been found with regard to standardized tests generally (Flaugher, 1978; Green, 1978) or individual intelligence tests specifically (Reschly, 1980; Reynolds, 1982; Sandoval, 1979) do not support Judge Peckham's conclusions.

If Judge Peckham's analysis of the issue of cultural bias was scanty and faulty, Judge Grady's can best be described as naive. At worst, it was unintelligent and completely devoid of empirical content. What it represented was a single person's personal judgment cloaked in the apparent authority of judicial robes. The court's opinion in *PASE* amply supports Reschly's (1980) conclusion, that with regard to item bias on the individually administered intelligence tests, "Subjective judgments appear to be unreliable and invalid in terms of empirical analysis . . . The only data confirming test bias that exists now is judgmental and speculative" (p. 127).

What makes Judge Grady's opinion interesting, if not precedent setting, is the fact that the published and easily accessible decision contains the questions and correct answers to every question on the WISC, WISC-R, and Stanford-Binet. Whether inadvertently or purposely, Judge Grady has given the test away. Although Judge Grady eventually upheld the tests as valid, his decision, to a far greater extent than Judge Peckham's in Riles II, may have the effect of invalidating the tests as they are presently used. The security of these tests may have, indeed, been seriously compromised, if not destroyed.

## The Child as Missing Person

The two cases just described, *Larry P.* and *PASE*, represent divergent views of two judges who both sought to advocate for the rights of children; but that advocacy was limited. One legal scholar (Kleinfeld, 1970, 1971) has distinguished between the right of persons to make various choices and the right of persons to be protected from the choices or initiatives of others. For the most part, children have benefited only from advances falling within the latter category. In psychological assessment and in almost all other aspects of life, children remain—like Ralph Ellison's hero—Invisible Persons whose views are infrequently evoked and whose wishes are rarely controlling. The concern of the legal system that children's interests be protected represents advocacy only of the second kind. Everyone is asked to serve children's best interests even if that means overriding their refusal to participate in psychological assessment when adults believe children will benefit from them. Children's right to choose "is not viewed as presently existing . . . but as maturing in the future" (Hirshberg, 1980, p. 225).

### Consent for Testing

One way of exemplifying how children are treated when they are referred for psychoeducational assessment in schools is to examine the consent process prior to placement for children in special education programs. The primary vehicle for federal regulation of informed consent in psychological assessment is through the Education for All Handicapped Children Act. The consent regulations implementing the act, (DHEW, 1977, pp. 42, 494-442, 495) have the intent of increasing parent involvement in educational decision making. They do so by requiring that school systems inform parents before they take certain actions and that they obtain affirmative permission before they engage in other, more intrusive, actions.

At a minimum, the school must notify parents when it wishes to identify, evaluate, or place a handicapped child in a special education program. It must also notify parents after they request these services and the school system refuses to perform them. Notice in these instances must be given to parents within a "reasonable time."

There are greater constraints when school systems propose to conduct a preplacement examination (or place a child in a special education program for the first time). While §615(b)(1)(C) of P.L. 94-142 merely requires that schools give "written prior notice to the parents . . . when . . . it proposed to initiate . . . the evaluation or educational placement of the child," the implementing regulations require affirmative, written consent at those times. Therefore, while the act apparently does not mandate that schools secure approval for testing or placement, the implementing regulations do. This disparity has not yet been seriously challenged by school systems and they appear to be abiding, in theory at least, by the regulations. Thus, when a particular child becomes the focus of an assessment whose effect or intent will be to recommend placement in a special education program for the first time, parental consent must be secured for all procedures involved in the psychoeducational assessment, including testing, interviewing, and observation.

In earlier drafts of the regulations, parents possessed an absolute veto both as to a proposed initial evaluation and placement. Without their consent, neither could occur. But those drafts failed to take into account that there may be adverse interests between a parent and a child in need of special education and related services. For arbitrary or unreasonable grounds, it would have been possible under the proposed rules for parents to have denied their children access to psychological services and subsequent remedial intervention by special educators.

The final regulations that now control are more cognizant of children's independent interests and provide for an alternative mechanism permitting schools to act as child advocates and to challenge parental refusal to consent. Depending on the nature of the laws prevailing in each of the states, school systems have two means for overriding a parent veto. Where state law requires consent prior to a preplacement evaluation, state procedures govern the school system's attempt to override parental refusal to consent, e.g., neglect laws. Where no such state law exists, the school system may use the procedural safeguards delineated in P.L. 94-142. Under the act, if an impartial hearing officer decides that the psychological evaluation may proceed, the school system may conduct the assessment even though the parents refuse to give their permission.

The implementing regulations define both in general and specific terms what parental consent entails. Generally, consent means that "the parent has been fully informed of all information relevant to the activity for which consent is sought, in his or her native language, or other mode of communication" (34 C.F.R. §300.500). More particularly, the consent letter must include "a description of the action proposed . . . by the agency, an explanation of why the agency proposes . . . to take the action, and a description of any options the agency considered and the reasons why those options were rejected." In addition, the school system must describe each evaluation procedure or test it proposes to use in the assessment (34 C.F.R. §300.505). According to the Office of Special Education, when the school does not know in advance what particular tests will be administered, it may exercise the alternative of describing the kinds of tests that will be used. But the regulations and implementing policy determinations emphasize that simply listing the names of tests without at least some minimal narrative explaining their nature does not meet the intent of the law.

As this rendering of P.L. 94-142 makes clear, minor children do not participate in the consent process at all. While the interests of parents and school systems are given direct expression, handicapped children are represented only through either one of these putative benefactors. In fact, while P.L. 94-142 is called the Education for All Handicapped Children Act, children themselves have little or no voice in its implementation. The only place within P.L. 94-142 where children may have an opportunity to relate their concerns is in those sections pertaining to the drafting of individual education programs (IEPs). The act requires a representative of the local school system, the child's current (or future) teacher, and one of the child's parents to attend the IEP meeting. In addition, at the discretion of either the parents or the school system, other individuals may be invited. Finally, the law states that one of the participants may be "The child, where appropriate" (34 C.F.R. §300.344). It offers no guidance at all as to what criteria are to be used in defining appropriateness or who is to make the decision to invite the child. However, in January 1981 the Department of Education issued policy interpretations of the IEP requirement. In that document, the department indicated that it is the parent who decides if the child attends, although it encourages the parent and the school system to discuss the decision together and to make some effort to persuade other handicapped children to participate (ED, 1981). But, at bottom, under the federal scheme, handicapped children have no right to consent, assent, or object to proposed psychoeducational evaluations. Moreover, there appear to be no federal laws requiring the consent of handicapped children for educational assessments.

## Children as Involved Participants

Under the federal scheme just described, children's interests are represented only through parents and the school; but this representation is severely limited.

Parents as custodians, the state as protector, and advocates who seek to act in what they perceive to be in the best interests of children, represent only in the sense of taking care of another. They may be said to act merely "*in* behalf of," that is, in the interest of or for the benefit of another. Those who act "in behalf of" are under no obligation to consult with those they take care of or to abide by their wishes. They do what they think best in the light of their trust obligations. Such a role is different from acting "*on* behalf of," which connotes that the advocate is acting on the part of, in the name of another, or as the one represented might act (Pitkin, 1967). If we are genuinely to urge the expanded rights of children, such advocacy must include the right of children to full-fledged participation in the decision-making process when their significant interests and future hang in the balance.

In the main, however, the law considers children generally incapable of knowing what is best for themselves. In their salutary goal to protect families from unreasonable state interference and in a more questionable desire to protect children from immature and potentially harmful autonomous decisions, the courts have presumed that parents, as preferred care givers, are competent to represent their children's interests. Only when this presumption is rebutted by evidence of significant injury to the child do courts replace parents—either permanently or for limited purposes—with alternative decision makers. But, although the right of parents to control the upbringing of their children has strong foundations in tradition and in the Constitution's preferences for minimal state interference in family life, "that right is nevertheless unusual among constitutional rights in that it protects the ability to control another person. Ordinarily, constitutional rights do not protect an individual's power to control someone else" ("Developments in the Law," 1980, p. 1353).

However, if parental prerogatives are founded on the premise that children are incapable of making informed decisions, it may be possible to rebut that premise also, making it permissible not only to shift decisions from parent to state but from parent to child. This has occurred in instances in which a particular class of rights, e.g., childbearing and contraception, have been considered so fundamental that parental control and intervention are judged to be unconstitutionally burdensome. Similarly, statutory and case law is presently affording adolescents greater freedom to seek medical and psychological help without parental permission, a change advocated by many writers and legal scholars in recent years (Bersoff, 1976-1977; Bricker, 1979;

Foster & Freed, 1972; Holt, 1974; Kleinfeld, 1970, 1971; Richards, 1980; Wald, 1974; see this text also).

Despite these developments, the right of children to seek aid (or reject it) by giving valid consent is far from universal. In light of the Supreme Court's overriding preference for parental control and its distrust of minors' ability to make mature judgments, it is unlikely that children will be granted the right to decide for themselves whether or not to be the subjects of psychoeducational evaluation. The majority view of the Supreme Court fails

> to recognize the single most important factor in the analysis of a child's right to (choose). It is the child who is at the center of this dilemma and it is his rights which should be accorded at least equal, if not greater, weight than those of the parents or the state. (Hirshberg, 1980, p. 225)

If prior cases are a guide, the courts will more likely employ the analysis used in *Wisconsin v. Yoder* (1972),[14] a case in which the Supreme Court upheld the right of Amish parents to violate state compulsory education laws and to keep their children at home once they completed eight grades. The exemption, the Court felt, was necessary to the free exercise of religion. In its positive light, the decision may be seen as allowing at least a limited class of parents the right to make decisions concerning family life even though it may interfere with a long-acknowledged state interest—in this case, compulsory education. On the other hand, it may be seen as another instance of adults' general failure to afford children the opportunity to articulate their own interests or to develop autonomy. Chief Justice Burger, who wrote the majority opinion, saw the case as involving only the "fundamental interests of the parents, as contrasted with that of the State" (p. 232). Justice Douglas, dissenting in part, was the only member of the Court to recognize that the critical interests at stake were those of the children.

> On this important and vital matter of education, I think the children should be entitled to be heard. While the parents . . . normally speak for the entire family, the education of the child is a matter on which the child will often have decided views. . . .
>
> It is the future of the student, not the future of the parents, that is imperiled in today's decision. . . . It is the student's judgment, not his parents', that is essential if we are to give full meaning to what we have said about the Bill of Rights and of the right of students to be masters of their own destiny. (pp. 244-245)

It is probably true that the decision to take a test is not quite so vital as that of total exclusion from schooling. But there is little argument that participation in many assessment programs also determines the future lives of children. Testing may determine whether a child is placed in academically—

or vocationally—oriented tracks in secondary school (e.g., *Hobson v. Hansen*, 1967); placed in elementary school classes for the educably retarded (*Larry P. v. Riles*, 1979); diagnosed as emotionally disturbed and separated from peers in institutions or segregated educational facilities (e.g., *Parham v. J.R.*, 1979,[15] and *Lora v. Board of Education of City of New York*, 1978[16]) or permitted to graduate from high school as minimally competent (e.g., *Debra P. v. Turlington*, 1979;[17] see generally Bersoff, 1979, 1982). Yet the tests upon which these decisions are based are of questionable validity for the specific purposes for which they are used. In that light, it does not appear justifiable to fail to permit children, within properly applicable developmental constraints, to at least share in the decision to become the subject of an educational assessment.

I personally believe that we should reverse our current presumptions. Rather than assume that children are too young emotionally, experientially, and cognitively to make "appropriate" decisions, we can alternatively presume that children are capable of making those decisions no more disastrously than adults. Only if there is a significant risk of irreversible damage, or clear and convincing empirical evidence that at particular ages children do not have sufficiently developed skills to exercise discretion, should parents and the state have the right to make unilateral decisions that meaningfully affect children. The burden would fall on those wishing to deny the right of children to choose; it would not fall to children and their advocates to show that children are capable. Such a proposal is in keeping with the legal doctrine that rights can be denied only after a showing of incompetency, as is true when those called mentally ill are no longer allowed to control their finances or when parents are required to relinquish custody of their children.

Of course, the question arises, do children have sufficient maturity and stability to make life-important decisions? Or are the courts correct in concluding that they do not? Justice Douglas, to support his claim in *Yoder* that students not only and the right but the competency to be heard, cited the work of major developmental psychologists and sociologists—such as Piaget, Kohlberg, Gesell, Kay, and Ilg—to the effect that cognitive capacity and moral judgment of young adolescents approximated that of adults. It must be said in the interest of intellectual honesty that while works cited by Justice Douglas lend substantial support to his assertion, many other scholars (e.g., Baer & Wright, 1974) who have reviewed the research of those cited are not in total agreement with their colleagues. However, the failure to corroborate centers mainly around adolescents' failure to evidence the judgment and reasoning associated with the most mature states of intellectual and moral development theoretically possible in adults. There is little evidence that those stages are reached by adults themselves.

The legal system, however, continues uniformly to assume that children are developmentally unable to render decisions equivalent to those of adults. But the increasing number of well-regarded, situation-specific, legally relevant studies indicates that law's assumption of a generally uncrossable line of eighteen years of age between dependence and autonomy is simply not empirically supportable. (Besides those studies reported in this text, see, e.g., Cohen & Harnick, [1980]; Melton, Koocher, & Saks, [1983]; Lewis, [1980].)

One of the few literature reviews to investigate systematically the issue of consent with regard to treatment decisions (Grisso & Vierling, 1978) concluded that minors below the age of eleven generally did not have the intellectual ability or sense of independence to give competent consent, but that those over fifteen were not any less competent than their adult counterparts. But this and more recent studies (e.g., Grisso, 1980), even though challenging the validity of arbitrary age-graded distinctions, assume that increased ability to make decisions is predominantly the product of development. An alternative hypothesis is that society in general and the law in particular, through reinforcement of parental authority (even as against the mature minor) have retarded children's ability to make appropriate choices. What seems to be a developmental incapacity may be more the result of a purposeful failure to teach children to be capable.

> When John Stuart Mill eloquently argued against the subjection of women, he accepted, *arguendo* that the women of his period were not effectively autonomous. He reasoned, however, that women . . . possessed the capacity for autonomy even though such a capacity might be constricted by traditional prejudices and conventions. (Richards, 1980, p. 10)

Courts, legislatures, parents, and other promulgators of standards and values who view their function primarily as child protectors may, in actuality, perpetuate and promote incompetency. While the child, properly, may be protected from taking actions that would preclude the development of independence (i.e., lead to death or irremediable damage), it is antagonistic to the expansion of autonomy to prevent children from engaging in conduct in which they "take risks and make mistakes—even clearly irrational ones— because responsibility for the sting of one's own mistakes is a crucial part of the kind of independence we associate with autonomy" (Richards, 1980, p. 19). The Supreme Court's heavy reliance on the privacy of the family is, from one perspective, a salutary one, when balanced against the alternative of intrusion by the state. But, when the Court talks of the primacy of "family" prerogatives, it is speaking only of mothers and fathers. In the final analysis, the child is given no say in this family decision. "Family," in reality, means only parents.

Whatever the outcome, we need data, even at the risk of discovering that the Supreme Court's presumptions are correct. I think current legal formulations fall far short of recognizing the autonomy of children in those instances where, as in psychoeducational assessment, their significant interests are at stake. I believe that we need developmental, social, community, and educational psychologists to produce situation-specific research to help the legal system make more reality-oriented decisions. The present status of children's rights will not advance significantly unless there is strong, valid evidence that our current presumptions are incorrect.

## *Notes*

1. San Antonio Ind. School District v. Rodriquez, 411 U.S. 1 (1973).

2. 347 U.S. 483 (1954).

3. Stell v. Savannah-Chatham Cty, Board of Education, 220 F. Supp. 667 (S.D. Ga. 1963), rev'd, 333 F.2d 55 (5th Cir.), cert. denied, 379 U.S. 933 (1964).

4. 269 F. Supp. 401 (D.D.C. 1967), aff'd sub nom. Smuck v. Hobson, 408 F.2d 175 (D.C. Cir. 1969).

5. Civ. No. 70-394-5 (S.D. Cal., filed Feb. 1971)—settled by consent decree, July 31, 1972.

6. Id. at 514.

7. Civ. No. 71-435 (D. Ariz., filed Aug. 1971)—settled by consent decree, Jan. 24, 1972.

8. C.A. No. C-70-37 R.F.P. (N.D. Cal., filed Jan. 1970)—settled by stipulation of the parties, Feb. 3, 1970.

9. Larry P. v. Riles, 495 F. Supp. 926 (N.D. Cal. 1979), appeal docketed, No. 80-4027 (9th Cir. Jan. 19, 1980).

10. PASE (Parents in Action on Special Education) v. Hannon, 506 F. Supp. 831 (N.D. Ill. 1980).

11. 343 F. Supp. 1306 (N.D. Cal. 1972), aff'd, 502 F.2d 963 (9th Cir. 1974).

12. Early in the Reagan administration the Department of Education issued proposed regulations modifying current rules in several significant respects. One of these modifications amended (a)(2) and would have merely required that tests be "professionally evaluated." The proposals were mired in political and professional controversy, and most of them were withdrawn.

13. 364 F. Supp. 913 (E.D. Pa. 1973).

14. 406 U.S. 205 (1972).

15. 442 U.S. 584 (1979).

16. 456 F. Supp. 1211 (E.D. N.Y. 1978) vacated and remanded, 623 F.2d 248 (2d Cir. 1980).

17. 474 F. Supp. 244 (M.D. Fla. 1979) aff'd in part, 644 F.2d 397 (5th Cir. 1981).

# References

American Psychological Association, American Educational Research Association & National Council on Measurement in Education. *Standards for educational and psychological tests.* Washington, DC: American Psychological Association, 1974.

Anastasi, A. *Psychological testing* (4th ed.). New York: Macmillan, 1976.

Baer, D., & Wright, C. Developmental psychology. In M. Rosenzweig & L. Porter (Eds.), *Annual review of psychology* (Vol. 25), Palo Alto, CA: Annual Reviews.

Berk, R., Bridges, W., & Shih, A. Does IQ really matter? A study of the use of IQ scores for the tracking of the mentally retarded. *American Sociological Review, 1981, 46,* 58-71.

Bersoff, D. Silk purses into sow's ears: The decline of psychological testing and a suggestion for its redemption. *American Psychologist, 1973, 28,* 842-849.

Bersoff, D. Representation for children in custody proceedings: All that glitters is not *Gault. Journal of Family Law, 1976-1977, 15,* 27-49.

Bersoff, D. Regarding psychologists testily: Legal regulation of psychological assessment in the public schools. *Maryland Law Review, 1979, 39,* 27-120.

Bersoff, D. The legal regulation of school psychology. In C. Reynolds & T. Gutkin (Eds.), *The handbook of school psychology.* New York: Wiley, 1982.

Bersoff, D. Social and legal influences in test development and usage. In B. Plake and S. Elliott (Eds.), *Buros-Nebraska Symposium on Measurement and Testing.* Lincoln: University of Nebraska Press, 1983.(a)

Bersoff, D. Children as participants in psychoeducational assessment. In G. Melton, G. Koocher, & M. Saks (Eds.), *Children's competence to consent.* New York: Plenum, 1983.(b)

Bersoff, D. Regarding psychologists testily: The legal regulation of psychological assessment. In J. Schierer & B. Hammonds (Eds.), *Master lecture series* (Vol. II) *Psychology and the Law.* Washington, DC: American Psychological Association, 1983.(c)

Bricker, S. Children's rights: A movement in search of meaning. *University of Richmond Law Review, 1979, 13,* 661-693.

Brim, O., Glass, D., Neulinger, J., Firestone, I., & Lerner, S. *American beliefs and attitudes about intelligence.* New York: Russell Sage, 1969.

Cleary, A., Humphreys, L., Kendrick, S., & Wesman, A. Educational uses of tests with disadvantaged students. *American Psychologist, 1975, 30,* 15-41.

Cohen, R., & Harnick, M. The susceptibility of child witnesses to suggestion. *Law and Human Behavior, 1980, 4,* 201-210.

Department of Education. Individualized education programs. *Federal Register, 1981, 46,* 5460-5474.

Department of Health, Education and Welfare. Implementation of Part B of the Education of the Handicapped Act. *Federal Register, 1977, 42,* 42474-42517.

Developments in the law. The Constitution and the family. *Harvard Law Review, 1980, 93,* 1156-1383.

Flaugher, R. The many definitions of test bias. *American Psychologist, 1978, 33,* 671-679.

Foster, H., & Freed, D. A bill of rights for children. *Family Law Quarterly, 1972, 6,* 343-375.

Glaser, R., & Bond, L. (Eds.). Testing: Concepts, policy, practice, and research. *American Psychologist, 1981, 36,* 997-1206.

Goldman, R., & Hartig, L. The WISC may not be a valid predictor of school performance for primary-grade minority children. *American Journal of Mental Deficiency, 1976, 80,* 583-587.

Green. B. In defense of measurement. *American Psychologist,* 1978, *33,* 664-670.

Grisso, T. Juveniles' capacities to waive *Miranda* rights: An empirical analysis. *California Law Review,* 1980, *68,* 1134-1166.

Grisso, T., & Vierling, L. Minors' consent to treatment: A developmental perspective. *Professional Psychology,* 1978, *9,* 412-427.

Haney, W. Validity, vaudeville, and values. *American Psychologist,* 1981, *36,* 1021-1024.

Heller, K., Holtzman, W., & Messick, S. *Placing children in special education: A strategy for equity.* Washington, DC: National Academy Press, 1982.

Hirshberg, B. Who speaks for the child and what are his rights? *Law and Human Behavior,* 1980, *4,* 217-236.

Holman, M., & Docter, R. *Educational and psychological testing.* New York: Russell Sage, 1972.

Holt, J. *Escape from childhood.* New York: Dutton, 1974.

Jensen, A. How much can we boost IQ and scholastic achievement? *Harvard Educational Review,* 1969, *39,* 1-123.

Jensen, A. *Bias in mental testing.* New York: Free Press, 1980.

Kirp, D. Schools as sorters: The constitutional and policy implications of student classification. *University of Pennsylvania Law Review,* 1973, *121,* 705-797.

Kleinfeld, A. Balance of power among infants, their parents, and the state (I, II, III). *Family Law Quarterly,* 1970, 1971, *4, 5,* 320-349, 410-443, 64-107.

Lewis, C. A comparison of minors' and adults' pregnancy decisions. *American Journal of Orthopsychiatry,* 1980, *50,* 446-453.

Melton, G., Koocher, & Saks, M. (Eds.). *Children's competence to consent.* New York: Plenum, 1983.

Messe, L., Crano, W., Messe, S. & Rice, W. Evaluation of the predictive validity of tests of mental ability for classroom performance in elementary grades. *Journal of Educational Psychology,* 1979, *71,* 233-241.

Meyers, C., MacMillan, D., & Yoshida, R. Validity of psychologists' identification of EMR students in the perspective of the California decertification experience. *Journal of School Psychology,* 1978, *16,* 3-15.

Neuberger, E. Intelligence tests: To be or not to be under the Education for All Handicapped Children Act of 1975. *Northwestern University Law Review,* 1981, *76,* 640-668.

Pitkin, H. *The concept of representation.* Berkeley: University of California Press, 1967.

The psychologist as expert witness: Science in the courtroom? *Maryland Law Review,* 1979, *38,* 539-621.

Reschly, D. Nonbiased assessment. In G. Phye & D. Reschly (Eds.), *School psychology: Perspectives and issues.* New York: Academic Press, 1979.

Reschly, D. Psychological evidence in the Larry P. opinion: A case of right problem—wrong solution? *School Psychology Review,* 1980, *9,* 123-135.

Reynolds, C. The problem of bias in psychological assessment. In C. Reynolds & T. Gutkin (Eds.), *The handbook of school psychology.* New York: Wiley, 1982.

Richards, D. The individual, the family, and the Constitution: A jurisprudential perspective. *New York University Law Review,* 1980, *55,* 1-66.

Sandoval, J. The WISC-R and internal evidence of test bias and minority groups. *Journal of Counseling and Clinical Psychology,* 1979, *47,* 919-927.

Sherman, S., & Robinson, N. (Eds.). *Ability testing of handicapped people: Dilemma for government, science and the public.* Washington, DC: National Academy Press, 1982.

Smith, E. Test validation in the schools. *Texas Law Review*, 1980, *58*, 1123-1159.

Wald, P. Making sense out of the rights of youth. *Human Rights*, 1974, *4*, 13-29.

Wigdor, A., & Garner, W. (Eds.). *Ability testing: Uses, consequences, and controversies.* Washington, DC: National Academy Press, 1982.

# 13

# Access of Handicapped Children to Educational Services

### Bruce L. Baker
*University of California, Los Angeles*

### Richard P. Brightman
*MAXXIS, Inc.*
*Los Angeles*

Approximately 10 percent of all children have a disability. This emotionally charged word embraces many handicapping conditions, including auditory, visual, speech, and orthopedic impairments; mental retardation and emotional disturbance; and the less visible learning disabilities or chronic health impairments. These childrens' parents share a passion that is at once common and unique. It is the passion parents reserve for their children, but it is unique in the degree to which it is tested. In seeing how the world behaves toward disabled people, each of these parents learns that his or her child is at high risk for discriminatory treatment. They may not yet know the precise nature of the obstacles that await their children when, as adults, they seek housing, employment, or government benefits, but they soon become familiar with the barriers that prevent their children from receiving the educational services to which they are entitled. Despite the passage in 1975 of a landmark federal law, the Education for All Handicapped Children Act (Public Law 94-142), many barriers remain. The following two examples were among our experiences during this past year:

Authors' Note: This chapter was prepared while the first author was a Visiting Scholar at the Judge Baker Guidance Center, Boston, and Visiting Professor of Psychology in the Department of Psychiatry, Harvard Medical School. The second author received support from grant 5T24 MH15901-03 from the National Institute of Mental Health. We appreciate Jan B. Blacher and Alan J. Brightman's critical review of this manuscript.

Mrs. L. is angry and in tears. She is aware that her six-year-old son with mental retardation has the right to a free and appropriate public education. Yet, after three meetings with district personnel, the only placement offered is a private nursery school for which the parents will be expected to pay.

Mr. and Mrs. M.'s son Daniel, who has Down's syndrome, maintained nearly age-appropriate development because of his participation in an early intervention program and their own teaching efforts. Now that he is 3 years old, the school district has denied schooling because he is not far enough behind. In this state, services for children aged 3 to 5 are discretionary. In this Catch 22 world, one staff member notes that if Daniel regresses without school, he may qualify.

The first example violates the letter of the law, while the second violates its spirit. Both highlight the fiscal binds and bureaucratic entanglements that can result in school personnel's becoming parents' adversaries. These parents, like countless parents of disabled children before them, are undergoing their own course of special education (see Boggs, 1978; Featherstone, 1980). It is a course that highlights the discrepancies between the intentions of social policy and the realities of public practice. It teaches, cruelly but effectively, that their children's handicaps stem only in part from their children's disabilities.

## Establishing the
## Right to Education

During the past decade, disabled citizens and their families have joined with attorneys and lay advocates to challenge abusive practices that lead to social exclusion of handicapped persons. We focus in this chapter on one aspect of the civil rights movement for this "last minority"—the right of disabled children to educational services. We will first examine efforts to establish the right to education, especially as it is presently articulated in the Education for All Handicapped Children Act of 1975. We will then ask, Is it working? We will consider the implementation of this far-reaching legislation and its impact, in particular, on parents and children.

### Exclusion from Public School

The policies that have resulted in exclusion of children from school are grounded in early court decisions. Almost a century ago a Massachusetts court ruled that a student could be expelled if he displayed "continuous disorderly conduct either voluntarily or by reason of imbecility."[1] In *Beatie v. State Board of Education*[2] the Wisconsin Supreme Court decided that a child could be expelled if he or she had "a depressing and nauseating effect on the teachers and school children." This tradition of investing school personnel with the broad discretionary power to determine who to educate became formalized in the school codes of every state. Despite compulsory education codes, numerous statutory exemptions enabled school officials to deny education arbitrarily and with impunity to children deemed different, most often those judged to have physical, mental, or emotional disabilities (Children's Defense Fund, 1974).

The magnitude of the exclusion problem is difficult to assess accurately. Criteria for defining types of disabling conditions vary widely (Hobbs, 1975), and school districts have not kept accurate statistics about unserved children (Children's Defense Fund, 1974). Nonetheless, the estimates that do exist are staggering. During the 1968-1969 school year, 19 states were reported to be serving less than 31 percent of their disabled children and 11 states 20 percent or less (Weintraub, Abeson, & Braddock, 1971). The most frequently cited estimates are those cited in Public Law (P.L.) 94-142 in 1975: Of the nation's 8 million disabled children, *more than half* were not receiving appropriate educational services, and 1 million were excluded from school entirely.

### Response to Exclusion

With its roots in such organizations as the National Association of Retarded Children (now Citizens), founded in 1950, an advocacy movement took hold in the early 1970s. Strategies borrowed from other minority groups' advocacy activities included formation of public interest groups (Edelman, 1973), documentation of abuse (Rivera, 1972; Task Force on Children Out of School, 1971), legislative lobbying (Budoff, 1975), and, especially, filing class action suits against state agencies deemed responsible for the exclusion problem.

Three court cases proved especially influential in advancing the disabled child's claim to a right to education. (For reviews of litigation prior to P.L. 94-142, see Cohen and DeYoung [1973], and Martin, [1979].) A powerful precedent was the classic civil rights case of *Brown v. Board of Education*,[3] which directly addressed the rights of racial minorities. Justice Warren's decision that guaranteed minority children access to equal public education was later adopted as a basis for P.L. 94-142.

Today, education is perhaps the most important function of state and local governments . . . In these days, it is doubtful that any child may reasonably be expected to succeed in life if he is denied the opportunity of an education. Such an education, where the state has undertaken to provide it, is a right which must be made available to all on equal terms. (347 U.S. at 493).

The first important "right-to-education" case involving disabled children was *Pennsylvania Association for Retarded Children (P.A.R.C.) v. the Commonwealth of Pennsylvania.*[4] Thirteen retarded children, their parents, and their advocates initiated a class action suit on behalf of 14,267 other retarded children whose exclusion from Pennsylvania's schools was construed as a violation of the equal protection clause of the Fourteenth Amendment. Decision by a consent agreement stipulated steps the Commonwealth was to follow to provide an appropriate education. A second case, *Mills v. Board of Education of the District of Columbia,*[5] was decided by a judgment against the defendant school board and extended the findings of *P.A.R.C.* to all disabled children. In brief, *P.A.R.C.* and *Mills* rendered the *Brown* decision applicable to disabled students.

Following these three landmark decisions, 36 right-to-education class actions were filed in 27 jurisdictions, indicating the need for the federal government to establish a clear standard (Martin, 1979). One result was the passage of Section 504 of the Rehabilitation Act of 1973. Described in its regulations (45 CFR 84, May 4, 1977) as "the first Federal civil rights law protecting the rights of handicapped persons," Section 504 read simply,

> No otherwise qualified handicapped individual in the United States shall, solely by reason of his handicap, be excluded from the participation in, be denied the benefits of, or be subjected to discrimination under any program or activity receiving Federal financial assistance. (29 U.S.C. 794, Supp. 1974)

Although Section 504 has been cited in public school cases, it has been used primarily by disabled adults seeking access to employment opportunities, higher education, housing, and rehabilitation services. An alternative legislative strategy focused on comprehensively revising federal special education laws. That effort culminated in President Ford's signing of P.L. 94-142, the Education for All Handicapped Children Act, on November 29, 1975.

### Education for All
### Handicapped Children Act

> It is the purpose of this Act to assure that all handicapped children have available to them . . . a free, appropriate public education which emphasizes special education and related services designed to meet their unique needs, to assure that the rights of handicapped children and their parents or guardians are protected, to assist states and localities to provide for the education of all handicapped children, and to assess and assure the effectiveness of efforts to educate handicapped children. (20 U.S.C. 1401)

The intent of P.L. 94-142 was to reverse the exclusionary practices of public schools, by providing *all* handicapped children, regardless of the nat-

TABLE 13.1    Children Served under P.L. 89-313[a] and P.L. 94-142,
                      by Handicapping Condition (school year 1981-1982)

| Type of Handicap | Number | Percentage |
|---|---|---|
| Learning Disabled | 1,627,344 | 38.4 |
| Speech Impaired | 1,137,919 | 26.9 |
| Mentally Retarded | 802,264 | 19.0 |
| Emotionally Disturbed | 341,786 | 8.1 |
| Other Health Impaired | 80,171 | 1.9 |
| Deaf and Hard of Hearing | 76,387 | 1.8 |
| Multihandicapped | 73,832 | 1.7 |
| Orthopedically Impaired | 59,958 | 1.4 |
| Visually Handicapped | 30,979 | 0.7 |
| Deaf and Blind | 2,642 | 0.1 |
| Total | 4,233,282 | |

SOURCE: The Association for the Severely Handicapped Newsletter, Vol. 9, No. 4,
April 1983.
NOTE: Sample consisted of children, ages 3-21, in the United States and territories.
a. Title I of the Elementary and Secondary Education Act.

ure or severity of their disability, with a free and appropriate public education. The range of handicapping conditions covered by P.L. 94-142 is shown
in Table 13.1, with recent statistics on the number of children served. To
encourage participation, the legislation provides for federal financial and
technical assistance to State Educational Agencies that comply with the regulations. For the 1980 fiscal year, the federal contribution came to $227 per
handicapped child served (Comptroller General of the United States, 1981).
Fundamentally, P.L. 94-142 guarantees all disabled children four basic
rights, which are detailed below.

    1. *The right to a free, appropriate public education.* This most
important right extends publicly supported education to all handicapped
children aged 3-21 (except where state laws or practices do not allow
serving children aged 3-5 or 18-21). If the public schools cannot provide an
appropriate education, then the public schools and the state must pay the full
cost of private schooling. The basic zero-reject provision of the law has had
enormous impact not only on thousands of children previously excluded
from school but also upon their families, who are freed from constant child
care. The interpretation of "appropriate" education causes some problems.
While this has not been seen as a guarantee of the best possible educational
program, it does mean that a child must be provided an adequate one
tailored to his or her individual needs. This program is detailed in the written
Individualized Education Plan discussed below.

2. *The right to placement in the least restrictive educational environment (LRE)*. Handicapped children are to be educated with nonhandicapped children to the maximum extent appropriate for the former (20 U.S.C. 1412,5,B). This integration, or "mainstreaming," was at first misunderstood by many persons to mean that all handicapped children must be placed in regular classrooms. Rather, LRE is best viewed as a continuum of possible placements. Some handicapped children can be educated best in the regular classroom, with the use of special aids and services. Others will benefit from a primary placement in the regular classroom and a period each day in a resource room, where a teacher who is specially trained in educational assessment, programming, and behavior management techniques works with a small group of children. Still others will learn best with a primary placement in a special classroom but some integration in the regular class for nonacademic subjects such as music, art, or gym. A very few handicapped students will require a separate classroom, separate school, residential setting, or home tutoring. Placements are to be reviewed at least annually. The assumption is that handicapped children should be in the most integrated setting possible, and school districts have the burden of showing why a child should be placed in a more restrictive environment.

3. *The right to supplementary aids and services*. The law also provides for those developmental, corrective, and other supportive services that are necessary to assist the child to benefit from special education. Related services that must be provided for the child if deemed necessary include physical education, psychological services, physical and occupational therapy, counseling, diagnostic and evaluative medical services, some types of special materials and equipment and speech and language services. A related service for parents is counseling or training in home management. A most important related service—frequently the source of conflict—is transportation. A child with spina bifida, for example, may not be able to meet the regular school bus; if the district does not provide special transportation, the child's parents could challenge this as denial of access to education.

To illustrate how related services can help to fulfill the previous two rights, consider 15-year-old Amy. She was born with a cleft palate that was surgically corrected in infancy. She has a severe hearing loss and has been termed legally blind. She has seizures, now controlled. In former days, this multihandicapped child would quite likely have been delayed intellectually, as a result of separate and academically inadequate schooling. Yet Amy is now in the tenth grade, and her entire schooling in Massachusetts (where a state law, Chapter 766, preceded P.L. 94-142 and was in many ways a model for it) has been in regular classrooms with individualized supportive services. For example, each teacher wears a clip-on microphone to transmit his or her voice to Amy's binaural hearing aids. Her typing teacher provides magnified script to make reading and copying easier. She participates for several hours a week in individual speech therapy. At present, Amy is an occasional honor roll student who participates with enthusiasm on the swim and track teams. She is looking forward to a career in journalism.

4. *The right to fair assessment procedures.* To eliminate perceived discriminatory practices of the past, P.L. 94-142 contains a number of provisions pertaining to assessment. Before a child can be placed in a special education program, a school district must notify the parents in writing, obtain their consent for assessment, and complete a thorough individual evaluation. The law holds that tests and procedures must not be racially or culturally discriminatory, must be in the child's native language, and must be valid for the purposes employed. Furthermore, no single test or criterion can be used to determine placement. Finally, if the child's parents disagree with the district's assessment, they may obtain an independent assessment; this can be at public expense unless the district can show in a hearing that a complete and accurate evaluation has been done (see also Chapter 14 of the law). In order to guarantee that these rights are not overlooked, the law provides two sources of protection to parents: the Individualized Education Program (IEP) and due process safeguards.

The IEP is the cornerstone of P.L. 94-142. A meeting to design the child's annual educational program is held each year but may convene sooner if parents or school personnel propose that placement, instruction, or services be initiated, changed, or terminated. The IEP meeting is conducted by the child's school district, and must include the special education admin-istrator or designee, the child's teacher, the child's parent, and (where appro-priate) the child. Whether the child is included depends upon factors such as age, ability to communicate, comprehension, behavioral appropriateness, and desire to participate. Others who have knowledge of the child may be invited to attend by the parent or the district.

The meeting results in a written plan. The usual initial topic of discussion is the child's *present level of performance.* Based on formal assessment results, informal teacher assessments, and classroom and home observa-tions, this discussion will focus on such areas as academic, social, percep-tual-motor, self-help, fine- and gross-motor, speech and language, and prevocational skills. These indications of present status and the participants' preferences and expectations about next steps serve as the basis for formu-lating *annual goals and short-term instructional objectives* in each skill area. These, in turn, suggest the type and frequency of *supplementary aids and services.* The IEP must also specify the child's *placement,* with a rationale for how it is consistent with the LRE provision and a statement of how much time, if any, the child will be integrated with nonhandicapped peers. Finally, the IEP includes a *statement of who will be responsible for implementation* of each component, *how progress will be measured,* and the *dates by which services will be initiated and terminated.* The IEP represents the school district's contract with the child, negotiated and signed by parents and professionals, all presumably acting with an uncompromising commitment to the chid's best interests. However, should disagreement about eligibility, assessment, program adequacy, or placement emerge as an unresolvable issue between parents and district personnel, the second source of protections may be utilized.

Due process protections are made up of administrative safeguards, central to which is the fair hearing. If at any point in the IEP process a parent or professional feels that the best interests of the child are being overlooked, a fair hearing may be requested. Both sides present their cases before an impartial hearing officer who decides the case. Should neither party file suit in civil court, the decision of the hearing officer is binding. Mrs. L., in our example at the beginning of this chapter, found that several meetings with school officials did not result in an agreement about educational placement. She decided that—despite the time, effort, and anxiety involved—she would "go to hearing," whereupon the district relented and agreed to her choice of placement. Due process procedures have been well-described elsewhere (Anderson, Chitwood, & Hayden, 1982). We will not go into further detail about the hearing and appeal processes, since very few cases actually go to fair hearing.

## Implementation and Impact

The implementation of P.L. 94-142 began on September 1, 1978. Few districts were prepared (Martin, 1979), and the first years were marked by considerable problems. Many school personnel had misgivings and misunderstandings about various provisions of the law (Saunders & Saltana, 1980), and reviews of the 1978-1979 school year revealed that many states were not in compliance with major requirements (Office of Special Education, 1980). Five years later substantial progress has been made. At a time when enrollment among nondisabled students is declining, increased number of children with disabilities are receiving special education and related services through the public schools.

Yet many challenges to full implementation remain. Numerous disabled children must still be identified, evaluated, and served, especially in the 3-5 and 18-21 year age ranges. However, shortages of trained personnel and state budget cuts or hiring freezes hamper these efforts. In many cases, placement decisions continue to be made on the basis of programs available rather than on the basis of child needs. Those most affected by P.L. 94-142 are, of course, parents of handicapped children and the children themselves, so the remainder of this chapter will consider how implementation is affecting them.

### The Parents

P.L. 94-142 empowers parents of handicapped children with crucial decision-making rights concerning their child's education. According to the law, parents are to play key roles as providers of information, as decision makers in the development of their child's educational program, as advocates in asserting their child's interests, and as partners with school personnel in implementing IEPs. Present evidence suggests, perhaps not surprisingly, that most parents are far from fulfilling these roles.

#### *Parental Participation*

The most critical of parental rights under P.L. 94-142 is participation in the IEP conference. The regulations underscore the significance of this right as follows:

> The IEP meeting serves as a communication vehicle between parents and school personnel, and enables them as equal participants to jointly decide what the child's needs are, what services will be provided to meet those needs, and what the anticipated outcomes will be. (Federal Register, 1981, p. 5462).

Yet one national survey found that only 77 percent of parents performed the specific, minimal, and legally mandated function of approving, either verbally or in writing, their child's IEP (Pyecha, 1979). Only 49 percent of parents actually served on the IEP committee and contributed to IEP development. More recent studies have noted higher parental attendance at IEP meetings (Scanlon, Arick, & Phelps, 1981) but parents still seem far from "equal participants." Another national survey of nearly 2500 parents (Salett & Henderson, 1980) found that in 52 percent of cases parents reported that the IEPs were completed before the meeting, a clear violation of the regulations. Considerable parental acquiescence may be inferred from the findings that 45 percent of parents felt that the annual goals in the IEP did not adequately meet their child's educational needs but only 5 percent refused to approve the IEP. Moreover, it is likely that these survey studies *overstate* parent participation, since it seems plausible that the more-involved parents would be more likely to return the questionnaire.

One study observed 14 IEP meetings to learn about the nature of parent participation (Goldstein, Strickland, Turnbull, & Curry, 1980). These conferences lasted an average of only 36 minutes, teachers spoke twice as much as parents, and the topics parents most often discussed were of a personal or familial, rather than curricular, nature. The authors generally characterized the conferences as "the resource teacher taking the initiative to review the already developed IEP with the parent, who was the primary recipient of the comments made at the conference" (p. 283). Equal participation suffers further in a study of who seems to be influential in IEP committee decisions (Gilliam & Coleman, 1981). Ratings completed by 130 participants in 27 IEP meetings indicated that parents were perceived as contributing little to the process and exerting little influence over decisions relative to other participants.

### Parental Satisfaction

These studies suggest that some parents are not even exercising their most basic P.L. 94-142 rights, while others are participating but with more passivity and acquiescence than the equal participation clause prescribes. What, then, do parents feel about the process? The U.S. Department of Education in its Fourth Annual Report to Congress indicated that only 0.1 percent of an estimated two million evaluations in 1979-1980 resulted in hearings, with the overstated conclusion that "this reflects parental satisfaction with more than 9,999 out of every 10,000 evaluations conducted, placements offered, or programs provided." On a smaller scale, Goldstein et al.'s (1980) parents reported satisfaction with the conference no matter what occurred during the meeting. Brightman and Sullivan (1980) provide a somewhat different picture based upon information provided through six intensive case studies and 26 structured interviews. Although these parents were generally satisfied with the *outcomes* of their IEP meetings, they were almost universal in reporting dissatisfaction with the *process*. They reported feeling intimidated, unwelcomed, and outnumbered, which resulted in their suppressing opinions and suggestions they believed might have been valuable. Paradoxically, they left their IEP meetings feeling disappointed and demeaned, even when pleased with the services the district promised to offer.

Moreover, the parents interviewed by Brightman and Sullivan realized that they were poorly prepared to act as the collaborators the law intended them to be. They knew little of what to expect of the process or their part in it. Ironically, in a meeting designed to focus on the needs of their children, these parents were out of their element. The authors stated, "In general, parents reported they didn't know that they should have known more" (Bright-man & Sullivan, 1980, p. 12). Parents seem to want more advocacy-related information. In a survey that questioned 283 parents about their advocacy-related needs, 64 percent requested more information about direct services, 50 percent wanted special training in advocacy-related skills, and 42 percent reported a need to become more assertive (Hartwell-Meyers and Haynes, 1978).

## Strategies for Increasing Participation

Despite this need, we find few evaluations of strategies designed to increase parent participation in the IEP process. Goldstein and Turnbull (1982) randomly assigned 45 families to one of two intervention conditions or to a control group. Interventions involved either (a) receiving in advance of the meeting a list of questions designed to help focus on topics that would be discussed; or (b) being accompanied to the IEP meeting by a guidance teacher acting in the role of parent advocate. Coded observations of the IEP conferences revealed that only parents accompanied by an advocate contrib-uted significantly more frequently than control parents. Parent satisfaction with the meeting did not relate to intervention condition. Although the use of school personnel acting in the role of parent advocate was apparently helpful to parents in this study, the potential for conflicts of interest arises when a teacher is placed in the position of serving two masters (Firth, 1981).

Numerous advocacy training programs for parents are available, but they have not reported systematic evaluations. An exception is the Parents as Advocates Program, developed by the UCLA Project for Developmental Disabilities (Brightman, in press). The aim is to improve parents' under-standing of P.L. 94-142 rights and procedures, and to improve their ability to use that knowledge when planning for and participating in their child's IEP meeting. Parents meet in groups of 6-12 families for six 2-hour weekly sessions. Limited didactic inputs are accompanied by filmstrip presenta-tions, handouts specifying parental rights, small-group problem-solving exercises, videotape analysis, and role playing with peer feedback. Parents complete several action-oriented homework assignments, such as locating their local special education coordinator or examining their child's school file. Outcome evaluation assesses parents' knowledge of P.L. 94-142 rights and procedures, ability to recognize violations of rights in written vignettes, and effective response to an IEP simulation measure. The last consists of 15 videotaped vignettes wherein special education professionals speak to the viewer about his or her child; each vignette denies a P.L. 94-142-granted right. The parent has 30 seconds to respond aloud to each. Audiotaped responses are coded for knowledge of the law, statement of desired outcome, and overall response effectiveness.

One study randomly assigned parents to either the Parents as Advocates program or a waiting-list control group. Trained parents demonstrated significantly greater gains on all three measures (Brightman, in press). Another study investigated whether observed changes were only nonspecific effects of being in any training program. Changes, however, were found to be quite program-specific. Advocacy trained parents gained significantly more on the advocacy measures than parents who were trained in a condition that focused on behavior modification teaching (Baker & Brightman, Note 1). Although parents who completed Parents as Advocates reported more satisfaction in subsequent IEPs, actual parent behavior following this training program has not yet been assessed.

Present law, then, grants parents of handicapped children a pivotal role in educational decisions—far more, in fact, than is granted to parents of nonhandicapped children. Some have accepted the concomitant responsibilities of informed and active participation. They garner what information they can and attend IEP conferences, although rarely as equal participants. They seem to want to trust in professionals and are generally acquiescent in IEP decisions. Yet, when they are interviewed privately, they express reservations, albeit about the process more than about the outcome.

It is important that formal conferences and hearings should not come to define the singular new parent-school relationship under P.L. 94-142, for many parents would prefer their involvement to take the form of more frequent and informal give-and-take with the teacher (Winton & Turnbull, 1981). These new rights, then, have had a paradoxical effect on parents; some have come to feel more empowered, but others, now faced with a host of new regulations and routines, may feel all he more confused and inclined to disengage.

### The Children

A critical review of this progressive legislation ultimately rests upon its manifestation in the classroom. The center of interest has been the LRE provision, resulting in increased integration of children with and without handicaps. Nobody asked nonhandicapped children if they wanted handicapped classmates, and that was probably just as well. A study just before the law took effect found that 26 percent of third and fourth graders reported knowing no disabled people, and an additional 51 percent reported knowing one or two at most (Brightman, 1981). Their answer, based on scant knowledge, might have been "no thanks." And nobody asked handicapped children if they wanted to leave the security of separate classrooms or their home for more integrated education. We don't know what they would have said.

It is important to reemphasize that the provisions of P.L. 94-142, especially regarding the education of handicapped and nonhandicapped children in integrated settings, did not grow from scientific or educational findings or even from a considered survey of all parties involved, but from the sociopolitical zeitgeist of the 1970s. The rationales offered for mainstreaming were not so much evidence-based predictions as expressions of hope—that in integrated settings handicapped children would better develop cognitive and social skills better, and/or would experience enhanced social status and self-esteem. A related expectation was that their nonhandicapped peers would also benefit from the experience, becoming more sensitive and accepting of differences.

With increased attention in recent years to an "appropriate education," the question of relative educational benefits of separate versus regular classrooms has become increasingly meaningless. Placement options embrace many levels of integration, and developmental progress depends as well upon wise establishment and implementation of long-term goals, short-term objectives, and related services. If individualized procedures are carried out as mandated, each child's progress is monitored and the program—which includes placement, goals, and related services—is periodically adjusted to maximize development.

One caveat, though, pertains to selection of criteria for evaluating placement effectiveness. Parents, teachers, administrators, and children may consider different criteria when they assess the outcome of integrated education (Peck & Semmel, 1982). Different values, for example, can be applied to the child's cognitive-developmental and social outcomes, to the child's preferences, or to the impact of the child's schooling on family functioning. Depending upon one's criterion, the degree of mainstreaming in a placement selected for the child could vary. For example, some have argued that even though children might benefit cognitively as much or more in a specialized setting as a mainstreamed one, the social advantages of integrated education outweigh this. In fact, we know little about the relative cognitive benefits. Early studies were clouded by methodological problems, such as lack of random assignment, and were inconclusive (MacMillan, 1982). Recent research has been primarily directed toward social outcomes.

## Social Outcomes of Mainstreaming

Researchers have considered questions such as, How much do nonhandi-capped children know about handicaps? How accepting are nonhandicapped children's attitudes and behaviors toward handicapped children? What interventions facilitate social interactions and/or peer acceptance? One crucial question has hardly been addressed directly: How does mainstreamed placement affect handicapped children's feelings of acceptance and self-esteem? This is generally inferred from measures of peer acceptance.

Studies have documented that elementary school children have many misconceptions about disabilities and predominantly negative attitudes toward disabled persons (Gottlieb, 1975; Cook & Wollersheim, 1976). Moreover, children evaluate mentally disabled persons more negatively than physically disabled persons (Gottlieb & Gottlieb, 1977; Parish, Ohlesen, & Parish, 1978; Willey & McCandless, 1973). Despite the hopes behind P.L. 94-142, simply exposing children to disabled peers, as in the context of a mainstreamed school setting, may not be sufficient to alter their negative attitudes and may even result in the handicapped child being less socially accepted (Goodman, Gottlieb, & Harrison, 1972; Gottlieb and Budoff, 1973). Most such studies have involved mentally retarded or emotionally disturbed children, disabilities most rejected by nonhandicapped peers, and most have involved elementary school children, old enough to have already formed opinions about handicaps. A frequent argument is that at the pre-school age, nonhandicapped children might be less aware of and potentially more accepting of differences (Turnbull & Blacher-Dixon, 1980). Several reviews, however, have found rejecting attitudes in preschoolers, although intentional intervention programs may be more successful at this age (Turnbull, 1982; Peck & Semmel, 1982).)

Within the past decade a number of programs have been developed to enhance children's knowledge about and acceptance of disabled peers. Donaldson (1980) discussed several strategies for producing attitude change, four of which have been investigated with respect to children's attitudes about disabilities: informational presentation, group discussion, disability simulation or role-playing, and structured contact. Evaluations of each of these single-strategy interventions have produced mixed results, with structured contact most consistently producing positive effects.

Many programs now utilize a multifaceted curriculum. Hazzard and Baker (1982) have reported a large-scale study of the nationally marketed Feeling Free multimedia program of disability-awareness films, simulation activities, discussions, and books (Barnes, Berrigan, & Biklen, 1978; Brightman, 1976; Brightman & Blatt, 1978; Sullivan, Brightman, & Blatt, 1979). Participants were children from 16 Los Angeles classrooms, grades 3 through 6. Two classes at each grade level were randomly assigned to the 6-session program and were compared on 5 outcome measures to the 8 remaining classrooms. Treatment children demonstrated increased knowledge about disabilities, more positive perceptions of disabled persons, and greater awareness of appropriate behavioral responses to disabled peers relative to controls. On two measures of children's acknowledged willingness to interact with disabled peers, however, treatment children showed little change.

It appears, then, that handicapped children may not experience a dramatic boost in social status simply as a function of integrated schooling. Yet, over time, the familiarity wrought by daily experiences may breed among nondisabled peers greater understanding of handicaps. We know elementary school children who delight in practicing sign language to communicate behind the teacher's back, and more than one child who has reminded a less-aware parent not to park in the space that belongs to handicapped people. Moreover, the integrated setting sets the stage for interventions aimed at increasing awareness and empathy. We can hope that with increased understanding will also come an increased ability to look beyond handicaps. An important focus for future research is long-term study of the effects of greater integration upon the handicapped child's self-esteem and successful adjustment. Yet we should note that all of these potential changes, in handicapped and nonhandicapped people alike, are very difficult to capture with our standard research designs and methods, for they may emerge not in weeks but in generations.

## Conclusions and Concerns

A handicapped child in the United States today has better access to a free and appropriate education than ever before. There are many caveats that could follow this statement. We'll conclude with two broad concerns, clustered under the general headings of dollars and sense. First consider the economics of P.L. 94-142. When President Ford signed the bill, he attached a message that began,

This bill promises more than the Federal Government can deliver and its good intentions could be thwarted by the many unwise provisions it contains.

> Everyone can agree with the objective stated in the title of this bill—educating
> all handicapped children in our nation. The key question is whether the bill
> will really accomplish that objective. (White House Press Release, December,
> 2, 1975)

This statement heralded two problems: inadequate federal funding to provide for full implementation; and attempts to alter, and usually to weaken,
provisions of the law. The law stipulates that the federal government will
assume an increasing proportion of the cost per student above what it costs
to educate a nonhandicapped student. By 1981 that was to have been 40 percent, but in fact it was still only 12 percent. Hence, a major obstacle to full
implementation is insufficient funding. Moreover, as we write this chapter,
the federal Office of Education is working to dilute many provisions of the
law. Thus far, strong citizen advocacy efforts have headed off some of the
most potentially devastating changes, but the struggle continues. Access to
education for handicapped children, it would seem, is never entirely won.

Much of the ultimate success of P.L. 94-142 will rest on the good will
and good sense of those centrally involved. There is a responsibility to balance the letter of the law with its spirit, rhetoric with empiricism, self-inter-
est with some consideration for the common good. There is a responsibility
to be sensible and fair, to avoid a backlash and some backsliding. For example, parents have the right to advocate for educational services; yet they
must also realize that there is a limit—that with limited resources, incredibly
expensive services for one child because his or her parents were very vocal
will likely result in less for others. It's not supposed to be that way, but with
fixed funding, it is. Moreover, school personnel must recognize parents'
right to involvement in their child's education and embrace as partners those
parents who wish to exercise these rights. Yet parents should also have the
right to only limited involvement if that is what they choose, without being
made to feel defensive and guilty (Turnbull & Turnbull, 1982). P.L. 94-142
expands the roles and responsibilities of professionals, parents, and children
alike. The eventual success may depend most upon good will and good
sense.

## Notes

1. Watson v. City of Cambridge, 1893.
2. Beattie v. State Board of Education, 172 N.W. 153 (1919).
3. Brown v. Board of Education, 347 U.S. 483 (1954).
4. Pennsylvania Association for Retarded Children v. Commonwealth of Pennsylvania,
334 F. Supp. 1257 (E.D. Pa. 1971).

5. Mills v. Board of Education of the District of Columbia, 348 F. Supp. 866 (D.D.C., 1972).

## Reference Note

1. Baker, B.L. and Brightman, R.P. *Training parents of retarded children: Program specific outcomes.* Submitted for publication, 1983.

## References

Anderson, W., Chitwood, S., & Hayden, D. *Negotiating the special education maze: A guide for parents and teachers.* Englewood Cliffs, NJ: Prentice-Hall, 1982.

Barnes, E., Berrigan, C., & Biklin, D. *What's the difference?* Syracuse, NY: Human Policy Press, 1978.

Boggs, E.M. Who is putting whose head in the sand or in the clouds as the case may be? In A.P. Turnbull & H.R. Turnbull (Eds.), *Parents speak out: views from the other side of the two-way mirror.* Columbus, OH: Charles E. Merrill, 1978.

Brightman, A.J. *Like me.* Boston, MA: Little, Brown, 1976.

Brightman, A.J. A little bit of awkward: Children's messages on mainstreaming. In A. Milunsky (Ed.), *Coping with crisis and handicap.* New York: Plenum Press, 1981.

Brightman, A.J., & Blatt, J. Feeling Free, Washington, DC: P.B.S., 1978.

Brightman, A.J., & Sullivan, M.B. *The impact of Public Law 94-142 on parents of disabled children: A report of findings.* Belmont, MA: The Cambridge Workshop, Inc., 1980.

Brightman, R.P. Training parents as advocates for their developmentally disabled children. In J.M. Berg (Ed.), *Perspectives and progress in mental retardation.* Baltimore: University Park Press, in press.

Budoff, M. Engendering change in special education practices. *Harvard Educational Review,* 1975, *45*(4), 507-526.

Children's Defense Fund of the Washington Research Project, Inc. *Children out of school in America.* Washington, DC: Author, 1974.

Children's Defense Fund. *94-142 and 504: Numbers that add up to educational rights for handicapped children. A guide for parents and advocates.* Washington, DC: Author, 1978.

Children's Defense Fund. *It's time to stand up for your children: A parent's guide to child advocacy.* Washington, DC: Author, 1979.

Cohen, J.S. and DeYoung, H. The role of litigation in the improvement of programming for the handicapped. In L. Mann & D.A. Sabatino (Eds.), *The first review in special education* (Vol. 1). Philadelphia: JSE Press, 1973.

Comptroller General of the United States. Disparities still exist in who gets special education, Report to the Chairman, Subcommittee on Select Education, Committee on Education and Labor, House of Representatives of the United States. September 30, 1981.

Cook, J. & Wollersheim, J. The effect of labeling of special education students on the perceptions of contact versus noncontact normal peers. *Journal of Special Education,* 1976, *10*, 187-198.

Donaldson, J. Changing attitudes toward handicapped persons: A review and analysis of research. *Exceptional Children,* 1980, *46*, 504-514.

Edelman, P.B. The Massachusetts Task Force reports: Advocacy for children. *Harvard Educational Review,* 1973, *43*, 639-652.

Featherstone, H.A. *A difference in the family,* New York: Basic Books, 1980.

Federal Register. January 19, 1981. Washington, DC: U.S. Government Printing Office.

Firth, G.H. "Advocate" vs "Professional Employee": A question of priorities for special educators. *Exceptional Children*, 1981, *47*, 486-493.

Gilliam, J.E., & Coleman, M.C. Who influences IEP committee decisions? *Exceptional Children*, 1981, *47*, 642-644.

Goldstein, S., Strickland, B., Turnbull, A.P., & Curry, L. An observational analysis of the IEP conference. *Exceptional Children*, 1980, *46*, 278-286.

Goldstein, S., & Turnbull, A.P. The use of two strategies to increase parent participation in IEP conferences. *Exceptional Children*, 1982, *48*, 360-361.

Goodman, H., Gottlieb, J., & Harrison, R. Social acceptance of EMRs integrated into a nongraded elementary school. *American Journal of Mental Deficiency*, 1972, *76*, 412,417.

Gottlieb, J. Public, peer and professional attitudes toward mentally retarded peers. In M. Begab & S. Richardson, *The mentally retarded and society: A social science perspective*, Baltimore: University Park Press, 1975.

Gottlieb, J., & Budoff, M. Social acceptability of retarded children in nongraded schools differing in architecture. *American Journal of Mental Deficiency*, 1973, *78*, 15-19.

Gottlieb, J., & Gottlieb, B. Stereotypic attitudes and behavioral intentions toward handicapped children. *American Journal of Mental Deficiency*, 1977, *82*, 65-71.

Hartwell-Meyers, L.K., & Haynes, J.D. *A data based approach to training parents of handicapped children as effective advocates* (E.D. 157 316). Tempe: Arizona State University, 1978.

Hazzard, A.P., & Baker, B.L. Enhancing children's attitudes toward disabled peers using a multi-media intervention. *Journal of Applied Developmental Psychology*, 1982, *3*, 247-262.

Herr, S.S., Arons, S., & Wallace, R.E. *Legal rights and mental-health care*. Lexington, MA: D.C. Heath, 1983.

Hobbs, N. *The futures of children*. San Francisco: Jossey-Bass, 1975.

MacMillan, D. *The mentally retarded in school and society* (2nd ed.). Boston: Little, Brown, 1982.

Martin, R. *Educating handicapped children: The legal mandate*. Champaign, IL: Research Press, 1979.

Moroney, R.M. Public social policy: Impact on families with handicapped children. In J.L. Paul (Ed.), *Understanding and working with parents of children with special needs*. New York: Holt, Rinehart and Winston, 1981.

Office of Special Education. *To assure the free, appropriate, public education of all handicapped children: Second annual report to Congress on the implementation of Public Law 94-142: The Education for All Handicapped Children Act*. Washington, DC: Author, 1980.

Parish, T., Ohlsen, R., & Parish, J. A look at mainstreaming in light of children's attitudes toward the handicapped. *Perceptual and Motor Skills*, 1978, *46*, 1019-1021.

Peck, C.A., & Semmel, M.I. Identifying the least restrictive environment (LRE) for children with severe handicaps: Toward an empirical analysis. *Journal of the Association for the Severely Handicapped*, 1982, *7*, 56-63.

Pullin, D. *Special education: A manual for advocates*. Cambridge, MA: Center for Law and Education, Inc. (Gutman Library, 6 Appian Way, Cambridge, MA 02138), 1982.

Pyecha, J. *A national survey of individualized education programs (IEPs) for handicapped children*. Research Triangle Institute, August 1979.

Rivera, G. *Willowbrook: A report on how it is and why it doesn't have to be that way*. New York: Vintage Books, 1972.

Salett, S., & Henderson, A. *A report on the education of all handicapped children act: Are parents involved?* Columbia, MD: National Committee for Citizens in Education, 1980.

Saunders, M.K., & Saltana, Q. Professional's knowledge of educational due process rights. *Exceptional Children*, 1980, *46*, 559,561.

Scanlon, C.A., Arick, J., & Phelps, N. Participation in the development of the IEP: Parents' perspective. *Exceptional Children*, 1981, *47*, 373-374.

Sullivan, M.B., Brightman, A.J., & Blatt, J. *Feeling Free.* Reading, MA: Addison-Wesley, 1979.

Task Force on Children Out of School. *The way we go to school.* Boston: Beacon Press, 1971.

Turnbull, A.P. Preschool mainstreaming: A policy and implementation analysis. *Educational Evaluation and Policy Analysis*, 1982, *4*, 281-291.

Turnbull, A.P., & Blacher-Dixon, J. The impact of preschool mainstreaming on parents. In J.J. Gallagher (Ed.), *New directions for exceptional children.* San Francisco: Jossey-Bass, 1980.

Turnbull, A.P., & Turnbull, H.R. Parent involvement in the education of handicapped children: A critique. *Mental Retardation*, 1982, *20*, 115-122.

Turnbull, H.R., & Turnbull, A.P. *Free appropriate public education: Law and implementation.* Denver, CO: Love Publishing Co., 1978.

Weintraub, F., Abeson, A., & Braddock, D. *State law and education of handicapped children: Issues and recommendations.* Arlington, VA: Council for Exceptional children, 1971.

Wiley, N., & McCandless, B. Social stereotypes for normal, educable mentally retarded and orthopedically handicapped children. *Journal of Special Education*, 1973, *7*, 283-288.

Winton, P., & Turnbull, A.P. Parent involvement as viewed by parents of preschool handicapped children. *Topics in Early Childhood Special Education*, 1981, *1*, 11-19.

# About the Contributors

**Bruce L. Baker** is Professor of Psychology at the University of California, Los Angeles, and is director of UCLA's project for developmental disabilities. Dr. Baker's research interests include mental retardation, parent training, and behavioral treatment for children. He has recently co-authored two books entitled *As Close as Possible*, and *Abnormal Psychology: Experiences, Origins and Interventions*. Dr. Baker received his doctorate in clinical psychology from Yale University.

**Donald N. Bersoff** obtained his Ph.D. in school psychology from New York University and his J.D. from Yale University. He is a partner with Ennis, Friedman, Bersoff & Ewing, the law firm that represents the American Psychological Association as well as other professional organizations. He is also coordinator of the NIMH-funded Joint J.D.-Ph.D Program in Law and Psychology at the University of Maryland and the Johns Hopkins University.

**Richard P. Brightman** received his Ph.D. in clinical psychology from the University of California, Los Angeles. He has recently completed a postdoctoral fellowship in mental health advocacy at the University of Southern California. Dr. Brightman's work has included service as a consultant to state agencies serving developmentally disabled citizens and extensive work with mentally retarded children and their families. He is also cofounder of MAXXIS, Inc., which offers training programs to maximize personal and professional effectiveness.

**Marcia Conlin** (J.D., St. Louis University) is a staff attorney at the National Juvenile Law Center, Inc., in St. Louis, where she advocates on behalf of unlawfully incarcerated children. She has served as an assistant public defender in the St. Louis County Juvenile Court, and she has provided extensive legal research to a major social science project investigating decision-making processes in the juvenile justice system.

**Ellen Greenberger** received a Ph.D. in clinical psychology from Harvard University. She is Professor of Social Ecology at the University of California, Irvine. Her research interests are in the area of social development and, increasingly, in developmental research that has policy implications for children, youth, and families.

**Thomas Grisso** (Ph.D., University of Arizona) is Professor of Psychology at St. Louis University. He is the author of *Juveniles' Waiver of Rights: Legal and Psychological Competence,* an empirical study of juveniles' abilities to understand Miranda rights. Currently he is engaged in research on decision making in the juvenile justice system, and on specialized assessment methods for forensic psychological evaluations.

**Robert D. Hunt** is Assistant Professor of Psychiatry and Pediatrics with the Yale University Child Study Center, and is also Director of Child and Adolescent Services at West Haven Mental Health Clinic of the Connecticut Mental Health Center. He obtained his medical degree at the University of California School of Medicine at San Francisco, and performed his training in psychiatry at Harvard Medical School and the UCLA Neuropsychiatric Institute. Dr. Hunt's interests focus on attention deficit disorder with hyperactivity, psychotherapy with abused children, and a range of subjects relating to child and family mental health services.

**Jean Ann Linney** received her Ph.D. in psychology from the University of Illinois at Urbana-Champaign. Currently, Dr. Linney is on the faculty of the Department of Psychology of the University of South Carolina at Columbia. Dr. Linney's interests are in the areas of community psychology, public policy, and children and youth. Dr. Linney recently completed work with the National Academy Science Panel on the Institutionalization of Youth, focusing upon alternative facilities for youth in trouble.

**John Monahan** is a psychologist and Professor of Law at the University of Virginia. He is a past president of the Division of Psychology and Law of the American Psychological Association. His most recent book, *Predicting Violent Behavior* (Sage, 1981), won the Manford Guttmacher Award of the American Psychiatric Association.

**Gary B. Melton** is an associate professor in psychology and law, and director of the law-psychology program at the University of Nebraska—Lincoln. Dr. Melton obtained his doctorate in clinical-community psychology from Boston University. His interests focus broadly on the application of psychology to law, with an emphasis on family, juvenile, mental health, and environmental law. Among his publications are three books on psycho-legal issues affecting children and families.

**Edward P. Mulvey** completed his Ph.D. in community psychology at the University of Virginia and was the recipient of the 1983 SPSSI award for outstanding doctoral dissertation on a social problem. During 1982-1983, he was a postdoctoral fellow in quantitative methods in criminal justice at the Urban Systems Institute at Carnegie-Mellon University. Currently he is Assistant Professor of Child Psychiatry at the Western Psychiatric Institute and Clinic in Pittsburgh.

**N. Dickon Reppucci** completed his Ph.D. in clinical psychology at Harvard in 1968. He was a faculty member at Yale for eight years, and became Professor of Psychology and the director of the Graduate Program in Community Psychology at the University of Virginia in 1976. For several years he has been a consultant to Virginia's Institute for Law, Psychiatry and Public Policy and is one of the co-founders of the Center for the Study of Children and the Law at the University of Virginia.

**Mindy S. Rosenberg** is currently Assistant Professor of Psychology in the child clinical psychology program at the University of Denver. Her interests focus on the area of family violence, with a particular emphasis on child abuse. Her current research investigates the impact of spouse abuse on children. She obtained her doctorate in community-clinical psychology from the University of Virginia.

**Elizabeth Scott** is co-founder and director of the Center for the Study of Children and the Law at the University of Virginia. She received her J.D. degree from the University of Virginia School of Law. Her primary area of interest is the application of social science to the development of legal policies relating to children and families. Current research interests include joint custody and sterilization of the retarded.

**Edward Seidman** is Professor, Director of Clinical and Community Psychology Training, and Associate Head of the Department of Psychology at the University of Illinois at Urbana-Champaign. He has served as a Senior Fulbright-Hays Research Scholar in Greece (1977-1978) and previously taught at the University of Manitoba. He is Chairperson of the Executive Board of the Council of Community Psychology Program Directors and a member of the American Psychological Association's Task Force on Public Policy. Professor Seidman has done extensive research in the area of psychotherapy as well as the development, implementation, and evaluation of a wide array of innovations in the areas of mental health, juvenile justice, and education. His current research and scholarship include the study of mutual help groups, economics and psychosocial dysfunction, primary prevention, and social policy. He is Editor of *Handbook of Social Intervention* (Sage, 1983).

**Lois A. Weithorn** received her Ph.D. in clinical psychology from the University of Pittsburgh. Currently, she is Assistant Professor in Psychology at the University of Virginia, and is affiliated with the University's Institute of Law, Psychiatry and Public Policy. Dr. Weithorn's research and scholarly interests are in the areas of informed consent; competency to consent to and refuse treatment; and children, families, and the law. Her current studies examine children's capacities to consent to psychiatric hospitalization, and the understanding and reasoning of pediatric cancer patients about their illness and its alternative treatments. Dr. Weithorn's earlier research on children's competencies was honored by the Society for the Psychological Study of Social Issues in 1981.